Photoshop 5.5:

Get Professional Results

Photoshop 5.5:
Get Professional Results

Ken Milburn

Osborne/McGraw-Hill

Berkeley New York St. Louis San Francisco Auckland Bogotá
Hamburg London Madrid Mexico City Milan Montreal New Delhi
Panama City Paris São Paulo Singapore Sydney Tokyo Toronto

2S4513
MAR 01 2001

Osborne/**McGraw-Hill**
2600 Tenth Street
Berkeley, California 94710
U.S.A.

For information on translations or book distributors outside the U.S.A., or to arrange bulk purchase discounts for sales promotions, premiums, or fund-raisers, please contact Osborne/**McGraw-Hill** at the above address.

Photoshop 5.5: Get Professional Results

1234567890 DOC DOC 019876543210

ISBN 0-07-212299-4

Publisher
Brandon A. Nordin

Associate Publisher and Editor-in-Chief
Scott Rogers

Acquisitions Editor
Megg Bonar

Project Editor
Emily Rader

Acquisitions Coordinator
Stephane Thomas

Technical Editor
Rick White

Proofreader
Linda Medoff

Indexer
Rebecca Plunkett

Computer Designers
Jani Beckwith, Mickey Galicia, Dick Schwartz, Roberta Steele

Illustrators
Robert Hansen, Michael Mueller, Beth Young

Series Design
Jill Weil

Cover Design
Dodie Shoemaker

This book was composed with Corel VENTURA™ Publisher.

About the Author

Ken Milburn is an award-winning graphic designer with several best-selling books to his credit, including *Flash 4 Web Animation f/x and Design* and *Digital Photography Bible*. He's written numerous articles on graphics and multimedia for national computer magazines over the past 13+ years.

Contents at a Glance

Contents

Acknowledgments

I would first like to thank Megg Bonar, my acquisitions editor, for giving me the opportunity to work on this book and to do it in a way that I think will give our readers the most "bang for the buck." Equally important were the contributions of the rest of the Osborne staff, who so carefully edited this book to make it a top-quality product—especially Emily Rader, project editor, who put in many late nights and a zillion phone calls; and Stephane Thomas, acquisitions coordinator, who did a brilliant job of greasing the wheels. It's the kind of editorial support that every author dreams of getting. And I wouldn't have been lucky enough to have had the chance to work with the folks at Osborne if it weren't for the fact that I have the world's best and most level-headed agent, Margot Maley Hutchinson, at Waterside Productions. She's going to make a great mom, too.

I'd never have managed to write 11 books without the love and support of my close friends: my former wife and good friend, Nancy Miller; my son, Lane; Janine Warner; Bob Cowart; Sonita Malan; Francisco Rivera; Sundeep Doshi; Terry Parker; Yolanda Burrell; Jane Lindsey; Zoe Zuber; Toni DiMarco; Mark Petrakis; Markus Baue; and Karen Serlin.

Nicole Crane and Stephan Schwinges wrote a pair of lovely "Advice from a Pro" features that, unfortunately, we couldn't make room for.

I also want to thank the publicity, beta testing, and product management teams at Adobe Systems for all the support and helpful information they provided me.

Finally, Rick White did a fine job of editing the book for technical accuracy, and of writing Chapters 10 and 14.

Introduction

Adobe Photoshop 5.5 is the latest in a parade of versions of the world's leading professional image-editing program. Since its beginnings, Photoshop has moved far beyond its original purpose as a mere digital darkroom. The program is widely used for prepress photograph preparation; for special effects; to reinterpret photographs as paintings; and for creating graphic elements for use in presentations, video, film, and print projects. Version 5.5 extends the program to make it even more useful for isolating subjects from their backgrounds to create what are called *knockouts.* In addition, for the first time, Photoshop is fully capable of preparing images for the Web and of creating interactive Web graphics.

We used to think of professional users of Photoshop as being either photographers, designers, or prepress production experts. As things have evolved, more and more business professionals of all sorts are discovering a critical need to do some or all of the things that Photoshop is best at. While this has always been true to some extent, two factors have contributed to making it more true today than ever: the ubiquitous nature of the Internet as a means of informing people and promoting businesses, and the convenience and speed of digital cameras.

The new features in Photoshop 5.5 give more power to both the business professional and the imaging professional:

- **Extract command**   This command allows you to extract images with transitional, semi-transparent edges, such as flying hair and gaps between leaves.

- **Background eraser**   This tool automatically erases portions of the image that fall within the user-specified range of brightness.

- **Magic eraser**   This tool allows you to manually define transitional edges and clean up the results.

- **Art history brush**   With this tool, you can choose a stroking method for cloning from a History palette snapshot.

- **ImageReady 2**   A new version of Adobe's popular program for preparing images for display on the Web. The program includes:
  - Simultaneous comparison of multiple levels and types of image compression (optimization) prior to saving the optimized image.
  - GIF animation, including automatic tweening and transitional effects
  - Image slicing
  - Javascripted rollover events
  - Image mapping
  - An even more Photoshop-like interface
- **Save for Web command**   This command lets you take advantage of ImageReady's optimization capabilities within Photoshop.

Whether you're new to Photoshop or you just want to improve the results you're getting using your existing skills, this book provides plenty of information on how to use Photoshop's features to achieve *professional* results.

What's Special About This Book

Photoshop 5.5: Get Professional Results covers all the essential Photoshop features you need in order to give your photographs a professional appearance—and then goes further to help you solve creative challenges that commonly plague individuals charged with making images suitable for professional publication or presentation. In that vein, this book contains dozens of Professional Pointer boxes aimed at making your workday routines easier and more gratifying.

This book is designed to include several features to help you comprehend the solutions given:

Tip: This feature offers you useful shortcuts and techniques. I give you some of my best advice here!

- **Numbered steps** clearly explain how to accomplish complex tasks. In many cases, I've provided sample images for you to download when working through these exercises. (You'll find these on the Osborne Web site, at www.osborne.com.)
- **Annotated figures** provide a visual guide to the steps needed to accomplish various tasks in Photoshop.

Cross-Reference: These notes help you to quickly find related material elsewhere in the book.

Professional Pointer

This feature is provided to guide you to the wisdom of professionals. It also offers a nice aside whenever information, albeit invaluable, goes into more depth than what is required to perform the example at hand.

Color Galleries

Unlike the color sections in many other Photoshop books, the ones in this book are there for more than decorative purposes. In full color, the "Image Gallery" explains which features were utilized to effect the end result, making it easy for you to learn to achieve similar results with your own photos. Most of the examples are from real-life assignments that had very specific professional requirements.

In addition, the second color section, which consists of the "Filter Gallery" and the "Mode Gallery," gives you color examples of Photoshop's filters and blend modes.

Who Needs This Book

This book was designed to help two distinct groups of people:

- *Business professionals* who need to bring their image-editing skills to a more professional level for a reasonable investment in time and money.
- *Experienced users of Photoshop** or other graphics programs who may need a solution to a problem that (though commonly encountered by other photographers and illustrators) is not part of their usual routine.

This is not the "Everything You Never Wanted to Know" guide to Photoshop. And it also is not a book that will leave you exclaiming, "Holy smoke! What on earth could I use that special effect for?" We have intentionally avoided covering every single aspect of Photoshop and have kept the size of the book within limits that would make it affordable. However, in order to ensure that you have access to all of the Photoshop essentials, we've put two bonus tutorials up on the Osborne Web site (www.osborne.com): "Working with Channels" and "Using Layers." Of course, you'll also use Photoshop's channels and layers in the course of completing several of the exercises in the book; as a result, you'll get a good idea of how to use the most needed capabilities of those two features without having to access these tutorials (although I heartily recommend them).

How This Book Is Organized

Photoshop 5.5: Get Professional Results starts with an overview of the interface environment and functionality, and then moves through the various specialized tasks

*[Ken: Yes, but even though I knew little about Photoshop when I began this project, I was able to learn a great deal by working through the tutorials while editing the book. Emily (project editor)]

[Thanks, Emily. Why don't you just leave this note in! Ken (author)]

that Photoshop is so good at performing. For those whose primary interest is in the new Web capabilities, you can start with the last two chapters and come back to the earlier chapters later.

- **Part I, "Image Processing,"** takes you through the Photoshop components, tools, and techniques for processing images. Chapter 1, "What's New in Photoshop 5.5," outlines all the new features in Photoshop 5.5; and Chapter 2, "Operational Basics," teaches you the basics of the interface. The balance of Part I explains image-processing basics: Chapter 3, "Making Image Adjustments," shows you how to change the brightness, contrast, color balance, and other overriding characteristics of an image. Chapter 4, "Image Retouching and Cleanup," explains how to retouch and recolor images. Chapter 5, "Cutting It Down to Size and Flipping Out," covers composition, cropping, and rotations.

- **Part II, "Image Compositing,"** walks you through procedures for making convincingly real scenes from multiple images. Chapter 6, "Making Selections and Masks," shows you how to isolate items from their original backgrounds; and Chapter 7, "Editing and Modifying Selections and Masks," goes on to show you how to isolate images in more sophisticated ways. You learn to distort images to make them fit into their new surroundings in Chapter 8, "Bending and Twisting the Image." This part concludes with Chapter 9, "Incorporating Text."

- **Part III, "Special Effects,"** shows you how to use filters and other Photoshop features to create special effects. In Chapter 10, you learn how to incorporate photographic effects such as blurring, lens flare, and other treatments. Chapter 11, "Creating Photopaintings", instructs you on techniques that can be used to abstract your photographs into impressionist illustrations.

- **Part IV, "Printing and Publishing Your Work,"** concludes the printed portion of this book by showing you how to prepare images, animations, and interactive elements using ImageReady 2, which is now included in the Photoshop 5.5 package. Chapter 12, "Managing Your Images," tells you how to organize and annotate your files. Chapter 13, "Optimizing Web Graphics," explains how to tweak images for the best possible performance on a Web site; and Chapter 14, "Using ImageReady for Special-Purpose Web Graphics," teaches you how to create animations, image slices, image maps, and rollovers.

How to Use This Book

If you are new to Photoshop, you should start from the beginning and read until you have a good feel for the functional structure of Photoshop. Don't be timid about trying out features as you read—just be sure to practice on copies of your valuable images until you feel your confidence building. Once you're familiar with the basics of editing an image, you can either get a solid grounding in the professional use of Photoshop by reading all the way to the end, or you can use the index to jump to solutions for particular problems.

Keypresses for Mac and Windows Users

Throughout this book I use a consistent convention for showing you what keystroke combinations to use so that both Macintosh and Windows users will understand exactly what to do on the machine they are using. In the process, you'll also learn how similar these two platforms really are, so that if you ever need or want to use Photoshop on the "other platform," you can do so fearlessly.

Equivalent keys are separated by a slash (/), with the Mac key given first: for example, OPT/ALT, CMD/CTRL, or DELETE/BACKSPACE. Keys that are the same on both types of computers, such as SHIFT, are only given once. The Mac CONTROL key is always spelled in full to distinguish it from the Windows CTRL key. When multiple keys have to be used, a plus sign (+) separates the keys, like this: OPT/ALT+CMD/CTRL+SHIFT+click.

Mouse operations

If you are expected to simply click the mouse key without holding it down, the instruction will be "click." If you are expected to click and hold down the mouse key while you move the mouse, the instruction will be "drag" (often, in this case, the "click" will be implied).

Note that the instruction to "click" always means to click the left mouse button if you're a Windows user and to click the *only* mouse button if you're a Mac user. On the other hand, if the instruction says "CONTROL+click/right-click," it means Windows users should click the right mouse button; while Mac users should press the CONTROL key and simultaneously click the Mac mouse button (the operation the Macintosh substitutes for the right mouse button function in Windows).

Have Fun!

In my opinion, Photoshop provides the second-most fun you can have in life. As serious an application as it can be, never miss an opportunity to have fun with it. You'll always end up discovering new solutions to difficult problems.

Part I
Image Processing

chapter 1

What's New in Photoshop 5.5

In this chapter, you:

- Learn how the new Extract command makes knockouts easier than ever

- Realize the power of two new erasers

- Find out how the art history brush differs from the history brush

- Get acquainted with the much-improved Contact Sheet II command and new picture package capability

- Learn how three new wizards improve the tasks of calibrating color, resizing images, and exporting images with transparent backgrounds

- Discover new typography controls

- Familiarize yourself with the new Web capabilities that result from the inclusion of ImageReady 2 in Photoshop

The Photoshop 5.5 package includes some important new Photoshop enhancements, as well as Adobe's ImageReady product, which provides Web preparation functionality. ImageReady 2 expands Photoshop beyond being a digital darkroom into becoming a state-of-the-art launching pad for Web images and graphic effects. This chapter covers all the enhancements specific to Photoshop, as well as those resulting from the inclusion of ImageReady.

Photoshop Enhancements

The most important enhancement to Photoshop 5.5 is its improved capability for handling *knockouts,* a term used in the printing industry to describe photographs of objects whose backgrounds have been eliminated. Version 5.5 allows you (with practice) to become an expert at this technique. In addition, Photoshop 5.5 has a number of other exciting new features, including the new art history brush tool, annotated contact sheets, picture packages, expanded wizards, updated PDF support, and more type controls. All of these are discussed in this section. Finally, to prepare you for the discussion of ImageReady, this section concludes by explaining how easily you can switch between the two interfaces.

Improved Handling of Knockouts

Professional photographers, graphic designers, and other media pros often like to use knockouts to isolate subjects from their original backgrounds. Version 5.5 of Photoshop does a much better job than previous versions of solving knockout problems in three areas:

- **Irregular and busy edges that trap the background inside them**   Hair and foliage are the culprits that come immediately to mind.
- **Multicolored and multitextured backgrounds**   These are especially problematic if the backgrounds consist of more objects like the subject. Think of knocking out a flower from a field of flowers or a model from a crowd of people.
- **Objects that are partially transparent or translucent**   Think of a goldfish bowl, or a glass of white wine, or the windows of a car. Transparent objects that reflect their surroundings are even tougher.

Three new tools in Photoshop—the background eraser, the magic eraser, and the Extract command—make it possible to knock out these sorts of difficult subjects. The two new erasers are found on a flyout attached to the eraser tool. The Extract command is found on the Image menu.

Cross-Reference: All three of these new features are fully covered in Chapters 6.

The background eraser works really well when you have a strongly contrasting solid-color background. It acts just like the magic wand, except that instead of making a selection, it deletes everything within its range (see Figure 1-1).

The magic eraser is much more intriguing than the background eraser. You set a range (of contrast with the items you want to keep) in its Options dialog and then decide whether you want the tool to keep adjusting the range as it moves, to maintain the range of pixels found at the first click, or to use the background color selection box. Then you just paint along the edges to eliminate the background under the brush. If the brush is feathered, you can get a very natural looking blend of the subject and any new background. You can see how well this works along the furry edges of the cat's hair in Figure 1-2.

These first two new tools are pretty neat, but wait till you try the Extract command. It can give Corel Knockout (formerly Ultimatte Knockout) a run for its money, it's much easier to use, and you don't have to buy a third-party program.

If you're not familiar with Corel Knockout, here's what that tool does: You indicate a border within which you want to keep certain items (such as wisps of hair or the reflections in the glass), while other items are those you definitely want

FIGURE 1-1   One click of the background eraser and all of the tones in the sky disappear.

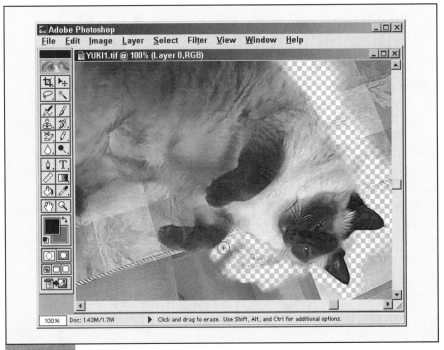

FIGURE 1-2 Notice how the magic eraser can even remove tones in the tablecloth that are similar to the color of Yuki's fur.

dropped. Then you indicate the areas that contain information that must be kept out and the areas that contain information that must be kept in. You then preview the image to see if you made your selections accurately. If not, you can make changes again and continue previewing and selecting until you see exactly the desired result. Then you click OK and move on.

To be fair, Corel Knockout gives you more control than Photoshop's Extract command, but you also need to invest more time in learning to use the Corel tool properly. In the Extract command, Adobe has added power without the accompanying time demands that Corel Knockout can require.

The added time and money invested in Ultimatte's tool may well be worthwhile if you're in a production situation or have a critical assignment that demands it. You have to weigh that against the fact that the Extract command in Photoshop 5.5 gives you most of that capability for no extra cost and with a much easier-to-use interface. As you can see in Figure 1-3, Photoshop's Extract command can give you a very professional result.

FIGURE 1-3   Finished knockout achieved with the Extract command

Art History Brush

The art history brush lets you paint from a snapshot, but the result is much different than simply using the history brush, as you can see in Figure 1-4. Although the art history brush is still taking its information from the snapshot, you can choose from a number of stroke styles and blend modes that "remix" the pixels in the snapshot.

Cross-Reference: The art history brush is described in detail in Chapter 11.

Annotated Contact Sheets

If you don't have a contact sheet–making program for managing your images, Photoshop 5.5 finally makes it practical to do without one by including the

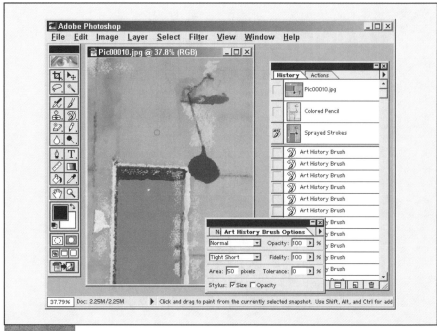

FIGURE 1-4 The image was painted from three different snapshots with the art history brush.

Contact Sheet II dialog (or feature), as shown in Figure 1-5. And this new feature is a great improvement and time-saver over the capabilities that were in Photoshop 5.02.

Cross-Reference: Contact sheets are covered in Chapter 12.

Tip: To avoid confusion, incorporate your file type into the filename. Better yet, get a third-party image-management program, such as Thumbnails Plus or Extensis Portfolio. Until you can justify the extra bucks, at least Photoshop 5.5 provides a workable alternative.

Photoshop 5.5 gives you the option to automatically add the names of files. It doesn't add the extension, so you'll still have a hard time with folders that contain five versions of the same file, each in a different format for a different purpose.

Picture Packages

Picture packages are what professional photo processing shops call those prints that give you a set of prints on a single sheet, such as a mix of two 4 × 5's and four 2¼ × 3¼ prints. Just in time for the age of the digital camera, Photoshop 5.5 lets you automatically produce your own picture packages from a single image, as shown in Figure 1-6.

Cross-Reference: Making picture packages is detailed in Chapter 12.

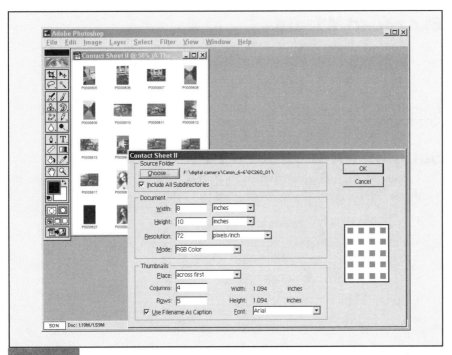

FIGURE 1-5   The Contact Sheet II dialog with the resulting contact sheet shown in the background

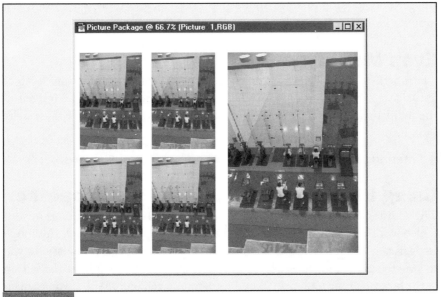

FIGURE 1-6   A picture package consisting of one 5 × 7 and four 2½ × 3½ prints on the same page

Expanded Wizards

Photoshop 5.5 offers a new and better wizard for performing color management, and it now resides on the Help menu. This is in addition to the 5.02 wizards for exporting a transparent image and resizing an image.

Cross-Reference: The use of all three wizards is fairly self-explanatory, but if you want to know more, see Chapter 2.

Support for Improved PDF Features

You can now open files stored in the new PDF 1.3 file format that's supported by Acrobat 4. PDF 1.3 offers improved support in the following areas:

- High-end print production
- PostScript 3 printing capabilities, including smooth shading (makes continuous tone blends at any resolution)
- Color management and embedded ICC profiles
- Font printing and embedding
- Late-stage edits

The most important thing about the improved PDF support is that it makes it much easier to move work between Photoshop and other Adobe applications, such as Illustrator and InDesign. You can configure either Photoshop or ImageReady to jump to other Adobe graphics programs. Only ImageReady can jump to GoLive, however.

Even More Type Controls

The functions of the Type Tool dialog have been amplified to offer four levels of anti-aliasing and "synthetic type styles." What's a synthetic type style? It refers to the ability to boldface, italicize, or underline typefaces that don't have those styles built in.

Cross-Reference: Entering text in Photoshop 5.5 is covered thoroughly in Chapter 9.

Using Photoshop and ImageReady Together

The addition of Adobe ImageReady 2 in the Photoshop 5.5 box brings to your table a world of new functionality in the area of Web preparation tools. Although ImageReady 2 is still a separate application, Adobe has made it very easy for you to switch back and forth between the two programs. There is a Jump To button at the bottom of the toolboxes of both programs (see Figure 1-7). If you're in either program and want to jump to the other, just click the Jump To button.

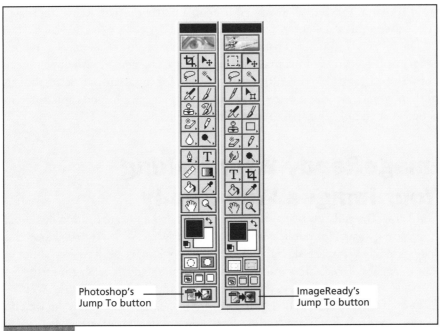

Photoshop's
Jump To button

ImageReady's
Jump To button

FIGURE 1-7 The Photoshop 5.5 and ImageReady 2 toolboxes each have a Jump
To button that takes you directly to the other application.

Photoshop will tell you it's temporarily saving the file and then bring up the
other application. Once you've made the jump, both programs remain open, and
the same nominal file is active in both programs. (If you're a Mac user, make sure
you've allocated memory between the two programs so that
this can happen.)

The best part is that you won't feel like a stranger in a
strange land after you've made the jump. Adobe has very
carefully designed both interfaces to be as similar as possible.
In fact, the only differences that exist are those that make it
easier for each program to do the work that it specializes in.
For instance, the ImageReady toolbox has a slice selection
tool but no history brush, pen, measure, or linear gradient
tools. Since you're more likely to create images in Photoshop
and since you still have the paintbrush, gaining the slice
tools in ImageReady is a worthwhile trade-off.

You can also move images back and forth between applications without having to make changes or lose information.

Layers stay the same and keep the same filenames. If you
bring in a TIF file and then optimize it in GIF format, you'll

Tip: When using the Jump
To button, you are required to
save the original version of the file
when you make the jump. You
can click a Save As button, which
makes a copy under another
name, or a Save button. The
second choice will overwrite the
original file. If you click the Save
As button, as soon as you find
yourself in the other program, you
are advised that there are differences
between the file that's currently in
the active window and the one in
the other program. You are then
given the option to update it or not.

still have your TIF file when you go back to Photoshop (you know the adage, "you haven't lost a daughter, you've gained a son").

The History and Actions palettes look and behave almost identically in both programs. You can even maintain all the history characteristics when you move between programs. However, this isn't the case for the Actions palette: though both programs' Actions palettes look and behave identically, you can't move an action created in Photoshop to ImageReady or vice versa.

ImageReady 2 for Making Your Images Web Ready

Until now, ImageReady was available only as a standalone application dedicated to prepping images for publication on the World Wide Web. At first glance, this may seem like a simple task; but, in fact, whole books have been written about it. There are gobs of available commercial and shareware standalone plug-ins that help you squeeze an image down to the smallest size that can be viewed on the Web.

Dozens more programs help you make an image map, slice a large image into smaller segments for faster loading, make an animation, or create JavaScript mouse rollover events.

ImageReady 2 brings all these tasks under one interface, and for the most part, it is an interface with which you are already familiar (that is, if you're already familiar with Photoshop). Figure 1-8 shows the ImageReady interface. You won't need to read all those books on making Web graphics to figure out how to do any of these things, either; the ImageReady interface is easy to understand.

That doesn't mean the program is lacking in features. First of all, it can do about 80 percent of what Photoshop can do. On top of that, it gives you quick and easy control over image optimization. Image optimization means making the best compromise between reducing an image to the smallest possible file size and keeping the quality of the image at an acceptable level. The problem is, the acceptable level for viewing depends on a number of highly variable factors, such as your own criteria, the physical size of the image, the bandwidth of the connection over which it's likely to be viewed, and the intended purpose for the image. For instance, an image that's going to be used as a background texture needs little fidelity to the original subject or qualities. On the other hand, an image for a photographer's or illustrator's portfolio had better be faithful to the original, or it's liable to embarrass its originator.

Many of ImageReady's features are duplicated in Photoshop 5.5, but those that are unique to it (because they're unique to the challenge of preparing Web graphics) are highlighted here.

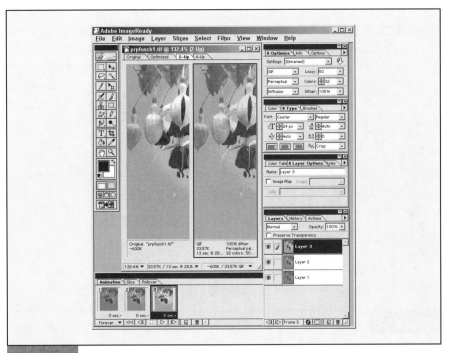

FIGURE 1-8 The ImageReady interface

Cross-Reference: Get detailed information about these ImageReady features and how to use them in Chapters 13 and 14.

Image Optimization Features

The bottom line is that you make the compromise between quality and file size through experimentation. What ImageReady does for you is to make that experimentation as painless as possible. The chief device for doing this is something that Adobe calls LiveView panels (see Figure 1-9). You see these in the ImageReady image window as folder tabs titled Original, Optimized, 2-Up, and 4-Up. All of these views are maintained simultaneously, and you can change any of the settings in any of the optimized tabs at any time without affecting the original. In the 2-Up and 4-Up views, you can change the level and type of optimization shown in any and all windows, so you can instantly compare the differences side by side.

The optimization settings are also very easy to make, and you quickly build an instinct for when you need to make changes because you see the results of those changes right away. You make the changes in an Optimize palette (shown in Figure 1-9) by making choices from pop-up menus and radio buttons. You can even

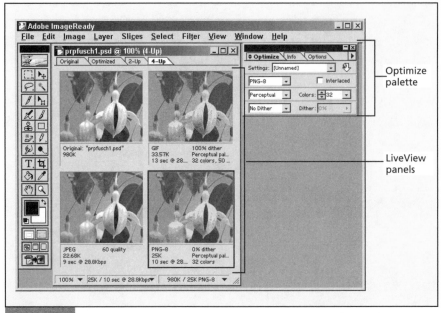

Each image in this 4-Up view is optimized in a different format and with different settings.

tweak the number of colors to be included in an optimized file by substituting a new color for anything in the palette, or by deleting all the colors that aren't actually used, or even by deleting colors that don't seem to contribute much to the overall effect.

ImageReady 2 also lets you choose from a wide array of palette types when you're optimizing to an indexed file format (GIF or PNG-8). You can apply a master palette to a whole series of images or force all the colors in the image to be Web safe. You can also choose to optimize the palette and image gamma for display on either Mac or Windows platforms. Of course, you can also create your own custom palettes.

Making user-defined image slices

By slicing images into subimages that will be displayed as a single seamless image when seen in a Web browser, you can ensure that individual sections of the image have been optimized to their best benefit. You also ensure that at least part of the image will start loading much faster than the whole image would. This way, while the viewer is taking in the content of one part of the image, another part can be loading.

You can also slice images in such a way that certain slices can be assigned links or JavaScript mouse rollover events, or they can be animated.

ImageReady makes slicing really simple. You can do it by dragging Photoshop's nonprinting alignment guides into position and then asking to slice along the guides. You can also drag a rectangular marquee into position and then ask ImageReady to slice the rest of the image accordingly. Once the image has been sliced, ImageReady 2 automatically numbers the slices for you, as shown in Figure 1-10. You can also change the status of slices so that they can have attributes (such as rollover scripts) attached to them. Finally, you can click any slice to select it, and then apply different optimization settings to each slice.

There are a few other things besides links and rollovers that you can do to image slices:

- Slices can be assigned as non-image slices, which can contain solid Hex colors or HTML text. Hex colors are derived from six-digit codes in HTML. What this means is that you can put content in a slice that can be viewed instantly. This allows you to make what appears to be a window of text inside a larger graphic.

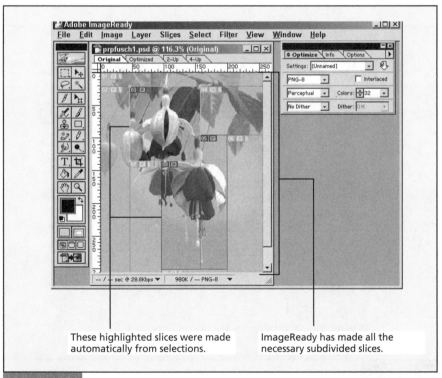

These highlighted slices were made automatically from selections.

ImageReady has made all the necessary subdivided slices.

FIGURE 1-10   ImageReady allows you to create slices automatically from selections.

- Alt tags can be used to load an alternate image if the current slice isn't compatible with a specific browser.

- ImageReady 2 makes it easy to change the automatically assigned JavaScript message to say anything you want it to say.

- All properties of any slice can be viewed.

- Slice files are automatically named by ImageReady, but you can control this, as well as choose the location of the folder they are saved to.

- Slices can be divided, merged with one another, rescaled, realigned, or deleted.

Creating JavaScript Rollover Effects

JavaScript rollover effects are compatible with virtually all browsers and Web graphics, so no special plug-ins are required to make them work. For that reason, they've become the most popular way to animate buttons and provide supplementary information or animation at a user's request. ImageReady 2 makes it possible to create these effects without writing a single letter of programming code, as shown in Figure 1-11.

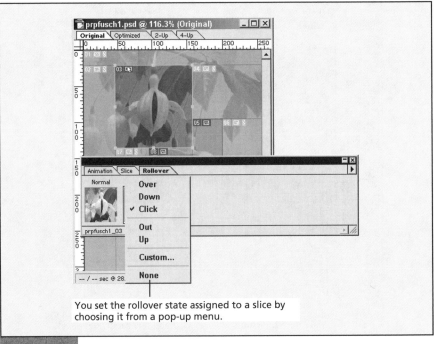

You set the rollover state assigned to a slice by choosing it from a pop-up menu.

FIGURE 1-11   Creating a rollover effect

ImageReady 2 makes creating rollover events fairly intuitive. You slice the image, and then use settings in the Animation and Layers palettes to set up the rollover states. Then you can make changes to the layers assigned to those states. Of course, this requires a specific set of steps.

JavaScript rollover effects can occur with the whole range of mouse events, such as the following:

- **Mouse over**   Any time the cursor passes over the targeted area.

- **Mouse down**   Any time the mouse button is depressed and held before the mouse passes over the targeted area.

- **Mouse click**   Any time the mouse button is clicked while the cursor is over the targeted area.

If you can write JavaScript code, you can further enhance the capabilities of ImageReady by adding other kinds of events. The events that follow are automatically accommodated in ImageReady:

- **Image changes**   For instance, a button can look as if it's being pressed when it is clicked. Or a larger image containing an instructional message can appear. Actually, the possibilities are endless.

- **Secondary rollover effects**   When the rollover event occurs over one area (that is to say, a specific image slice), something happens in another area. For instance, an animation window could pop up.

- **Changes in a layer's visibility or layer effects**   You can make the layer fade or take on a layer effect when the event occurs.

A Full-Featured GIF Animation Palette

ImageReady also contains a full-featured palette called Animation, which easily creates a sequentially numbered set of still GIF files that are embedded into HTML code to make them appear at a given interval and place on the target Web page. Where they appear and the method by which they replace one another contributes to making the applications for animated GIFs quite variable: anything from a movie clip, to flying text, to preprogrammed slide shows. Animated GIFs are far and away the most popular means of creating animations on Web pages. This popularity is due to the fact that until now, GIFs have been the one animation method that was close to universally readable.

L▶ Tip: *Flash animations,* animations produced using a vector-based technology created by Macromedia, are very close to becoming universally readable. However, they aren't always appropriate for the effect desired. For one thing, they're vector based, while GIF animations are bitmapped (just like Photoshop files).

ImageReady's Animation palette makes it very easy to create animations from the layers in Photoshop files. This means that you can position the contents of layers visually because you can adjust and readjust their transparency. For instance, you can see the direction a limb moves when you want to animate the photograph of a person. You can also paste a variety of photos on different layers, drag them into any relative positions you like, and then have the Animation palette show them at a slow frame rate and without replacing the previous frames. The result will appear to be a stack of photos, slowly dropped atop one another.

Cross-Reference: You'll get much more detailed information about the possibilities and techniques for GIF animation in Chapters 13 and 14.

ImageReady's animation program resides in the Animation palette, shown in Figure 1-12. The content for the frames is supplied by the layers in any open image windows. You can also import frames from QuickTime movies.

The Animation palette shows each frame in a timeline and permits you to control numerous characteristics of individual frames, as well as the entire movie. The palette lets you experiment with your "movie" by previewing it at any time and then continuing to work. For openers, it allows for such advanced animation optimization techniques as saving only those pixels in a frame that have changed from the previous frame.

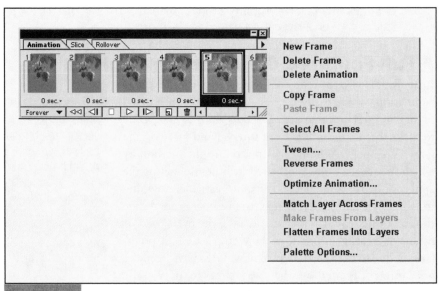

FIGURE 1-12 The Animation palette and its flyout menu

The Animation palette also has several tweening controls. *Tweening* is animator-speak for drawing the frames between the start of a movement and its peak. This allows you to automatically insert frames that change in value (for example, position, opacity, and layer effects) over time.

HTML Code Automatically Updated

Many capabilities of ImageReady 2 will automatically generate HTML code to support the features you've implemented. Generally, you will then paste that HTML code into code that you generated (either by hand or in a program for Web page creation, such as Adobe GoLive! or Macromedia Dreamweaver). Now, here's the rub. Ordinarily, any subsequent change you make in the image or the codes assigned to it would have to be reedited by hand in the target HTML file. ImageReady 2 tags its files so they can be automatically associated with changes you make in an image. Make a change, and ImageReady 2 can automatically update the parent HTML code. This can be a major stress reliever.

Features You Might Have Missed Since Your Last Upgrade

If you're skipping a revision of Photoshop or haven't had any experience with ImageReady, there are some noteworthy features you might have missed. Don't worry, they'll all be thoroughly covered in this book. Nevertheless, you might want to know right now what the most essential of these features are.

- **The History palette**   This palette controls multiple undos and instantly returns images to specific image states.

- **Layer effects that can be changed or edited at any stage**   These are especially useful for creating text and buttons, and they include beveled and rounded edges, embossed borders, drop shadows, and inner and outer glows. You can also apply combinations of these effects to the same image layer.

- **Support for designating a spot color**   This makes it possible to perfectly match colors for such things as company logos and other corporate colors.

- **Color management that complies with ICC (International Color Consortium)**   Adobe sees this as the most promising way to ensure consistent color calibration across devices such as digital cameras, scanners, monitors, and printers.

- **Editable text layers**   These make it possible to correct spelling or to change the content of text after a little time has passed.

Professional Skills Summary

This chapter has introduced you to Photoshop 5.5's many new features, including a variety of production time-savers. You learned about Photoshop's two new tools and a new command for isolating objects from their backgrounds. The new art history brush allows you to give a "painting-like" look to your images. In version 5.5, making job prints and contact sheets is fully automated, and you have better control when entering text. Adobe's bundling of ImageReady 2 in the Photoshop 5.5 package means that now you can easily prepare photos and other bitmapped graphics for use on the Internet or for sending as e-mail attachments. Brand-new features in version 2 of ImageReady include the ability to see 2-Up and 4-Up views of the same image at different levels of optimization, to slice and map images, and to perform JavaScript rollovers like a pro.

Operational Basics

System Setup and Monitor Calibration

If you're just getting into Photoshop (believe me, there are professionals who are just getting into Photoshop), make sure your computer meets the minimum system requirements. I've run the program on slower machines with less memory than Adobe recommends, but you don't really want to do that unless your work is all for the Web and you don't have to do a lot of fancy image compositing. Realistically, plan on using a computer with a processor that's not more than one or two generations old, and see that it's equipped with at least 64 megabytes of RAM and 125 megabytes of hard drive space. You'll also need a CD-ROM drive. At least that's what Adobe recommends. Here's what you'll really benefit from:

- As much RAM as the bank will bear.
- At least 7 or 8 gigabytes of hard drive space—especially if you use Windows. That's because Windows will never give you an out-of-memory error as long as you have plenty of scratch disk. If you own a digital camera, get an even bigger hard drive. You'll find yourself storing photos by the gazillions.
- A Trinitron-based monitor for editing your pictures and another monitor for displaying toolboxes, palettes, and dialogs. (Windows users will have to upgrade to Windows 98 or 2000 to do this.) I'm recommending the Trinitron for images for two reasons: the screens are flatter, so there are fewer reflections, and their ICC phosphor profile is already built into Photoshop and to the modern operating systems. Knowing your monitor's ICC profile makes basic calibration much more reliable. Trinitron tubes are sold in monitors made by many manufacturers, though the patent is held by Sony.

Calibrating Your Monitor

Eventually, you will want to calibrate your whole system so that you can come as close as possible to WYSIWYG—that is, so you end up with a print that looks like the image you saw on your monitor. This means you will eventually want to calibrate your scanner and printer, but you won't be able to do either successfully unless you first calibrate your monitor.

Photoshop 5.5 is fully compliant with Apple's ColorSync, and the built-in Adobe Gamma color correction seems much more accurate than it is in earlier versions. I could give you step-by-step instructions on using Adobe Gamma, but frankly it's much easier to simply choose Help > Color Management. A wizard will appear, as shown in the following illustration, that "holds your hand" through a step-by-step process. You should repeat this process every time you are operating your computer in different ambient light conditions. (Portable users, if your LCD can be adjusted, listen up!) You should also repeat it about once a month to compensate for changes in your monitor's phosphors.

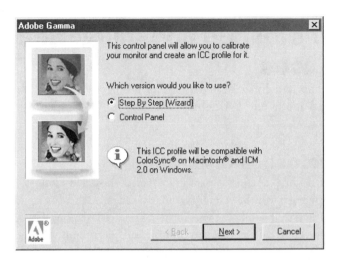

Professional prepress-quality monitor calibration is best accomplished by buying a whole monitor calibration product, including the monitor, from a single vendor, such as Miro's Radius PressView XL. Systems like this include a 21-inch monitor, a professional colorimeter, and everything else you need to automate calibration to an exacting degree. If you need that level of accuracy and have the business to pay for it (it costs around $3,000), by all means do so.

Short of that, any system that uses a suction cup device to read a color target directly from the face of the monitor is likely to be more precise than any system that is purely software based. Systems that use a suction cup are also necessary if you have several computers and want them all to match. At the recommendation of several professional print makers, I've been using the ProveIt! calibration software and their hardware colorimeter. The whole package costs less than $300, making it the most reasonably priced hardware calibration yet. The software, which is also excellent as a software-only calibrator and profiler, comes in versions for both Windows and Macintosh.

Professional Pointer

PressView also comes with a black hood that attaches to the top and sides of the monitor. Its purpose is to cut down on stray light reflections that alter your perception of accurate color. You can do the same thing for your monitor, regardless of how much you paid for it, for very few bucks. Buy some black masking tape, a mat knife, and a piece of black matte mounting board. Neatly cut three strips about 12 inches wide. One should be exactly as long as the top of your monitor; the other two exactly as long as its sides. Use the masking tape to hinge the sides to the top, and then tape the hood to your monitor. You will get a big boost in monitor accuracy and eye comfort.

The Photoshop and ImageReady Interfaces

The Photoshop and ImageReady interfaces are nearly identical. In this book, anything said about one is true of the other—unless a specific difference is mentioned.

The Photoshop Interface

Let's start with a map of the Photoshop interface, shown in Figure 2-1. These interface components will be referenced many times in this book, and it will be taken for granted that you know what is being referred to, as well as the main purpose for all the components of a certain type, such as menus. For the Photoshop interface, as well as for any components that are shared with ImageReady, each of the components is described here.

Menu bar

The menu bar is the repository of Photoshop's major commands, each of which resides on a menu. Menus are titled by category: File, Edit, Image, Layer, Select, Filter, View, Window, and Help.

Menu

A menu appears as soon as you click its name in the menu bar. It contains commands.

Submenu

Many commands have variations, called subcommands. For instance, the New Layer command has five subcommands: New Layer, New Adjustment Layer, New Background Layer, New Layer Via Cut, and New Layer Via Copy. Subcommands are found on submenus.

Toolbox

The toolbox is the repository for all the area-specific brushes, selection tools, erasers, pens, and so forth. It is also the home of the color selection boxes, the edit and screen mode buttons, and the Jump To button for switching to other image editors.

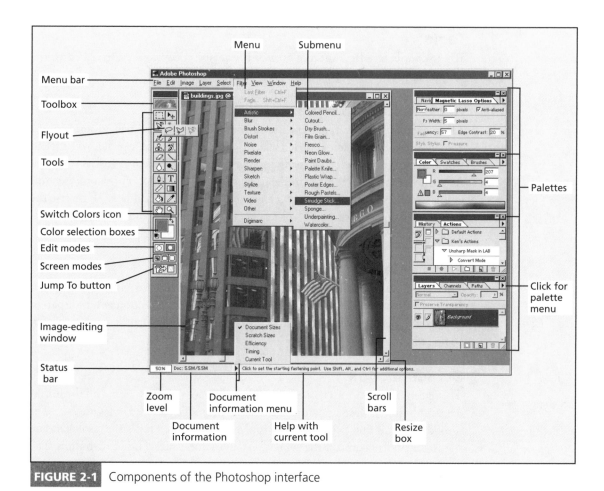

Components of the Photoshop interface

You can show and hide the toolbox and any visible palettes by pressing the TAB key.

Flyout

Flyouts are the submenus of the toolbox. Any tool that has variations has a flyout. The visual indication that a flyout exists is a small black arrowhead in the lower-left corner of the tool button.

To reach a tool on a flyout, either press SHIFT and the shortcut key to rotate through the flyout tools, or click and drag the tool button. As you drag, the flyout appears. Then you just click the tool you want to select.

Tools

You use tools to edit a specific area of the image. Each tool is described in the chapter appropriate to its use.

Color selection boxes

The two larger squares represent the current foreground and background colors. To choose a different color, click a selection box, and the color picker will appear. The default colors are black for the foreground, and white for the background. Any time you want to restore the defaults, click the Default Colors icon (the miniature swatches) in the lower-left corner of the color selection box. To reverse the foreground and background colors, click the Switch Colors icon (the double-headed arrow) in the upper-right corner of the color selection boxes area.

Edit modes

These two buttons allow you to switch between standard editing mode and Quick Mask mode. The latter lets you see and edit any selection as a transparent red mask. This is often referred to as a *rubylith*, in reference to its counterpart in analog photography.

Screen modes

The screen mode buttons make it possible to fill more of the screen with the image. The first button is the Standard Screen mode (the mode pictured in Figure 2-1). The second button is Full Screen Mode with Menu Bar, which hides the scroll bars and status bar and maximizes the window at the same time. The third button, Full Screen Mode, also maximizes the edit window and even removes the menu bar.

The shortcut key for screen modes is F. To toggle between one screen mode and another, press SHIFT+F.

Jump To button

If you don't change the settings, the Jump To button will save your image file and then open it in ImageReady. You can also use this button to jump to other image-editing applications. If you're in ImageReady, you can also jump to HTML editing applications. Jumping to other applications and to HTML editing software is covered in detail later in this chapter.

When you jump between Photoshop, ImageReady, and other applications, a copy of the current file is left open in the window you were originally working in.

Image-editing window

The current state of your image file displays in the image-editing window. You can have multiple image-editing windows open at once, each containing either different files or duplicates of files. Anything you do in Photoshop will be limited to the currently active image-editing window. The currently active window is the one with the title bar whose color is different from the color of the title bar of all the other open windows (usually darker).

To make an image-editing window active, click its title bar. You can also activate it by clicking inside it with any tool, but you risk accidentally making a brush stroke or other edit. You can also switch between windows by choosing from a list of open windows in the Window menu.

Status bar

The status bar contains several fields that inform you about the current state of your document.

ZOOM LEVEL   This field displays the current image magnification. You can change this level at any time by reentering a different number to represent the percentage of zoom. To do so, highlight the number currently in the field, and then type a new number representing the percentage of magnification. You don't need to enter a percent sign. Press RETURN/ENTER to execute the change.

DOCUMENT INFORMATION   This area normally displays two versions of the file's size. The first number is the size the file would be if it were flattened. The second (after the slash) is the file size including all layers and Alpha channels. You can also use the document information menu to change the category of information shown here (see the next topic).

DOCUMENT INFORMATION MENU   The document information menu lets you choose among five types of information to be displayed in the document information space on the status bar. The options are Document Sizes, Scratch Sizes, Efficiency, Timing, and Current Tool.

- *Document Sizes* tells you the byte size of the document.
- *Scratch Sizes* displays the total memory required to display all open images on the left and the total memory allocated to Photoshop on the right. If the number on the left is greater than the number on the right, Photoshop is using the hard drive as a substitute for RAM. This dramatically slows performance.

- *Efficiency* displays the percentage of operations being performed in RAM versus RAM and a scratch disk.
- *Timing* displays how much time it took to complete the last operation.
- *Current Tool* shows the name of the currently chosen toolbox item.

HELP WITH CURRENT TOOL   This status bar field instructs you on how to use the current tool and tells you what modifier keys can be used.

Dialogs

Dialogs (often called dialog boxes) allow you to make settings that affect the way a command is applied. Choosing any menu command that is followed by ellipses (for example, Image > Duplicate) will result in the display of a dialog. Except in the Text dialog, pressing RETURN/ENTER will result in accepting the default settings.

Scroll bars

You can use the scroll bars to move a document from left to right and top to bottom inside the image-editing window.

Resize box

Drag this to resize the image-editing window. It does not affect the size of the image.

Palettes

Palettes provide the means of controlling options in your image-editing environment. They often duplicate menu commands but provide a handier place to find them. By default, palettes appear in group windows in order to save space on your screen. You can drag them from one group window to another. You can also drag them out of a group window, and they will create a window of their own.

All palettes have a row of icons across the bottom that let you execute the commands most frequently associated with that palette. All palettes also have a menu. Finally, you can find many commands related to the operation of specific commands in context menus.

PALETTE MENUS   All palettes have their own menus of commands. To reach a palette's menu, click the small right-facing arrowhead in the upper-right corner of the palette. Although many of these commands duplicate commands found on the palette's icons or commands located on the menu bar, many are unique to their respective palette menus.

The ImageReady Interface

As stated earlier, the Photoshop and ImageReady interfaces have been carefully designed to be as similar as possible. Except where it's specifically noted, the instructions you are given for performing an operation in Photoshop will work in the same way when you happen to be in ImageReady.

The ImageReady interface is pictured in Figure 2-2, and descriptions of the components follow. Only those functions of the interface that are unique to ImageReady are labeled.

Slices menu

Slices are rectangular sections of the image that are treated by HTML as individual images. ImageReady automatically places these images into an HTML table so that they can be seen on the Web as a unified image. The advantage is

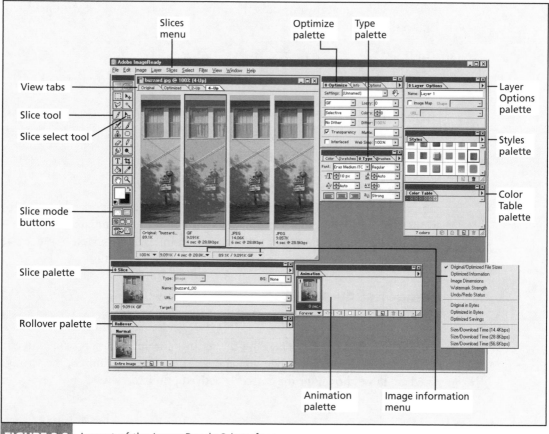

FIGURE 2-2 Layout of the ImageReady 2 interface

twofold: (1) You have a larger image that appears to load much faster because individual slices can be optimized to different degrees. (2) You can assign links and mouse rollover effects to individual slices.

The Slices menu contains commands that are specific to creating and modifying slices.

View tabs

View tabs give you the choice of viewing the original in its original file format, the currently chosen Web-optimized version of the image, two versions of the image, or four versions of the image.

Slice tool

You use the slice tool to draw a rectangle designating the principal slices. ImageReady then automatically draws any slices needed to fill the spaces in the HTML table. ImageReady calls the principal slices *user-slices*. Automatically drawn slices are called *auto-slices*.

Slice select tool

When you want to select a slice for modification, use the slice select tool.

Slice mode buttons

These buttons are used to show or hide slices. Hidden slices will show the HTML background color of the Web page.

Image information menu

The choices on ImageReady's image information menu are considerably different from those on Photoshop's document information menu and are self-explanatory. You can show different image information for each open view of the image by making a different choice in each of the information menus.

ImageReady palettes

The following are palettes unique to the ImageReady 2 interface.

OPTIMIZE PALETTE   These are the settings for optimization as seen in any given view of the image. When you choose File > Save Optimized, the settings used are those chosen for the currently active optimized view.

TYPE PALETTE   This Type palette is much different from Photoshop's because it must control the appearance of type on an HTML page.

LAYER OPTIONS PALETTE   You use the Layer Options palette to rename the layer, change transparency and blend mode, and control the brightness levels of this and the underlying layer as regards blending.

STYLES PALETTE   This palette lets you choose preset layer effects.

COLOR TABLE PALETTE   This palette shows the colors for an optimized PNG-8 or GIF view of the image.

ANIMATION PALETTE   This palette contains the interface for creating animations from layers.

SLICE PALETTE   Here you'll find the interface for assigning links and HTML characteristics to image slices.

ROLLOVER PALETTE   This palette contains the interface for making rollover events. Rollover events are visual changes to the screen that occur when the mouse is in a particular state as regards the portion of the image that the event is assigned to. A typical rollover state would be Mouse Down (meaning that the mouse button had been depressed), and a typical event would be a change in the size or color of the object.

Using Context Menus

A context menu is so called because its contents depend on the location of the cursor. Context menus are the same for both Mac and Windows versions of Photoshop, but they are accessed somewhat differently. Mac users have only one mouse button. Therefore, they must press the Macintosh CONTROL key (not to be confused with CTRL, the Windows control key) while clicking. Windows users press the right mouse button. In this book, you are instructed to CONTROL+click/right-click.

Context menus are associated with the tools or locations in the Photoshop interface. These same menus are available in ImageReady whenever the two programs share the same interface component.

You access a context menu in the same way, regardless of type. You must be actively in the context of that menu. That is, if you want the context menu for a tool, you must have that tool selected. If you want the context menu for what you can do with the contents of a selection, you must click *inside* that selection. If you're using Windows, you always right-click. If you're using a Mac, you press CONTROL and click. For example, this menu is available for the marquee and lasso tools whenever the cursor is located inside an active image-editing window and no active selection has been made:

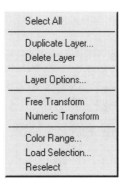

This menu is available for the marquee and lasso tools whenever the cursor is located inside an active selection marquee:

Setting Preferences

The Preferences dialog is where you make Photoshop settings that will remain in effect for all of your work, unless you change them. I recommend that you leave most of these settings at their defaults, until a particular job requires that you deviate for a specific reason or you know your own requirements demand a different setting. Many of the settings can be changed as you work; others won't take effect until you close and reopen Photoshop.

One change I do recommend is that you turn on the Brush Size option in the Display & Cursors preferences. The command sequence for doing this is File > Preferences > Display & Cursors. Select Brush Size in the Painting Cursors area and click OK. Now, when you use a brush, you will see a circle on the screen that describes the area of paint that will be applied by the brush.

To reach the Preferences dialog, choose File > Preferences. There are eight subdialogs or commands: General, Saving Files, Display & Cursors, Transparency & Gamut, Units & Rulers, Guides & Grid, Plug-Ins & Scratch Disks, and Memory & Image Cache. Any of these is directly accessible from any of the others by opening the pop-up menu and clicking another command.

It's a good idea to take a long look at each of these dialogs to understand what each does. Most of the settings are self-explanatory. Those that are not are explained under each of the dialogs shown.

General

The General Preferences dialog, shown next, lets you set those characteristics of Photoshop that most affect your overall operation of the program: which color picker you want as your default; the type of interpolation you want to employ when you rescale an object and whether the sliders instantly preview the currently chosen color; whether the program should beep at you when it has finished a specific job; and how Photoshop handles and recalls the placement of palettes.

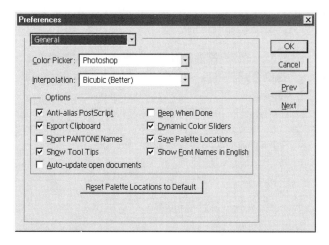

Here's a description of the purpose of each of these settings:

- **Color Picker** Choose between Photoshop's color picker and your system's (Macintosh or Windows) color picker. Using Photoshop's color picker is recommended because you will get better conversion between color modes and more accurate representation of spot colors.

- **Interpolation** Choose Bilinear, Bicubic, or Nearest Neighbor methods of recalculating pixel colors when images are transformed (resized, rotated, etc.). Bicubic interpolation is generally considered to be most accurate. Use Nearest Neighbor when you intentionally want to show pixelization.

- **Beep When Done** Select this if you tend to run long action routines or complex special effects filters—especially if you have a slow processor and limited RAM. The beep will tell you when it's time to go back to work.

- **Dynamic Color Sliders** Preview colors instantly as you move the sliders in the color picker. Turn this feature off if you want to speed performance.

- **Save Palette Locations** Select this box if you want Photoshop to remember where you left a palette just before you closed Photoshop last time.

- **Reset Palette Locations to Default** Click this button to make all of the palettes accessible through their tabs and rearrange them in their group windows. You don't have to restart Photoshop for this to take effect.

Saving Files (Photoshop Only)

The Saving Files Preferences dialog, shown next, lets you choose the settings associated with how files are saved. This includes deciding whether you want to be asked whether and how previews are saved when a file is saved, whether you want to force the addition of file extensions according to file type, and whether you want to save a flattened version of the file in order to make it compatible with programs that can't read layered files.

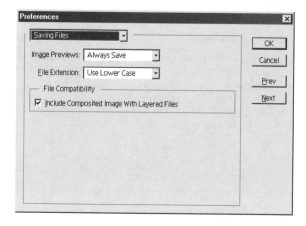

Here's a description of the purpose of each of these settings:

- **Image Previews**   This menu gives you three choices: Ask When Saving, Never Save, and Always Save. Image previews add data to the file, which costs download time when files are transmitted across networks or the Web. On the other hand, they save a lot of blind searching for the right file when you're trying to load files. I like to leave the Ask When Saving choice on; then I'm always reminded *not* to save a preview when I'm saving a Web image. However, this isn't as important as it used to be, because if you use the new Save for Web command, Photoshop will automatically leave off the preview.

- **File Extension**   You can choose to require that file extensions (a requirement for Web graphics and many Windows programs and, therefore, a good habit to get into) be either upper- or lowercase.

- **File Compatibility**   The meaning of this one is obscure, but if you save a flattened version of the file along with any Photoshop layers, you'll be able to open the file in programs that are compatible with Photoshop files but not Photoshop layers. I'd rather just save a separate TIF file. Otherwise, you bulk up your PSD files when you may need that bulk only a small percentage of the time. Of course, if you're an illustrator who uses Photoshop mainly for composing images that will be traced in an illustration program, you can ignore that advice.

Display & Cursors

The Display & Cursors Preferences dialog, shown here, lets you decide on settings that affect how your image is displayed and how different types of Photoshop cursors look:

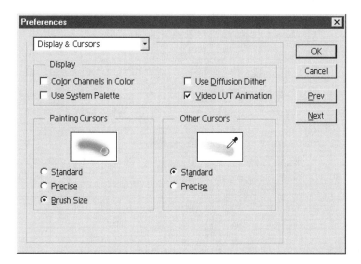

Here's a description of the purpose of each of these settings:

- **Color Channels in Color** This option lets you view color channels in color, which, in my opinion, makes it harder to judge the brightness values in these channels. Seeing the channel in color doesn't help you to judge the color values, either. That's all a function of brightness. The one advantage is that you can see which channel you're editing without referring to the Channels palette.

- **Use System Palette** This option only works with 8-bit color displays. It substitutes the system palette for the Photoshop palette.

- **Use Diffusion Dither** If you're using an 8-bit display, you probably want to select this box so that your display can attempt to simulate a full range of colors.

- **Video LUT Animation** If you experience problems with your video card when you're previewing color changes made by image or filter adjustments, be sure this box is not selected.

- **Painting Cursors and Other Cursors** Choose Standard to show the icon of the chosen tool as the cursor, or choose Precise to show the cursor as a crosshair. If you're serious about what you're doing, you probably want your painting cursors to show the precise brush size so you'll know exactly what areas your strokes are affecting.

Transparency & Gamut

The Transparency & Gamut Preferences dialog, shown next, lets you change the color and size of the checkerboard grid that displays in transparent areas of the image. It also lets you decide whether the program will substitute a contrasting color when CMYK colors are out of gamut, and how opaque that color will be.

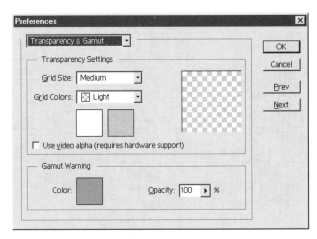

Here's a description of the purpose of each of these settings:

- **Grid Size** Lets you choose the size of the squares in the checkerboard grid that shows through in transparent areas of the image.

- **Grid Colors**   Lets you choose both the color of the grid and whether the grid will be light, medium, or dark.
- **Color swatches**   Let you choose any color in the color picker as the contrasting colors in the transparency grid.
- **Gamut Warning, Color and Opacity**   Choose a color that will sharply contrast with your images so you can easily see areas of out-of-gamut (printing range) colors when working in CMYK mode.

Units & Rulers

The Units & Rulers Preferences dialog, shown next, lets you choose the type of unit (inches, centimeters, etc.) that will be used as the basic unit of measurement, the width of columns (when columns are used as a unit of measurement), and whether points and picas will be sized for traditional or PostScript printing specifications.

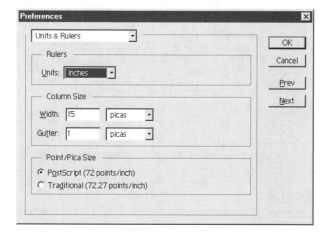

Here's a description of the purpose of each of these settings:

- **Units**   Choices for the units of measurement that will be used in the rulers and in the Info palette are pixels, inches, centimeters, points, picas, and percent. You don't need to restart Photoshop for these settings to take place. In fact, you can watch the figures in the Info palette change as you change the unit type in the dialog.
- **Column Size, Width and Gutter**   The numbers you enter here determine the measurement that Photoshop uses when you open a new file and specify columns as the unit of measurement. If you specify more than one column, the width of the gutter (space between columns) will also be taken into account in determining the overall image size.
- **Point/Pica Size**   Here, you determine whether to measure for digital output on PostScript devices or for traditional analog print shot output.

Guides & Grid

The Guides & Grid Preferences dialog, shown next, lets you choose the color and appearance of guidelines and grid lines. It also lets you choose the distance and unit of measurement for the interval between grid lines and the number of subdivisions for each grid interval.

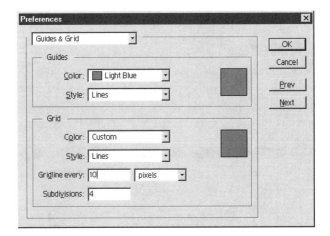

Here's a description of the purpose of each of these settings:

- **Guides, Color and Style**   Choose the guideline color from any of the nine color swatches on this pop-up menu. You can also click in the color swatch to pick any custom color from the color picker.

- **Grid, Color and Style**   Choose the grid line's color and line style from the pop-up menus, or choose a custom color. Choices and the method of choosing are the same as for guidelines.

- **Gridline every**   Enter the number of units that will separate the grid lines. Choose the type of unit (pixels, inches, centimeters, points, picas, and percentage of image size) from the pop-up menu at the immediate right of this field.

- **Subdivisions**   Enter the number of subdivisions for each grid line interval. Then, when you choose View > Snap to Grid, the cursor will snap to either the grid intersections or to the intersection of any of the subdivisions.

Plug-Ins & Scratch Disks

The Plug-Ins & Scratch Disks Preferences dialog, shown next, is used to set the folder in which any Photoshop-compatible plug-in software will be stored. Photoshop will automatically find applications that are stored in subdirectories of the designated plug-in folder. You can also designate up to four different drives where Photoshop will automatically look to find any empty space to use as a scratch disk. A scratch disk doesn't have a fungus. It is used to temporarily store needed data that exceeds the amount of RAM available to Photoshop.

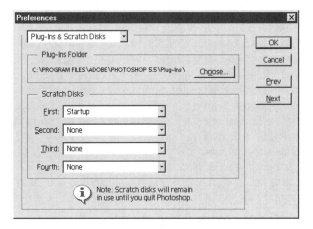

Here's a description of the purpose of each of these settings:

- **Plug-Ins Folder**   Click the Choose button and browse to any folder you want to designate as your plug-ins folder.
- **Scratch Disks**   Designate as many as four different drives from the list of currently active hard drives on each of the four pop-up menus in this box.

Memory & Image Cache

The Memory & Image Cache Preferences dialog, shown next, lets you determine the image dimensions that Photoshop will subsample from the original. These subsamples (smaller images) will be used for calculating the effects of filters and other commands that affect the entire image when the image is seen at less than 100 percent.

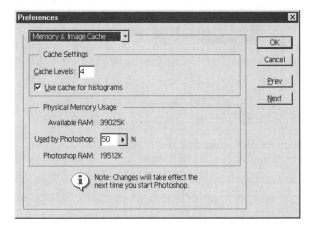

Here's a description of the purpose of each of these settings:

- **Cache Levels and Use Cache for Histograms** You can enter a number of subsamplings of the image that Photoshop should make. Then, whenever you are working in a zoomed-out window, Photoshop will recalculate only the pixels in the subsampling closest to the size of the preview window. This can greatly speed the processing of filters, transformations, and other operations that require a lot of recalculation in the previews. Of course, the recalculation has to occur on all of the pixels at the real resolution of the file itself; but since those pixels aren't being displayed, their recalculation progresses much more quickly anyway. If you always work on small images and have limited memory (lots of Web authors work this way), you should keep the number of caches to a minimum. Also, more than four or five is overkill except on the very largest images and on machines with more than 256MB of RAM. Unless absolute accuracy in histograms is important to you (as in some scientific applications), you'll want to select the Use Cache for Histograms box, too.

- **Physical Memory Usage (Windows only)** Windows applications automatically use as much memory as they can find, but you may want to force a certain percentage of memory to be allocated to Photoshop. If so, this is the place to do it. Either enter a percentage or drag the slider.

Using the History Palette

The History palette records each of your Photoshop actions—anything from a command to a stroke of the brush—as you do them. As long as you don't go over your specified number of recordable actions, you can instantly return to any image state by clicking the History State bar for an earlier stage of the image. A map of the History palette, with instructions on how to use it, can be seen in Figure 2-3.

As shown in Figure 2-3, you reach the History Options dialog from the History palette menu. There are three settings: Maximum History States, Automatically Create First Snapshot, and Allow Non-Linear History, as shown here:

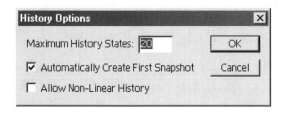

Just how much history you track should depend on the amount of RAM you have installed and the size of the images you're dealing with. If you have more than 128MB of RAM or are dealing mostly with small images for the Web, you can probably get away with more than the default 20 history states.

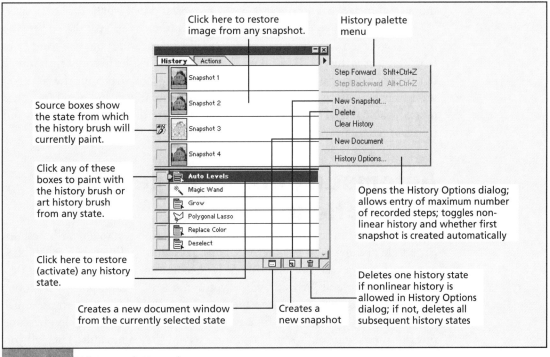

FIGURE 2-3 History palette and menu

You should almost always leave the Automatically Create First Snapshot box selected. It's good insurance, since you can always return to or duplicate a snapshot. However, you should also remember to take more snaps whenever you make a major change in the appearance of your file or whenever you want to create an effect that you may brush in later.

Select the Allow Non-Linear History box if you want to be able to create a new effect several steps before the last step in the list but don't want to dump the steps that follow. The new step will still come at the end of the list, but you will be able to go back to those that came in between. You can always toggle this; so if you decide later that you want to dump all the steps that occur after a certain point, you can reopen the Options dialog and deselect the check box.

Special Effects with the History Brush

You can get some very nice (sometimes ethereal) effects by painting in effects created by filters or textures that come from other images. To do this from a special effects layer, duplicate the layer you want to filter and then run the filter. To do it from another image, open the other image and use the move tool to drag it into the current image. It will appear on its own layer, and that will be the active layer. Take a snapshot when the new image or filtered layer is selected; then delete the filtered layer (you don't have to, but it keeps it from covering your work and saves RAM for better things). Now all you have to do is click the history brush source box in the History palette to the left of the new snapshot, make sure the layer you want to paint onto is selected, set your brush transparency and blend modes as desired, and paint. If at first you don't succeed, delete the history brush steps and try again. Exciting stuff. Possibilities without end.

Automating Boring Repetition with Actions

Now here's one of the most productive things you can learn to do in Photoshop. *Actions* are nothing more than recorded macros. Adobe polishes their capabilities with each new revision of Photoshop. It's become such a popular activity that there are now several Web sites where you can download and play with actions that were created by experienced Photoshoppers. You don't need to use other people's actions, though. Any time you find yourself doing essentially the same three-or-more-step routine, get smart and record the commands. Then all you have to do is press a function key or click a menu bar to execute the whole routine at several times the speed that you could do it by hand.

Actions have been improved quite a bit since they were introduced in version 4. All actions that were created in version 4 can be played in current versions of Photoshop, but actions created in Photoshop 5 and 5.5 cannot be played in Photoshop 4. Most commands and some tools can now be recorded. Exceptions are the painting and toning tools, tool options, view commands, and preferences. Commands that can't be recorded can be inserted. An inserted command doesn't execute until the action is played, so those commands won't affect the file that was used to record the action. Furthermore, no values are specified for the command when it is inserted, so the command pauses during playback to let you make settings according to the moment.

There are also some tools and palettes that can now be recorded: the marquee, crop, move, lasso, polygon, magic wand, line, type, gradient, and paint bucket tools, and the Paths, Channels, Layers, and History palettes. Also recordable are the Actions menu's Play and Batch commands. This makes it possible to have actions record actions. Are we having fun yet?

To reveal the Actions palette, choose Window > Show/Hide Actions. The Actions palette is shown in Figure 2-4. The left column shows a series of check marks indicating whether a command will be executed. You can toggle these check marks on and off by clicking them. So if you want to run an action but

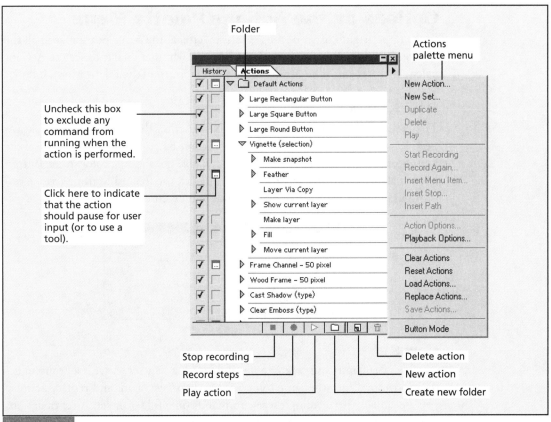

FIGURE 2-4   Actions palette and flyout

don't want to include one of the commands in that action's list, just turn off that command's check box. If you're creating a complex action, you may be able to make it do multiple variations, simply by turning some command on and off just before running the action.

The middle column is the "break" column. If you click this check box, the adjoining command will pause for user input.

The wide right-hand column holds the names of the actions. Click the right-pointing arrow for an action, and you see all the individual commands contained in the action. Click the right-pointing arrow (aka the Expand icon) for a command, and you will see all the option settings for that command.

The Actions palette actually has two modes (a word Adobe seems to adore): List and Button. Button mode lists the actions as a stack of buttons. You simply click the button to run the action. List mode shows the list of available actions in the three-column format shown in Figure 2-4.

Options on the Actions Palette Menu

In the upper-right corner of the Actions palette, at the same location as in all the Photoshop palettes, is a right-facing black arrowhead. Click it to see the Actions palette flyout menu. The commands on this menu, and their definitions, follow.

New Action

The New Action command opens the New Action dialog. This dialog, shown next, lets you type in a name for the new action, assign it a function key (or if the Shift box is selected, a SHIFT+function key), give the action a color in the Button Mode palette, and begin recording. As you click the Record button, actions will start remembering any "legal" commands you execute.

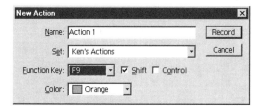

New Set

The New Set command creates a new folder for a new set. A set is a group of actions organized into the same folder. When you save, load, and replace actions, you are actually performing these commands on a folder or set. A set of actions can be created by anyone on any computer running Photoshop. You can then open that set of actions on your computer. The dialog, which simply lets you name the new folder, is shown here:

Duplicate

The Duplicate command duplicates the selected, previously recorded action. Then you can edit steps in the action to create a new action. The duplicated action will have the same name, followed by "copy." You can change the name (or any of the other associated options) by double-clicking the filename.

Delete

Click the Delete command, and a dialog will ask you, "Delete Selected Action?" Click OK, and it's gone. This can also be used to delete a single command within an action.

Play

The Play command causes the commands in the action to be executed in the sequence in which they appear in the action. This has the same effect as clicking the Record button in the VCR-style controls. The command can also be used to play an action starting with the selected command.

Tip: The Play Only command that appeared in Photoshop 4 is gone. You can still play only one command in an action by highlighting that command in the Actions palette and clicking the Play button.

Start Recording

The Start Recording command lets you start recording. More importantly, it lets you start recording again after you've paused (clicked the Break icon) to insert a command or to use a nonrecordable tool.

Record Again

The Record Again command is a quick way to change all the settings in an action in order to produce a new variation of the result. It automatically steps you through each command in an already-recorded action and lets you change the settings in each of the associated dialogs.

Insert Menu Item

The Insert Menu Item command lets you insert any command from Photoshop 4's main menu. You can also insert some commands from the various palette flyouts. Flyout commands that can't be inserted will be grayed.

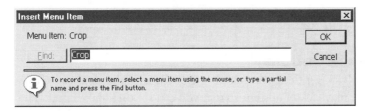

Insert Stop

The Insert Stop command causes the action to pause when it is played back. Stops let you perform nonrecordable tasks, such as painting with a brush. When you execute the Insert Stop command, the Record Stop dialog appears, as shown in the following illustration. You can type any instructions you like in the Message area. Selecting the Allow Continue check box places a Continue button in the message dialog so that the user can continue playing the action after following the suggestions in the instructions box.

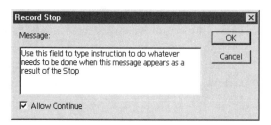

Insert Path

The Insert Path command lets you specify a path within an action. In this way, the action can be performed so that it includes loading, saving, or changing a file located in a particular directory path.

Action Options

The Action Options command opens the dialog for the selected action, as shown next. If a command within the action is selected, you will still get the Options dialog for the parent action.

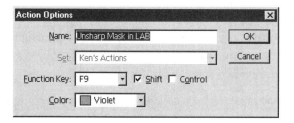

Playback Options

The Playback Options command opens a dialog that lets you choose to slow down the playback of options so that you can see them take effect. This can help you judge how to fine-tune actions. In addition to the default Accelerated playback, you can choose to see each step as it is processed, or to pause for a specified number of seconds after each action is completed.

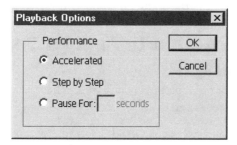

Clear Actions
The Clear Actions command removes every action set you've stored on your Actions palette. Don't worry, you can always reload them, one at a time, as long as you remembered to save them.

Reset Actions
If you've used the Clear Actions command, you can restore all the Photoshop 4 default actions with this command. You can also use it to clear all but the default actions: RGB to Indexed Color, Reduce Graininess, Drop Shadow, Vignette, Image Size, and Revert.

Load Actions
The Load Actions command places any chosen action set saved to disk on the Actions palette list.

Replace Actions
The Replace Actions command lets you replace all of the currently loaded action sets with one from a previously saved disk file.

Save Actions
The Save Actions command saves an entire set of actions. When you want to save a single action, delete all the others in the set. Remember, you can always reload any set you've saved.

Button Mode

The Button Mode command toggles between List mode and Button mode. A check mark appears before the command when Button mode is active.

Creating an Action to Apply a Sepia Tone to a Photograph

The following exercise will give you a good idea of how easy it is to create an action that you can use over and over.

1. Open an image to which you would like to apply a sepia tone, such as a portrait of your grandmother taken when she was a girl.

2. From the main menu, choose Window > Show Actions (unless the Actions palette is already visible). From the Actions palette flyout, make sure Button Mode is not checked.

3. From the Actions palette flyout, choose New Action. In the dialog, enter the name **Sepia tone**. Click the Record button.

4. From the main menu, choose Image > Adjust > Hue-Saturation. The Hue-Saturation dialog appears. Choose Master from the Edit pop-up menu. Slide the Saturation slider to the left until it reads –100 (or type that figure into the Saturation box). The other two sliders should remain at 0. Make sure the Colorize box is not selected. Click OK. The command Hue/saturation will appear on the Actions list. This command has removed all the color from the image, but the image is still in RGB mode so that you can add color later.

5. From the main menu, choose Image > Adjust > Color Balance. The Color Balance dialog appears. Make sure the Midtone radio button is chosen. Move the top slider toward red until it reads approximately 46. Leave the middle slider at 0. Move the bottom slider toward yellow until it reads approximately –33. Make sure the Preserve Luminosity box is selected—if not, the adjustments you've made will cause the image to fade slightly.

6. Stop the recording. You can either click the VCR-style Stop button at the bottom of the Actions palette or choose Stop Recording from the Actions palette menu.

That's all there is to recording an action.

To use an action that has been recorded, from the Actions palette menu, load the set to which the action was recorded (of course, you won't have to do that if the action is already loaded). Then all you have to do is play the action. You can do that by following this procedure:

- Highlight the action, and then click the Play button at the bottom of the Actions palette.
- Choose Play from the Actions palette menu.

- Press a function key assigned to the action in the Action Options dialog. You access the Action Options dialog by double-clicking the action's name bar in the Actions palette.

- Choose Button Mode from the Actions palette menu, and then click the button bearing the name of the action.

Using the Info Palette

Whenever you need to know the exact values of primaries in a color, the coordinates of the cursor in respect to the upper-right corner of the image, or the pixel dimensions of a selection marquee, have a look at the Info palette. If you don't see it onscreen, choose Window > Show Info. Instructions on how to use the Info palette are in Figure 2-5.

Professional Pointer

You will often want to measure the size of a portion of your image—perhaps to see how it will fit a particular layout or whether it will fit inside another element or layer. Use the rectangular marquee tool to make a selection around the area you want to measure. Once you've written down the measurements, press CMD/CTRL+D to drop the selection.

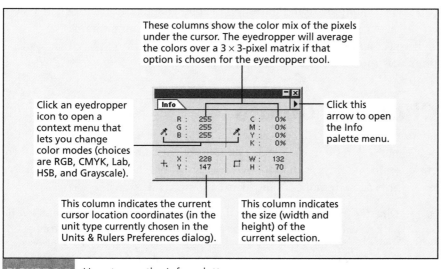

These columns show the color mix of the pixels under the cursor. The eyedropper will average the colors over a 3 × 3-pixel matrix if that option is chosen for the eyedropper tool.

Click an eyedropper icon to open a context menu that lets you change color modes (choices are RGB, CMYK, Lab, HSB, and Grayscale).

Click this arrow to open the Info palette menu.

This column indicates the current cursor location coordinates (in the unit type currently chosen in the Units & Rulers Preferences dialog).

This column indicates the size (width and height) of the current selection.

FIGURE 2-5 How to use the Info palette

Jumping Between Image-Editing Applications

Adobe has been hard at work making its application interfaces more and more integrated. The latest trick is a button at the bottom of the toolbox that lets you instantly (well, almost) take your current file into another application. Both Photoshop and ImageReady have this button, and Adobe plans to add it to its other products as well.

The Jump To button is not the only method for jumping between applications. Using either a keyboard shortcut (CMD/CTRL+SHIFT+M) or choosing File > Jump To > Graphics Editor or File > Jump To > HTML Editor (ImageReady only) makes it possible to jump between Photoshop and ImageReady—or from either of these products to any other graphics product that can accept Photoshop file input. All it takes to set this up is making a shortcut (Windows) or an alias (Macintosh) and placing it inside the Jump to Graphics folder.

If you jump using the File > Jump To command, you'll see a submenu that lists all the applications whose shortcuts you've placed in the Jump To folder (or folders, if you're in ImageReady).

If you jump using the shortcut keys, you'll always jump to whatever application has been designated as the default. ImageReady is the default designated Jump To application for Photoshop and vice versa. To change the designation, go to the Jump To folder and rename the shortcuts so that the default is enclosed by brackets, like this: [Adobe Photoshop 5.5]. The brackets should be curly brackets ({ }) if you're jumping from Photoshop to another application and square brackets ([ ]) if you're jumping from ImageReady to another application.

If you're jumping from ImageReady to an HTML editor, place that application's alias/shortcut inside the Jump to HTML folder.

Choosing Colors

Photoshop lets you choose colors in virtually any way you find convenient. You can even choose colors from schemes that don't match the current mode. However, there are four principal ways of choosing color: directly from the image, from one of several color pickers, from the Color palette, and from the Swatches palette.

- **Directly from the image**   You choose colors directly from the image by clicking with the eyedropper tool, as shown in Figure 2-6. The Eyedropper option also provides a check box so that you can average the color of pixels over a 3 × 3 matrix. This gives you a way to pick a solid color that comes closest to

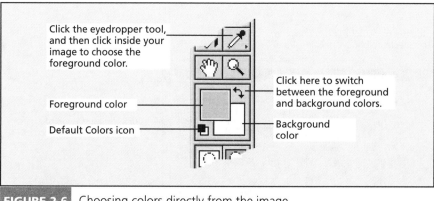

Click the eyedropper tool, and then click inside your image to choose the foreground color.

Foreground color

Default Colors icon

Click here to switch between the foreground and background colors.

Background color

FIGURE 2-6 Choosing colors directly from the image

matching dithered colors or the color of sky or pavement that is actually made of several close pixel values.

- **From one of several color pickers** It is best to choose color using the Photoshop Color Picker dialog, shown in Figure 2-7, for several reasons. The most important is that it will give you accurate representation of all your swatch book color choices (see the next section, "Choosing Pantone and Other Swatch Book Colors"). It is also a cross-platform color picker, which means that others who deal with your images are more likely to see the same colors. You can also choose from your operating system's color picker. Select your preferred color picker from the Color Picker pop-up menu in the General Preferences dialog, shown in the "Setting Preferences" section under the "General" heading, earlier in this chapter. To open Photoshop's Color Picker dialog, click the foreground (or background) color selection box on the toolbox.

- **From the Color palette** The Color palette gives you access to the full range of colors available to you (except for custom colors) in a less space-hungry format. See Figure 2-8 for a visual tutorial on using the Color palette.

- **From the Swatches palette** The Swatches palette lets you choose colors from any indexed color palette, even when you are working in True-Color (24-bit color). It's an easy way to make sure you're picking a Web-safe color. It's also an easy way to ensure that you always pick the same shade of a given color. Figure 2-9 shows the Swatches palette.

The chosen colors are always shown in the color selection boxes in the toolbox. The foreground color is the one on top (no kidding). Guess which is the background color?

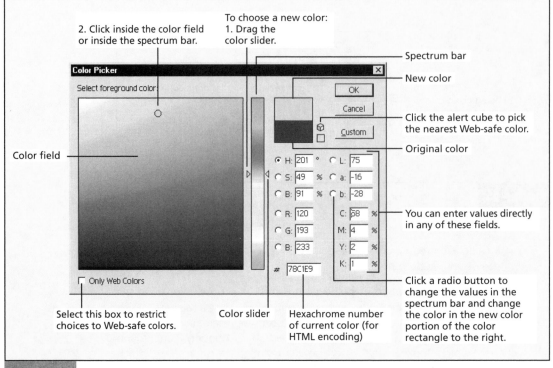

To choose a new color:
1. Drag the color slider.

2. Click inside the color field or inside the spectrum bar.

Spectrum bar

New color

Click the alert cube to pick the nearest Web-safe color.

Original color

Color field

You can enter values directly in any of these fields.

Only Web Colors

Click a radio button to change the values in the spectrum bar and change the color in the new color portion of the color rectangle to the right.

Select this box to restrict choices to Web-safe colors.

Color slider

Hexachrome number of current color (for HTML encoding)

FIGURE 2-7 Choosing colors from Photoshop's Color Picker dialog

Professional Pointer

You can choose the closest Web-safe color at any time, regardless of whether you are using indexed color, using ImageReady, or are currently working on an image destined for the Web. Choosing a Web-safe color is an excellent idea if you're picking colors for solid-color areas such as frames, logo backgrounds, and type. Then you know that these important elements will translate properly to Web usage when viewed on virtually any computer system. To do this, click one of the color selection boxes to bring up the Color Picker dialog. Select the Only Web Colors check box in the lower-right corner. The color picker will then display only Web colors, so that's all you can choose.

Choosing Pantone and Other Swatch Book Colors

You can pick swatch book–specific colors from the following color-matching systems:

- PANTONE Coated, PANTONE Uncoated, PANTONE Process, and PANTONE ProSim custom colors

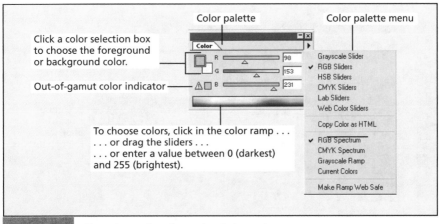

FIGURE 2-8 Choosing colors from the Color palette

- TRUMATCH
- FOCOLTONE
- TOYO Color Finder 1050
- ANPA-COLOR ROP Newspaper Color Ink Book
- DIC Color Guide

To choose from any of these systems, follow the instructions in Figure 2-10.

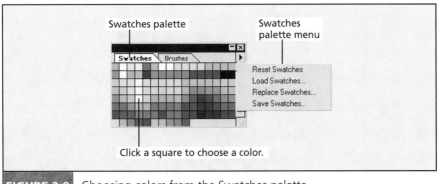

FIGURE 2-9 Choosing colors from the Swatches palette

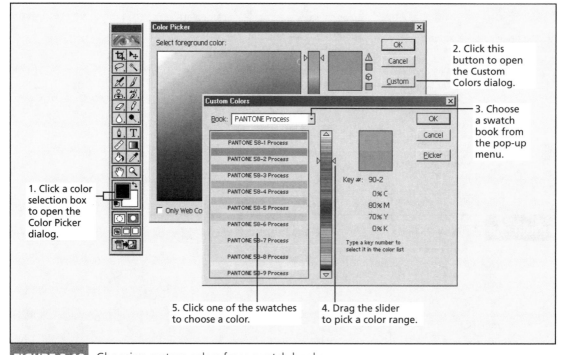

1. Click a color selection box to open the Color Picker dialog.

2. Click this button to open the Custom Colors dialog.

3. Choose a swatch book from the pop-up menu.

5. Click one of the swatches to choose a color.

4. Drag the slider to pick a color range.

FIGURE 2-10 Choosing custom colors from swatch books

Choosing Screen Modes

Photoshop lets you work in seven different color spaces: Bitmap, Grayscale, Duotone, Indexed Color, RGB Color, CMYK Color, Lab Color, and Multichannel. To choose a color mode (everybody but Photoshop calls these color *models*—no real difference), choose Image > Mode, and then choose any of the color models listed. Here's the Mode menu:

A brief discussion of each of these modes follows. It's meant to advise you as to the appropriateness of using different modes for different circumstances and purposes. They are listed in the order of the frequency with which you're likely to need or use them.

RGB (Red, Green, Blue)

RGB mode contains the colors of light, otherwise known as *transmissive* color. RGB is also called *additive* color because all of the colors in its spectrum are made up by adding its primary colors together. Devices that use RGB color are monitors, slides, digital cameras, and the Web. (Well, many Web graphics stick to indexed color, but that's a lowest-common-denominator thing to make sure that even the worst-equipped color monitors stand a reasonable chance of viewing the colors as they were originally composed.)

In this mode, the full range of 24-bit colors are viewable and editable on monitors. Furthermore, all Photoshop commands and tools are available in RGB color. Unless you are working with an image that was scanned on a high-end CMYK scanner, you should almost always do your Photoshop full-color editing and composing in this mode. RGB is also compatible with more raster image file formats than any other color mode.

The drawback to RGB is that it can make more colors visible than are printable. However, you can always preview your colors in CMYK without converting them (thereby causing a loss of data). To preview, choose View > Preview > CMYK.

Lab (Lightness, a-channel, b-channel)

Lab color is neither additive nor subtractive and is completely device independent. It also has a wider gamut than RGB—so wide, in fact, that it covers all the colors available to both RGB and CMYK. You can also access all the Photoshop commands in this mode. In fact, it's Photoshop's native mode. I don't use it as much as RGB for editing (and I suspect others don't) because we're just not used to the idea of mixing colors by using the *a* (blue-yellow) and *b* (red-green) channels. Another reason Lab may not be used as much as RGB is that it's risky if your end result is print because it's even easier to create colors that are way out of gamut.

There are definite advantages to using Lab for correcting certain problems, particularly with digital and digitized photos. Those cases will be brought to your attention as appropriate in other chapters of this book.

CMYK (Cyan, Magenta, Yellow, and blacK)

CMYK is the color model for anything you view by reflective color—such as all the flowers in the field and everything that appears in print. What Photoshoppers are mostly concerned with is the "everything that appears in print" part. If print is

Tip: Before converting from Lab or RGB to CMYK, be sure you have calibrated your monitor as well as the state of your personal technology allows. In other words, at least use the Adobe Color Management Wizard described at the beginning of this chapter. Otherwise, you are definitely going to lose more data in the translation than is necessary.

the destination for your images, you will definitely want to end up in this color mode before you send your file to your print shop or service bureau.

Indexed Color

Indexed color gets its name from the fact that each color in the image is assigned to a specific row and column coordinate in a palette of limited colors. Change the color of one of the palette's cells, and you change all instances of that color throughout the image, as well as in any other images assigned to that palette—for instance, other frames in an animation.

You rarely want to use indexed color for photographs, as the limited (256 maximum) number of colors tends to cause a loss of detail and shading. Colors tend to flatten out into bands of color in an effect generally referred to as *posterization*.

On the other hand, most navigational and informational Web graphics, as well as thumbnail images, are assigned to the GIF file format. The GIF file format accepts only indexed color. Another thing to keep in mind where Web graphics are concerned is that GIF offers the only (nearly) universal guarantee that an image with a transparent background will be viewable.

Grayscale

This is the mode for what we have become accustomed to calling "black-and-white" photography. If you're aiming for a black-and-white end product, you'll find working in grayscale mode much faster than working in color. That's an especially worthwhile tip if you're short on horsepower or memory. However, given today's fast processors, I find I'd rather keep all the data in the image for as long as possible. There's always the possibility that I can pull a little more detail out of one of the color channels.

You can convert from any color mode to grayscale and back again as many times as you like. Of course, you won't be able to retain the color you had in the image before it was converted to grayscale. However, there's a certain charm to hand-colored grayscale images. (All it takes to hand color a monotone image is converting that image to RGB mode and then choosing Color as the blend mode for your brushes.) You could even sepia-tone the image before you hand-color it to get a really classic look.

Bitmap

Most of us refer to all photo and paint program files as bitmaps, so it's a bit confusing that Adobe refers to a pure black-and-white image as a bitmap. Nevertheless, that's

Professional Pointer

It may not be in your best interest to convert from the composite channel of a color mode to grayscale. Take a look at the grayscale interpretation in individual color channels. Each of these looks like a black-and-white photo taken through a colored filter. Thus the range of tones may actually be more dramatic than the composite's range of tones. If you convert to grayscale while a color channel is selected (that is, while it is being viewed in the image-editing window), Photoshop retains the gray values as they were in that color channel.

what they mean here. This is actually one of the most complicated color mode conversions. First, you can't convert directly from a color mode. You have to first convert the image to grayscale. Second, rather than showing you an instant conversion, a dialog appears that requires you to make several choices. Figure 2-11 shows you the dialog and explains each of those choices.

The result of applying each of the conversion methods is shown in Figure 2-12 and discussed here. First, Figure 2-12a shows the grayscale image we're converting from.

- **50% Threshold** Uses 50 percent gray as the division between absolute black and white. This makes for a very high contrast image, as shown in Figure 2-12b. You may find uses for this image as a masking channel.

- **Pattern Dither** Mixes pixels into a diagonal pattern that is hard to imagine a use for (see Figure 2-12c). There are no options for varying this pattern.

- **Diffusion Dither** Clumps black-and-white pixels into an irregular pattern, as shown in Figure 2-12d, in order to simulate grayscale with only two shades of gray.

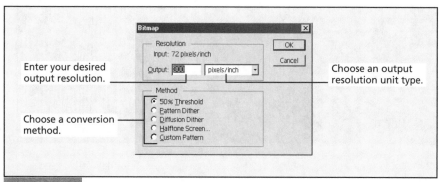

FIGURE 2-11 The Bitmap dialog and how to use it

- **Halftone Screen** Presents a dialog that gives you quite a bit of flexibility in determining the lines per inch, pattern angle, and dot shape of the halftone. Figure 2-12e shows the effect of using this option on the building image.
- **Custom Pattern** Allows you to apply a custom pattern if you have made a rectangular marquee selection and then chosen Edit > Define Pattern. (Otherwise, it will be grayed.) A pattern so defined is then applied in making the

a. Original grayscale image   b. 50% Threshold   c. Pattern Dither

d. Diffusion Dither   e. Halftone Screen   f. Custom Pattern

FIGURE 2-12 Bitmap mode options applied to the building image

halftone. You can use all sorts of noise and special effects filters to create texture patterns and then use these patterns to make an endless variety of mezzotint effects. The pattern in Figure 2-12f was made from the vertical lines in one of the buildings.

Duotone

The Duotone color mode allows the creation of images that print with more than one ink, thus greatly increasing the number of tones possible in an image. In printing, a single ink can only reproduce about 50 levels of gray. So each additional ink adds another 50 levels. Photoshop will also let you specify different colors of ink, which can make the apparent dynamic range even greater.

In order to convert an image to Duotone mode, you must first convert it to Grayscale mode.

Multichannel

Multichannel mode is used for spot color channels or for multicolor images that use special inks for special effects. If you want to create a duotone wherein one part of the image is restricted to a specific tonal range, you can also convert the duotone to Multichannel mode. You could then erase or otherwise manipulate the output of the individual inks by editing the channels to which they are assigned.

Installing Plug-Ins

Most third-party, Photoshop-compatible plug-ins use automated installation routines that are the same as those used for installing any other software on your system. You can also download many public-domain and shareware plug-ins from the Internet. To install these plug-ins, simply place them in the folder that you chose in File > Preferences > Plug-Ins & Scratch Disks.

Using the Help Menu

Photoshop's help feature is one of the best indexed and most complete in the business. The Macintosh Help menu looks like this:

The Windows Help menu is the same minus the first two items related to balloon help. That's because the Windows equivalent, in-context help, is always turned on. Also, the Windows Help menu has an item called About Plug-In that gives you a menu of all the installed plug-ins. Choose a plug-in and you get its splash screen, which shows you the program's version number and publisher, and often provides information about the authors and displays the serial number. Mac users can get the same information under the Apple menu when the plug-in is running.

The use of the rest of the Help menu items, with the exception of Color Management (because it's covered at the beginning of this chapter), is explained in the following sections.

Help Topics

Choosing Help Topics gives you access to the entire text of the Photoshop, ImageReady, and supplementary manuals online. You can also execute this command by simply pressing F1. You can search by using the table of contents, any topic in the index, or any keyword in the text. If you can't find a topic by using one of these three methods, chances are, it doesn't exist.

Each search method has a tab in the Topics dialog. The Macintosh version has a greater capability for Boolean searching. You can add to or subtract from the number of possible choices by pressing the appropriate button. This is the part of the help interface I rely on most often. It takes a little longer, but you get all the references to your keywords, no matter what their context, in one search. I feel that in the long run it is the most direct and time-saving route.

How to Use Help

This is the menu choice that gives me an excuse to keep this section of the chapter to a minimum. After all, if you want to know more about using Help, the needed information can be found right under this menu choice.

Export Transparent Image (Photoshop Only)

This is one of three wizards on the Help menu that take you through multiple-step tasks that most of us find a need to do over and over: monitor calibration, resizing images (particularly in preparation for Web optimization), and exporting transparent images for use on the Web. Yet we may not do them often enough to remember the exact routine for producing the best results. These wizards act much like modern software installation programs. They present you with the logical sequence of steps and ask you to make choices when there are choices to be made.

Export Transparent Image lets you knock out a portion of the image to a transparent background and then put it into the proper format for either print or the

Web. When you choose Help > Export Transparent Image, a series of wizard dialogs appear. Each asks you a question and then lets you either go back to the previous step (unless you're at the first step) or forward to the next step. Here are the questions, along with my help on some of the answers that may not be self-explanatory:

1. Which option best describes your image?

   - **My image is on a transparent background.** In order to qualify, the selected image layer must be transparent outside the shape of the image.

   - **I have selected the area to be made transparent.** Careful here—don't choose this unless you have selected the area you want to keep and then *inverted* the selection to include everything else.

   - **I need to select the area to be made transparent.** If you select this, you will have to cancel the wizard, make your selection, and then restart the wizard.

2. What will this image be used for?

   - **Print.** Choose this one and the image is exported with a clipping path to an EPS file for inclusion in a page layout program.

   - **Online.** Lets you choose between GIF or PNG formats. If you choose GIF, you'll have to pick a method for reducing color (see Chapter 15). If you choose PNG, you can have 24-bit color, but many Web browsers will require a plug-in in order to view the file. The wizard will give you a fairly complete range of choices, such as number of colors, dithering method, matting colors, and whether or not to use interlacing. However, if you're just learning to optimize GIFs, you could expect better results by experimenting in multiple views from inside ImageReady.

Resize Image (Photoshop Only)

This wizard makes it easy for a beginner to properly size images for the desired quality of output with as much precision as a pro could do it. It doesn't matter

Professional Pointer

Always use this wizard before jumping to ImageReady. That way, you'll accomplish several things at once: (1) The wizard automatically creates a duplicate, guaranteeing separate Web and original copies of the image, so you'll always retain the maximum amount of image information. (2) It's faster than manually resizing the image. (3) You can work much faster in ImageReady if your images are already sized for the Web when you start.

whether that output is for print or the Web. As is the case with the Export Transparent Image command, you're asked all the right questions for either situation.

Using Adobe Online

If you click the eye logo at the top of the toolbox and your computer is wired to the Net, you'll go straight to Adobe's Web site. It's not a bad habit to get into, to try one of the online tips each week. Some are excellent—and they'll probably inspire you to invent new tips on your own. Of course, there's all sorts of information posted about other Adobe products, the latest news, and even a set of links to other sites that specialize in Photoshop.

You should click the logo every once in a while because it will automatically search the Adobe site for any updates to your version of the program and then (with your click of permission) download them for you. Once you get past the update stage, you see this navigation window:

Professional Skills Summary

This has been a chapter to guide you through the use of Photoshop tools and features that you will need to employ across many of the operations covered in the other chapters of this book. Novices will have learned about some basics, but more advanced users are also likely to have learned some useful tips and advice.

chapter 3

Making Image Adjustments

In this chapter, you:

- Trim, or crop, your image to eliminate visual distractions
- Use the Auto Levels command
- Make proper use of Photoshop 5.5's new Auto Contrast command
- Correct exposure with the Levels, Curves, Brightness/Contrast, and Hue/Saturation commands
- Work with adjustment layers
- Correct for white balance after the photo has been taken
- Adjust color balance for dramatic effect
- Adjust exposure for small details within the image
- Apply different exposure and color controls to different parts of the image
- Change the size of the image
- Get details in highlights and shadows in high-contrast scenes

About Image Adjustments

Whether you shoot your pictures on film and then scan them, or shoot them with a digital camera, a good percentage of your photos will need corrections (or at least, changes) for both color balance and tonal (exposure) balance. If you're the artist (as opposed to a prepress production person), you'll want to correct your images no matter how well you've calibrated your digital equipment. There are several reasons for this:

- You can't always control all the elements of light and still hope to shoot fast enough to capture the moment.
- The "rules" (especially for exposure and color balance) don't always pertain. There will be times when you will have your own artistic and subjective reasons for wanting to make a change.
- There are too many variables in the precision and calibration of contributing equipment (for example, studio strobes, reflective walls, lens coatings, scanner settings).
- You will find it easier to compensate for minor variations in color and contrast once you have the image in Photoshop than to meticulously calculate the difference in color between four o'clock sunlight and five o'clock sunlight or the sudden intervention of a wispy cloud between your subject and the sun.

I could have titled this chapter "The Digital Darkroom," since the material I'll cover is analogous to choosing the development time of your film, the contrast of the paper you're going to print on, the exposure of the enlarging paper, the time of development, and so forth. The difference is that the processes are much faster and easier when you do the job digitally in Photoshop. You will also have much more control over the results you produce.

A Logical Sequence for Making Corrections

There are no absolute laws by which you must abide when doing any aspect of digital imaging. However, if time is money to you and if your reputation rests on your ability to produce consistent results, there is a sequence of events that is most likely to work best for you.

If you want to minimize duplication of effort and avoid making mistakes that will be harder to undo later without affecting subsequent steps, you will want to work in the following order:

1. Crop the image.
2. Correct overall exposure.
3. Correct overall color balance.
4. Correct exposure in image details.
5. Correct color balance in image details.

6. Retouch your image (see Chapter 4 for these details).

7. Impose additional photographic effects (see Chapter 10 for these details).

8. Do any desired compositing (as described in Part II).

9. Create artistic effects (see Chapter 11 for these details).

Cropping Your Images

Cropping the image is the single most effective change you can make to strengthen the composition (and therefore, the message) in your photograph. Digitally speaking, it also has a pair of major side benefits:

- You minimize your memory requirements. This means you will have more "horsepower" available for working in multiple layers, running filter effects, and performing many other image-processing chores.

- You eliminate the need to process and retouch all the detail that you eliminated when you made the crop.

In Figure 3-1 you can see the dramatic difference that cropping can make in one photo.

Many professional jobs require that the dimensions of the image be of a certain proportion. This may be because you want to mount a display using images that fit a uniform frame and mat. It is often because your publication, advertisement, or Web site demands a particular layout.

Cross-Reference: Detailed information on cropping images can be found in Chapter 5.

Original   Crop

FIGURE 3-1 The image before and after cropping

L▶ Tip: Exposure adjustments work only on the currently active layer unless they are used in the context of an adjustment layer (see "Working with Adjustment Layers," later in the chapter) or unless all layers are flattened before making the adjustment. However, it's wise to make your initial adjustments to the overall image *before* you create layers. Doing so will ensure that layers made from the original image will match.

Adjusting Exposure

Adjusting exposure after the shot is made is much more than just a matter of making the overall picture lighter or darker. It's true that it's usually necessary to do that, but you will also want to make sure you still get solid blacks in the darkest shadows, detail in all but the very brightest highlights, and desirable tonal values in between. When I refer to adjusting exposure, I'm talking about the cumulative effect of several adjustments, including levels, curves, and brightness and contrast.

First of all, adjusting exposure is an extremely simple operation as long as your photo is already reasonably well exposed. You just choose one of Photoshop's automatic adjustment commands. These are the Auto Levels and Auto Contrast commands, as well as the Auto buttons found in the Levels and Curves commands' dialogs. All of these are pictured in Figure 3-2.

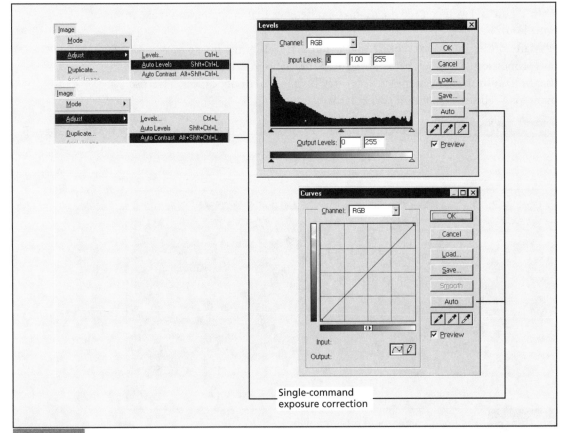

Single-command
exposure correction

FIGURE 3-2 Four ways of automatically correcting exposure

Using the Auto Levels Command

- **Advantage:** ☑ Very quick, single-click autocorrection of tonal range and color balance.
- **Disadvantage:** ☒ Algorithm isn't very sophisticated at "guessing" when major areas of the image need tonal emphasis.

It's always a good idea to start by executing the Auto Levels command. It gives you a quick idea of what the potential might be for the image. If you don't like the result, you can always press CMD/CTRL+Z to undo it. More often than not, however, the correction you'll get for anything that's noticeably off base is at least a more acceptable, more readable result. If the result of the Auto Levels command looks horrible, you'll have a much better idea of how you want to use the other controls to adjust the image. Here is the original photo and the photo after using the Auto Levels command:

Before

After

The result of using the Auto buttons in the Image > Adjust Curves and the Image > Adjust Levels commands is exactly the same as using the Image > Adjust > Auto Levels command.

Using the Auto Contrast Command

- **Advantage:** ☑ Automatically finds the white, black, and midpoints in the image and adjusts the overall contrast of the image so that you get a technically correct result.
- **Disadvantage:** ☒ Results can be so similar to the Auto Levels command that choosing which to use can be confusing.

The Auto Contrast command is new in Photoshop 5.5. It makes a great follow-up command to the Auto Levels command for testing where you might want to go with corrections and for making corrections that would be good enough for proofing purposes. The following illustration shows the same flower as the previous illustration. On the left, the flower is shown after treatment with the Auto Levels command, on the right, after treatment with the Auto Contrast command.

Auto Levels   Auto Contrast

When using either of these commands, the difference between the original and the corrected image will be quite subtle if the image was properly exposed and scanned.

Using the Levels Command

- **Advantages:** ☑ Generally produces the most effective results with the least effort. ☑ Can't accidentally create blocked-up areas of brightness.
- **Disadvantage:** ☒ Can't control brightness in two noncontiguous areas of the image.

If your automatic corrections don't produce the result you want (they may make snowscapes too dark or a shot at dusk look like daylight with the lights on), the next easiest command to use is the Levels command. To call up the Levels dialog, choose Image > Adjust > Levels. Follow the steps in Figure 3-3, and you'll get an overall correction that pleases you about 95 percent of the time.

You probably noticed that there are more controls in the Levels dialog than were described in the step-by-step callouts. These are special-purpose controls that are used less frequently. Their purpose is described in Figure 3-4.

1. Select the Preview box to see instant results of your adjustments.
2. Choose the channel you want to adjust. RGB and CMYK adjust all channels at once.
3. Drag to indicate the level of the blackest point.
4. Drag to indicate the whitest (no detail) point in the image.
5. Drag to indicate the 50 percent gray point (midtone).

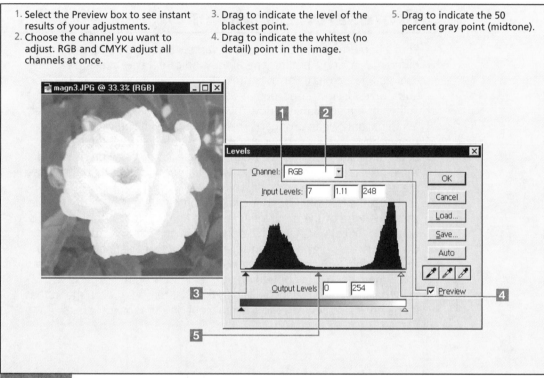

FIGURE 3-3 Making adjustments in the Levels dialog

Black, mid-, and white points can be typed directly instead of dragging sliders. Enter any number between 0 and 255.

This menu allows a choice of channels for setting levels. Each color channel can be adjusted individually. The present choice indicates that all channels will be adjusted equally.

This button opens the File Open dialog where you can indicate a file to apply previously saved Levels settings.

This button opens the Save As dialog to save settings to a file.

Another way to pick white, mid-, and black points is to click an appropriate dropper image.

Indicates lightest and darkest levels that will be seen in print or on screen

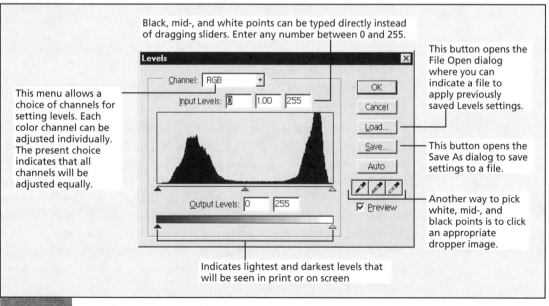

FIGURE 3-4 Special-purpose controls in the Levels dialog

Professional Pointer

Photoshop uses eyedropper icons at various places to designate slightly different functions, but in general they indicate a way to sample something (such as color or lightness) from the image itself. In the Levels and Curves dialogs, eyedroppers are used to designate the spots where you want the absolute shadow (black dropper), midtone (gray dropper), and highlight (white dropper). The pixels on which you click actually represent the areas at either end of the brightness spectrum to show any detail at all and take into consideration an average of all pixels within a three-pixel radius. Any pixels that were lighter or darker than the chosen areas will be absolute black or white.

Using the midtone dropper can be a bit dangerous because it actually shifts the tone of the pixel you choose to be gray. If that tone happens to be a little bit colored, all the colors in the image will shift to gray. Now, if the spot wasn't gray because the color balance of the image was off, that's terrific. You get automatic color balancing as a bonus. But if you just happened to pick something that really isn't quite gray, the whole color balance of the image will shift. For that reason, I recommend that in the beginning you stick to the highlight and shadow droppers.

Using the Curves Command

- **Advantages:** ☑ Highest level of control of any command. ☑ Ability to control brightness or balance color in specific portions of the brightness spectrum. ☑ Ability to color balance to medium gray with a single click. ☑ Ability to draw freehand curves for brightness balance. ☑ Perfect for creating bizarre spontaneous effects.

- **Disadvantages:** ☒ Really easy to mess up. ☒ Very complicated interface. ☒ Can be time consuming.

The Curves command is executed by choosing Image > Adjust Curves and then making settings in the dialog. Curves give you more control over the contrast between tones within a specified range. So you can, for instance, raise the level of brightness in the highlight above, say, a value of 180; lower the brightness values between 85 and 125; and entirely block up all the levels of brightness below 50. Furthermore, you can do all of this within the same dialog at the same time. If you like, you can even draw the curve freehand, which allows you to produce some really bizarre results. In short, the Curves command gives you nearly unlimited control over brightness levels. The steps for typical use of the Curves dialog are shown in Figure 3-5.

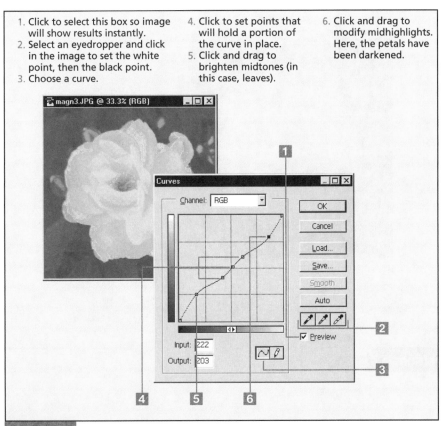

1. Click to select this box so image will show results instantly.
2. Select an eyedropper and click in the image to set the white point, then the black point.
3. Choose a curve.
4. Click to set points that will hold a portion of the curve in place.
5. Click and drag to brighten midtones (in this case, leaves).
6. Click and drag to modify midhighlights. Here, the petals have been darkened.

FIGURE 3-5   Typical procedure for using the Curves command

Using the Brightness/Contrast Command

- **Advantages:**   ☑ With only two controls to use, this is a quick and easy process.   ☑ Great for burning and dodging within a selection.   ☑ Results preview instantly.   ☑ Easily understood effect.

- **Disadvantages:**   ☒ No control over specific parts of the brightness spectrum.   ☒ No way to control highlights and shadows.

The Brightness/Contrast control affects the entire image, rather than a specific brightness range. You reach this dialog by choosing Image > Adjust > Brightness/Contrast. Using these controls is quite simple. Figure 3-6 shows how to use the controls.

Tip: You can make any of the image adjustment commands operate only on specific color channels if you go to the Channels palette and turn off one or more channels (click the eye icon). This is also true of many other commands in Photoshop.

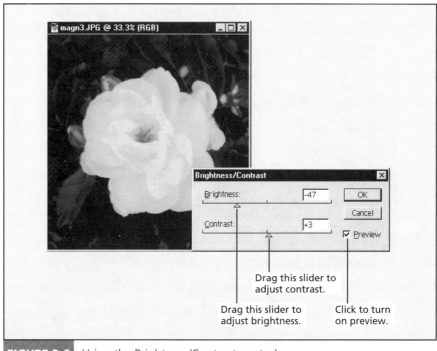

FIGURE 3-6 Using the Brightness/Contrast controls

Using the Hue/Saturation Command

- **Advantage:** ☑ Can be used while you're controlling color saturation or tint.
- **Disadvantage:** ☒ Doesn't control contrast.

The Lightness slider in the Hue/Saturation dialog can be used in conjunction with Hue and Saturation or independently. It affects all values in the brightness spectrum equally, and there is no contrast control.

You reach the Hue/Saturation dialog by choosing Image > Adjust > Hue/Saturation. Figure 3-7 shows you how to adjust exposure with the brightness control. Normally, you would not do this unless you were also making at least one of the other adjustments permitted by this dialog (Hue and Saturation), since you can't also adjust the white point or the black point or make any contrast adjustment to compensate for the change in overall brightness.

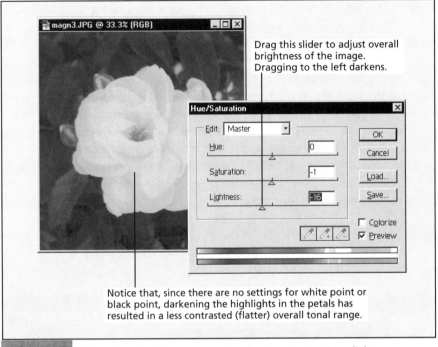

Drag this slider to adjust overall brightness of the image. Dragging to the left darkens.

Notice that, since there are no settings for white point or black point, darkening the highlights in the petals has resulted in a less contrasted (flatter) overall tonal range.

FIGURE 3-7 Using the Brightness control in the Hue/Saturation dialog

Working with Adjustment Layers

- **Advantage:** ☑ Adjustment layers work on all underlying layers to equal effect. This makes it possible to change the adjustments at any time.

- **Disadvantage:** ☒ You can only select layers that you don't want to be affected by dragging them above the adjustment layer in question. Unfortunately, this can result in having a cutout shape appear in front of something that it should be behind.

An adjustment layer is a special type of layer that lets you use virtually any of the commands found under the Image > Adjust menu to affect equally all the layers that are temporarily stacked beneath the adjustment layer. As long as the adjustment layer isn't merged with any image layers, you can change the settings in the adjustment dialog for that layer.

Adjustment layers can be used to create special effects by influencing them with Photoshop's blend modes (see the "Using Layers" tutorial on the Osborne

Web site, for information on blend modes). Adjustment layers don't add to the file size unless they contain a mask. You can control the area over which the adjustment takes place (and the degree to which it takes place) with a mask. You can also adjust the intensity of the effect with a transparency slider. You can have multiple adjustment layers that contain different versions of the same settings stored in the same file. You can then compare the effect of adjustments by turning layers on and off. You could also use this capability to print actual test strips.

When you want to change brightness values or the overall color balance, you can either change them for a single layer or for all the layers below what is called an adjustment layer (see Figure 3-8). Adjustment layers provide a means of making virtually all of the commands on the Image > Adjust submenu apply to all the layers that are below the adjustment layer.

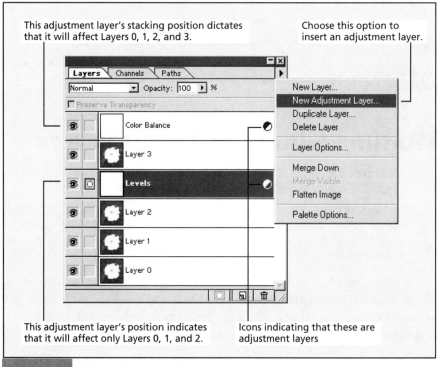

FIGURE 3-8 Using adjustment layers

To insert an adjustment layer, choose Layer > New > Adjustment Layer, or choose New Adjustment Layer from the Layers palette menu. The New Adjustment Layer dialog will appear:

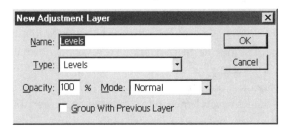

Select the type of adjustment you want to make in the Type pop-up menu. You will see a new dialog specific to that adjustment. It will be the same dialog you would see if you chose Image > Adjust and selected that same adjustment type, except that it will affect multiple layers instead of only the currently active layer.

Professional Pointer

I have to modify what I said about not being able to make adjustment layers affect only specific underlying layers. You can link individual layers to an adjustment layer and then merge the linked layers. This will cause the adjustment layer to affect only the formerly linked layers. However, the adjustment then becomes permanent.

After-the-Shot White Balance

White balance settings correct for the color of ambient (overall) lighting so that the color of familiar objects (such as skin tones) looks natural to us. Okay, this one's a little hard to show on a black-and-white page. See the Image Gallery example for Chapter 3, which shows the difference between a balanced and unbalanced image.

Those of you who use a digital camera—particularly if it's of the point-and-shoot variety—will quickly discover that its automatic white balance settings don't produce the results you visualized when you took the picture. Even when your picture-taking process produces technically perfect color-balanced pictures, you may want warmer-looking skin tones, a later-in-the-day feeling (often suggested by the prevailing color of light), or simply a warmer (more red/yellow) or colder (more blue/green) mood.

The method you use to alter the color balance of an image will most often be determined by the end result you have in mind.

Creating That Natural Look in Your Images

Often, deep shade, an overcast sky, or a brightly colored nearby wall will cause the overall cast of your subject to be a bit off balance. Sometimes, it's hard to judge the quality of skin tones if they aren't too far off normal. We just know they're not quite as "healthy" as they could be. Look for something in the image that you know is neutral in tone.

Photoshop provides several methods for balancing color; but if it's natural color or subtle changes you're after (rather than startling effects), the two most useful methods are Image > Adjust > Variations and Image > Adjust > Color Balance. Both of these methods allow you to control the color balance of highlights, midtones, and shadows separately. You'll want that level of control if the imbalance you want to correct exists only in areas of a limited brightness range. A good example would be specular highlights that are reflections of a nearby object or the blue that sometimes occurs only in deep shadows.

Adjusting Color with the Variations Command

- **Advantages:** ☑ Very easy for novices to do color balancing. ☑ Provides a quick visual comparison between different balances of color. ☑ Makes it possible to control overall brightness and color balance at the same time.

- **Disadvantages:** ☒ Slow and indirect, especially in situations in which complex controls need to be employed. ☒ Precision adjustment requires extra steps. ☒ Doesn't preview the results in the original image. ☒ Can't be used on adjustment layers, so will affect only one layer at a time.

It's really easy to adjust color using the Variations command, as shown in Figure 3-9. You look at a screen full of thumbnails, each showing a variation in color balance or brightness (thus, the name Variations). Click a thumbnail, and the color balance of the original changes to that of the thumbnail.

Start by choosing Image > Adjust > Variations. The Variations dialog takes over all of your available screen real estate. The color balance and brightness of the Current Pick thumbnail changes each time you click a thumbnail in either the color balance previews at lower left or the brightness previews at lower right.

If one of the thumbnails seems to exhibit the desired color balance, click it. The color balance of the Current Pick thumbnail will change accordingly; so will the color balance of all the other thumbnails. So you can continue to change the color balance by continuing to click thumbnails until you see what you like.

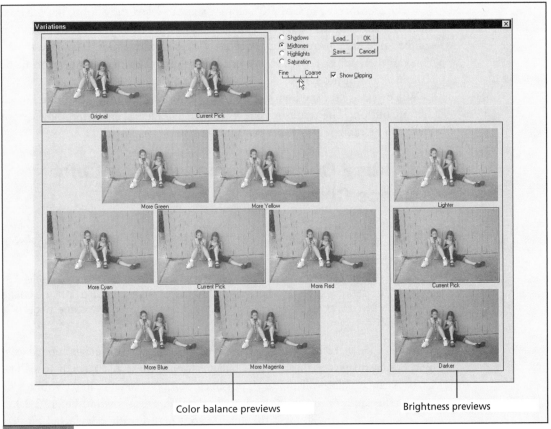

Color balance previews   Brightness previews

FIGURE 3-9 The Variations dialog

If you want to change color balance over only part of the brightness spectrum (say you just want to change the color balance of the white sneakers), click the radio button for the desired tonal range. You can adjust for each of the three parts of the brightness spectrum individually, and the results will be cumulative on the Current Pick thumbnail.

You can often give the image a better balance in tonal values by choosing the Highlights or Shadows radio button and changing the brightness level in that area by clicking the lighter or darker thumbnails.

One of the most annoying aspects of working with variations is that the default settings are often too coarse. That's easy to correct. Just under the radio buttons you will see a Fine to Coarse scale. Move the pointer to a lower setting, and you'll immediately see the results reflected in the thumbnails. You can use this scale to make coarse adjustments up to a point, then finer adjustments for fine-tuning. Or you can drag the pointer to a low setting and click thumbnails to add up fine adjustments until you get exactly what you want.

If you are working in CMYK, you may want to select the Show Clipping box. This will cause a garish color to appear at any point where the color of an item will be impossible to reproduce accurately after making color separation plates. You can then adjust color balance until the clipping colors disappear from the Current Pick thumbnail.

When you are satisfied with the way the Current Pick thumbnail looks, click the OK button. The result of your Variations choices, as shown in the Current Pick, will be rendered to your active image layer.

Adjusting Color Balance with the Color Balance Command

- **Advantages:** ☑ Precise control over shifts in each of the primary colors. ☑ Very quick to exert controls. ☑ Changes can be previewed in the main image window.

- **Disadvantages:** ☒ No side-by-side, before-and-after preview. ☒ Makes it too easy to settle for a correction that may seem acceptable until the image is viewed alongside others shot at the same time on the same page in a publication.

More experienced users will want to adjust color balance the old-fashioned way: by choosing Image > Adjust > Color Balance (or just pressing CMD/CTRL+B). The Color Balance dialog will appear. If possible, position it so you can see your image at the same time you make adjustments in the dialog, as shown in Figure 3-10.

Select the Preview box (it's the default, so it may already be selected), unless you are working with either a humungous image or a very slow computer—or unless you already know exactly the settings you want to use. Make sure the Preserve Luminosity box is also selected if you want to balance color without changing the brightness values in the image. Again, this is the default, so it's probably already selected.

There are two ways to change the color balance: enter positive or negative numbers in the Color Levels fields (they represent Red, Green, and Blue in left-to-right order), or just drag the sliders for each color. Drag the slider in the direction of the color you want to add.

Tip: You can actually add more color than the sliders will allow. Just drag the slider to its max, click OK to render the change in balance, and then repeat the command.

Usually, changing the color balance for the midtones will suffice. If you want to refine your changes, click the radio button(s) for Shadows or Highlights, and make any needed changes before you click OK.

Tip: If your desktop or your Photoshop background is set to a neutral gray and your monitor has been properly calibrated, you can use the neutral gray background to judge the neutrality of colors in your image. The sidewalk in Figure 3-10 is a case in point.

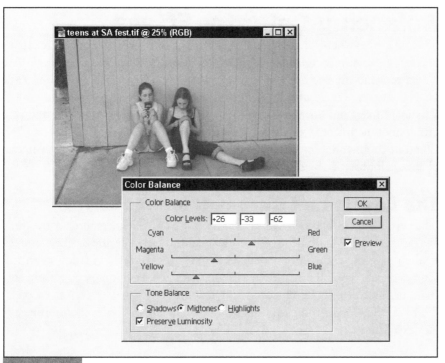

FIGURE 3-10   Using the Color Balance dialog

Professional Pointer

If you are shooting a series of images in the same location, you should be able to adjust the color balance for all of the images according to the adjustment you made for one image. You will have an easier time doing this if you can place a Kodak 18 percent gray card in one of the shots. Then you balance for the gray card, write down the numbers in the color fields, and simply type the same numbers into the Color Balance dialog for each image. Better yet, use the Actions palette to record the settings when you balance for the gray card. Then you can just run a batch script for the remainder of the images in the series. For more info on creating action scripts and using batch commands, see Chapter 2.

Balancing Color for Effect

There are times when you may want to balance color to create a nightmare, a psychedelic experience, a dream state, or an artistic effect. The Photoshop tools best suited to achieving such effects are all found in the Image > Adjust submenu: Levels, Curves, Hue/Saturation, Desaturate, Replace Color, Selective Color, Channel Mixer, and Posterize. You can also use color controls to create duotone and monotone images from color pictures or to colorize grayscale images. The Duotone command is found under the Image > Mode submenu. Finally, you can change color balance by directly editing the color channels.

The Levels and Curves Commands

The Levels and Curves commands are usually used for overall gamma correction. However, they can both be used to correct color in very specific brightness areas in the image. If you distort the curves severely (or draw them wildly with the Curves pencil), you can use the Curves command to create some very bizarre colorations. To reach the Levels command dialog, choose Image > Adjust > Levels. To reach the Curves command dialog, shown in Figure 3-11, choose Image > Adjust > Curves.

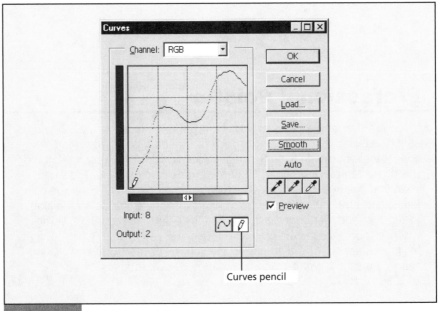

Curves pencil

FIGURE 3-11   The Curves dialog

The Hue/Saturation Command

The Hue/Saturation command can be used to create monotones or to make dramatic shifts in the overall color balance exclusively in one color direction. To reach the Hue/Saturation command dialog, shown in Figure 3-12, choose Image > Adjust > Hue/Saturation.

The Desaturate Command

The Desaturate command can be used to age a picture or as an alternative method for turning it into black and white. You would want to use this method to turn the image into black and white (grayscale) if you wanted to hand color the image. That's because, although the image's tones are all shades of gray, you're still in the color mode that you were in when you executed the command.

There's no dialog for the Desaturate command. As soon as you choose the command, the image loses all its color. To reach the Desaturate command, choose Image > Adjust > Desaturate. To hand color a desaturated image, choose Image > Adjust > Channel Mixer and select the Monochrome check box. Now use the painting tools as you normally would, except be sure to choose Color as the blend mode in the brush's Options palette. This will retain the underlying brightness values in the image while changing the color of the pixels as you paint.

The Replace Color Command

Replace Color is used to exchange one range of color for another. It is most often used to change the color of a catalog item or to change the color of an item in an

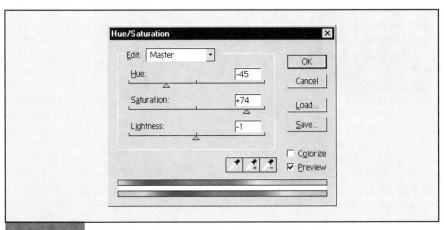

FIGURE 3-12 The Hue/Saturation dialog

ad. I once worked as assistant to a photographer who shot a fair number of car ads on location. We were once shipped a real car that was painted in several layers of peel-off paint. Then we could make it appear as though a different car had been used in different locations by peeling off a layer. We could have done the same thing with Photoshop and a gray car.

To reach the Replace Color command, choose Image > Adjust > Replace Color. To hand color a desaturated image, see the steps in Figure 3-13.

1. Select the portion of the image you wish to recolor.
2. Choose Image > Adjust > Replace Color. The Replace Color dialog will appear.
3. Select this dropper. Click in the image to indicate the main color to change.
4. Click to switch between these droppers to add or subtract tones from the range that will be replaced.
5. Drag to change color.
6. Drag to adjust color intensity (Saturation) and brightness (Lightness).
7. Your choice will be previewed here.

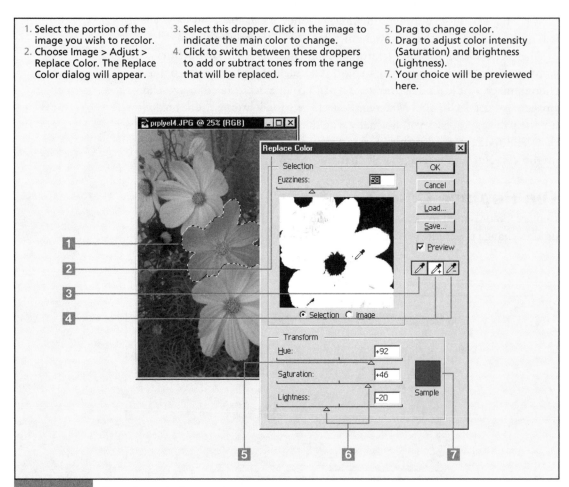

FIGURE 3-13 Steps for replacing a color range

The Selective Color Command

The Selective Color command changes the balance of a specific range of colors according to the adjustments you make in the Cyan, Magenta, Yellow, and Black primary colors settings (you don't have to be in CMYK color mode to do this, either). This command can be useful for correcting an area of problem color—the ruddiness in my Irish face, for instance. More often, it is used to create an effect in a selected area of the image—for instance, changing the balance in a blue sky (and, simultaneously, in all the surfaces that reflect that color) to give the feeling that the photo was shot at dusk or dawn.

Use the Selective Color command by choosing Adjust > Image > Selective Color, choosing a color range to be modified, and then following the steps shown in Figure 3-14.

The colors you adjust can be made to change only the colors in the range you select (absolute) or all colors in proportion to the amount of that color that they contain (relative).

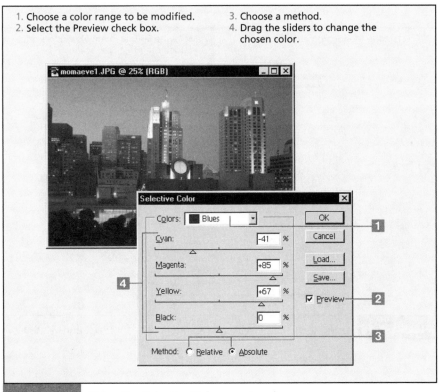

1. Choose a color range to be modified.
2. Select the Preview check box.
3. Choose a method.
4. Drag the sliders to change the chosen color.

FIGURE 3-14 Using the Selective Color command

The Channel Mixer Command

The Channel Mixer command changes the balance of color for each primary color channel over the full range of brightness. It can also be used to convert an image to monochrome grayscale, and then the brightness of individual tones can be altered according to the colors in a specific channel. You could use this effect to produce results similar to using color filters with black-and-white film. To do this, choose Image > Adjust > Channel Mixer, and then follow the instructions in Figure 3-15.

If you want to use the Channel Mixer command as an alternative method of changing the overall color balance of the image, choose one of the primary colors for the color mode you're in (usually Red, Green, or Blue), select the Preview check box, and move the sliders until you're happy with the result you see.

Cross-Reference: For more detailed information on channel operations, see Chapter 2 and the tutorial "Working with Channels" on the Osborne Web site.

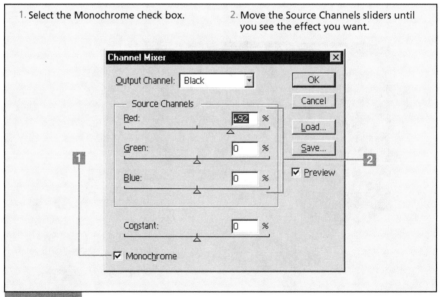

FIGURE 3-15 Using the Channel Mixer to imitate a filter for black-and-white film

The Posterize Command

Posterize reduces the number of colors in the image to a fixed number. This results in shaded colors becoming one solid color. Posterization is often a quick way to reduce file size by cutting the number of colors. It is also very useful for generating layer effects. You can make a duplicate layer, reduce the number of colors in the duplicated layer, and then use blend modes and the transparency slider to combine the two layers into one with more dramatic characteristics. Posterization is also a good preliminary to exporting an image to be autotraced into vectors by such programs as Macromedia Flash or by illustration programs. The resultant drawings have simpler, easier-to-edit shapes. This is especially important for Flash because that program is usually used to produce content for the Web, where less data means faster uploading and animations. To posterize an image, choose Image > Adjust > Posterize and follow the instructions in Figure 3-16.

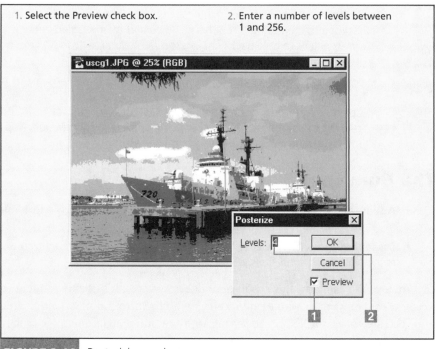

FIGURE 3-16   Posterizing an image

Correcting Small Details

There will be times (actually, lots of times) when you just want to lighten, darken, or change the color intensity of a small area of the image. This may be the case even when the picture is, technically speaking, perfectly exposed. Nevertheless, you'll want to lighten a shadow to minimize a wrinkle or force a specular highlight (sparkle) to focus attention on a particular spot. You might also want to change the brightness of an area more for reasons of composition or emphasis than to make the scene more accurately reflect the in-person experience.

The three "spot" tools that Photoshop dedicates to shading small areas of the image are burn, dodge, and sponge. All three of these tools get their names from traditional photochemical darkroom techniques.

L▶ Tip: The burn, dodge, and sponge tools work best with very small areas. If you get uneven results, try selecting the area whose values you want to change and then using whichever of the controls covered earlier in this chapter seems most appropriate.

- *Burning-in* is the act of cupping one's hands under the enlarger lens so that only a spot of light gets through. Pieces of cardboard with holes punched through them are also popular for this purpose. Burning-in results in darkening a small area.

- *Dodging* gets its name from the use of a small piece of cardboard that is taped to the end of a coat hanger wire and then wiggled under the enlarger lens to hold back light in a specific small area. Dodging results in lightening a small area.

- *Sponging* takes place during the development of the enlargement. A small sponge is soaked in hot developer or ice water. If hot developer is applied to an area, it increases in contrast (or color saturation in the making of color prints). If cold water is applied, it shortens development, causing a loss of intensity and contrast.

The Burn Tool

- **Advantages:** ☑ Can add to the illusion of depth in a picture. ☑ Minimizes attention to darker areas.

- **Disadvantage:** ☒ Very easy to overdo it, making the result look obviously manipulated and even sloppy.

When you're using the burn tool (or dodge or sponge), it's usually prudent to keep the tool moving so as to blend its effect with its surroundings. To the same end, be sure to set the Exposure setting to a low number (around 10 usually works for me). You can then affect the area progressively by continuing to stroke. To use the burn tool, follow the steps in Figure 3-17.

1. Select the burn tool from the flyout and double-click it to bring up the Options palette.
2. Click here and drag the slider to set the exposure to a low level (or enter a number between 1 and 100).
3. Choose Midtones for most images. You can repeat the operation for Highlights and Shadows.
4. For pressure-sensitive pads only—select one or both of these to make the pen pressure reflect the brush size, the exposure (intensity of the effect), or both.
5. Stroke in areas where you want to remove color.

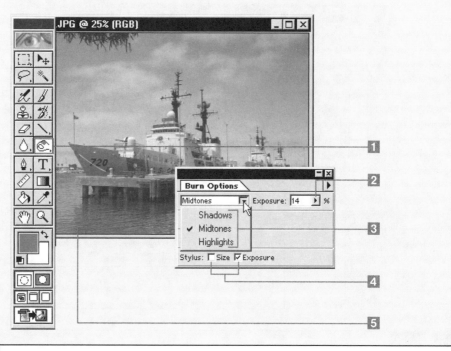

FIGURE 3-17 Using the burn tool

The Dodge Tool

- **Advantages:** ☑ Can minimize defects by lightening shadows. ☑ Calls attention to details by lightening them in contrast to their surroundings.

- **Disadvantages:** ☒ Very hard to keep exposure even and blended over larger areas. ☒ Tends to add some color shifting as area worked on gets lighter.

The dodge tool is especially capable of overdoing it, so be extra careful about setting the Exposure settings. This is a great tool for making up for the lack of fill flash in contrasting lighting situations such as bright sunlight. It's also an excellent choice (along with the rubber stamp tool) for wrinkle removal. Those techniques are demonstrated together in Chapter 4. To use the dodge tool, follow the steps in Figure 3-18.

1. Select the dodge tool from the flyout and double-click it to bring up the Options palette.
2. Click here and drag the slider to set the exposure to a low level (or enter a number between 0 and 100).
3. Choose Midtones for most images. You can repeat the operation for Highlights and Shadows.
4. Select one or both of these to indicate the behavior of pressure-sensitive pens (optional).
5. Stroke areas you want to lighten.

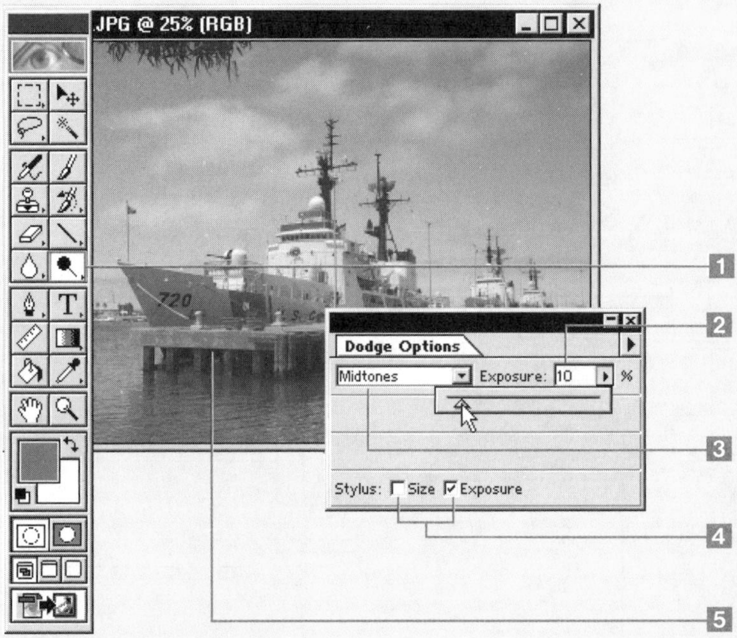

FIGURE 3-18   Using the dodge tool

The Sponge Tool

- **Advantages:** ☑ Excellent for reducing color of objects that you want to recolor with the Hue/Saturate command. ☑ When used in saturate mode, excellent for intensifying the color of small, meaningful objects.

- **Disadvantage:** ☒ You must take care not to make the effect obvious.

The sponge tool is used to increase or decrease the saturation of colors in the image. It gets its name from the fact that in photochemical printmaking, a sponge full of ice water is used to slow development in some parts of the print in order to lower contrast and saturation. If the sponge is soaked in hot developer, development is accelerated, and saturation and contrast increase. To use the sponge tool, follow the steps in Figure 3-19.

1. Select the sponge tool from the flyout and double-click it to bring up the Options palette.
2. Click here and drag the slider to set the exposure to a low level (or enter a number between 0 and 100).
3. Choose Saturate or Desaturate, depending on whether you want to intensify or dilute the color.
4. Select one or both of these to indicate the behavior of pressure-sensitive pens (optional).
5. Stroke areas where you want to intensify or remove color.

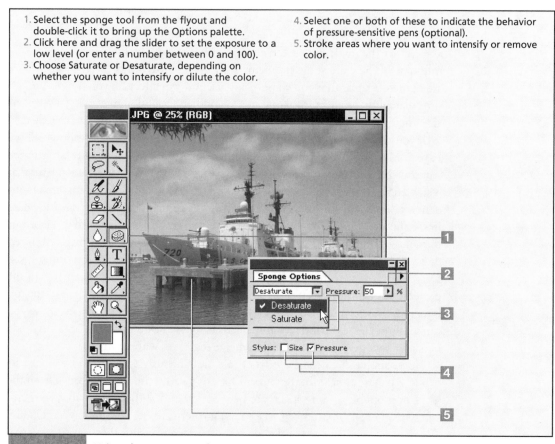

FIGURE 3-19 Using the sponge tool

In the example in Figure 3-19, the sponge tool was used in Desaturate mode to take color out of the water in the foreground in order to give the photo a feeling of added depth.

Applying Different Exposure Controls on Different Parts of the Image

There will be times when you'll want to interpret different parts of the image using entirely different sets of values and with different tools. Usually you would do this because the brightness spectrum in your subject is too wide for anything but the human eye to record. Also, as with all other Photoshop controls, there will be times when you just want to do it for dramatic effect.

You can introduce great dramatic effects by making a selection around the area you want to control so that the effect is isolated from the rest of the image. You can also feather the mask so that the changes you make gradually blend with the surroundings. There are some problems with this approach, however. First, if there are numerous areas that you want to apply a uniform effect to, you'll have a tough time matching the effect from one area to another. Second, it may help you to visualize the final result if you adjust whole images, and then blend them together.

If you should find this second effect appealing, simply choose Window > Show Layers. Make as many copies of the layer you want to manipulate as there are adjustments you want to make. Click the eye icon in the name bar of each layer that is stacked above the layer you are going to adjust so that your adjustments aren't hidden by other layers. Adjust each layer individually until it shows very desirable values in specific areas of the image (perhaps you want to emphasize the tweed in a fabric or the color of the wildflowers in a field). When you've finished adjusting each layer, drag the layer that's closest to the overall look of the image to the top of the stack. Drag the image with the second-highest number of acceptable adjustments to the position just beneath it. Turn off all the other layers. Click the name bar of the top layer to activate it, and then drag the transparency slider to around 40 percent so you can see through the top layer. (Remember, changing the transparency or blend mode of a layer isn't permanent unless you merge that layer with another.)

Next, double-click the eraser tool to simultaneously select it and to make its Options palette appear. In the Eraser Options palette, choose Paintbrush from the Type pop-up menu. Set Opacity to between 50 and 70 percent so that your erasures are gradual (if you need to exercise greater care, set it even lower). Choose Window > Show Brushes, and choose a soft-edged brush so that your strokes will blend away the image where you touch down. Erase away until the underlying layer shows through in the parts where you made a different tonal adjustment that you want to include in the overall picture (maybe it's the flowers or the tweed). When you've finished with the top two layers, return the opacity of the top layer to 100 percent. Link the top two layers and merge them (see how in the section "Cleaning Up the Environment," in Chapter 4). The two merged layers become the top layer. Now you can repeat this process for each underlying layer in turn.

Changing the Size of the Final Image

Changing the size of a digitized photo is always a lossy proposition. Each detail in the image is represented by a pattern of a specific number of specifically colored picture elements (pixels). Think of pixels as square dots. Any time you change the size of the picture, it becomes necessary to add or expunge dots, which alters detail in the image.

The effect of making the picture smaller is almost always less noticeable because most of us just aren't as conscious of tiny details anyway. Make the picture larger, and the picture starts to get blocky or hazy. Photoshop has some nifty tricks up its sleeve, though. It is very good at bridging the colors between old and new pixels so that we're less likely to be aware of blockiness—the phenomenon that has come to be known as jaggies.

Whether or not you can get away with resizing your images is going to depend on how critically demanding you and your clients are. In a photograph, most of us will find that a resolution of around 120 pixels per inch produces a quality that would be acceptable in an amateur snapshot.

Because the original laser printers printed at 300 dpi, keeping archival images at that resolution became a sort of industry benchmark. It's still not a bad one. An 8½ × 11-inch 300 dpi photograph can be enlarged to at least 16 × 20 inches and still look thoroughly professional. This is because we tend to view larger images from a greater distance, so we aren't critical of slight blurriness or pixelization. On the other hand, we can generally reduce that same image to fit a Web page without any objectionable degradation.

Preserving Detail in Highlights and Shadows in High-Contrast Scenes

One of the toughest challenges is keeping detail in highly reflective or brightly lit areas of an image. Some examples are heavily shaded main subject areas with areas of interest in bright sunlight, white lace on a white wedding gown, or the delicate shape of white petals.

First of all, all of the examples just mentioned prove the wisdom of exposing for the highlights—particularly when you're shooting with a digital camera. If highlights are blocked up (that is to say, totally opaque), the only way you're going to get any detail into the area is to fake it. You might be able to clone detail in from an adjacent but more shaded area, or composite it in from another frame that just happened to be underexposed.

Tip: Actually, it's not a bad idea to shoot an intentionally well-underexposed version of a scene that is full of contrast, just for the purpose of cloning in highlight areas after the fact. You can always control the opacity of the rubber stamp tool so that the effect is naturally subtle.

Anyway, we're drifting here. You don't really have to go to all that trouble as long as you remember to expose for the highlights. If you shot the image on film, scan it in 32- or 36-bit mode, and import it into Photoshop as 16 bits per channel. (Of course, you will need a scanner that can scan at more than 8 bits per channel.) This will ensure that you have as much dynamic range data as possible. Be sure to adjust the scanner exposure so that you get as much detail into the highlights as possible. Make your dynamic range adjustments in 16-bit-per- channel mode. Then, when you are happy with the results, you can convert your image to 8-bit mode.

Of course, some subjects, such as the proverbial black cat in a coal bin, have no normal highlights—only brighter shadows. When that is the case, it's wise to overexpose. Then you can get detail in nearly the blackest of blacks. Once again, it's wise to scan in more than 8 bits per color (the more the better), make your adjustments, and then convert down to 8 bits per color.

Of course, you're probably wondering why on earth you'd want to convert down to 8-bit color at all. Well, first of all, the file size of 16-bit-per-color images is roughly twice that of 8-bit-per-color images. Once you've got the dynamic range interpretation that you've been looking for, it's wasteful to keep the image in 16-bit-per-color (aka 48-bit) mode, because you have way more color than any screen or printing device can reproduce. Another very important consideration is that you won't be able to take advantage of the full range of Photoshop commands unless you're in 8-bit-per-color RGB or LAB mode.

Professional Skills Summary

In this chapter, you have learned to perfect the color balance and dynamic range in your photographs through the use of Photoshop's image adjustments and tools for controlling the exposure of small sections of the image. In Chapter 4, you will further improve your ability to perfect your images by using Photoshop's retouching tools.

Image Retouching and Cleanup

One of the greatest benefits of working with digital images is the ability you're given to get rid of anything you'd rather not include in your images: dirt, skin blemishes, trash on a lawn—even large objects that detract from the composition or block your view. This chapter shows you how to clean up most any sort of mess. Retouching is one of the first things you should do in the creative process because you will avoid having to retouch copies you make on individual layers or pieces that you use as composite parts of other images.

Cleaning Up the Small Stuff (Spots and Scratches)

It is nearly impossible to keep the surfaces of film or the flatbeds of scanners spot-lessly clean. The result is that there are often spots and scratches on the image. You can get rid of these in two ways: automatically or by hand. Of course, when I say "by hand," I don't mean you should resort to using spotting tools on your negatives. Photoshop's brush tools are much better at doing that sort of thing.

Tools for Retouching by Hand

The tools you will use for hand retouching are all found in Photoshop's toolbox. In order of the frequency with which you're likely to use them for retouching, these are the rubber stamp (also called *clone*), paintbrush, dodge, burn, and sponge tools.

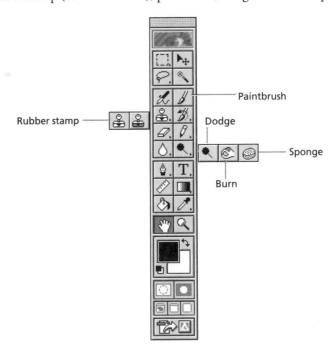

Retouching with the rubber stamp tool

- **Advantages:** ☑ Covers blemishes with the contents of the surrounding areas. ☑ Can be applied with any brush shape, opacity, or blending mode.
- **Disadvantage:** ☒ You have to remember when to reset the sampling (pickup) point, or you may find yourself having to retouch your retouching.

The rubber stamp tool copies whatever parts of the image fall under the sampling point to the brush stroke area. This makes it very easy to maintain the grain structure and texture of the area you are retouching.

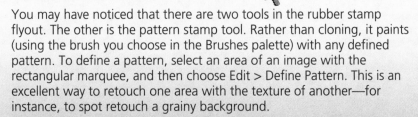

Professional Pointer

You may have noticed that there are two tools in the rubber stamp flyout. The other is the pattern stamp tool. Rather than cloning, it paints (using the brush you choose in the Brushes palette) with any defined pattern. To define a pattern, select an area of an image with the rectangular marquee, and then choose Edit > Define Pattern. This is an excellent way to retouch one area with the texture of another—for instance, to spot retouch a grainy background.

To use the rubber stamp, double-click the tool so that its Options dialog, shown here, appears:

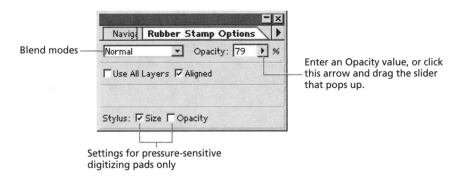

Set the Opacity and blend mode as desired (a few tips follow), and then click the Aligned check box to toggle the checkmark. As always, if the box is checked, the option is on. Finally, choose Window > Show Brushes, and choose the brush size and shape you want to use.

Professional Pointer

You can change brush sizes or shapes while you're stroking by pressing the bracket ([and]) keys. The [key chooses the brush to the left of the currently chosen brush, and the] key chooses the brush to the right. So, usually, pressing the [key would select a smaller brush; but if you were already on the smallest feathered brush in the default Brushes palette, you would have chosen the largest unfeathered brush. If you keep the Brushes palette visible while you're working, you'll be able to see what would happen if you press one of these keys.

Press OPT/ALT and click to set your sampling point, and then stroke to retouch. You'll get a better feel for this in the upcoming section "Retouching an Image: The Professional Solution." Also, check out the illustration here.

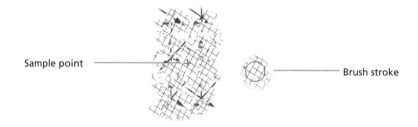

Sample point —————————— ———— Brush stroke

If the sample point and the brush stroke are aligned, the sample point will maintain its original distance and angle from the brush stroke. This is the way to copy a whole area of the image from one location to another. If you deselect Aligned in the Rubber Stamp Options dialog, the brush will always sample from the original point. Working with alignment turned off is a good way to make multiple copies of an area appear in different areas of the image.

Professional Pointer

It's a very good idea to choose File > Preferences > Display and Cursors, and then choose the Brush Size radio button. From then on, the cursor for any brush will be a circle the size of your brush. Then you'll be able to tell exactly what area your stroke is affecting.

In order to blend your strokes, you may want to lower the opacity of the stroke slightly. However, you don't want to make opacity so low that you have to make multiple strokes to get them to match in lightness. Play with this a bit.

Retouching with the paintbrush tool

- **Advantages:** ☑ Lets you paint soft-edged strokes in solid colors with any brush and at any level of transparency.   ☑ You can also use a full range of blend modes.

- **Disadvantages:**   ☒ Can't build up color (use the airbrush tool for that) and can't fill in single pixels with an undiffused edge (use the pencil tool for that).

The paintbrush, airbrush, and pencil tools serve similar functions. All three place color in your image. The main difference is that the airbrush paints with softer edges, the strokes usually fade faster (but you can control that in the options), and the tool will build up color if you continue to press in one spot—just like a real airbrush (almost). The pencil draws with perfectly hard edges, so you can see jaggies in the curves.

The paintbrush is the most commonly used of the three, probably because it's the most versatile and its use is easily understood. Strokes made with the paintbrush, thanks to the aliased and/or feathered edges of its strokes, can be made to blend quite nicely.

You can see all the paintbrush tool options in the dialog shown here:

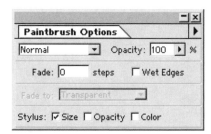

Most retouching will require that you use the default options shown in the illustration. If you have a pressure-sensitive digitizing pad, you can have pressure indicate size, opacity, color, or any combination of the three.

In retouching, you will use the brushes to spot grainless areas of solid color and (if you're a good enough artist) to create objects and textures that weren't there in the original.

Retouching with the dodge tool and burn tool

- **Advantage:** ☑ Maintains the texture and color of the surrounding area while matching areas of blotchiness or the shadows from wrinkles with the highlight areas.

- **Disadvantage:**   ☒ It takes practice to learn to blend the effects and to keep streaks out of the retouching.

The dodge and burn tools are simply opposite facets of the same function: controlling the brightness of small areas in the image. The dodge tool brightens all tonal values while maintaining the original brightness relationship of pixels to one another; the burn tool darkens.

Professional Pointer

Once you get very good at judging how the primary color channels affect the overall (composite) color balance, you can make clever use of the dodge and burn tools to influence the color balance of very small areas by using them on the individual color channels. You can experiment with this by choosing Window > Show Channels. Click the name bar of the channel you want to lighten or darken. Then burn or dodge in the monochrome image that results. To go back to the composite image, click the composite channel's (RGB, CMYK, or what-have-you) name bar.

When you're using the burn and dodge tools, you definitely want to have the Options palette in view:

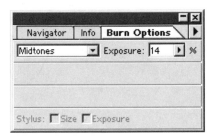

The Options palettes for the burn and dodge tools are identical except for the name on the tab. The reason you want to keep the palette in view is so that you can easily adjust opacity—though that's not much of a problem if you are using a digitizing pad (personally, I can't imagine trying to do any production work without one). Also, there will be times when you'll want to work only on deep shadows or brilliant highlights. If this is the case, you'll minimize the chances of streaking the image by choosing the appropriate mode from the pop-up menu on the left.

Retouching with the sponge tool

- **Advantage:**   ☑ Lets you control color saturation in small areas without having to select them first.
- **Disadvantage:**   ☒ Same tendency to streak or blotch as other hand tools.

The sponge tool is wonderful for taking the excess redness out of tired eyes or for making the red roses stand out in the composition. The only controls available in the Sponge Options dialog are Pressure (same as Opacity) and a pop-up menu that makes the tool either intensify (Saturate) colors or gradually remove (Desaturate) color:

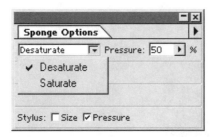

Retouching an Image:
The Professional Solution

The problem posed here is a common one: the photograph with the expression and pose that your client likes has a number of problems. It wouldn't be acceptable to either the photographer's or the client's purpose to leave these problems alone. Therefore, we must fix them. We have to do it in such a way that the results don't look manipulated or unnatural. We also have to do it in a reasonably short time.

You can download the photograph used in this example (shown in Figure 4-1) from the publisher's Web site, at www.osborne.com. It is called RTCHTONI.JPG. However, you could use any portrait of your own as a substitute—it's best if you pick a scan of a portrait that shows some dirt and scratches.

1. First, we'll get rid of the tiny linear scratches that were made by a dirty film transport. Select the rubber stamp tool. Double-click the rubber stamp tool icon to make sure its Options palette is visible. The apply mode should be Normal, the Aligned option should be selected, and the Opacity setting should be 100%. These are the defaults.

2. We want to make sure we don't retouch any area that doesn't need retouching. Zoom in tight enough (press CMD/CTRL++) to see the scratches clearly, and place a rectangular selection marquee around each of the scratches. (Press SHIFT while dragging to add more than one marquee if there is more than one scratch.) In addition to protecting the rest of the photograph, the marquees make it easier to see the scratches we need to retouch.

We'll eliminate scratches in the background.

The sponge tool will help with some redness in the corners of the eyes.

We'll remove any spots caused by dirt on

Nose flaws and a wrinkled elbow can also be touched up.

FIGURE 4-1   Unretouched studio portrait for an ad

3. From the Brushes palette (Window > Show Brushes), choose a small, soft-edged brush that's just a little larger than the scratches you are going to retouch. (If the spots vary greatly in size, retouch as many of the same size as you can before switching brush sizes. You'll save significant time.)

4. Set the pickup point immediately to one side of the scratch. To set the sample point, press OPT/ALT+click. Place the brush cursor so that it is centered over the scratch at a 90-degree angle from the sample point. Most transport scratches are perfectly straight, as long as you haven't rotated the image. So you may want to hold the SHIFT key as you stroke to keep the brush perfectly aligned with the scratch. If the surrounding area is fairly plain (like the seamless backdrop in this shot), you'll be able to retouch the whole scratch in one stroke. If it's passing through textured detail (such as the facial features), you'll want to blend by alternating the sample point from one side of the scratch to another.

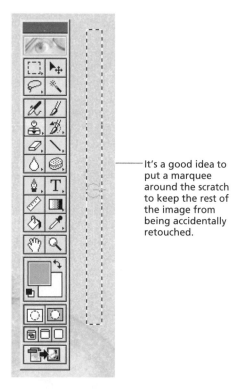

It's a good idea to put a marquee around the scratch to keep the rest of the image from being accidentally retouched.

5. Be sure to press CMD/CTRL+D to deselect, so that you're no longer protecting any of the image. Otherwise, you'll find the next steps have no effect.

Professional Pointer

Make sure the brush cursor is an actual size circle. If it isn't, from the main menu, choose File > Preferences > Display & Cursors. In the Preferences dialog, click the Brush Size radio button. You do not have to restart the program for the change to take effect. For most of the brushwork you do, this is the most accurate cursor mode. It's a good idea to leave it as your regular Preferences setting.

6. Now, let's get rid of some of the larger freckles and other skin irregularities. The rubber stamp tool should still be active. If not, choose it again. Move the cursor to an area close to the blemish that is the same tone and texture that you want for covering the blemish. Press OPT/ALT+click to pick up the color and texture under the cursor. Repeatedly move and click the cursor to cover the blemish without smearing the cloned tone and pattern. If the blemish intersects two or three pattern/tone areas, clone from each of those areas and work your way inward with a smaller brush. If the blemish sits directly on the border between light and dark areas, align the pickup point (press OPT/ALT+click) at the same border and as close to the blemish as possible (without including it). That way, you pick up the pixel pattern of the transition.

7. When you've taken out all the original blemishes, there may still be some unevenness in tonal values. These are best removed by altering their intensity with the burn and dodge tools. You should choose a brush that is slightly smaller than the blemish. Zoom in very tight, so that you can easily see the area that the brush is blending. In the Options palette, set the transparency to about 10% and watch carefully to see when you have blended the intensity. The following illustration shows one blemish before and after being dodged.

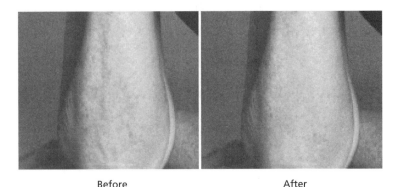

Before   After

8. Sometimes, in the process of lightening and darkening to get rid of strong shadows (such as those in the wrinkles and muscles), the lightened area will turn out to be a slightly different color than its surroundings. You can fix that by choosing the brush tool. In the brush tool Options palette, choose Color as the blend mode. Press OPT/ALT to turn the brush into the eyedropper tool, pick up color from the surrounding area, and then paint with the brush in the off-color area. The brightness values will stay the same—only the colors will change.

9. There is some redness in the corners of the eyes that we'd be better off without. Zoom in very tight on one eye. Select the sponge tool. In the Sponge Options dialog, choose Desaturate from the tool operations menu. Also, drag the Pressure slider to about 50 percent. Now, slowly take the red out of the corners of the eyes.

10. You might want to use the dodge tool to lighten the whites of the eyes slightly.

11. Finally, use the rubber stamp tool to remove any spots caused by dirt on the image.

Plastic Surgery, or Major Retouching Work

There will be times when you need to do more than fix a small blemish. You may actually need to reshape something in the scene. This seems to come up more in photographs of glamorous people than at any other time. In the instance of our example photograph, there is a slight bump in model Toni DeMarco's nose that resulted from a childhood accident, and the way she's leaning on her left elbow has made the skin push out unattractively. Here's how both of these problems were fixed:

1. You can straighten out the bump on the nose by using the burn tool to pull the shadow from the straight part of the nose into the flattened part of the nose. Use the dodge tool to widen the highlight into the flattened part of the nose. Right here we get a "lessonette" in how highlights and shadows influence our perception of shape and depth in a two-dimensional image. See the "before and after" in the illustration:

 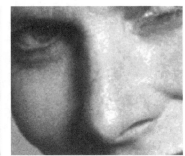

Before   After

2. I've saved what might appear to be the toughest job for last: fixing the elbow where resting it on the backdrop has caused a distorted wrinkle. Use the lasso tool to draw a freehand marquee that outlines the shape of the elbow as it should be. Be sure to include a good portion of both the upper arm and forearm in the selection.

3. When you have finished making the selection, choose Select > Feather, and when the dialog appears, enter about 3 pixels in the Feather Radius field. Use a large brush and the rubber stamp tool to paint over the wrinkled portions of the arm that are inside the selection. When that looks good, press CMD/CTRL+SHIFT+I to invert the selection. Now use the rubber stamp tool to cover the saggy part of the skin with the background and shadow. It's going to take some practice to get this right, but that's exactly how the finished version, shown in Figure 4-2, was done.

Professional Pointer

Save your image to a new filename each time you complete a complex task, such as the one in this exercise. (A good technique, which I've been using in this example, is to add a number to the original filename so you can remember the sequence of work.) Then you can always go back to an older version as your work progresses. This one precaution could be responsible for saving a client or a career, because you can still make a deadline after making a big boo-boo.

FIGURE 4-2 Retouched portrait

Cleaning Up the Environment

There's not really a lot of difference between cleaning up a portrait and cleaning up a landscape. We don't always have time to call the EPA (or hire a stylist) before we take a photograph, so we have to use Photoshop to do the job for us.

As you might suspect, Photoshop's rubber stamp tool can do a large part of this job. There are also times when you can more easily cover up an area by just overlaying another section of the image. In our example, shown below, we're going to move part of a parking lot over to cover up a car that's weakening the composition. Then we'll use the rubber stamp tool to blend the edges. If you want to follow along with the steps in the book, get the image named THEATRE.JPG from www.osborne.com. If you want to use your own photo, just find one with a similar problem. (Maybe you want to get rid of a trash can on a lawn?) Here's the unretouched photo:

We'll cover up this car, which detracts from the composition.

1. Select the rectangular marquee tool and make a selection. Press CMD/CTRL+C and then CMD/CTRL+V. You have copied the selection to the clipboard and then pasted to a new layer in Photoshop. The new layer is already the one selected.

2. Now you want to move the selection to cover up the car (or whatever you want to cover up). Select the move tool, but rather than dragging the selection, move it with the arrow keys to keep it in perfect horizontal alignment with its original location. Generally speaking, this will make it easier to keep the lighting consistent and to keep matching elements aligned. The following illustration shows the whole process:

New layer selected
in the Layers palette

Move tool

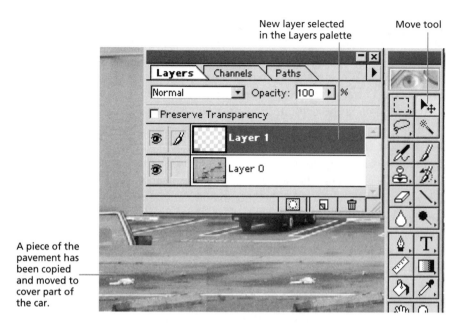

A piece of the
pavement has
been copied
and moved to
cover part of
the car.

3. Notice that we haven't attempted to cover the entire car—only that part of it that we could cover in a fairly seamless way with other elements in the picture. I say "fairly seamless" because there is a seam and we need to use the rubber stamp tool to blend out the seam, and get rid of much of the top half of the car. (There's also a rag that we should have cloned out of the original selection, but you can do that now.) Since the areas we want to blend together are on separate layers, we'll have to merge them. Assuming that the layer containing the copied selection is still active, choose Merge Down from the Layers palette menu. (In case you don't know, you reach palette menus by clicking the small arrowhead in the upper-right corner of any palette.)

4. Zoom in tight on the area you want to blend. Double-click the rubber stamp tool to select it and to bring up the Options palette. Deselect the Aligned box. Set the sample point in an area that is the color and texture you want to move into another area. Now each time you click to start a stroke, the sample point will originate at the same spot. By changing the sample point from time to time, you can clone in color and texture from inside and outside the selection until it becomes seamless.

5. Now get rid of the car by using the rubber stamp tool. I used a very large brush with the Aligned option turned on to paint in the seam between the theater wall and the parking lot asphalt to cover the roof of the car. Then I used a combination of aligned and unaligned strokes to cover the rest of the car. It would take too long to describe each stroke, but practice a little and you'll get the idea pretty quickly. You can see the finished lotscape here:

Changing the Color of an Item in Your Composition

In car, fashion, and catalog photography, it's often desirable to be able to change the color of items to match those of the colors offered in a given line, or change the color of merchandise to match the logo in an ad. In fine arts and illustration, you may want to change the color of an object for purely expressionist reasons. Whatever your motive, the techniques are the same.

Accurately Selecting the Area for a Color Change

The biggest challenge in changing the color of an item is selecting it. In fact, making accurate selections is one of the biggest challenges in digital photography. That's why two chapters of this book, Chapters 6 and 7, are devoted to the subject. For now, there are a couple of things to keep in mind:

- If you copy the area containing the object you want to recolor to a new layer, you can experiment without risking the integrity of the original image. You'll also be able to use transparency and blend modes when reapplying the recolored portion to the whole photograph.

- If you use an adjustment layer to change image brightness temporarily, you can see enough detail in shadows and highlights to be able to accurately select the edges of the objects you want to recolor.

Making the Color Change

To demonstrate how to change the color of an image in your composition, we're going to go back to that photograph of Toni and change the color of her bathing suit. I've used the version with the finished retouching changes, but if you haven't saved yours, you can make the changes on the original. You might learn even more if you use the same (approximate) steps to change the color of a friend's shirt. Anyway, once you've loaded the image into Photoshop, follow these steps:

1. Make a rough selection (or a marquee selection) around the item(s) whose color you want to change, and press CMD/CTRL+C to copy and then CMD/CTRL+V to paste. The copy will appear in perfect register over the original item, but in its own layer. Be sure you don't select the move tool while this layer is active, or you will risk getting the copy out of register with the underlying image.

2. From the Layers palette menu, choose New Adjustment Layer. The Adjustment Layer dialog will appear.

3. Choose Levels, Curves, or Brightness/Contrast so that you can lighten the shadows. You should choose the one you're most comfortable with, since your use of this layer is only temporary. I've chosen Levels, which opens the following dialog:

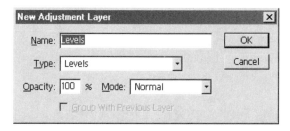

4. Use the adjustments to lighten the shadows so that you can clearly see the edges of the swimsuit where it would otherwise blend into the shadow areas.

5. Now you are going to select the item you want to change. The exact method by which you do this is immaterial, as long as the end result is accurate to the outlines you're trying to select. Also, keep in mind that the efficiency of different selection methods will be appropriate to different types of shapes and their edges (see Chapter 7). For this image, I selected the magic wand. In the Magic Wand Options palette, I entered 35 in the Tolerance field. Click in the largest area of similar colors. Press SHIFT and continue to click until you've

added the entire swimsuit. When you near the edges of the suit, there may be some selection of material outside the edge. If it's minor, you can trim it with the lasso tool (next step). Otherwise, press CMD/CTRL+Z to undo and enter a lower number in the Tolerance field.

6. Once you have the suit pretty well selected, select the lasso tool. Zoom in tight on the areas you want to trim. Press SHIFT to add to the selection or OPT/ALT to subtract from the selection, and use the lasso to trim it to the exact shape. Now you should have the suit perfectly selected. Save the selection so that you can retrieve it in case you accidentally drop it.

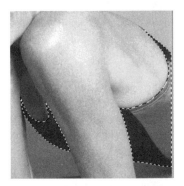

7. Trash the adjustment layer (drag it to the trash icon at the bottom of the Layers palette). Your image will return to normal.

8. Now you want to get rid of everything on the layer that you don't want to re-color. Press CMD/CTRL+SHIFT+I to invert the selection (or choose Select > In-verse); then press DELETE/BACKSPACE to erase everything outside the original selection.

9. To make sure you don't have any little smudges left over outside the selec-tion, make the Background layer active by clicking its eye icon in the Layers palette. If you see any artifacts in the transparent area of the layer, select the eraser tool and erase them. Click the Background layer's eye icon to make that layer visible again.

10. Make sure the swimsuit layer is still the active layer (it will be highlighted in the Layers palette—if not, click it). Near the top of the Layers palette, you will see a check box labeled Preserve Transparency. Make sure this is selected.

11. Now you're going to recolor the suit. I'm going to give you two ways to do it, each with a slightly different purpose. First, we'll just change the colors in the suit but keep the highlights, stitching, and so forth. This lets us identify it as the same object. Second, we'll recolor it to cover up the details—so that it looks more like the top of an evening gown.

12. Click the foreground color selection box in the toolbox to bring up the Color Picker dialog, and choose the color you want to change the suit to.

Cross-Reference: Choosing colors is covered in Chapter 2.

13. Choose Edit > Fill. The Fill dialog will appear. Choose the settings shown below and click OK.

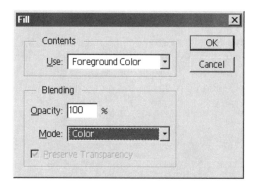

14. You will see that the swimsuit has changed color, though you don't notice much of a change in the areas that were totally black anyway.

15. Now we'll completely change the suit to a solid black, so that it looks more like an evening gown. Choose Black as your foreground color by clicking the Default Colors icon just below and to the left of the background color selection box in the toolbox.

16. In the Layers palette, choose Normal for the blend mode.

17. Choose Edit > Fill and change the settings in the Fill dialog to match those shown here:

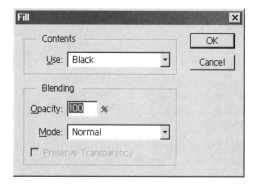

18. Click OK in the Fill dialog. You will see that the swimsuit has turned a solid black. If you want, you can experiment with changing the transparency of the layer and with using different blend modes to see their effect. In the meantime, the results of this second method for recoloring will look like those shown in Figure 4-3.

19. From the Layers palette menu, choose Flatten Image. This will ensure that you don't accidentally move the layer that contains the recolored swimsuit. If you

FIGURE 4-3   The suit is now a solid black and looks more like the top of an evening gown.

are going to change the swimsuit to other colors, save the file under a new name and use the History palette to undo the layer flattening; then repeat the steps above.

Removing Backgrounds

One of the most commonly encountered retouching problems, particularly for digital camera users, is an ugly background in a photograph that otherwise captures an attractive moment with an engaging subject. This is particularly true for digital cameras because their short focal length lenses produce extreme depth of field. The result is that everything is at least recognizably sharp from about eight inches to infinity. Conventional photographers often keep attention focused on the subject by throwing the background out of focus. If you use a digital camera, you'll have to learn to use Photoshop to throw the background out of focus.

Another common reason for eliminating backgrounds is that the photographs will be used in catalog or Web pages—for example, the designer might want to wrap text around the object and have its background appear to be the same as that of the text. I'll show you how to do both techniques in Photoshop here.

There are many techniques for background removal. You can simply use the brushes to paint out a background by hand. If you're a good enough artist, you can even paint in a compatible image or backdrop. For the most part, however, you will want to substitute one background for another, using a new photograph or creating a new background layer and filling it with a solid color. That's usually just a matter of making a fairly elaborate selection (the edges of what you want to select are seldom smooth and sometimes even transparent or translucent). So removing backgrounds is mostly a matter of tuning up your selection techniques.

In addition, the following exercise shows you a revolutionary new selection technique that has just been introduced into Photoshop 5.5. However, the main objective here is to show you some alternatives for dealing with the background.

Cross-Reference: Chapters 6 and 7 show you how to perfect your selection techniques to remove backgrounds.

You can use the example image, LILIES.JPG, if you want to download it from Osborne's Web site. As always, however, I encourage you to use your own image as you follow because most of us learn more by doing than just by reading.

1. Open a file that features a strong central subject—anything you've shot of a person, pet, flower, or product usually qualifies.

2. Make sure the Layers palette is visible. If it isn't, choose Window > Show Layers.

3. Drag the layer that contains the main image (probably Background) to the New Layers icon at the bottom of the Layers palette (it looks like a turning page). Click the new layer to select it.

4. Choose Image > Extract (or press OPT/ALT+CMD/CTRL+X) to open the Extract dialog, shown in Figure 4-4.

5. Select the edge highlighter tool. Paint a thin line around everything you want inside the image. If there are translucent or tiny details (such as small leaves or hairs or peach fuzz) that protrude from the edge, make sure the edge highlighter covers them—in other words, use a wide brush. If there are small areas of highlight or shadow that define the edges, make sure they are mostly inside the selection (you'll discover that you don't need to be absolutely accurate in this respect). In the close-up, shown here, you can see how the highlighter is being applied. Be sure to enclose everything that you want to keep in the foreground.

Professional Pointer

You are defining an area that contains some pixels that should be kept inside the foreground and some that should blend into the background. Anything that's completely contained inside the selection will be kept, as will any pixels that are the same color as any of the pixels inside the selection. Everything outside the selection will be dropped entirely. Any pixels whose colors are the same as the background's colors will be dropped, unless they are also contained in the foreground. The result is a transition area that blends with the background.

Eyedropper · Fill color menu · Eraser · Highlight color menu (choose marker color here) · Fill tool · Brush size menu · Force chosen color to foreground (can pick up with eyedropper) · Edge highlighter

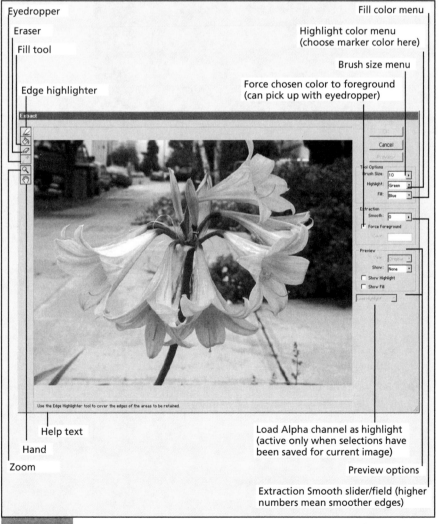

Help text · Hand · Zoom · Load Alpha channel as highlight (active only when selections have been saved for current image) · Preview options · Extraction Smooth slider/field (higher numbers mean smoother edges)

FIGURE 4-4 The Image > Extract dialog and the meaning of its components

6. When you have finished marking off your foreground image, select the fill tool and click inside all the areas that you've completely surrounded. The area will fill with the fill color. Zoom in to make sure you haven't filled any background areas.

7. If you have filled background areas or if the fill spills out into the background, you'll have to edit your selection. Select the fill tool again (if necessary) and click in the fill. It will disappear. Now correct your edge highlighter area with the edge highlighter and eraser tools; then fill and check again. Keep this up until you're pretty sure you've got it. The image in the preview area should look something like this:

8. Click the Preview button. It will take some time, but eventually the background will disappear, and all you'll see will be the transparency pattern and your foreground image. If you decide you can do better, choose Original from the View menu and select the Show Highlight and Show Fill check boxes. You're then back to the pre-preview state and can continue to edit your transitions and fills. Repeat the process as often as necessary in order to achieve perfection. Most of the time, you'll get it right on the first or second try.

9. Okay, so now you have your foreground image as you like it. Click OK and you'll find yourself back to your original image. Since your knocked-out image is on a separate layer and is in the foreground, it will appear as though nothing has happened at all. Don't worry.

10. Next, you want to throw the background out of focus to a much greater extent than is already the case (see Figure 4-5). Activate the background layer. Choose Filter > Blur > Gaussian Blur. In the Gaussian Blur dialog, select the

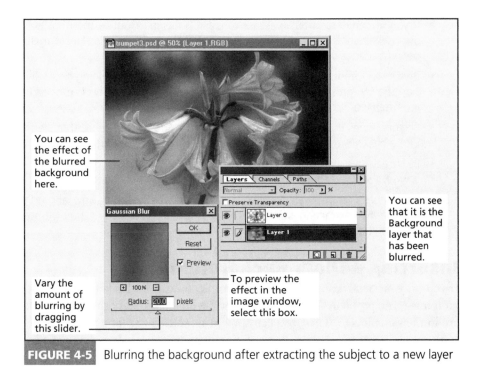

You can see the effect of the blurred background here.

You can see that it is the Background layer that has been blurred.

Vary the amount of blurring by dragging this slider.

To preview the effect in the image window, select this box.

FIGURE 4-5 Blurring the background after extracting the subject to a new layer

Preview box and drag the Radius slider until the background is as fuzzy as you'd like it to be; then click OK.

Tips for Using the Extract Command

Using the Image > Extract command will take a little getting used to, especially if you're a veteran Photoshopper. It's a little like suddenly jumping into another program. Here are a few things I've come to understand about how to make it work best for me:

- You can change the size of the edge highlighter or eraser with the bracket ([and]) keys, just as you can change the size of the brush when working in Photoshop.

- You can switch marking tools with the same single-letter keys you'd use in Photoshop. Press B to select the edge highlighter, E for the eraser, K for the fill tool, I for the eyedropper, Z for the zoom tool, and H for the hand (pan) tool.

- If you're debating about whether to leave pixels in or out of the transition area (whatever is covered by the edge highlighter color), there's at least an 80 percent chance you'll be better off leaving it in.

- Be sure all foreground colors are represented at least once as being clearly inside the foreground area (not covered by the highlighter). This is especially important for highlighted and shadowed edges.

- Be sure edges that are transitional, such as the anti-aliased edges that blend into a background, are entirely contained inside the edge highlighter area.

- Be sure to cover small holes in the foreground with the edge highlighter. Otherwise, the background colors will be considered part of the foreground.

- Remember that you can switch back and forth between preview and edit modes when extracting an image. This gives you a chance to fine-tune before you commit.

Inserting a Plain Background

If you (or your boss) would rather have a simple, solid-color background behind your image, no problem. You can even show the image so that both backgrounds are in the same image. Then you can show it to your client (or a future client) both ways. Clients feel that you're providing them with real value when you give them a chance to make choices.

Here's how you insert a plain background behind your image. Let's just pick up where we left off with the previous image.

1. In the Layers palette, click the eye icon next to the layer that contains the blurred background. It is now part of the file, but not visible.

2. Choose Window > Show Swatches and pick the color you want for a background (or you can use the color picker or a custom color book if you'd rather).

3. Press X to switch the foreground and background colors. The color you've chosen is now the background color.

4. Choose Layer > New > New Background. Yikes! Your image suddenly has a new, solid-color background, as you can see in Figure 4-6.

FIGURE 4-6 The lilies with a solid background

Professional Skills Summary

This chapter taught you everything you need to know about basic retouching using Photoshop 5.5. You learned how to remove scratches, dust, defects, and artifacts. You also learned to retouch with the burn and dodge tools. You even had some lessons in digital plastic surgery and making background knockouts. Of course, everything Photoshop does can contribute to retouching, so there is no end to where we could go with this.

In the next chapter, you will learn about cropping and transformations. You'll be surprised to discover how much there is to know about these two subjects.

chapter 5

Cutting It Down to Size and Flipping Out

In this chapter, you:

- Learn about transformations, including commands that scale, rotate, slant, stretch, and change the perspective of selections, layers, and paths

- Discover how to straighten images and eliminate keystoning

- Understand different reasons for cropping

- Find out how to size and crop an image for use in a montage

- Learn three different ways to crop an image

This chapter is about cropping and transformations, both of which have more important implications than the simplicity of their operation might at first lead you to suspect. Often, in order to straighten the image and to correct perspective distortion, you will want to make transformations before you crop the image. So we'll cover transformations first, then cropping.

Transformations

Transformations include anything that changes the size, shape, or orientation of a layer within the boundaries of the current image. You can also transform the contents of any selection. As soon as you make the transformation, the contents of the selection are automatically and temporarily copied, and the copy is pasted in place when the transformation has been completed. The reason I bring up the "within the boundaries" business is that Photoshop has commands that will cause the boundaries of the image or the image and its boundaries to shrink or grow. Specific transformations that can be made within Photoshop without the aid of third-party filters include Size, Stretch, Rotate, Skew, Distort, and Perspective. You can also rotate in 90-degree and 180-degree increments and use the Flip command to reverse the image horizontally or vertically.

Like most Photoshop commands, transformations work only on one layer unless you first link layers together, as shown here:

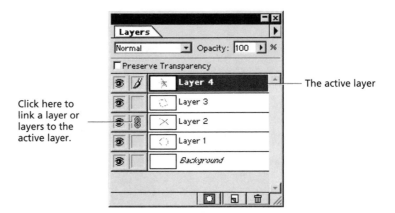

Click here to link a layer or layers to the active layer.

The active layer

Free Transforms

- **Advantage:** ☑ Lets you scale, rotate, slant, distort, or apply perspective in one overall operation, just by dragging handles. This results in higher pixel fidelity because pixels are resampled only once.

- **Disadvantage:** ☒ You can't apply precision, so you can't make two different files (or unlinked layers) distort to the same measurements.

To transform a selection, you press CMD/CTRL+T or choose Edit > Free Transform. At that point, the nature of your transformations will depend on which keys you press while dragging the handles of the free transform bounding box. The possible types of transformations are shown in Figure 5-1.

Here's how to use the Free Transform option (shortcut: CMD/CTRL+T) with no modifier key:

> **▶ Tip:** By default, transformations are made in relationship to the center point of the transform bounding box. You can change the effect of the transformation by moving the center point. To move the center point, drag it while the transform bounding box is visible.

Drag the cross-hair to change the center of the image.

Drag a corner marker to rescale disproportionately.

With the cursor slightly away from the corner handle, drag to rotate.

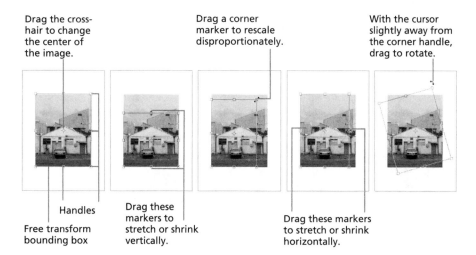

Handles

Free transform bounding box

Drag these markers to stretch or shrink vertically.

Drag these markers to stretch or shrink horizontally.

Here's how to use the Free Transform option while pressing CMD/CTRL:

To distort, press CMD/CTRL and drag a corner handle.

The arrow changes shape when CMD/CTRL is pressed.

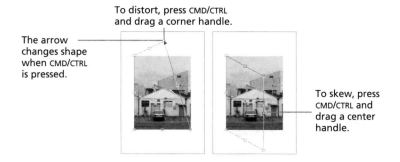

To skew, press CMD/CTRL and drag a center handle.

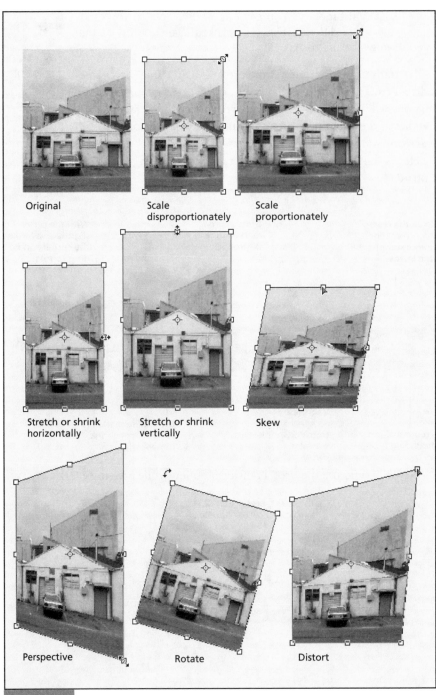

Original

Scale
disproportionately

Scale
proportionately

Stretch or shrink
horizontally

Stretch or shrink
vertically

Skew

Perspective

Rotate

Distort

FIGURE 5-1 Effects of each of Photoshop's transformations

Here's how to use the Free Transform option while pressing OPT/ALT:

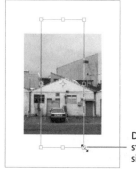

Drag a corner handle to stretch or shrink all four sides from the center.

Here's how to use the Free Transform option while pressing CMD/CTRL+OPT/ALT+SHIFT:

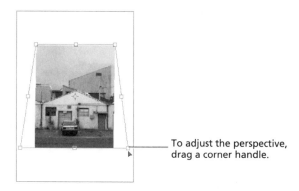

To adjust the perspective, drag a corner handle.

To apply a transformation, either double-click inside the free transform bounding box or press RETURN/ENTER.

Transforming a Path or Selection

You can transform a path or selection without transforming the contents of that path or selection. This is an excellent way to select with the rectangular or elliptical marquee tool, and then slant or size the path to the exact degree you want.

To transform a selection, follow these steps:

1. Make a selection using any of the selection tools.
2. While the selection is still active, choose Select > Transform Selection. A free transform bounding box will appear around the selection.

3. Use any of the Free Transform operations, described in the previous section, to alter the selection. Here, the selection is being rotated:

If you want to move the selection, choose one of the selection tools (if one isn't already chosen) and drag from inside the selection boundaries.

To transform a path, follow these steps:

1. Create the path using the pen tools.

2. Make sure the path you want to transform is selected. (Select the direct-selection tool from the pen tools flyout and drag a marquee around the path or double-click it.)

3. Choose Edit > Free Transform Path, or choose Edit > Transform Path and select any of the transformation types on the submenu shown here:

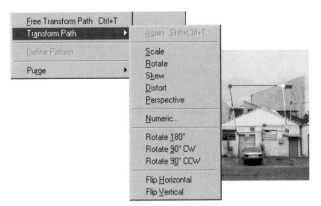

4. Use any of the operations described in the following sections for transforming a layer. However, in this instance, only the path itself will be transformed. The image inside the path will be unaffected.

Using the Transform Again Command

If you're not sure to what degree you want to transform the layer, you can make a small transformation, and then choose Edit > Transform Again to repeat the transformation. Of course, this means you will change the pixels in the image several times, which can result in loss of data and the introduction of artifacts. *Artifacts* are clumps of pixels that don't contain image data but are invented by a program that is automatically rearranging pixels in some way. Heavily compressed images often exhibit lots of artifacts.

Scaling the Image

The Scale command changes the overall size of the image in both dimensions, though not necessarily equally. If you hold the SHIFT key while scaling in Free Transform mode, you will scale proportionately. Scale is also used to stretch the image. Stretching refers to scaling on only one axis, either horizontally or vertically. You can stretch an image in Free Transform by dragging the center handle on any side.

   To stretch or scale interactively, choose Edit > Transform > Scale. A transform bounding box will surround the layer, as shown here. Drag the corner handles to scale the image and the center handles to stretch it.

Corner handle

Center handle

Rotating the Image

The Rotate command (Edit > Transform > Rotate) spins the image about its (moveable) center. In Free Transform mode or with the Rotate command, the image is rotated visually. That is, you turn the transform bounding box until your eyes tell you that you've found the right position. In the Numeric Transform dialog, you can rotate the selection by entering either positive or negative numbers between 0 and 360 (degrees) or by dragging the dial to indicate the approximate angle.

   To rotate in Free Transform mode, choose Edit > Free Transform. Drag just outside the corner handles. When the image has been rotated to the desired angle, double-click or press RETURN/ENTER to cause the transformation. If you're in Free Transform mode, you may wish to perform other types of transformations before confirming.

Skewing the Image

Skewing the image causes it to lean like the Tower of Pisa. The edge you drag and its opposite stay parallel and straight, while the other sides slant. In Free Transform mode, you can stretch and slant at the same time.

Distorting the Image

Tip: Dragging to distort is often a better way than using Perspective to straighten perspective or architectural lines in a photograph that has been taken with a hand-held camera. That is because the perspective distortion is often horizontal and vertical, and because it is not always clear to a novice where the center of distortion is.

The Distort command stretches all the pixels to meet the repositioning of one corner of the transform bounding box. However, when dragging to distort, you can drag one corner and then the other until you get exactly the effect you want. It is most useful for correcting perspective distortion typically found in hand-held photos. This is because you can use it to correct horizontal and vertical distortion independently. (See "Setting It Straight and Correcting Perspective Planes," later in the chapter.)

Using the Perspective Command

Perspective distortion stretches opposite corners of the same side of the image equidistantly from the center of that side. If you are making a perspective correction by dragging, you can simultaneously shrink and stretch the image.

Using the Numeric Command

When you need to perform one or more types of transformations simultaneously, and those transformations have to meet absolutely precise measurements, you can enter those dimensions (and angles, if they pertain) into a dialog. All of the types of transformations that you have checked will then take place at once. This means that far less data is lost than if you make several transformations by trial and error or if you make each of several types of transformations.

To stretch or scale numerically, choose Edit > Transform > Numeric. The Numeric Transform dialog will appear, as shown in Figure 5-2.

Tip: You cannot adjust Perspective or Distort in the Numeric Transform dialog.

Position units can be pixels, inches, centimeters, points, or picas. Scale units offer the same choices plus the opportunity to enter a percentage (this can be more than 100 percent).

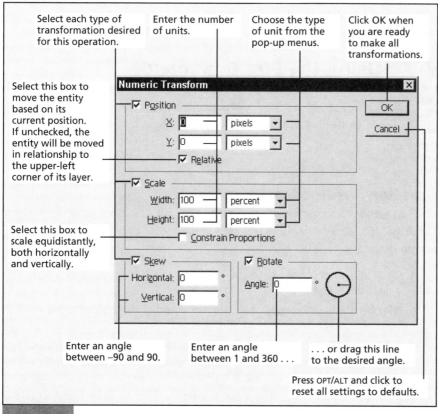

Select each type of transformation desired for this operation.

Enter the number of units.

Choose the type of unit from the pop-up menus.

Click OK when you are ready to make all transformations.

Select this box to move the entity based on its current position. If unchecked, the entity will be moved in relationship to the upper-left corner of its layer.

Select this box to scale equidistantly, both horizontally and vertically.

Enter an angle between –90 and 90.

Enter an angle between 1 and 360 . . .

. . . or drag this line to the desired angle.

Press OPT/ALT and click to reset all settings to defaults.

FIGURE 5-2 How to make a numeric transformation

Using the Rotation Commands

The Rotate 180 command is often mistakenly thought to be the same as flipping. However, in this case, the image is spun 180 degrees rather than flipped, as shown here:

The advantage of using this command over free rotation is that it turns the image exactly upside down. This is very useful if you are creating a semisymmetrical shape by drawing only half the shape.

Tip: The two Rotate 90 commands are very useful for righting images shot in portrait aspect (taller than wide) on digital cameras.

The Rotate 90 CW command flops the image on its right side, and the Rotate 90 CCW command flops the image on its left side.

Using the Flip Commands

Flip Horizontal creates a left-to-right mirror image of the original. This command is ideal for flipping scans of film that were made with the emulsion facing in the wrong direction. Flip Vertical creates an upside-down mirror image of the original—an essential part of the solution for creating reflections.

Creating a reflection in water

You can greatly enhance the mood of a photograph shot over water if you show the image of what's on dry land reflected in the water. Photoshop makes it fairly easy to create this effect.

1. Select the area of the image you want to see reflected in the water (or on a rain-drenched street).

2. Press CMD/CTRL+C to copy the selection to the clipboard and CMD/CTRL+V to paste it to a new layer.

3. Make sure the new layer is selected (it should be if you just created it, but you can tell by checking to see if it's highlighted in the Layers palette). If the Layers palette isn't showing, choose Window > Show Layers.

4. Now you want to flip the image upside down. Choose Edit > Transform > Flip Vertical.

5. Select the move tool and drag the image so that it occupies the correct position over the water. If you copy an area that overlaps outside the area in which you want the reflection, you can use the eraser tool to make the reflection fit.

6. In the Layers palette, choose Multiply as the blend mode (the menu at upper left), and lower the transparency to around 20% with the Opacity slider.

7. As a final touch, you may want to try using one of the Distort filters, such as Ocean Ripple, to give a watery texture to the reflection layer, as shown here:

Setting It Straight and Correcting Perspective Planes

Now that you know how to make transformations, you're better prepared to start cropping. Often you'll need to straighten the image before cropping because (in your hurry to "capture the moment") you didn't level the camera too carefully before pushing the shutter button. Also, if the photo is of something architectural, chances are you're experiencing something called the *keystone effect*, or *keystoning* for short. It simply means that lines that should be perfectly parallel, such as the side of a building, seem to converge. Transforming your image before you crop can make it look as though it were shot with a professional's expensive view camera. Here's how:

1. Make the window bigger than the picture. There are several ways to do this; the easiest is to select the magnifier tool, press OPT/ALT, and click in the center of the image to zoom out until there's a border around the image.

2. Now you have room to rotate the image so you can straighten it. First, assuming you just opened the image from the original scan or digital image, you'll have to put it on a layer. You can't transform the background layer. Choose Window > Show Layers and double-click the Background layer name bar when the Layers palette opens.

3. When the Layer Options dialog opens, enter a new name for the layer (if you wish—it's not absolutely necessary), and then click OK. You now have no background layer, but you probably won't need one.

4. Next, you want to know what's absolutely horizontal and vertical. Photoshop lets you use temporary guidelines, which takes out the guesswork. Choose to show rulers and guidelines by choosing View > Show Rulers and then View > Show Guides.

5. Select the move tool and click and drag from the vertical ruler to display a vertical guideline, and from the horizontal ruler to display a horizontal guideline. Then move each guideline, respectively, to where horizontal and vertical perspective should match, as shown here:

6. Now you're going to "level the camera." Press CMD/CTRL+T to put the layer into Free Transform mode. Drag a little outside the corner handles of the transform bounding box to rotate the image (as shown in the following illustration), until you've made the best compromise between having the horizontal lines parallel to the horizontal guidelines and the vertical lines parallel to the vertical guidelines. It's not likely you'll get a perfect (or even a very good) match—you just want to come as close as you can. We'll fix the rest by using the Freeform Transform command to distort the image.

7. Choose Edit > Free Transform. The transform bounding box will appear. Press CMD/CTRL to make it possible to distort the transform bounding box. Drag whichever corners of the image will straighten the horizontal and vertical lines, as shown next. A little practice will sharpen your instincts for this to the point where you can do it perfectly. Now double-click to complete the transformation.

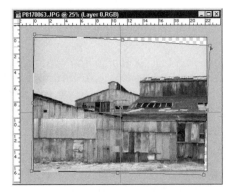

8. Now that your image is all straightened out and looks like it was shot by a seasoned pro, select the crop tool and drag diagonally to place a cropping marquee in the image. Next, drag the handles to place the crop lines exactly where you want them, and then double-click inside the marquee. Your image will be cropped.

Cropping to Eliminate Unwanted Detail

The primary example of cropping to eliminate unwanted detail is to get rid of the "other" person in the photograph—the one with whom, thank heavens, you no longer have a relationship. Actually, getting rid of unwanted detail is one of the first things you should do to strengthen the message of your photography. If you are selling real estate, nobody wants to see the recycling bins on the sidewalk.

Cropping isn't the only way to get rid of unwanted detail. There are times when you need the area occupied by the blemishes in order to be able to see the face. For the cure, see Chapter 4. On the other hand, cropping is the easiest way to get rid of unwanted detail, and it may improve your composition as well.

For example, take a look at the following before-and-after images. The geometry of the building makes a much stronger statement without the extra pavement, tree, and phone wires, which have been cropped out in the right-hand image. Cropping out the foliage at the left edge of the building would make the image even stronger.

Before   After

Cropping to Improve Composition

One of the main reasons for cropping is to strengthen the impact of the picture. Often, you can do that by cropping so that elements in the picture point to the center of interest. At other times, you may want to use the rule of thirds. The *rule of thirds* says that if you place the center of interest in any portion of the image that would fall at the intersection of lines that divide a picture by thirds, the eye will be naturally attracted to that point.

The first rule of composition is that there are no hard-and-fast rules. Breaking a rule can surprise us just enough to pique our interest. However, we can break the rules more successfully when we understand instinctively how the rule works. So if you have the patience, try placing several of your photos under a rule-of-thirds grid. It is very easy to do this in Photoshop, thanks to the fact that Photoshop has layers.

1. Open a new image that's about 20 percent smaller than your average digitized photo. Choose File > New. The New dialog appears.

2. Choose Inches for the Width and Height units; then enter dimensions that are easily divisible by three (six units by nine units is a good start).

3. Choose Window > Show Layers to reveal the Layers palette, and then click the New Layer button at the bottom of the palette.

4. Choose View > Rulers. Rulers will appear at the top and left margins. Drag guidelines from the rulers to the number of units that would divide the image into thirds, both vertically and horizontally.

5. Select the line tool. Double-click it to make the Line Options palette visible, and choose a weight of 4 or 5. Click in the foreground color selection box in the toolbox to bring up the color picker, and choose a color that will contrast sharply with your image.

6. Choose View > Snap to Guides. Draw lines to match your guidelines. Now select the move tool and drag the guidelines back to their parent rulers, so that they're out of the way.

7. In the Layers palette, double-click the Background layer. When the Layer Options palette appears, click OK. Your grid is now on a layer.

8. Next you want to get rid of the white so that you can see past the grid. Double-click the magic wand to select it and display its options. In the Options palette, enter **2** as the Tolerance. Now click in each quadrant of the grid. When the selection marquee appears, press DELETE/BACKSPACE. You will see the checkerboard pattern that indicates layer transparency, as shown here:

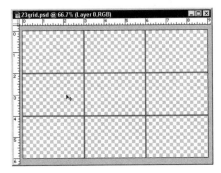

9. Save this image under a name and in a directory where you will be able to re-trieve it easily. You will be able to use it to check most any image. Don't close the image after you've saved it.

10. Open the image you want to test.

11. Select the move tool and drag the grid onto the image.

12. Drag the new layer with the image on it below the layer with the grid on it.

13. Move the grid around until the center of interest falls under one or more of the points of interest in the grid.

14. Choose Edit > Free Transform, and then move and size the grid so that you can put the main point of interest over a focal point in the image (there may be several—you can play with this), as shown here:

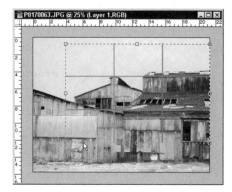

15. Use the rectangular marquee tool to place a rectangular selection around the grid, and choose Image > Crop.

16. Click the eye in the Layers palette to hide the grid, and see if you don't think your picture makes a stronger statement than the original.

The rule of thirds works for many pictures, but that doesn't mean other fac-tors, such as contrast, unusual subject matter, line, and shape in the image itself, won't do as much or more to lead the viewer's eye to your point. It is a rule that often works, and you should build an awareness of it. Also, the center of interest really only needs to fall in the general area of the one-third intersections.

Cropping to Match a Layout

If you are shooting for advertising, catalog, or cover illustrations, the paramount cropping consideration is going to be making your image fit the layout. Once again, Photoshop's layers come to the rescue. Put the layout and the areas occu-pied by type and logos onto an independent layer above the photograph (just as you did the grid in the exercise in the previous section). Then use the move tool to

Professional Pointer

You will occasionally take a shot that's not big enough in one dimension to fill the layout. To expand the background, look for another shot that includes more of the background on that side of the image. Put it on another layer, and then scale it so that you can blend it seamlessly with your current background (see the next section, "Making It Fit into a Composition"). What works even better is a panoramic image-stitching program. Crop off the part of the second image that you definitely don't want, and then stitch the two images together. Then you can crop the stitched image and have all the background you need.

position the layer so that the image makes the best fit. If necessary, choose Edit > Free Transform to resize the layout layer, and then trim as in the previous section.

Making It Fit into a Composition

One job that Photoshop is capable of doing brilliantly is combining multiple photographs into a single composition. If this is what you want to do, it will speed operations if each image is cropped to include only as much of the image as will be used in the target composition. That way, Photoshop can use the memory for processing, rather than for storing useless data.

Before you combine one image with another, open both the target image and the image you'll be adding to it. The first thing you should do is crop the image you want to combine so that it includes only what you will be combining. Use the crop tool. (If you save this cropped image, be sure to use Save As to save it under another name. Otherwise, you won't ever be able to recover the parts of the image you cropped out.)

Next, compare the image size of each. Then you can resample the image so that you're not importing a larger (more data) image than you actually need. You can do that with either the Info palette (choose Window > Show Info) or by taking a look at the Image Size dialog (choose Image > Image Size). I prefer the latter because there are fewer steps. You don't have to issue a Select All command in order to see the image size, as you do with the Info dialog. Furthermore, you're probably going to want to change the size of the image anyway, and you can do it in the same dialog. Figure 5-3 shows you visually how to change image size.

You are probably going to want to eliminate the background from objects (such as the flower in Figure 5-3) that you are planning to add to your montage. If that is the case, it is better to open, size, and crop all the images you'll be combining. Then open one at a time (except for the image that is the background),

Chapter 1: **What's New in Photoshop 5.5**

© Ken Milburn
IMAGE 1-1A

Many things happened to the original photo (not shown) on its way from a proof made on a flatbed scanner to a finished portrait. The most important of these was knocking the subject out of its original background with the use of the new Extract command. (The knockout is shown at left.)

Chapter 1 provides an overview of all the new features Adobe has introduced in Photoshop 5.5.

© Ken Milburn
IMAGE 1-1B

© Rick White   **IMAGE 2-1A**

This was a hot-selling poster photographed 20 years prior to the current ad campaign for milk. It looked a little soft after the transparency was rescanned for this book, but the fix was an easy one. First, some of the scanning artifacts were cleaned up in the b channel of the Lab color mode. Then the Levels command's white eyedropper was used to choose the highlight in the glass as the brightest point in the image, and the black eyedropper was used to choose the darkest part of the eye makeup as the darkest point in the image. Based on these levels, Photoshop made the resulting changes in contrast and detail.

Screen modes are first introduced in Chapter 2, along with other Photoshop basics such as setup, interface elements, important palettes, recordable actions, and color selection methods.

© Rick White   **IMAGE 2-1B**

Chapter 3: **Making Image Adjustments**

First the Auto Levels command was used to correct the white balance. Then the Levels command was used to lower the overall effective exposure by about 1 stop. The handball court was then masked and darkened with the Levels command. Finally, the dodge tool was used to add some detail to the t-shirts.

Chapter 3 explains how to adjust exposure and color with the Adjust commands, adjustment layers, and toolbox tools.

© Ken Milburn

IMAGE 3-1A

© Ken Milburn

IMAGE 3-1B

Chapter 4: **Image Retouching and Cleanup**

© Ken Milburn

IMAGE 4-1A

A selection was made for the opening in the window, and the Levels command was applied to it. The selection was then inverted, and the Levels command reapplied to suit the tonal values of the exterior. The cat's eyes were lightened in order to draw more attention to them. The rubber stamp tool was used to retouch all the spots and scratches.

Chapter 4 provides techniques and tutorials for retouching and recoloring images, and for removing backgrounds.

© Ken Milburn

IMAGE 4-1B

The Free Transform command was used to straighten the keystone effect. Part of the curb was lifted to a new layer and moved over to cover the meter in the foreground; then the meter was cloned out. The Levels command (Chapter 3) added some snap, and the Unsharp Mask filter (Chapter 10) was applied to make the edges crisp.

Chapter 5 details cropping and transformations.

© Ken Milburn   IMAGE 5-1A

© Ken Milburn   IMAGE 5-1B

IMAGE 6-1A

The Hue/Saturation command (Chapter 3) and various selection tools were employed to bring out details of the tree and the foreground grass. Then the black eyedropper tool in the Levels dialog was used (Chapter 3), with one click in the blackest area, to balance the tonal coloration of the image.

Chapter 6 discusses selections, paths, and masks, and how they are used to isolate portions of layers for editing or creating knockouts.

IMAGE 6-1B

Chapter 7: **Editing and Modifying Selections and Masks**

This was shot in early evening, but the camera's autoexposure made it look almost as though it was daylight. To create a moodier and more interesting sky, the original sky was removed with the Color Range command and a more interesting sky placed on an underlying layer. The neon sign on the Fairfax theater was sharpened with the Unsharp Mask filter (Chapter 10). The cyclist was moved a bit further into the picture by lifting him to another layer and then using the Extract command. The original cyclist was then cloned out (Chapter 4). Various areas were selected, feathered a great deal, and then adjusted with the Levels controls (Chapter 3). Many of the selections were edited as masks.

Chapter 7 explains how to edit, move, feather, and save selections and masks. It also shows you how to create instant knockouts and how to paint masks.

© Ken Milburn

IMAGE 7-1A

© Ken Milburn

IMAGE 7-1B

Chapter 8: **Bending and Twisting the Image**

© Ken Milburn IMAGE 8-1A

These easy manipulations emphasize the color of the winter sky and the autumn leaves. The trick here was in making selections with the magic wand tool to select the sky. The Contract command (Chapter 7) was used to shrink the selection by a couple of pixels, and the sky was darkened with the Brightness/Contrast controls (Chapter 3). The selection was reversed and then saved. Next, the selection was subtracted from so that only the red leaves were left, and the leaves were brightened slightly. The houses and trees were selected and darkened by lowering the brightness and by painting the white house dark gray so that the viewer's eye would focus on the red autumn leaves. Finally, the image was distorted with the Pinch filter.

The distort filters, including Pinch, are covered in Chapter 8.

© Ken Milburn IMAGE 8-1B

Chapter 9: **Incorporating Text**

This manmade desert island was shot near Key Largo for a barbeque tools product photo. It was really a "cartoon-sized" island, and the ad's layout allowed only a cramped area for the barbecue. Reshaping the island was accomplished by cloning areas using assorted selection tools (Chapter 6) and the rubber stamp tool (Chapter 4). Text was then added and was shaped and enhanced with the Bevel and Emboss command.

Chapter 9 focuses on entering, editing, and importing text, as well as on creating text effects.

© Rick White   IMAGE 9-1A

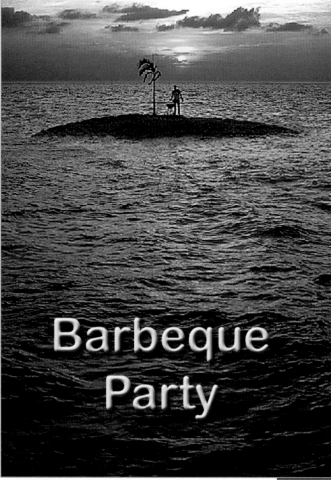

© Rick White   IMAGE 9-1B

Chapter 10: **Photographic Effects**

IMAGE 10-1A

To create the final composite of two photographs, a model was first photographed in a static pose. Then the background was knocked out using the Extract command. The model was given the appearance of movement using the Motion Blur command.

Chapter 10 shows you how to incorporate blurring and other photographic effects in your images using Photoshop's filters, tools, image commands, and layers.

IMAGE 10-1B

Chapter 11: **Creating Photopaintings**

The contact proof was used as the original image and resized 800% in order to keep photographic detail to a minimum. The model was removed from the background with the Extract command (Chapters 4 and 6), a new background layer was added, and then a new background pasted in. Next, the image was flattened and that layer copied three times. Each layer was then filtered with a different Artistic filter. Various blend modes were applied between the filters, and the eraser was used to make some layers more prominent in certain areas of the image.

Chapter 11 shows you how to create these and other painterly effects; it also includes tutorials on making custom brushes and brush palettes, and on using the history brush and art history brush tools.

© Ken Milburn   IMAGE 11-1A

© Ken Milburn   IMAGE 11-1B

TAMEGRET TAMRUNRS vanboard2

wdaisy1 wdroad WNDWBOX1

whflwr2 whpnkbrst2 whtice

whtroses willow1 yelily2

raw freeform selection or move selection outline. Use Shift, Alt, and Ctrl for additional options.

IMAGE 12-1

Now Photoshop 5.5 can add filenames as titles to a contact sheet. Contact Sheet II is a batch command that makes thumbnails of all the images in a given folder and places them in the number of rows and columns that you specify.

With the Picture Package command, Photoshop 5.5 has also automated the task of reproducing several sizes of an image on a single page, similar to portrait packages that you get from a professional studio.

© Ken Milburn

IMAGE 12-2

You learn these and other image management techniques, including how to create Web photo galleries, in Chapter 12.

Chapter 13: Optimizing Web Graphics

No longer do you have to guess what level of compression to use to get the best compromise between Web performance and image quality. The inclusion of ImageReady 2 in Photoshop 5.5 makes it possible to view the original image and three levels of optimization (in GIF or JPEG format, or a mix of the two) before deciding which to save and publish.

Chapter 13 outlines the techniques involved in optimizing graphics for the Web.

© Ken Milburn

IMAGE 13-1

IMAGE 13-2

Chapter 14: **Using ImageReady for Special-Purpose Web Graphics**

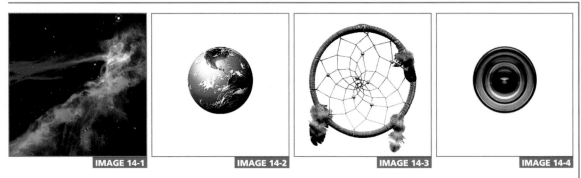

IMAGE 14-1   IMAGE 14-2   IMAGE 14-3   IMAGE 14-4

The graphical image elements above were used to create the following animation frames. The elements consist of two stock astronomy photos, a dreamcatcher scanned on a flatbed scanner, and a Nikon lens placed facedown and scanned on a flatbed scanner. The animation was achieved by first creating four layers in Photoshop and then animating those layers as frames in ImageReady's Animation palette.

Chapter 14 takes you step-by-step through the process of creating this animation sequence, and also provides tutorials on slicing images, creating interactive rollovers, and making image maps.

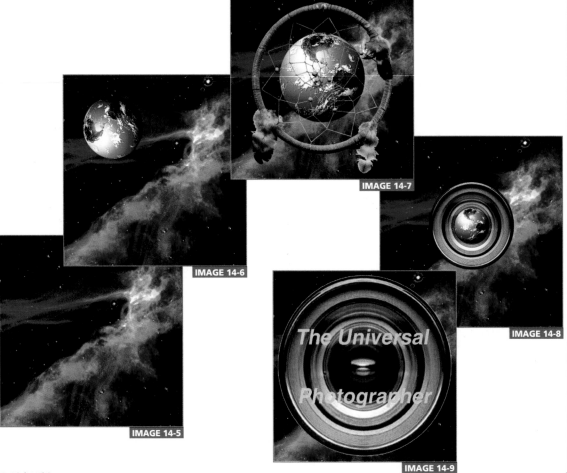

IMAGE 14-7

IMAGE 14-6

IMAGE 14-8

IMAGE 14-5

IMAGE 14-9

On the Web: **Working with Channels**

In this image, the man's bright clothing needed more detail. The Red channel showed better detail than did the Green, so the gown and hat were selected in the Red channel and copied to the same location in the Green channel.

Download "Working with Channels," on the Web at www.osborne.com, for a tutorial on how to work with channels.

© Rick White

IMAGE WEB1-1A

© Rick White

IMAGE WEB1-1B

On the Web: **Using Layers**

IMAGE WEB2-1A

The original image was shot in the late evening, so there was still enough light to supply some detail in the landscape; however, the image was fuzzy, so the picture was sharpened using very high settings in the Unsharp Mask filter (Chapter 10). The detail in some of the darker areas was enhanced by copying the layer, adjusting the new layer, and then erasing parts of it to retain some of the background layer where the original image was more important.

Download "Using Layers," on the Web at www.osborne.com, for a tutorial explaining everything you need to know about layers: types of layers, how they work, and how to create, combine, and group them.

IMAGE WEB2-1B

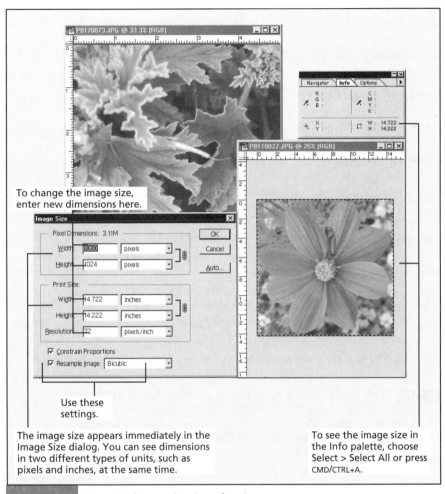

To change the image size, enter new dimensions here.

Use these settings.

The image size appears immediately in the Image Size dialog. You can see dimensions in two different types of units, such as pixels and inches, at the same time.

To see the image size in the Info palette, choose Select > Select All or press CMD/CTRL+A.

FIGURE 5-3 How to change the size of an image

and remove the background in the individual files. When you've finished, you can open one file at a time and drag each one into place above the background file.

Cross-Reference: See Chapters 6 and 7 for more information about removing backgrounds.

Three Methods for Cropping

As is often the case with any type of Photoshop operation, you can crop in multiple ways. Each of the following methods has advantages and disadvantages in particular situations.

- Using the crop tool
- Using the rectangular marquee tool
- Placing a larger image into a smaller image

Using the Crop Tool

- **Advantage:** ☑ You can easily and quickly adjust the size of the crop before executing, simply by dragging handles.
- **Disadvantages:** ☒ Not suited for making trims close to the edge, because the tool will snap to the existing edge.   ☒ Always crops all the layers simultaneously, making it unsuitable for cropping portions of layers.

The crop tool is found on the flyout for the shape selection tools in the upper-right corner of the toolbox. Click whatever tool is currently shown in that position and drag until the crop tool is available. Once you have chosen the crop tool, simply drag diagonally to make a marquee that's roughly the desired size and proportion. To change the size of the cropping marquee proportionately, drag a corner handle (the small squares at the corner of the marquee). To move a single side, drag the center handle for that side. To make the actual crop, double-click inside the marquee when you have the marquee positioned and sized just as you like. Figure 5-4 shows you how to crop an image using the crop tool.

Using the crop tool with the Fixed Size option

- **Advantages:** ☑ Lets you crop in the units of measurement of your choice.   ☑ Automatically resamples the image to meet the measurement and resolution specifications.
- **Disadvantage:** ☒ You may inadvertently increase or decrease your file size, as there is no warning when the file will be resampled.

If you need to crop an image to a specific size and then resample it to fit a specific page layout, using the crop tool with the Fixed Size check box selected cuts the number of steps required. This option crops and resamples simultaneously. So it's not quite like cropping to a fixed size using the rectangular marquee. When you drag the cropping marquee, it always stays in proportion to the final image size, but the size of the final image is determined by the resolution you specify.

To use the crop tool with the Fixed Size option, follow the steps shown in Figure 5-5.

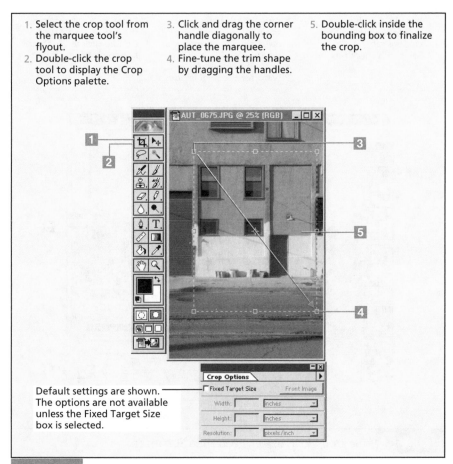

1. Select the crop tool from the marquee tool's flyout.
2. Double-click the crop tool to display the Crop Options palette.
3. Click and drag the corner handle diagonally to place the marquee.
4. Fine-tune the trim shape by dragging the handles.
5. Double-click inside the bounding box to finalize the crop.

Default settings are shown. The options are not available unless the Fixed Target Size box is selected.

FIGURE 5-4 Basic steps for using the crop tool

Using the Rectangular Marquee Tool

The rectangular marquee tool is typically used for making rectangular selections or for painting a rectangle by stroking it (see Chapter 6). However, if you make a rectangular selection, there are a couple of ways you can crop with it. You can either crop the image to the exact size of the selection, or you can invert the selection and delete the contents of the inversion. The latter lets you crop an image that's on a layer within another image.

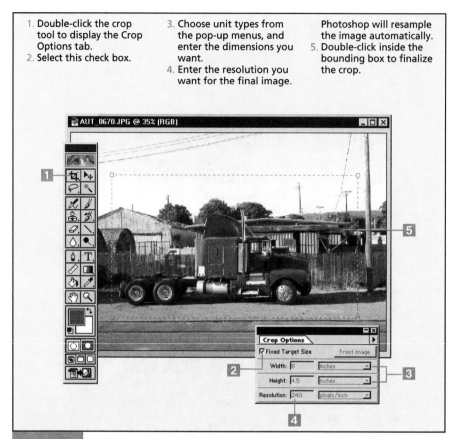

1. Double-click the crop tool to display the Crop Options tab.
2. Select this check box.
3. Choose unit types from the pop-up menus, and enter the dimensions you want.
4. Enter the resolution you want for the final image.

Photoshop will resample the image automatically.
5. Double-click inside the bounding box to finalize the crop.

FIGURE 5-5 The crop tool is used here in Fixed Size mode.

Using the rectangular marquee tool with the Crop command

- **Advantages:** ☑ Slightly quicker to access the rectangular marquee because it comes up when you press M. ☑ Won't automatically snap to the edges of the image (unless you've chosen View > Snap to Grid to toggle Snap on). ☑ Doesn't require double-clicking to finalize the crop—in case your digitizing pad isn't very responsive to double-clicking.

- **Disadvantages:** ☒ Impossible to adjust the proportions of your selection without dropping the selection and reselecting. ☒ Only choice for measurement units is pixels.

To use the rectangular marquee with the Image > Crop command, follow the steps shown in Figure 5-6.

Using the rectangular marquee tool with the Constrained Aspect Ratio option

- **Advantages:** ☑ Provides a means for cropping to a specific aspect ratio, regardless of the actual image dimensions or the final resolution to which you may or may not resample the image.   ☑ Provides a means for cropping several images to a given aspect ratio through a Photoshop action.

- **Disadvantage:** ☒ Does not provide you exact final dimensions in a single step.

1. Double-click the rectangular marquee tool to select it and display the Marquee Options palette.

2. Choose Normal, which is the default, from this pop-up menu. From the main menu, choose

Image > Crop to finalize the crop.

Optional: Drag from inside the marquee to reposition the marquee without changing its size.

Optional: Enter a number of pixels for the width of the soft edge here.

FIGURE 5-6 Cropping with the rectangular marquee tool and the Image > Crop command

You will find the instructions for using the rectangular marquee tool with a constrained aspect ratio in Figure 5-7.

If you want an aspect ratio of 2:3, enter **2** in the Width field and **3** in the Height field. When you click and drag within the image, the marquee will have the same height and width proportions regardless of the size you drag it to. Drag to position it so that the portion of the image you want preserved is surrounded by the marquee (see Figure 5-7). You cannot change the position of the sides of the marquee because that would alter the aspect ratio of the final crop.

Using the rectangular marquee tool with the Fixed Size option

- **Advantages:** ☑ Lets you crop the image to a specific pixel width and height. ☑ The image is never resampled, so there's no danger of accidental resampling. ☑ Allows processing of multiple images when placed into an action script.

- **Disadvantage:** ☒ Only choice for units is pixels.

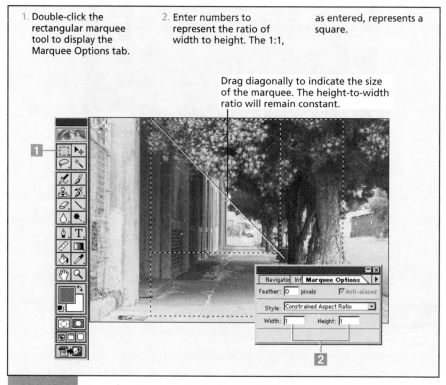

1. Double-click the rectangular marquee tool to display the Marquee Options tab.

2. Enter numbers to represent the ratio of width to height. The 1:1, as entered, represents a square.

Drag diagonally to indicate the size of the marquee. The height-to-width ratio will remain constant.

FIGURE 5-7   Cropping to a constrained aspect ratio

You will find the instructions for cropping to a fixed size in Figure 5-8.

You should be aware of a couple of things when you use the rectangular marquee tool. It's a little startling to see the whole marquee appear the instant you click anywhere on the image. If you've put the marquee in the wrong place, there are a couple of things you can do: either press CMD/CTRL+D to drop the selection, or drag from inside the marquee to move it wherever you want. Oh, yes, you can also move the marquee with the arrow keys. Each keypress moves the marquee one pixel. If you want to move it faster, pressing SHIFT+arrow key moves it ten pixels at a time. Once you have chosen Image > Crop, the image is instantly cropped. If you goofed, press CMD/CTRL+Z, or delete the step from the History palette (see Chapter 2).

1. Double-click the rectangular marquee tool to display the Marquee Options palette.
2. Choose Fixed Size from this pop-up menu.
3. Enter the width and height. Pixels are the only units allowed.
4. Click anywhere in the image to place the marquee. The entire marquee will appear at once.
5. Click anywhere to move the upper-left corner of the marquee, drag to refine its placement, or move it one pixel at a time using the arrow keys. When you have included what you intend to include, choose Image > Crop.

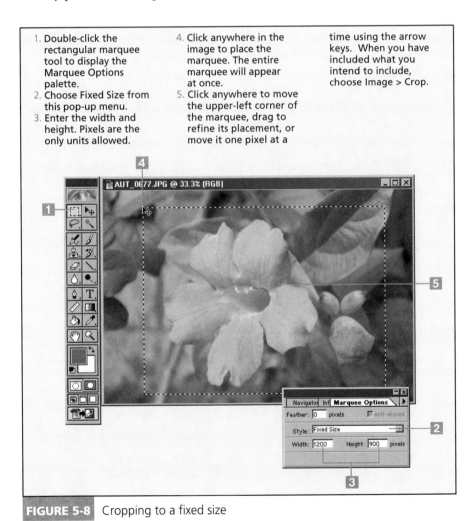

FIGURE 5-8 Cropping to a fixed size

Pasting an Image into a Smaller Image (or Selection)

- **Advantages:** ☑ Provides immediate visual feedback because the pasted-in image is automatically previewed in relationship to the size of the active window.   ☑ Perfect for fitting current resolution into a predetermined frame size.   ☑ If you use the new file method, you can also automatically change the color mode of the resultant copy.

- **Disadvantage:** ☒ You can't change the size or shape of the cropping frame.

Use the "paste into new image" method when you want to create a new file for the cropped image that is sized for a particular purpose. This method is commonly used when you want to visually and interactively place an image inside a mat board cutout of a given size (because you ordered 50 of them) or because you need to place images inside a frame of a given size for use on the portfolio page of your Web site.

You will want to know the exact dimensions of your current image as well as the exact dimensions of your target image. Be sure you have chosen the appropriate units in the File > Preferences > Units & Rulers dialog. To determine the units for your current image, choose Image > Image Size and write down the dimensions reported there.

To crop an image using this method, choose File > New from the menu bar (or press CMD/CTRL+N). The New dialog appears.

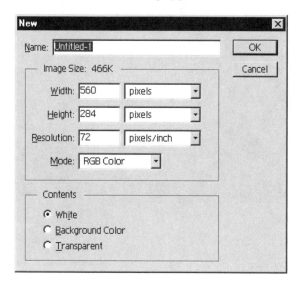

In the Width and Height fields, enter pixel dimensions that are smaller than the image(s) you want to crop. Remember that these dimensions are also going to be the final dimensions of the image. Since the result of this crop is going to be a new file, you may want to enter the new filename in the Name field—otherwise you can rename the default filename later. Enter the resolution for the final image (if in doubt, enter 300 dpi for printed hard copy or 72 dpi for screen resolution—as in multimedia and Web images).

If you want to keep your new file in the same color mode as it currently is (probably RGB), make sure the correct color mode has been chosen in the New dialog's Mode pop-up menu. You can automatically convert the image to a new color mode by choosing the new mode from the same menu. This is especially handy if you're preparing a bunch of images for offset printing (because they need to be in CMYK format) or when you want to convert a bunch of images to grayscale for black-and-white printing (or just because you find the effect appropriate to your intent).

If you like, you can automatically frame images that are smaller than the new file by specifying a background color that is the color you want the frame to be. Then click the Background Color radio button in the New dialog.

Once you have set the desired dimensions and specifications for the new file, click OK. A new window will appear. From the Window menu, choose your original file. Its window will become the active window. Double-click the hand tool. This will size the window so that you can see its contents entirely within the screen area. Click to activate the new file's window, and, once again, double-click the hand tool to make sure that it, too, fits entirely within the viewable area of the Photoshop window.

Select the move tool from the toolbox. Click in the original image and drag it into the window of the new image. Release the mouse button so that you can see the image appear. With the move tool still active, continue to position the image until it fits the window frame as desired. When the file is positioned as you like it, press CMD/CTRL+SHIFT+S to execute the File > Save As command. In the Save As dialog that results (see the following illustration), navigate to the directory where you'd like to keep the file, enter the name you'd like to use, and click OK.

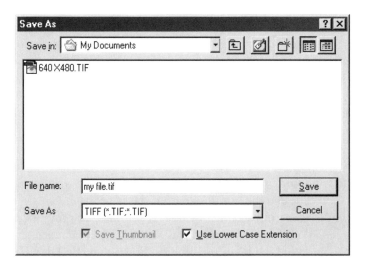

Professional Skills Summary

In this chapter, you have learned both the purpose and the techniques for applying transformations and for cropping. You've also learned the techniques for which each of these is most appropriate. This chapter concludes the section on the basics of using Photoshop. Starting with the next chapter, you'll learn to combine images into montages and collages. Montages are composite images made to look like a single image. Collages are composite images that are obviously composed from multiple sources.

Part II
Image Compositing

chapter 6

Making Selections and Masks

In this chapter, you:

- Learn the difference between selections, masks, and paths

- Discover how to choose the right selection tool

- Get acquainted with the uses and strength of the three new masking features in Photoshop 5.5

- Find out when and how to use paths for making selections

- Learn to choose and use pen tools

- Learn to paint and draw with paths

Selections and masks serve two purposes:

- They isolate portions of a layer so that you can apply Photoshop tools and commands to only that part of the layer.
- They allow you to make the area outside the selection transparent, so that part of the image can be combined seamlessly with other layers.

Making selections and masks is an art unto itself. Because these operations (along with layering and channel operations) are critical to any effects that involve montage or collage, selections and masking deserve a chapter of their own. Selections can be any shape. The shape of a selection is always shown by a marquee (a.k.a. "marching ants"). A selection marquee is so called because it is a blinking dashed line that looks a bit like the cycling bulbs on a Broadway marquee.

Making selections is such an important part of creating special effects that Adobe wisely gives you many different tools and commands for making selections. You can also make selections by painting on a mask (using any of the brush tools in Quick Mask mode) or by silhouetting your subjects with vector pen tools (much like those in illustration programs such as Illustrator and FreeHand).

This chapter will cover where to find selection tools and commands and why they are on two different menus, including a quick reference table. In addition, the purpose of each selection tool is defined by category: geometric, lasso, magic wand, and Color Range. Each of these categories is accompanied by a practical application exercise. Then there's a discussion of how to use Quick Mask mode, both for retouching masks made by other methods and for creating masks by painting them in. Finally, this chapter talks about using the pen tools for making selections.

The Difference Between Selections, Masks, and Paths

Masks and selections are almost the same thing. Selections are temporary, whereas masks are permanently stored as grayscale images in alpha channels. Another important distinction is that you can use any of Photoshop's tools to edit a mask; you can't do this with a selection, which is just a marquee. Selections and masks are both used to confine the effects of Photoshop's tools and commands to a limited area within a chosen layer.

Selections are also different from masks in that you can draw with them. You do this by using the Stroke command in the Edit menu. You'll find a full explanation of stroking selections later in this chapter. Here we see a selection (the dotted line) that has been stroked (the solid line):

Selections and paths are also very closely related. Paths are vector geometry, and you create them in virtually the same way that you draw when using an illustration program. In fact, you can move paths from Photoshop to illustration programs and back (but that's a topic for later). Paths are perfectly smooth, very precise, and their shapes are easily changed and scaled. Any path can be converted to a selection, and any selection can be converted to a path.

Tip: All of the tools in this chapter have Options palettes that let you change the settings for various characteristics of that tool. To reach the Options palette for any tool, double-click that tool's icon in the toolbox.

Selection Tools and Their Talents

The selection tools are used to draw a "marching ants" marquee around the part of a layer's image that you want to isolate. You'll find the selection tools at the top of the toolbox, in three of the upper four slots, as shown here:

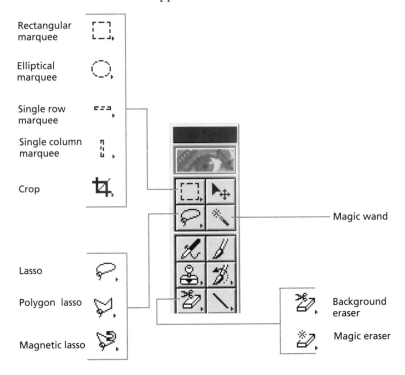

The presence of a small, right-facing arrow in the lower-right corner of a tool icon indicates that multiple tools can be accessed when that button is clicked.

In addition to these toolbox selection tools, there are three other means of making selections: Quick Mask mode and layer masks, The Select > Color Range command from the menu bar, and selections made from a color channel by duplicating the channel. You can also erase portions of a layer to transparency. This amounts to another means of making a selection, since the transparent areas of that layer won't be affected by any of Photoshop's tools and commands (unless the Preserve Transparency check box in the Layers palette is not selected).

Rectangular Marquee

- **Advantages:** ☑ Quick and easy way to make areas for signs, buttons, and frames. ☑ Useful for adding a large area to an irregularly shaped area. ☑ Useful for tracing and making edge effects for buttons.
- **Disadvantage:** ☒ It's too square, man.

The rectangular marquee is the tool to use if you want to make a selection within a rectangle or a rounded-corner rectangle. The shape of this tool can be constrained to a square by pressing SHIFT while dragging the rectangular marquee. You can also specify a constrained aspect ratio or a fixed size. To specify a constrained aspect ratio, choose Constrained Aspect Ratio from the Style pop-up menu in the Marquee Options palette, and then type a width and height ratio in the appropriate fields.

Anti-aliased is always selected in the Marquee Options palette for the rectangular marquee; so if you rotate a rectangular selection, the edges of the slanted lines will still be smooth.

To make a rounded-corner rectangle selection (very useful for making navigation buttons for Web and multimedia applications), simply drag a rectangular marquee, and then choose Select > Modify > Smooth. In the Smooth Selection dialog, enter a number of pixels for Sample Radius. Because there's a limit of 16 pixels for smoothing, this doesn't work very well if you need a good-size rounded rectangle in a large, high-resolution file. Here's how to get around that: Make a rounded-rectangle selection in the proportion you want. Use Edit > Transform > Scale to scale the selection to the size you want to use. Make sure the rectangular marquee tool is still chosen. Place the cursor in the center of the selection and drag it into the position where you would like to use it. If you want to use this selection to make repeated buttons and signs in this image, be sure to save the selection.

The settings in the Marquee Options palette are the same for both the rectangular and elliptical marquees. They are shown in Figure 6-1.

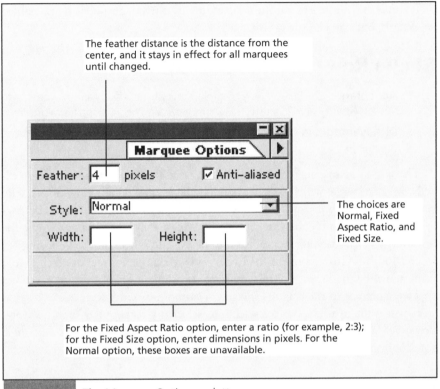

The feather distance is the distance from the center, and it stays in effect for all marquees until changed.

The choices are Normal, Fixed Aspect Ratio, and Fixed Size.

For the Fixed Aspect Ratio option, enter a ratio (for example, 2:3); for the Fixed Size option, enter dimensions in pixels. For the Normal option, these boxes are unavailable.

FIGURE 6-1 The Marquee Options palette

Elliptical Marquee

- **Advantages:** ☑ Can be used to quickly make any oval selection. ☑ Useful for cutting holes and curves into rectangular selections.
- **Disadvantage:** ☒ Not suitable for irregular-shaped selections.

The elliptical marquee is the tool to use if you want to make a selection within a circle or oval. The shape of this tool can be constrained to a circle by pressing SHIFT while dragging the circle. You can also specify a constrained aspect ratio or a fixed size. To specify a constrained aspect ratio, choose Constrained Aspect Ratio from the Type pop-up menu in the Marquee Options palette, and then type a width and height ratio in the appropriate fields.

Because the outlines of elliptical selections are curved, anti-aliasing is enabled by default; but you can turn it off.

Single Row/Column Marquee

- **Advantage:** ☑ Makes it easy to stroke straight lines of a given thickness or to run some third-party filter effects, such as glows and neon, along a straight line.
- **Disadvantage:** ☒ Makes the selection marquee the full width or height of the image.

The single row marquee and single column marquee tools make a selection exactly one pixel wide, which is either perfectly horizontal (single row) or perfectly vertical (single column) and the full width or height of the layer. This seems useless at first, because the marquee isn't even wide enough to see a gap. Actually, however, you can expand the selection to be as wide as you like by choosing Select > Modify > Grow from the menu bar and typing the number of pixels. More important, the single row/column marquee is excellent for retouching scratches that were present in the original image—a common occurrence.

If you want to use a shorter selection, select the rectangular marquee tool, press OPT/ALT, and drag so that the rectangular marquee cuts off the single row/column marquee.

Crop Tool

- **Advantage:** ☑ You can continue to change the size of the marquee by dragging handles.
- **Disadvantage:** ☒ It's not a selection tool.

The crop tool makes it easy to select exactly the portion of the image to which you want to crop. If you need to crop to exact dimensions, choose Window > Show Info from the menu bar. The Info palette shows the exact dimensions of the crop marquee. Dimensions are reported in the units you set in the Units and Rulers dialog (File > Preferences > Units & Rulers). You can adjust these dimensions proportionately by dragging the corner handles of the crop marquee, or you can adjust height or width by dragging the center handles.

Lasso

- **Advantages:** ☑ Can be made to follow any outline form, regardless of the color of underlying pixels. ☑ Perfect for editing the shapes selected by faster, more automated selection tools.

- **Disadvantage:** ⊠ Initial selection tends to be either too painstaking or woefully inaccurate (but inevitably improves with experience and drawing talent).

The lasso is the true freehand selection tool. You just draw with it, the way you would draw freehand with a pencil. More often, it's used as a tracing tool to outline the edges of a curvy, organic object, like a flower or apple, or area you want to isolate from the rest of the image.

You can change the behavior of the lasso tool by using it in conjunction with modifier keys. Press SHIFT to add to anything that's already been selected—regardless of what tools made the initial selection. Press OPT/ALT with the lasso tool to subtract from the current selection.

Professional Pointer

It can be difficult to trace the edges of a shape precisely, and yet that's absolutely necessary if you hope to produce realistic results in editing and compositing. This is especially true if you're not using a pen pad. You'll work much faster if you make your initial selection without being overly concerned about accuracy. Save this first selection, and then use the modifier keys to add and subtract from the selection wherever you need to make corrections. This way, you only spend time making accurate selections on the parts you missed. On the second pass, zoom in very tight on the original selection, and use the Navigator palette or the hand tool (activated any time you press the SPACEBAR) to move the image along the marquee path. You'll be able to make your corrections very accurately without having to worry about the interior of the selection.

Polygon Lasso

- **Advantages:** ☑ Follows straight edges perfectly. ☑ Much quicker at making rough freehand selections than the lasso.

- **Disadvantage:** ⊠ You're restricted to selecting straight lines (unless you hold down the ALT key, which automatically switches to the lasso tool).

The polygon lasso tool is often the tool to use when making the preliminary quick selection, even of curvy, organic shapes. You can quickly click around the shape's perimeter and then move in to make corrections with the lasso and polygon lasso tools. Despite the fact that Photoshop 5.5 has lots of tools that automate the selection of irregular shapes, some must be hand traced. Hand tracing is usually required because there are different edge characteristics along various sections of the edge, which defy the settings chosen for automated selection tools such as the magic wand or background eraser. Once you've made a rough selection, it is easy to zoom in and edit the edges with the lasso tool.

Professional Pointer

Some shapes are best selected with a combination of the lasso and polygon lasso tools. This is quite easy to do, because either tool acts like the other if you press OPT/ALT while tracing. Just be sure you don't press OPT/ALT before tracing, or you will start subtracting from any selection you've already made.

Magnetic Lasso

- **Advantages:** ☑ Can greatly speed freehand lasso selection, especially in areas where edges are highly irregular (bumpy or jagged). ☑ Fastest method for selecting objects when edge contrast of subject to be selected is obvious.

- **Disadvantages:** ☒ Easy to inadvertently select too much or too little. ☒ Takes practice to learn to use fluently.

The magnetic lasso is either a lifesaver or a major frustration builder, depending on how well you learn to use it and on the nature of the shape you're trying to select. The idea is that you drag along the vicinity of the edge you want to select, and the magnetic lasso automatically finds the best pixels that define the edge you're trying to isolate.

It's a good idea to learn to use the magnetic lasso's options, particularly Lasso Width, Frequency, and Edge Contrast. These three controls determine how the magnetic lasso will draw the selection along the chosen edge. Lasso Width determines the pixel radius around the cursor where the magnetic lasso will look for edges that are within the chosen contrast range. Frequency is the number of pixels between which the tool lays down control points. These control points anchor the selection so that it won't accidentally disconnect from the edge as you move the cursor around. Edge Contrast is the percentage of lightness that must change between an edge and its surroundings.

Magic Wand

- **Advantage:** ☑ Great for selecting large areas of similar lightness, such as blank skies, walls, or seamless studio backgrounds.

- **Disadvantage:** ☒ It can be difficult to select transitional edges (those that are partly transparent, reflective, or that contain colors in the background) accurately.

The magic wand tool is so named because all you have to do is flick (well, click) it, and it manages to select everything you wanted to select—or almost everything. What it really does is select everything within a certain range around the item you picked.

The magic wand isn't perfect in its magic, though. It actually selects colors within a lightness range of 1–255. It will select other colors if you set the range past a certain point, because all colors, if they pass 50 percent brightness, contain all three primary colors.

The magic wand tool is best for selecting areas of similar color that contrast fairly sharply with the areas of color you don't want to select. It can be especially good for selecting complex shapes photographed against a fairly evenly lighted, seamless paper background or for selecting objects from an overexposed sky.

It is typical, when making magic wand selections, for the tool to select something more or less than you want; however, if most of the selection is correct, you're way ahead of using the lasso or other "manual" selection tools to make the whole selection.

Background Eraser

- **Advantages:** ☑ Excellent for making natural-edged knockouts of complex edges, such as hair, or semitransparency in small areas. ☑ Nearly the perfect tool for retouching the results of the Extract command.

- **Disadvantages:** ☒ It takes practice to understand how to use the settings so that you don't erase too much or too little at a time. ☒ Learning when it is or isn't a time-saver is also an acquired instinct.

The background eraser is one of two brand-new selection tools in Photoshop 5.5, the other being the magic eraser. Strictly speaking, neither of these is really a selection tool. What they do is erase portions of a layer to transparency. They differ in how large a portion gets erased at a time and in how you control the tool.

The background eraser erases the background pixels over the width of the chosen brush—up to the edge of the pixels outside the range of the pixels you've chosen to erase in the Background Eraser Options dialog. Its closest relative is the magnetic lasso.

Magic Eraser

- **Advantage:** ☑ Excellent for removing large areas of similar lightness.

- **Disadvantage:** ☒ Not entirely instinctive because it will require that some areas be "fenced off" with a selection marquee if the contrast between background and subject doesn't fall within a uniform range.

The magic eraser works just like the magic wand except that it erases, instead of simply selecting, the area that falls within the range chosen in its Options palette. Its obvious use is for instantly removing boring backgrounds, such as seamless backgrounds and sky, but this works best if the contrast between background and subject is pronounced.

There is some overlap in function with the Extract command (covered later in this chapter in the section "Selecting with the Extract Command"), given that there is a Contiguous check box in the Options palette. If selected, this option makes it possible to remove background color from "holes" in the edges of shapes (such as the space between hairs or leaves). However, you will still need to be careful that you don't inadvertently erase colors inside the subject that must be kept. Just in case you do, keep one hand near the CMD/CTRL+Z keys so that you can quickly undo any goofs.

To protect an area of the image from too much erasing by the magic eraser, as shown in Figure 6-2, select the area you want to protect. Then invert the selection by pressing CMD/CTRL+SHIFT+I. Now everything that you've selected except the original selection is susceptible to your next command or stroke—in this case, the application of the magic eraser.

The checkerboard pattern is the selected area.

Original image

Image after magic eraser was used without selection protection

Image after protecting the center of the flower

FIGURE 6-2 Three views of the same image

Selection Commands

Not all selections are made with the selection tools just described. Some are made with the pen tools (covered later in this chapter), and some are made with menu commands—most notably, the new Extract command.

Commands that select can be found in several places. Often, the same command is found in more than one place:

- The Select menu, shown here:

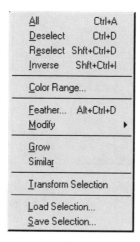

- The Image menu, shown here:

- The context menu. To reach the context menu for selections, one of the selection tools must be selected (active). Press CONTROL+click/right-click inside the selection.

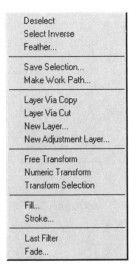

You can also make a selection from a channel by selecting the channel in the Channels palette and clicking the Save Selection as Channel button:

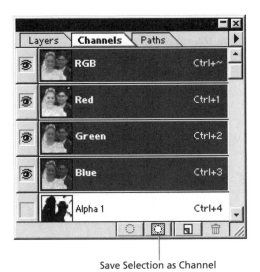

Save Selection as Channel

Cross-Reference: For information on channels, including making selections from channels, see the tutorial "Working with Channels," on the Osborne Web site.

Command	What It Does	Location	Shortcut
All	Selects the entire layer.	Select menu, context menu	CMD/CTRL+A
Deselect	Drops all selections so you can edit the entire image without restrictions from a mask.	Select menu, context menu	CMD/CTRL+D
Reselect	Reselects a selection after being deselected.	Select menu, context menu	CMD/CTRL+SHIFT+D
Inverse	Inverts the selection; very useful when you want to magic wand–select something on a more or less solid-color background or when you need to eliminate the background from a selected subject.	Select menu, context menu	CMD/CTRL+SHIFT+I
Color Range	Selects all the colors in the image that are within the specified range; excellent for selecting complex shapes (such as lace or hair) from a background.	Select menu	None
Extract	Causes the Extract dialog to open, which you can use to make very complex selections. See "Selecting with the Extract Command," later in the chapter.	Image menu	OPT/ALT+CMD/CTRL+X

TABLE 6-1   Functions and Locations of Photoshop's Selection Commands

It would be nice if all these commands could be found on the same menu, but Adobe does offer several other ways to access them, so you can use whichever method you prefer. To alleviate some confusion, Table 6-1 lists all the commands for making selections, showing where they can be found and what they do.

Five Ways to Automate Making Selections

The headline may be a bit misleading: nothing Photoshop can do will guarantee you that you won't have to edit the result of the selection. However, Photoshop does offer several commands and methods to speed up the process. In fact, if you're lucky enough to have an image with edges that aren't too difficult to distinguish from those of overlapping objects, you may even be able to do the whole job in a click or two.

Professional Pointer

You should be aware that any of these automated methods of extracting selections from their backgrounds has the potential to erase portions of the image (particularly along the edges) that you didn't intend to erase. Photoshop's History palette makes it easy to back up and start over. You can undo several steps by simply selecting an earlier state. It also offers another way that may be even more helpful: the snapshot and the history brush. If you remember to take a snapshot before you extract the image (that is, delete the area outside the selection), you will be able to use the art history brush to paint details back in whenever needed. (To take a snapshot, choose New Snapshot from the History palette flyout.) You'll find a detailed explanation of how to use the history brush in Chapter 9.

Selecting by Color Range

- **Advantages:** ☑ Can select multiple shades of colors throughout the image. ☑ Good for picking background color out of "holes" (such as sky between leaves or phone wires).
- **Disadvantages:** ☒ Difficult to control in subtle areas. ☒ May take more editing than other methods, such as Image > Extract.

The Color Range command is one of the most powerful tools in the Photoshop arsenal. Because it allows you to add several colors to the mix of colors it will select, you can select many very complex shapes in only a few steps. After you specify the colors to be added (which you do by clicking on them and specifying a "fuzziness" between 0 and 200), they are selected wherever they appear in the image. Think of it as a combination of the magic wand tool and the Select Similar command—but with more controls to ensure greater accuracy.

Color Range isn't a toolbox tool, though it acts much like the magic wand. To access this tool you have to choose Select > Color Range. What pops up is a dialog different from any other in Photoshop, as shown in Figure 6-3.

When the Color Range dialog opens, you will notice a large frame (Adobe calls this the *preview area*) in the center. The preview area shows you either the mask that results as you select colors or the image surrounded by the mask. You determine which by clicking either the Selection radio button or the Image radio button, just below the preview area. The preview area will probably start out completely black and change to reveal the selection mask as you choose colors with the eyedroppers. The leftmost eyedropper chooses the base color that will be

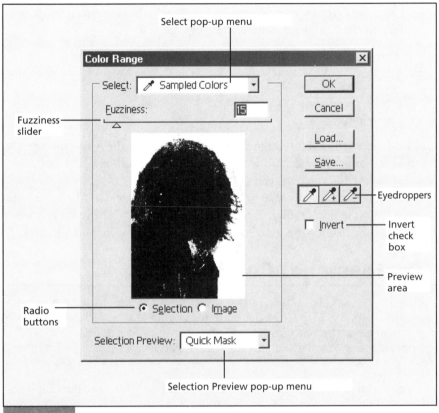

Select pop-up menu

Color Range   [×]

Select: [/] Sampled Colors [▾]

OK

Cancel

Fuzziness: [15]

Load...

Save...

Fuzziness slider

Eyedroppers

[/] Invert

Invert check box

Preview area

Radio buttons

⊙ Selection ○ Image

Selection Preview: Quick Mask [▾]

Selection Preview pop-up menu

FIGURE 6-3 The Color Range dialog

selected. The middle (+) eyedropper adds colors to the selection, while the rightmost (–) eyedropper subtracts colors from the selection.

In the Fuzziness slider just above the frame, you set the allowable brightness range of the colors you select. If you select the Invert check box, the selection will be inverted. Above and below the preview area are two pop-up menus, Select and Selection Preview. In the Select menu, you can choose to do one of four things:

- **Sampled Colors**   Select from eyedropper-sampled colors
- **Color boxes**   Select all of one of the primary or complementary colors at once
- **Area boxes**   Select all the shadows, midtones, or highlights
- **Out of Gamut**   Select the *out-of-gamut colors,* the range of colors that a computer cannot display or print.

The Selection Preview menu controls the color in which the main image window previews the mask while you're selecting colors:

- None
- White
- Black
- Quick Mask

Quick Mask assigns a color to the mask, so when you see the mask, you see it in the assigned color. (The default is red to imitate a rubylith mask.) Finally, you can load or save the current selection criteria.

If you have photographs of several objects that were shot with the same lighting and the same background, save the selection criteria. Then you can select them simply by loading the selection criteria you saved for that background.

Professional Pointer

Feather and anti-alias settings may have been set in the lasso Options palette. If so, this may affect the accuracy of your selection. Since you are not warned of this when making a Color Range selection, be sure to select these options before making a Color Range selection.

As powerful as Color Range selection is, you can get a lot more out of it if you understand how to employ a few other Photoshop commands with it. The first thing to understand is that Color Range can save you hours of time even without making exactly the selection you ultimately want. If you're selecting the silhouette of a tree from the sky, for example, Color Range can probably do at least 60 percent of the job within minutes. Within another few minutes, you can probably finish 80 or 90 percent of the job by hand. If you spend even an hour in hand retouching at the end, that's still several hours less than you would have spent by using the lasso tools.

On the other hand, I don't want to give you the impression that Color Range is the universally fastest and easiest selection method. In the real world, virtually everything in every scene contains some colors from other things in the scene. Because only you can possibly know which of these areas or objects you want selected (and how carefully), there are many times when it is simpler to trace your selection by hand.

Making a knockout with the Color Range command

As explained in Chapter 1, a *knockout* is a photograph of an object whose background has been eliminated. In this section, we're going to prepare artwork for a movie theater brochure, in which we'll create a more dramatic sky by knocking out the original one. To do this, we want to create a mask that will knock out the sky without having to select each speck of sky between the leaves.

We can select the sky and create a mask for it quickly and easily by employing one or two nifty selection tricks along the way. This works best when the color of the subject is completely different from most of the colors in the background. If this is the case, you will be able to select your subject pretty quickly by simply adding colors to the selection with the plus eyedropper tool in the Color Range dialog. After you've made the basic selection, you will save it. Then select the saved channel and clean the stray pixels out of the mask. This happens fairly quickly by using the Color Range dialog again to select the sky, inverting the selection, contracting it a bit so as not to harden soft edges, and filling the selection with white. Next, load this selection and copy its contents to a new layer. Another new layer is created between the original background and the frame and filled with a solid color so it is easy to see any faults in the selection. Finally, you'll clean up the edges of the selection.

Here's the procedure, step by step:

1. Open a file that features a leafy tree against an open sky or a piece of hardware against a fairly plain background. If you don't have such a file, you can download FAIRFAX.JPG, shown in Figure 6-4, from the Osborne site (www.osborne.com).

2. Zoom in so you can clearly see edges and holes. In the Fairfax image, you want to look at the edges of small leaves around the fringe of the image. Once you have started using the Color Range command, you won't be able to zoom, so it's important that you do it now. You will be able to pan around the image with the hand tool, however.

3. Choose Select > Color Range. The Color Range dialog will appear. Select the eyedropper and click a section of sky or background in your file. (You can also select colors from the preview area in the Color Range dialog, but that's hard to do when the preview image is all black.)

4. Choose an option in the Selection Preview pop-up menu at the bottom of the Color Range dialog. Your choice here determines how your image file will preview the selection. Choose each of the selections in turn to see how they affect the preview. I usually find that Quick Mask does the best job of showing me what's been selected. I also find it helpful to switch around.

5. Drag the Fuzziness slider to the right until you see that most of the sky has been selected, but be careful not to let too much of what you want to keep in the foreground get selected.

6. In the Color Range dialog, select the plus eyedropper to add more colors to the selection. Continue to click on all the colors that you don't want to keep in the foreground subject. If you click on a color that causes too much of the

FIGURE 6-4 Original image of the movie theatre

foreground subject to be selected (remember, your goal is to do as little mask editing as possible), select the minus eyedropper and reselect the color that caused the overselection. Eventually you'll arrive at a point at which the preview image seems to represent the proper selection. Hint: Look closely at the edges of the foreground objects in the zoomed-in preview area. If there are fringes of the selection around the edges of the foreground object, click with the eyedropper as shown in Figure 6-5. If by doing this you can get large areas of the interior of the subject selected, what's left will be much easier to fix—and that's important so you don't have to spend hours retouching tiny edges in the selection.

7. From the Selection Preview pop-up menu, choose Quick Mask. A red, 50 percent transparent mask now appears on the frame. Press CMD/CTRL++ several times to zoom in to about 300 percent on the frame. Press the SPACEBAR to activate the hand tool so you can move around the frame. Try moving the Fuzziness slider up until the preview starts to show parts of the frame. Keep previewing and adjusting until you have a mask that is a happy balance between tightly masking the frame's profile and including too much interior detail on the frame.

FIGURE 6-5 Zoom in close to pick colors to be included in the selection

8. When you're satisfied, select the Invert box in the Color Range dialog and click OK. You will see a selection marquee surrounding your foreground object. Of course, unless you have a pretty clearly delineated foreground object, you'll probably have to make some corrections in this selection.

9. Placing the cursor inside the selection, press CONTROL+click/right-click to bring up the context menu. Choose Select > Save Selection. Then press CMD/CTRL+D to drop the selection.

10. Choose Window > Show Channels. Select the mask channel (channel 4, unless you've saved other selections). The image window changes to display only the mask. In this black-and-white image, it is quite easy to spot areas the mask doesn't fully cover (called *holidays*). In this image, this would be any black or gray areas. Now we'll eliminate the "schmutz" inside and outside the mask that resulted from stray colors.

11. You could get rid of these artifacts by simply painting the white areas whiter and the black areas blacker. Sometimes, in fact, that's the best option. In this instance, however, you can save yourself a lot of time by using the magic wand. Double-click on the magic wand icon to bring up the Magic Wand Options palette. Set Tolerance to 200. Click in the largest gray area, and then SHIFT+click to add any other interior gray areas to the selection.

12. Press D (to choose Default Colors). Your background color is now white. Press DELETE/BACKSPACE. You have just filled the selection with solid white. If you haven't, choose Edit > Fill from the menu bar and make sure Mode is set to Normal and Opacity is set to 100%. Then click OK.

13. You may still have some edges that need cleaning up. In the Channels palette, click the Load Channel as Selection button. Your selection marquee will appear. Now click the RGB channel so that you can see the full color image. For the Fairfax image, we still have parts of the theater selected that we don't want selected, and there are some fringes around the leaves. We can clean these up manually in Quick Mask mode.

14. Click the Edit in Quick Mask Mode icon (□) in the toolbox.

15. As soon as you enter Quick Mask mode, your selected area will turn 50 percent red (less than 50 percent if there are transparent areas in the selection). You can alter the mask by painting on it with any of the brushes. Black applies a mask, white removes the mask. A feathered brush causes a graduation from black to white, so the mask becomes gradually transparent along those edges. If you've selected new colors for any reason, press D to get the default colors—black and white. You can switch from foreground color (white) to background color (black) by pressing X. Now use the brush to do whatever retouching seems necessary.

16. When you've finished retouching in Quick Mask mode, click the Edit in Standard Mode button (□) in the toolbox. It's just to the left of the Quick Mask button. You can also switch by pressing Q (which actually toggles between Standard and Quick Mask modes). A selection marquee will replace the Quick Mask. Be sure to save the modified selection to a new channel (choose Selection > Save Selection and click OK when the Save Selection dialog appears).

17. Chances are, you now have a perfect mask; however, you need to do a visual check to find out. In the Channels palette, select the RGB channel. The whole image reappears. The selection marquee should still be showing. Press L, move the lasso cursor over the selection, and CONTROL+click/right-click. From the context menu, choose Layer Via Copy.

18. Click the foreground color selection box in the toolbox to bring up the color picker, and pick a color that contrasts strongly with the foreground image.

19. In the Layers palette, select the Background layer. Choose Edit > Fill. In the Fill dialog, select Foreground Color from the Use pop-up menu. Zoom in to 200 percent (or more) and examine the edges of the frame for any excess pixels. If you find them, erase them with the background eraser. In Figure 6-6, the background eraser is being used to erase the holidays (in this case, the white pixels showing over the background) in the selection between the leaves. You'll find instructions on how to use the background eraser under "Selecting with the Background Eraser," later in this chapter.

20. Once you've cleaned up all the edges with the background eraser, you can replace the background with any image you like. I replaced this one with a much more dynamic sky, taken from another photograph.

You can see the finished composite image in Figure 6-7.

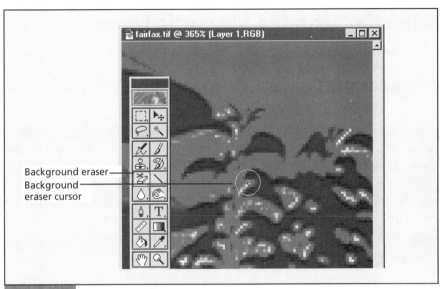

Background eraser
Background
eraser cursor

FIGURE 6-6 The background eraser removes all instances of the color under the crosshair in the center of the circle.

FIGURE 6-7 Finished composite image of the theatre

Selecting with the Magnetic Lasso

- **Advantages:** ☑ Automatically finds edges within the boundaries of the chosen settings. ☑ Makes a definite selection along the border it chooses.
- **Disadvantage:** ☒ Not as fast at making the initial selection as the magic wand tool and the Color Range and Select Similar commands.

The magnetic lasso was introduced in Photoshop 5. It lets you specify a width, in pixels, for the cursor. After that, you only need to come within that distance for the lasso to automatically find the edge that you want the selection to adhere to. The more pronounced the contrast between your subject's edges and the color of surrounding objects, the wider you can safely set your lasso width. In the illustration that follows, you can see that as long as the magnetic lasso cursor is within 10 pixels of the edge of the rose, it will automatically select the edge of the rose.

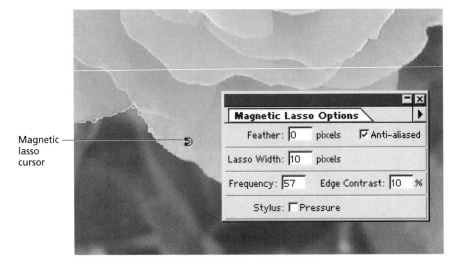

Magnetic
lasso
cursor

Also, as you can see in the illustration, the Magnetic Lasso Options palette allows you to specify a percentage of contrast between pixels that will be considered as an edge. The higher the contrast, the harder the edge must be before the selection is made. Another options field is Frequency. You enter the number of pixels between anchor points. The magnetic lasso lays down anchor points at specified intervals so that you don't accidentally deselect portions of the edge that you've already found to be well selected. Otherwise, any time you back up, the selection marquee peels away from the edge as though you were removing tape from a surface. If you want to back up past an anchor point, press DELETE/BACKSPACE, which you can repeat for as many anchor points as you like.

To make a selection with the magnetic lasso, select it from the toolbox and click when the tip of the lasso cursor is exactly on the edge you want to select. You don't need to hold the mouse button as you move the mouse (or pen) to apply the selection marquee. However, it's a good idea to click whenever there's a sharp reversal in the marquee's path (for instance, where the petals of the rose overlap). Clicking forces an anchor point and will keep the path from wandering away from the corner—particularly if you have specified a wide path.

The magnetic lasso produces clean edges that seldom need retouching. The rose in this next illustration was selected entirely with the magnetic lasso, and no retouching was done at all. However, you should always closely inspect the edges of any selection to make sure that it doesn't require editing before you use the magnetic lasso's selection to trim a shape from its background.

Selecting with the Background Eraser

- **Advantage:** ☑ Lets you quickly erase halos and stray pixels left over after automatic selections made with Extract, Color Range, the magic wand tool, and Select Similar.

- **Disadvantages:** ⊠ Not well suited for erasing entire backgrounds. ⊠ Can erase past edges without warning.

The new background eraser tool allows you to erase a range of colors in relationship to the color under the tool's sampling spot, or *hotspot,* and within the radius of the tool's chosen brush size. In addition to size, the amount of feathering in the chosen brush also affects the percentage (or transparency) of the erasure at the edges of the brush shape.

When you select the background eraser, the cursor changes to a circle representing the brush size, with a crosshair in the center representing the hotspot. The settings in the Background Eraser Options palette determine how the erasure behaves in relation to the pixel under the hotspot. The Background Eraser Options palette is shown in Figure 6-8.

When using the background eraser, it's important to understand that the crosshair indicates the pixel on which your other settings are based. So if you click or drag over a light-colored pixel that's surrounded by other light-colored pixels and your Tolerance is set to a fairly wide range, all pixels that are inside the brush shape will be erased. Also, if you have set Sampling on Contiguous and you drag the hotspot past the edge you are keeping, you'll start erasing pixels inside your edge.

Tolerance describes the percentage of brightness variance that can occur for pixels that are to be erased.

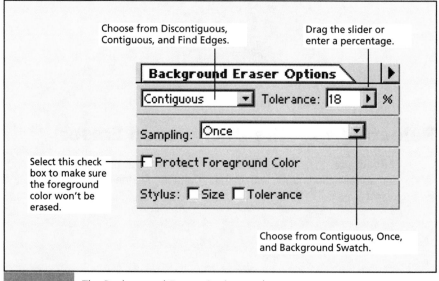

FIGURE 6-8   The Background Eraser Options palette

The Brush menu (that's what Adobe calls it, for some mysterious reason) at the upper left of the Options menu provides three settings that determine how much erasing will spread from the hotspot: Discontiguous, Contiguous, and Find Edges. Discontiguous erases pixels as they fall within the Tolerance range of the hotspot pixel, as long as you keep dragging—even if they are interrupted by pixels that are outside the range. Contiguous will erase everything that is within range of the hotspot pixel until it encounters pixels that are outside that range. If you want to erase the same shade of pixel in another location, you must click (and optionally drag) again to resample. Find Edges stops erasing when it encounters an abrupt change in pixel brightness.

The Sampling menu lets you choose different methods by which the program will decide what to erase. The choices are Contiguous, Once, and Background Swatch. If you choose the Contiguous option, the hotspot will sample from every pixel you drag it over. The Once option will only erase pixels that were under the hotspot when you click to begin dragging. The Background Swatch option will only take into account colors that are within Tolerance in relation to the color of the background color selection box (at the bottom of the toolbox).

Selecting with the Magic Eraser

- **Advantage:** ☑ Very fast at eliminating backgrounds from images. With luck, it can do its work in a single click.
- **Disadvantages:** ☒ Too easy to erase too much or leave too much edge editing to do. ☒ Not very useful when edges have pronounced transitions (such as flying hair or liquid in a glass).

As stated earlier, the magic eraser is much like the magic wand, but instead of making a selection, it erases the selection to transparency. It is very handy if you have a clearly defined subject with hard edges that is in pronounced contrast to a close-to-single-color background. It can be an excellent tool for removing blank skies from outdoor scenes—especially if used in conjunction with the background eraser.

Before you use the magic eraser, you will want to set its options so that you don't erase too much or too little. Figure 6-9 shows the Magic Eraser Options palette and the magic eraser cursor in an image.

The Tolerance field determines the range of colors (from 1 to 256) that will be chosen for erasure when the cursor is clicked, based on the color of the pixel on which it is located. The Opacity field determines the degree of transparency of the erasure (with 100% causing a complete transparency, and a lower percentage causing a partial transparency). The Opacity setting makes the magic eraser unique in its ability to partially erase large areas of the image. You will find this

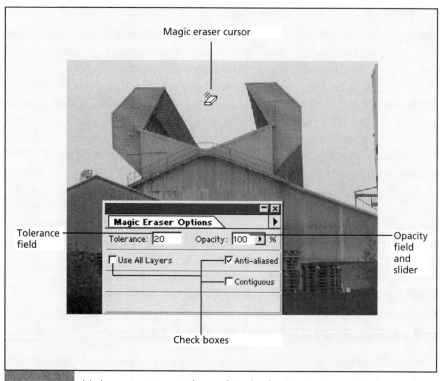

Magic eraser cursor

Tolerance field

Opacity field and slider

Check boxes

FIGURE 6-9 It's important to set the options in the Magic Eraser Options palette so that you don't erase too much or too little in an image.

particularly handy when composing collages or montages in which images or images and textures are meant to blend together.

There are also three check boxes: Use All Layers, Anti-aliased, and Contiguous. As is true of all check boxes, if the box is selected, the command is activated. If it's not selected, the command has no effect. Use All Layers indicates that the data that determines what will be erased will be sampled from all visible layers. You will still erase pixels only from the currently chosen layer. The Anti-aliased check box indicates that the edges of the erased area will be blended with the pixels in underlying layers. Be careful to deselect this option if the eventual color of the background will be noticeably different from the current background—otherwise you'll see a strange halo around your selection. The Contiguous check box is a new option for the magic wand and magic eraser tools. It will let you select all the "holes" that contain the background color. For instance, the magic eraser immediately erased all the spaces between the banisters when it erased the sky in the illustration. Here's the result of using the magic eraser on the factory image, using the settings shown in Figure 6-9:

Professional Pointer

Watch out when you turn off the Contiguous option to be sure that you don't accidentally make holes within your foreground selection, such as the reflections on metal surfaces or the glint in your subject's eyes. You can be sure to avoid this if you first make a selection inside the border of the area you want to select so that transitional areas (those with holes such as the space between leaves or latticework) are outside the selection. Then press CMD/CTRL+SHIFT+I to invert the selection, and use the magic eraser inside the selected area. The area that is not selected (thanks to your selection inversion) will be protected.

Selecting with the Extract Command

- **Advantages:** ☑ Capable of making realistic edge transitions. ☑ No special background or lighting required. ☑ Relatively easy to learn and use.
- **Disadvantages:** ☑ Proper use takes practice, practice, practice. ☑ Not every image is a candidate.

Aside from Web features, the really big news in Photoshop 5.5 is the Image > Extract command. This is the first time Photoshop has included a masking capability that can take edge transitions into full account. The bad news is that until you learn to second-guess it pretty well, you're likely to come up with amazingly disappointing results. The good news is that it's easy to reject a preview and edit your selection so that you come up with good results.

This is the second time the Extract command has come up in this book. Part of the reason is to give you more than one approach to learning this tool. Another is to give you a more detailed explanation of the tool's settings and functions.

Strictly speaking, Extract isn't a masking tool. As its name implies, it extracts the image you select and places it on a new layer. If you want to keep an intact version of that layer, it's best to copy the layer (drag it to the New Layer icon button at the bottom of the Layers palette), and then extract the image from the copy. You could also take a snapshot in the History palette and then use the history brush to paint portions of the image back in if necessary.

The Extract command works on a layer. If you start with an image whose only layer is the background, Photoshop will automatically convert it to Layer 0. You can then drop a new background onto a new layer and drag that layer below Layer 0 in the Layers palette.

To access the Extract command, choose Image > Extract, or press OPT/ALT+CMD/CTRL+X. Your screen will be filled with the Extract dialog. The entire dialog is shown in Chapter 4, Figure 4-4, with all its components labeled.

The Extract toolbox

The Extract dialog has its own toolbox, as shown here. This toolbox is the Extract command's equivalent to the Photoshop toolbox. Its tools are discussed next.

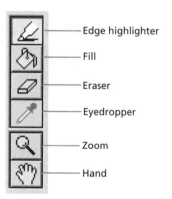

EDGE HIGHLIGHTER Use this to highlight the area over which transitional edges occur. If the edge is a sharp, tight edge, choose a small brush and paint a narrow path. If the edge is highly transitional (transparencies, reflections, hair, fur), use a wide brush and be sure to cover the entire transition. It paints like a highlighter, so you can see through the marking. You can choose any color you like for the highlighter. Pick one you can see through easily but that contrasts sharply with the image so that you can easily see its borders.

Be sure to enclose the entire foreground. Make sure all the colors (including shades of colors) that are definitely meant to be in the foreground are included in some part of the area that's not covered by the highlighter. As much as possible, do the same for colors that are definitely to be included only in the background. Colors that fall into both camps are those that you will have to retouch later.

There are two ways to change the size of the edge highlighter's brush. You can either press the] and [keys or you can use the Brush Size slider in the Tool Options area of the Extract dialog's control panel, as shown here. I find the second option to be much quicker when making a major change in brush size. Small changes are quicker with the bracket keys.

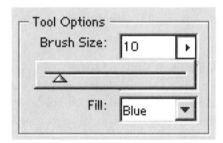

FILL The fill tool tells the Extract command which colors to consider as belonging strictly to the foreground. Anything that is not covered by the fill tool's color will be considered to belong strictly in the background.

The fill tool covers the entire foreground in a single click. If it fills the entire image, you have left holes in the highlighter border. If that's the case, click again with the fill tool, and the foreground highlight color will disappear. Use the highlighter to repair the border, and then click again with the fill tool.

You cannot preview the image (the Preview button is grayed) until you have filled the foreground.

ERASER The eraser is used to fine-tune the transition area by erasing all or parts of highlighter strokes. Its brush size is always the same as the highlighter's; so if you switch back and forth (press E for eraser and B for highlighter), you'll maintain the same brush size.

The only way to get rid of the entire border highlight is to erase it all with the eraser tool, but you can do it in practically no time by choosing a very large brush.

EYEDROPPER The eyedropper is used to force a particular color to be the foreground color. To use it, you have to select the Force Foreground box in the control panel and then click a color with the eyedropper.

ZOOM You will find the zoom tool (magnifier) indispensable when you have images with wildly transitional edges, such as those used in the example illustrations that accompany this section. To zoom in, select the zoom tool and click in the image. The zoom will be centered where you click. To zoom out, press OPT/ALT+click with the zoom tool. The keyboard zoom in and out also works the same in the Extract dialog as in Photoshop: press CMD/CTRL+− TO ZOOM OUT, CMD/CTRL++ to zoom in.

HAND Use the hand tool to pan and scroll a zoomed-in image around in the image window. The hand tool works the same way in the Extract dialog as in Photoshop, except that you can't double-click it to fill the dialog with the whole image.

The Extract control panel

On the right side of the Extract dialog is the control panel, shown here. Its options are explained next.

BRUSH SIZE FIELD AND SLIDER This is a field and a slider. You can enter any whole number of pixels up to 999 for the brush radius, or you can drag the slider to indicate brush size. All brushes are circular and feathered. You cannot choose a brush shape from the standard brushes palette.

HIGHLIGHT MENU This pop-up menu lets you change the color of the highlight marker. Choices are Red, Green, Blue (regardless of what color mode you're in), and Other. If you choose Other, you can pick any color you want from the standard Color Picker dialog. Your choice of color doesn't affect the quality of the border selection, but choosing a color that's easily seen and easy to see through helps you to edit the transition area more accurately.

FILL MENU The choices for fill colors are the same as for the highlight marker. Choose a color that can be easily distinguished from the highlight. I've found the default green highlighter and blue fill to be workable about 80 percent of the time. However, if you often have greenery as a background, you may want to pick a different highlighter color.

SMOOTH FIELD AND SLIDER The setting here determines how jagged the extraction will be. I've found higher settings to be best for scenes with lots of flying hair and wide transitional borders. Still, you have to realize that every picture is composed of a different set of pixels, and so you'll need to experiment with your settings. This is another field/slider combo. You can enter any whole number between 1 and 100.

FORCE FOREGROUND CHECK BOX   This option is best used on subjects that have a single-color foreground with lots of holes. Take a sample of the main color with the eyedropper, select the Force Foreground box in the control panel, and then cover the entire object with the highlighter marker and click Preview.

Forcing the foreground on subjects that don't have a mono-colored foreground can produce some truly bizarre (sometimes gorgeous) results—so you may want to do some experimenting.

FOREGROUND COLOR SELECTION BOX   This is the color that Force Foreground will use if it's selected. You can use the eyedropper to pick up the color from the foreground of the image. You can also click the color selection box to open the Color Picker dialog, and then choose any arbitrary color.

VIEW   Lets you view either the original image or the extracted image. You must click the Preview button before this option will be available.

SHOW   Lets you see the image against several different backgrounds or as a grayscale channel mask (which, unfortunately, you cannot save). The choices are Black, Gray, White, Other, and Mask. If you choose Other, the Color Picker dialog opens, and you can choose any color background, which helps if you want to preview your image against a color that will dominate in your final composite image. If you choose Mask, you will see a grayscale mask of the area you've chosen. Unfortunately, there's no means of editing or saving this mask. It wouldn't be much of a stretch to imagine that capability in a future version of Photoshop, though.

SHOW HIGHLIGHT   This shows the transitional border as outlined by the highlight marker. It's very helpful to be able to turn the highlight on and off with this control so that you can better judge how well you've covered the transition area and whether you need to uncover areas that should definitely belong to the background.

SHOW FILL   This shows the fill color that designates what will definitely be kept in the foreground.

Making a knockout with the Extract command

You need a magazine cover photo of an up-and-coming woman director. The art director has called for a solid-color (or near solid-color) background so that the type for the cover will stand out clearly. Unfortunately, your only chance to photograph this director is on the set between breaks in the shots, and you have to do it over lunch. To make matters even more challenging, the shot you feel expresses this director's personality most engagingly is one in which her hair is flying in all directions. Masking all that hair in order to get a plain background will prove to be a real challenge.

The shot I use in the example is a very real challenge because some of the colors in the background are the same as some of the colors in the foreground. As a result, it is going to be difficult to get a perfect extraction, so you'll learn a bit here about how to fix that. You'll learn even more about how to fix such problems in Chapter 7, which is all about editing and retouching selections and masks. If you want to download this shot, you will find it on the Osborne site as DIRECTOR.PSD. Better yet, use a shot of your own that poses similar problems. I will assume you have opened the photo in Photoshop 5.5. Here's the photo I used:

Step by step, here's how you go about making a knockout with the Extract command:

1. Choose Image > Extract, or press OPT/ALT+CMD/CTRL+X. The Extract dialog will consume most or all of your screen, and you will see the preview of your image in the center.

2. In the control panel, make sure the Show Highlight and Show Fill boxes are selected.

3. Choose the highlight marker. You will notice a lot of fine, flying hair, through which you can see chunks of the background. Use the brush slider to choose a big brush, and paint a highlight wide enough to cover the space between hair that's totally in the foreground and even the wispiest of hairs that are flying out into the background.

4. Choose a much narrower brush size and continue to use the marker to cover borders that are very "tight"—that is, those where the foreground and background meet without much of a transition. Make sure the foreground is completely enclosed. You don't have to surround the entire foreground with the

highlighter as long as it runs into the border on both sides. Here is a pretty good example of how it should look at this point:

5. Select the fill tool and click in the center of the face (which, in this instance, is the foreground). The entire area inside the highlighter turns blue (or whatever the foreground color is). Be sure the fill color doesn't spill out onto the background. If it does, click in the foreground again with the fill tool, and then select the highlighter and paint over the gap. Now fill with the foreground color again. You may have to repeat this process a few times to find all the gaps in the border, but eventually you'll get it. The result should look like this:

6. Now you're almost ready to preview your extraction. First, drag the smoothness slider to about 50 (or enter 50 in the field). Then select the Preview check
box. Now, unless you have a very fast computer and lots of RAM and no other
applications running, you may want to make yourself a cup of coffee. Of
course, if your image is smaller than the typical 20–40MB, that will help, too.
Sooner or later, you'll see something that looks more or less like this:

7. It's surprisingly good, considering that we had a few objects whose colors
were in both the background and the foreground. If you think you can improve on this, choose Original from the View menu. Reselect Show Highlight,
and use the eraser tool and the edge highlighter tool to modify the highlight.

8. You can alternate previewing and editing the highlight as many times as it
takes until you feel you've done the best you can. When that time comes,
click OK. You'll find yourself back at the Photoshop editing window. Your
foreground subject will be seen against a transparent background (unless, of
course, you had other layers beneath it).

9. Since this particular extraction is less than perfect, you will want to use the
background eraser, eraser, and history brush (on the original snapshot) to
clean things up.

Once you've cleaned up the selection, you'll want to put in your solid-color
background. Don't do this by selecting the foreground, inverting the selection, and
pressing DELETE. That won't create a new background; it will simply fill the inverted part of the selection, and then you won't be able to see any background you
create later unless you repeat this entire operation. Bet you don't want to do that.

FIGURE 6-10 The finished extracted photograph of Louise Middleton, director and screenwriter

10. Of course, you can place anything you like on a separate layer and then drag it below the extracted layer, and the result will be a new background. You could have a photograph, painting, or texture as the background. All I did to create this one was create a new background layer (choose Layer > New > Background) after making sure my background color was the one I wanted for the new background. I then used the Lighting Effects filter (choose Filter > Render > Lighting Effects) to "light" the background. You can learn all about the Lighting Effects filter in Chapter 14. You can see the finished work in Figure 6-10.

Using Paths to Make Selections

Using the selection tools isn't always the best way to draw a selection. If your subjects have well-defined, smooth edges, you're likely to have the best luck most of the time with Photoshop's pen tools. This is especially true if you're experienced at using illustration programs such as Illustrator, Macromedia FreeHand, or CorelDRAW!. Those programs use vector-defined Bezier curves to draw shapes. Figure 6-11 shows you the anatomy of a Bezier curve.

Bezier curves make it possible to create selections with perfectly smooth edges. This is because their shapes are stored in the computer as mathematical formulae rather than as resolution-dependent pixel maps. After you have studied path

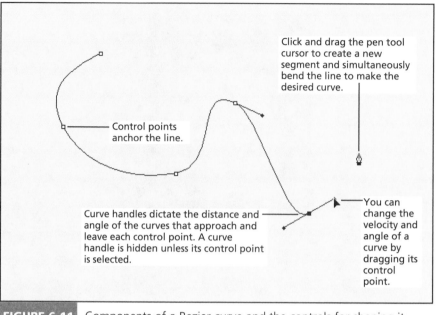

Click and drag the pen tool cursor to create a new segment and simultaneously bend the line to make the desired curve.

Control points anchor the line.

Curve handles dictate the distance and angle of the curves that approach and leave each control point. A curve handle is hidden unless its control point is selected.

You can change the velocity and angle of a curve by dragging its control point.

FIGURE 6-11 Components of a Bezier curve and the controls for shaping it

selections a bit, you begin to realize they're a very quick way to do most of the work in making a complex selection, which can then be fine-tuned with the lasso tools.

The process of working with pen tools is nearly identical to that of working with an illustration program—such as Adobe Illustrator, Macromedia FreeHand, or CorelDRAW!—because paths drawn with the pen tools are vector-based drawing objects (instead of Photoshop-type bitmaps). These objects aren't actually part of the Photoshop image but simply float above it—as if printed on a separate cellulose layer. On command, the drawing on that layer can be transferred to Photoshop in either of two ways: (1) as a marquee selection or (2) as an integral part of the underlying bitmap (pixel mosaic), either filled or stroked.

It is easy to make part of a selection with the pen tools and the remainder by some other method. You will often encounter shapes that are partly geometric (such as furniture or cars) and partly organic (such as people, pets, or trees). Often, this mixture results from two items overlapping when you want to select them both. First, select the geometric part of the shape with the pen tools. Make a selection from the path, and then press SHIFT while you add to the selection with one of the other tools.

Making Paths with the Pen Tools

To select the currently visible pen tool from the keyboard, press P. To select any of the others, press SHIFT+P repeatedly until the specific tool you want appears in the pen tool slot. To select a pen tool from the toolbox, click the pen tool slot and drag across the resulting flyout buttons until the tool you want is highlighted. The various pen tools are shown here:

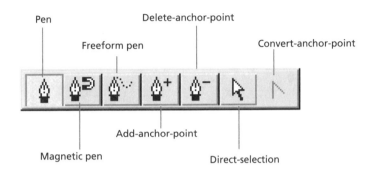

Following are descriptions of what each of the pen tools does and, where appropriate, tips on how best to use them.

Pen

The pen tool is the basic path-drawing tool. It lays down anchor points and, at the same time, creates a line between the preceding anchor point and the one just created. If you click and drag when creating a control point, the curve control handles will extend, and you can drag them to influence the direction of the curve.

You can change the pen tool to several of the other tools by pressing a modifier key (for example, CTRL or ALT) or positioning the pen cursor at a particular spot. If you place the pen cursor atop an existing point, it automatically becomes the delete-anchor-point tool. If you place the pen cursor atop an existing line, it automatically becomes the add-anchor-point tool. When working in an image, you can convert the pen tool to the direct-selection tool by pressing CMD/CTRL. Similarly, you can convert the pen tool to the convert-anchor-point tool by pressing OPT/ALT.

Magnetic pen

The magnetic pen tool behaves just like the magnetic lasso except that it creates a path as the cursor passes within the chosen radius of an edge. Just in case it isn't obvious, you can't use this tool unless you're tracing an image. It needs to see contrast between the edge pixels in a bitmapped image.

Before you use the magnetic pen, be sure to double-click it to bring up its Options palette, shown in Figure 6-12.

The two options that will have the greatest effect on the accuracy of the path you want to trace will be Edge Contrast and Pen Width. If you have soft edges against an out-of-focus background consisting of many objects that contain similar colors, set your edge contrast range and your pen width fairly low. If your

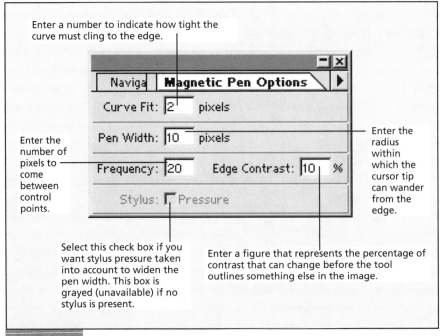

Enter a number to indicate how tight the curve must cling to the edge.

Enter the number of pixels to come between control points.

Enter the radius within which the cursor tip can wander from the edge.

Select this check box if you want stylus pressure taken into account to widen the pen width. This box is grayed (unavailable) if no stylus is present.

Enter a figure that represents the percentage of contrast that can change before the tool outlines something else in the image.

FIGURE 6-12   The magnetic pen options and how to use them

subject stands in stark contrast to the background, set contrast and width to a higher number, and you'll be able to trace your path much more quickly.

To trace a path with the magnetic pen, follow the steps in Figure 6-13.

If you wander too far away from the edge, drag the cursor back to the last anchor point. The path will follow the cursor backward, so you can start over by sticking closer to your edge. If you need to back up more than one control point, back up to the control point you want to delete and press the DELETE/BACK-SPACE key; then continue backing up and deleting until you get to the place where you want to start again. If you need to narrow the magnetic pen's radius in order to stick closer to the line at certain points, you can change the size of the path as you draw. Press [to narrow the radius and] to increase it—just as you would choose a larger or smaller brush while painting.

There will be some edges that you simply can't trace very well with the magnetic pen because there isn't enough edge contrast. In those cases, the human eye will be a better judge of where the edge should be. You can switch to the freeform pen as you trace by pressing OPT/ALT.

Freeform pen

The freeform pen tool lets you create a path by drawing just as you would with the pencil tool. The only difference is that you'll end up with a Bezier-curve path rather than a pixel stroke that blends with your image.

1. Double-click the magnetic pen tool.
2. The Magnetic Pen Options palette will appear.
3. Enter settings here.
4. Drag the cursor within 10 pixels of the edge.

FIGURE 6-13 Tracing a path with the magnetic pen

At first, it may seem that the freeform pen tool would always represent the easiest way to draw a path. The problem is, if you are even slightly nervous, you may create way too many control points to make the line easy to reshape. You may also discover that you need to add control points because the program decided that you didn't need one right at the spot where you'd like to reshape the curve. Practice will tell you when it is and isn't a good idea to use the freeform pen. Here is a path being made with the freeform pen:

Add-anchor-point

The add-anchor-point tool will insert a new control point on an existing path. It is handy because you can create a very rough outline with the pen tool by clicking at various points along the circumference of a shape to get the general outline; then click to add control points and drag to reshape the lines with the control handles. Try outlining an object this way. Experience will show you that this is often the fastest way to work. This illustration shows the preliminary outline and the curve that's been modified after points have been added:

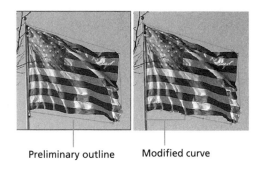

Preliminary outline   Modified curve

Delete-anchor-point

The delete-anchor-point tool deletes any existing point when you click it. It is handy for smoothing lines made with the magnetic lasso and the freeform pen tools when they get a little too "bumpy" to suit you.

Direct-selection

The direct-selection tool is used to select the active path or control point and to drag the control handles to reshape a curve. All of its functions are shown in Figure 6-14.

Convert-anchor-point

The convert-anchor-point tool switches a control point among one of three types:

- **Symmetrical curve**   The curve approaches the control point and leaves the control point from diametrically opposite angles.

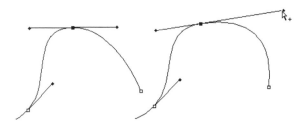

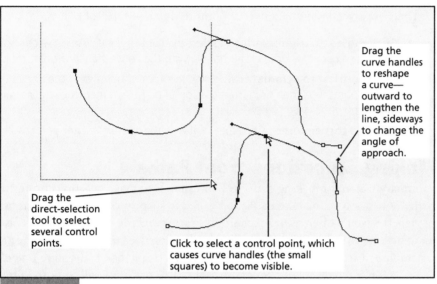

Drag the curve handles to reshape a curve—outward to lengthen the line, sideways to change the angle of approach.

Drag the direct-selection tool to select several control points.

Click to select a control point, which causes curve handles (the small squares) to become visible.

FIGURE 6-14 Using the direct-selection tool

- **Asymmetrical curve** The curve approaches the control point from an angle independent of the angle from which it leaves, but there is still a smooth curve as it passes through the control point.

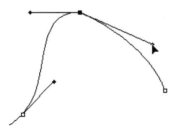

- **Corner point** The curve makes an abrupt turn as it passes through the control point. There are no curve control handles.

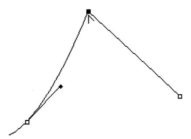

There are several ways to convert a point to different types of points:

- **Symmetrical to asymmetrical**   Select the control point. The curve control handles will appear. Drag either handle with the convert-anchor-point tool.
- **Asymmetrical to symmetrical**   Click the control point with the convert-anchor-point tool; then drag from the corner point. Symmetrical handles will appear on either side.
- **Curve to corner point**   Click the point with the convert-anchor-point tool.

Making Selections from Paths

A primary reason for making paths in Photoshop is to make selections from the paths. When you are making masks to be used to shape picture frames, buttons, or vignettes, you'll often want a technically exact geometric shape. It is much easier to make such a shape with paths than by drawing freehand—unless you're an accomplished technical draftsperson with a rock-steady hand. If you're one of those, you're a rare beast and congratulations. The rest of us will want to know how to make selections from paths.

There's another reason for making selections from paths—you want a very smooth outline for your knocked-out subject. In traditional illustration, knock-outs were done to make the subject more obvious and to make it easier to surround it with easily readable text. There will still be times when you want to do that in Photoshop, but you'll also want to knock out subjects so that they can be used in montages and collages. In these applications—particularly montage—it is important that the subject look as though it were always a part of its adopted surroundings. Selections made from paths may look too severe. On the other hand, if the subject is a piece of hardware, such as the car shown in Figure 6-15, paths may be the only way to preserve a strictly geometrical silhouette.

To convert a path to a selection, follow the steps shown in Figure 6-16.

Making Paths from Selections

If you want a really quick way to draw a path around a photographic subject, photograph it against a solid background, select the background with the magic wand, invert the selection so that it is the object that is selected (CMD/CTRL+SHIFT+I, or choose Select > Inverse), and then convert the selection to a path. You can now edit the path into a really smooth, tight-fitting path, and then turn the path back into a selection. Figure 6-17 shows you how to turn a selection into a path.

The selection is automatically converted to a path.

Of course, you won't see both the path and the selection at the same time. I've used Photoshop to combine the before-and-after stages of this operation. Notice

FIGURE 6-15 In this example, the car has been knocked out of its background.

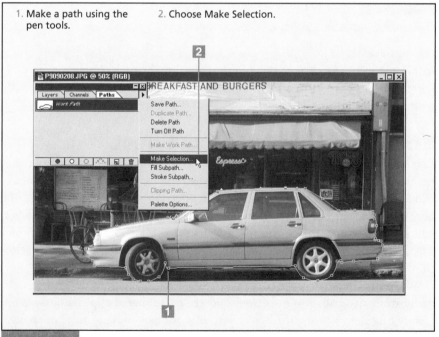

FIGURE 6-16 A knockout of the car selected with the pen tool. The background has been filled with a gradient.

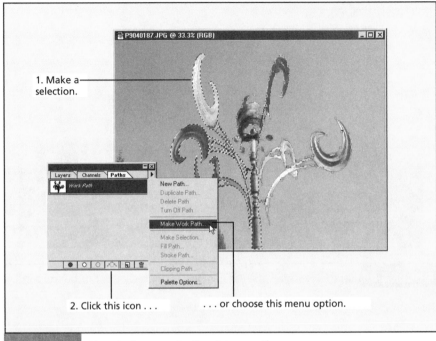

1. Make a selection.

2. Click this icon . . .

. . . or choose this menu option.

FIGURE 6-17 How to turn a selection into a path

that in some of the tighter curves of this sculpture, the path contains quite a few more control points than are actually needed. You can eliminate these quickly with the delete-anchor-point tool.

Stroking a Path to Add an Effect

Photoshop lets you turn a path or selection into a bitmapped brush stroke that becomes part of the image. It's a perfect way to draw with an absolutely steady hand. Photoshop calls it "stroking a path or selection." Although you can stroke both paths and selections, the results can be quite different. This is because when you stroke a selection, you can only choose a color and a stroke width and whether to stroke inside or outside the path or to center the stroke on the selection. Stroking a path is a much more versatile proposition.

When stroking a path, the stroke can be made with any of the following tools: paintbrush, airbrush, eraser, background eraser, rubber stamp, pattern stamp, history brush, art history brush, smudge, blur, sharpen, dodge, burn, or sponge. This is a great way to make a stroke take exactly the shape, intensity (opacity), and any other settings for a given tool with a perfectly even and steady effect.

Following is a very simple application of path stroking, using the paintbrush tool. Try the technique on your own subject, and you'll begin to see how many different ways this technique can be applied. This exercise assumes that you are starting with a single-layer image and that you've already drawn a path around the subject. Here are the steps:

1. Select the path, and then convert the path to a selection (click the Make Work Path button at the bottom of the Paths palette).

2. Press CMD/CTRL+C to copy the contents of the selection to the clipboard. Make sure the selection is still active, and choose Edit > Paste Into. This will paste the contents of the selection onto a new layer but will leave its position intact.

3. Make sure the original layer (probably the background) is selected by checking the Layers palette to see if it's highlighted. If it's not, click the layer name to select it (the layer name will be highlighted).

4. Double-click the paintbrush to select it and simultaneously reveal the paintbrush options. Set your brush options to reflect your preferences (here, Opacity was 100% and blend mode was Normal).

5. Choose Window > Show Brushes to reveal the Brushes palette.

6. Choose a large, soft-edged paintbrush.

7. From the Paths palette menu (click the small arrow in the upper-right corner of the Paths palette), choose Stroke Path or Stroke Subpath (depending on whether you chose a path or a subpath). Photoshop paints for you. In Figure 6-18, you can see that Photoshop has painted a glow effect around the flower.

FIGURE 6-18 Painting by stroking a path

Selection Tips and Tricks

This section guides you through some of the subtleties of working with selections and masks.

Floating a Selection

Perhaps there are times when you don't want to make a permanent new layer but would like to suspend the contents of the selection over the rest of the image temporarily. (Frankly, I think it's safer to lift the contents of a selection to a permanent layer, but some people are used to what they had to do before layers were available in Photoshop.) This is called *floating a selection*, and there are three ways to do it:

- **Cut the selection to a floating selection**   Select the move tool and drag the selection.
- **Copy the selection to a floating selection**   Select the move tool and press CMD/CTRL, or press CMD/CTRL+OPT/ALT and click. (This floats the selection without moving it.)
- **Drag the contents of the selection**   You can use this technique to float the selection without moving it. Press M to select the move tool, and then press the LEFT ARROW once and the RIGHT ARROW once. This moves the selection exactly one pixel, which makes it a floating selection, and then moves it back exactly one pixel to where it was.

Remember that a floating selection instantly becomes part of the image beneath it if you click anywhere outside the selection while a selection tool is active or if you press CMD/CTRL+D to drop the selection. Either of these operations is called "dropping the selection" and can be disastrous if you didn't intend to do it. Should you accidentally drop a floating selection, immediately press CMD/CTRL+Z to undo.

Moving a Selection Marquee

Moving a selection marquee so you can select another part of the image is easy in Photoshop. Simply move the selection tool cursor inside the selection, and drag. Only the marquee moves, not its contents.

Moving selection marquees is a handy way to repeatedly draw the same shape by stroking the path. You can change the style of the path and the color of the path any time you stroke it.

Copying and Pasting

Photoshop 5.5 has the same Copy and Paste commands as almost all desktop computer applications, but Paste behaves differently by always creating a new layer. To copy an area or a layer, simply select it with any of the tools described in this chapter, and then issue the Edit > Copy command (or press CMD/CTRL+C). To paste what you've copied into a new layer (whether in the same document or another open document), execute the Edit > Paste command (or press CMD/CTRL+V).

Matting Layers

Layer Matting is a process that eliminates unwanted pixel colors from the edges of a selection after that selection has become a layer. To reach Layer Matting, go to the menu bar and choose Layer > Layer Matting. There are three choices on the flyout menu, each described here.

- **Defringe**   Brings up a dialog in which you can choose a number of pixels to be "sliced" from the periphery of the image shape on the selected layer.

- **Remove Black Matte**   Removes any black pixels that border the image shape on the selected layer. This command is used mainly to remove black pixels mixed into the border by anti-aliasing at the time the subject was removed from a black background.

- **Remove White Matte**   Removes any white pixels that border the image shape on the selected layer. This command is used mainly to remove white pixels mixed into the border by anti-aliasing at the time the subject was removed from a white background.

Professional Skills Summary

In this chapter, you have learned Photoshop's more sophisticated selection and masking techniques. You've also been given a number of tips and tricks related to making successful selections and masks. In Chapter 7, you will further improve your selection and masking skills by learning how to edit your initial selections and masks.

Editing and Modifying Selections and Masks

In this chapter, you:

- Learn to make one-step selections
- Edit a geometric selection to select a shape with complex curves
- Eliminate ugly halos from Web graphics
- Make instant knockouts with the magic wand
- Learn how modifier keys can help you edit selections
- Change some characteristics of the entire selection
- Move and copy the contents of selections to other files and layers
- Move selection marquees without moving their contents
- Find out about the uses and subtleties of the Modify commands
- Discover various means of softening the edges of selections
- Edit a selection by painting a mask

You will rarely—even given the power of the new selection and extraction tools—make a selection in Photoshop that doesn't need some editorial tweaking. This is especially true if you hope to make it good enough to fool people into thinking that the elephant in Times Square was actually there and that you just happened to be at the right place at the right time.

The Power of One-Step Selections

Strictly speaking, this first section of this chapter should have been included in Chapter 6 on making selections. After all, this chapter is really about *editing* selections. There are two reasons why the geometric and magic wand selections are included here: (1) I ran out of space in Chapter 6. (2) Making these selections is often a good start for making a selection that will be refined by editing. You can use one-step selections to select a large area, and then use the editing procedures described in this chapter to more carefully pick the exact edge from a zoomed-in view of the subject. Because, in the professional world, time is money, I am always looking for ways to save time.

The geometric selection tools are the rectangular marquee tool, the elliptical marquee tool, and the single column marquee and single row marquee tools. You'll find the general information regarding the use of these tools in Chapter 6. The material here concerns particular problems that can be solved with the use of the rectangular and elliptical marquee tools.

Basing Selections on the Rectangular or Elliptical Marquee

You'll encounter lots of times when the best way to select a complex item is just to trace it with a combination of the lasso tools. However, nine times out of ten, you'll find that you need to zoom in to at least a 100 percent (I prefer about 150 percent) view of the edge in order to be able to trace it accurately. (Don't zoom in too far because you're liable to get disoriented as to which pixels define which shapes and shades.) Making edges when you're zoomed in poses a problem though. It becomes difficult to be sure you haven't accidentally clicked and lost edges you've already traced. If you start with an overall selection, as I've done with the apple, shown here, you can just trim it by adding to and subtracting from the selection while zoomed in.

 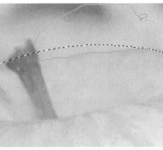

If you lose the selection, you can immediately undo it, go back a step or two in the History palette (see Chapter 2), or choose Select > Reselect (CMD/CTRL+SHIFT+D). Any of these three choices will restore all the out-of-the-window work you've done up to that point.

The rectangular and elliptical marquee tools are also excellent for trimming away a large portion of a layer to transparency. Doing so will reduce file size when you have small items floating over a large background area. You've previewed how to do this in a couple of the earlier chapters, but just to remind you (and to keep you from having to flip pages so often):

1. Select the rectangular or elliptical marquee and drag its shape to enclose the object you want to keep.30

2. Press CMD/CTRL+SHIFT+I to invert the selection.

3. Press DELETE/BACKSPACE.

Using a shape as the basis for a complex selection

The primary use of geometric selection tools is for creating perfectly geometrical ovals, rectangles, or lines. These selection tools enable you to "paint" the shape into your image by filling with a color, pattern, image, or filter. Typical uses are for navigation buttons, flowchart symbols, and text backgrounds.

You need to make six navigation buttons, identical in size and shape, for your company's Web site. Furthermore, the buttons need to be rectangular with rounded corners. You've made many attempts to select the needed shape with a combination of lasso and polygon lasso tools. Even with the new grids and guide-lines and snaps, however, it's nearly impossible to keep the lines perfectly perpen-dicular or keep all four corners rounded to the same degree. You've also tried the pen tool without much success.

There is another problem associated with making these buttons that's not directly associated with making a selection. Many buttons are made with drop shadows or glows. The selections that make these have highly feathered edges. Because most Web buttons are exported in GIF 89a format, which allows a shade of only one color (out of 256) for transparency, you'll need to avoid mixing the wrong pixels from the current background into the feathering. If they get mixed, you'll get an unattractive, jagged border around your button when you superimpose the button on your Web page. I call what you see in this illustration "ugly halo syndrome (UHS)":

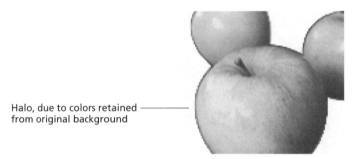

Halo, due to colors retained ————— from original background

Eliminating ugly halos

To avoid UHS, you first need to make a new file that exactly matches the color of the background on your Web page. If the Web page is either black or white, no problem—just open a new file with a pure white or black background. If it's not black or white, open the target Web page, in either your HTML editor or your Web browser, and capture the screen. Open the screen capture and your new file in Photoshop. Use the eyedropper tool to pick up the color from the Web page background. Activate the window for the new file and fill it with the picked up color. This is the point at which you should start the following exercise.

For readers already familiar with Photoshop, here's a synopsis of what follows: You will make a rectangular selection of the correct size in the new file, round the corners with the Smooth command, and save the selection to a new channel. You will then use the selection to make one of the buttons in a color that contrasts with the background and has a drop shadow. Finally, you will repeat the procedure six more times, using the saved mask channel to make the new selection each time and then filling the new button with a new color and new text.

Here's the step-by-step exercise:

1. Close the screen shot file and activate the new file window, which now uses the Web page's background color. From the menu bar, choose Window > Show Info. Drag the Show Info palette to a location where you'll be able to see it while you work and where it won't be covered by the tool's Options palette.

2. Choose File > Preferences > Units & Rulers. From the Units pop-up menu, choose Pixels and click OK.

3. Select the rectangular marquee tool from the toolbox. If that tool is not showing in the upper-left corner of the toolbox, place the cursor in that position and hold the mouse key until the flyout appears. Then drag to select the rectangular marquee tool.

4. Double-click the rectangular marquee tool to activate the Marquee Options palette. Choose Constrained Aspect Ratio from the Style pop-up menu. Set Width to 3 and Height to 1, as shown here:

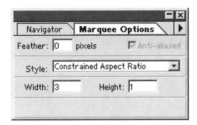

5. In the workspace, drag from corner to corner until the selection is the right length (the height is automatically correct because you are in Constrained Aspect mode).

6. Look at the lower-right corner of the Show Info palette to find the exact dimensions for your button. Write them down. The dimension I chose was 135 × 45 pixels. As long as you've written down these dimensions, you can always create a new button of the same size by calling up the Marquee Options palette, choosing Fixed Size from the Style pop-up menu, and then entering these pixel dimensions. Pixels are the only units of measurement that the Height and Width fields will accept when Fixed Size is selected, as shown in this illustration:

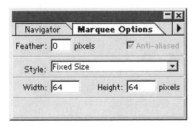

7. Choose Select > Modify > Smooth. In the Smooth dialog box, set Sample Radius to 16 and click OK. The selection now has rounded corners. (Actually, they are so round that the selection has rounded ends.) Save the selection to a new channel. To do so, CONTROL+click/right-click inside the selection and choose Save Selection from the context menu.

8. With the selection still active, CONTROL+click/right-click inside the selection and choose Layer Via Copy from the context menu. Don't be alarmed if your

button seems to have disappeared—it will reappear by the time you finish the next step. Choose Window > Show Layers. You will see a layer called Layer 1. Double-click its name bar. In the Layer Options dialog, shown here, enter **Button 1** in the Name field, leave all other choices at their defaults, and click OK.

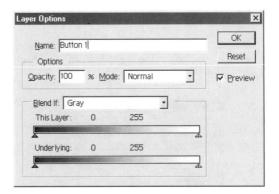

9. In the Layers palette, select the Preserve Transparency check box. Choose Window > Show Swatches. When the Swatches dialog box appears, choose a color for your button. While the Button 1 layer is selected, press OPT/ALT+ DELETE/BACKSPACE to fill the layer with the foreground color.

10. CONTROL+click/right-click the Button 1 layer. From the context menu, choose Duplicate Layer. In the dialog box, rename the layer **Button 1 Shadow**. Leave the rest of the settings at their defaults, and click OK. Make sure the Button 1 Shadow layer is selected.

11. Press D to restore the foreground and background colors to their black-and-white default. Select the Preserve Transparency check box in the Layers palette. Press OPT/ALT+DELETE/BACKSPACE to fill the new button with black. The new button now completely covers the old button.

12. Now you want to blur the black button so it will look more like a cast shadow. With Button 1 Shadow as the selected layer, deselect the Preserve Transparency toggle in the Layers palette. Choose Filter > Blur > Gaussian Blur. In the dialog box, set a blur radius of about 2 pixels, and click OK.

13. In the Layers palette, drag the Button 1 Shadow layer below the Button 1 layer. Leave the Button 1 Shadow layer selected. Press V to select the move tool from the toolbox. Drag the Button 1 Shadow layer down and to the right to create a drop shadow. (You can automatically create drop shadows with Layer Effects, but using this method ultimately gives you more control and begins teaching you a bit about layers—so stick with me for the moment.)

14. Select the Button 1 layer. Press T to select the type tool. Click the cursor over the button. In the dialog that appears, choose a font you like (Arial and Helvetica read especially well on monitors), set the point size so the type will be proportionate to the button size, and type your button label in the text box. Choose Crisp or Strong from the Anti-Alias menu. Click OK. The Type Tool dialog is shown here:

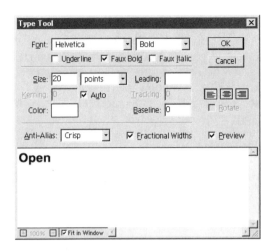

15. To make additional buttons, simply duplicate the original button and shadow layers for the number of buttons you want. Rename each layer so you know which layer pertains to which button. Use the move tool to position the buttons and drop shadows. Select the layer for each button, select Preserve Transparency in the Layers palette, and fill with a new color (if you need to change the colors of the buttons). Now add the new text.

16. When you have all the buttons you want, you will need to convert from RGB to indexed color, because you want to save these buttons as GIF files (no need for GIF 89a—no transparency is involved here). Choose Image > Mode > Indexed Color. A dialog box appears asking if you want to flatten layers. Click OK. The Indexed Color dialog appears. You are now going to reduce colors to the minimum you can get away with and still maintain the look of your button. The point is to make the file size of all your Web graphics as small as possible, so your pages will load into your visitors' browsers quickly. Choose Adaptive from the Palette pop-up menu and Web from the Forced pop-up menu, as shown in the following illustration. The Colors setting is now at 16 (if you type in any other number, the color depth changes accordingly). Be sure Diffusion is chosen in the Dither pop-up menu. Click OK.

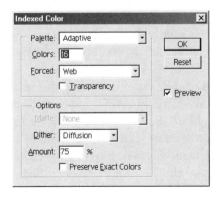

17. If you have several buttons in a single file, select each with a rectangle selection that comes as close to the edges of the button and shadow as possible. Press CMD/CTRL+C to copy the button to the clipboard. Press CMD/CTRL+N to bring up the New dialog. Because the file is already the size of the file in the clipboard, just click OK. A window for a new file opens. Press CMD/CTRL+V. The button appears in the new window. Press CMD/CTRL+SHIFT+S to bring up the Save As dialog. In the File field, type the filename and choose Compuserve GIF as the file format. Be sure to deselect the Save Thumbnail check box. Once more, the idea is to keep file size to a minimum. Click Save.

You can see the finished buttons (before being saved separately and alongside the Layers palette) here:

Instant Knockouts with the Magic Wand

The magic wand tool selects everything that's within the brightness range (Tolerance) setting that you choose in the Magic Wand Options dialog. It's even more versatile in Photoshop 5.5 because now you can choose all of the areas in the image that fall within that range, whether they adjoin one another or not. All you have to do to make that happen is deselect the Contiguous check box in the Magic Wand Options dialog.

The trick in using the magic wand successfully lies in adjusting the Tolerance setting so that the wand selects everything right up to the wanted border, but doesn't start wandering into that edge. You also want to choose a subject with well-defined edges that contrast with a background of a more or less uniform color. Place the Magic Wand Options palette somewhere on the screen where it can be easily accessed, set the Tolerance at a fairly high setting (around 100 is often a good start), and click somewhere within a few pixels of the edge you want to select. If the result is obviously too large a selection, immediately press CMD/CTRL+Z to undo, and drag the Tolerance slider to a slightly lower setting. Repeat the process until you come very close to getting exactly the selection edge that you want (see Figure 7-1). The later sections of this chapter will show you numerous ways to edit that selection, if it isn't close enough, but first we'll go through the steps to make the selection.

Quickly selecting objects from a plain background

The challenge in this instance is simple. You have photographed many catalog objects on seamless paper. Tracing these complex shapes with the lasso tool simply takes too long. How can you select them quickly? The photograph shown in Figure 7-1 is ideal for demonstrating this frequently encountered situation. The trick is to set the magic wand's tolerance high enough to cover a large portion of the background, but not so high that it starts infringing on the subject. You can discover what that tolerance is by starting at a high number and clicking near the subject. If the selection bleeds into the subject, the number is set too high. With a little practice, you'll usually make the right guess the first time. After you've selected a workable tolerance, start by selecting the part of the background farthest in distance and color from the subject. Press SHIFT to add to the selection, and click just outside its borders. The selection will "march" toward the subject until

FIGURE 7-1 The finished selection

the entire subject is selected. Finally, do whatever cleanup is necessary by using the other selection tools.

Here are the steps:

1. Open a file consisting of a fairly smooth-edged subject photographed against a single-color, contrasting background.

2. Press w to select the magic wand tool. In the Magic Wand Options palette, set Tolerance to 80 and click the background in a medium shadow area. As you can see in the following illustration, this tolerance is too high. Press CMD/CTRL+D to drop the selection, and then repeat this step with a lower number until the apple is selected. Don't worry if there are minor errors in the marquee outline or if all the background is not selected. The result of too high a magic wand tolerance setting can be seen here:

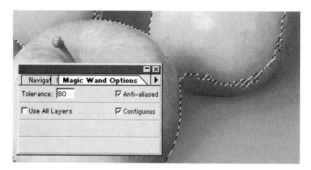

3. Adjust the Tolerance slider to a lower setting, and try again. Since the results also depend on *where* you click, you might also try a different location. At first, this trial-and-error method will seem unreasonably time consuming. By the time you've done this successfully two or three times, you'll be able to make more educated guesses about how much tolerance to use and where to click. This time, your results will probably look more like this:

4. Press SHIFT and click in several more areas until the entire background is selected. Stop when the selection meets the border smoothly. It's a good idea, at this point, to save your selection, so that if you goof and drop it while editing, you'll be able to retrieve it.

Professional Pointer

The History palette (introduced in Photoshop 5) makes it much less necessary to constantly save selections, since you can always back up a few steps. Remember, however, that you will probably have to limit the number of steps saved in the History palette in order to conserve memory. Take more steps than that after making the selection and you will have lost it. Also, if you quit and then reopen the file, all the History steps will have been lost. So stay in the habit of saving your selections as you go along. To save a selection, choose Select > Save Selection.

5. Place the cursor inside the selection and CONTROL+click/right-click. From the context menu, choose Select Inverse. Now the apples are selected. CONTROL+click/right-click again, and choose Save Selection from the context menu.

6. Zoom in tight (at least 150 percent magnification) on your edges. I find the quickest way to do this is to enter **150** in the leftmost field in the status bar at the bottom of the window (if you don't see the status bar, choose Window > Show Status Bar). Select the hand tool, and move the window around so that you can inspect the edges of the selection carefully.

7. Edit any near misses out of the edges. You can either paint them smoother in Quick Mask mode (discussed at the end of this chapter in the section "Changing a Selection Using Quick Mask Mode") or use the modifier keys and the lasso tools.

8. When the selection looks perfect, save it. If you want to lift the contents of the selection to a new layer, place the cursor inside the selection and press CONTROL+click/right-click. The context menu, shown here, appears. Choose Layer Via Copy (to copy the contents of the selection and place them in the same location on a new layer) or Layer Via Cut (to remove the contents of the selection from the original layer and place it in the same location on a new layer). You can now open another image and drag and drop it into it.

9. The imported image will appear on its own layer. In the Layers palette, drag the name bar of the new image below the layer that now contains your subject. Use the move tool to position the new layer, or the layer without your cutout subject, so that it takes its rightful place in your intended composition.

Using Modifier Keys to Make and Edit Selections

You've probably already caught on to the idea if you've read the preceding material in this chapter, but one of the easiest and most useful ways to refine the shape of a selection is to use the modifier keys to change the behavior of a selection tool. (SHIFT, CMD, and OPT are the Mac's modifier keys; Windows' are SHIFT, CTRL, and ALT.)

These keys are consistent in how they change the nature of a selection, no matter which selection tool is being used. In Figure 7-2, a lasso tool and a geometric selection tool (the rectangular marquee or elliptical marquee) have been used to modify each initial selection shown in Figure 7-2a.

Here are the modifier keys you press in order to use one selection shape to alter another:

- **SHIFT to add to a selection**   To manually reshape a selection by adding to it, press SHIFT, and then use the selection tool of your choice (see Figure 7-2b).
- **OPT/ALT to subtract from a selection**   To manually reshape a selection by carving away parts of it, press OPT/ALT, and then use the selection tool of your choice (Figure 7-2c).
- **OPT/ALT+SHIFT+drag to intersect one selection with another**   To leave only as much of a selection as the overlapping portions of shapes made by

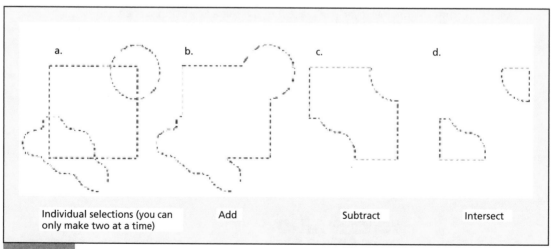

| a. | b. | c. | d. |

Individual selections (you can only make two at a time)   Add   Subtract   Intersect

FIGURE 7-2   You can modify individual selections (a) using appropriate modifier keys: SHIFT to add (b); OPT/ALT to subtract (c); and OPT/ALT+SHIFT+drag to intersect (d).

selecting two different areas, press OPT/ALT+SHIFT while creating the second selection (Figure 7-2d).

Modifier-Key Behavior Before and After Making a Selection

You have to be aware of when you use a modifier key as you're making selections. The keys behave differently depending on whether you have already made a selection, or no selection exists. If nothing is selected and you press SHIFT before using the rectangular marquee or elliptical marquee tool, the selection will have a square or circle aspect ratio (that is, 1:1). On the other hand, if you already have an active selection and want to add a circle or square (rather than a rectangle or ellipse), press SHIFT, start to drag, release SHIFT, and then press SHIFT again. If you just want to add a rectangle or ellipse, press SHIFT before you start to drag. The aspect ratio of your selection will depend on the angle of the drag.

If you want to subtract a square or circle from an existing selection, start with the normal OPT/ALT+drag—but before you finish dragging, press SHIFT while continuing to hold down the OPT/ALT key. The shape being subtracted will assume a 1:1 aspect ratio.

To subtract a marquee from the center out, place the cursor at the desired center point and press OPT/ALT. Then drag a very short distance (so you'll still remember where the center was), release the OPT/ALT key, and immediately press it again. The marquee will center itself at the spot where you first began to drag.

Adding and subtracting straight-sided polygons with the lasso follows similar procedures. To add a straight-sided selection with the lasso, press SHIFT and start to drag; then immediately press OPT/ALT, and drag and click to make your straight-sided polygon. To subtract a straight-sided selection with the lasso, press OPT/ALT and start to drag; then immediately release the OPT/ALT key, and then press it again.

Changing the Whole Selection

Photoshop also provides numerous ways to change the overall characteristics of a selection. You can drop it, hide it, select everything that's not selected while deselecting what is selected, change the selection into a mask or layer mask, transform the selection (without affecting its contents), or move the contents of the selection.

Dropping the Selection

There are two ways to drop a selection (so that you can apply tools and commands anywhere in the image):

- Click (be sure not to drag) anywhere when any of the selection tools are active.
- Press CMD/CTRL+D (or choose Select > Deselect).

Dropping the selection is so easy that it can be too easy. Since you can sometimes spend hours making the selection in the first place, only to accidentally lose the whole thing, Photoshop gives you three ways to recover:

- Press CMD/CTRL+Z or choose Edit > Undo. You have to remember to do this before you do *anything* else.
- Choose Select > Reselect (CMD/CTRL+SHIFT+D).
- Use the History palette and return to the command where you made the selection.

Hiding the Selection

There will be lots of times when you want to keep the selection active, but would like to hide the marquee so that you can better judge the effects of blending, blurring, retouching, filtering, and the like.

To hide a selection, press CMD/CTRL+H or choose View > Hide Edges. It would also be handy to have this command on the selection context menu, but alas, it isn't.

Professional Pointer

If you hide your selections, you may suddenly find some of your tools behaving erratically. For instance, you can't paint with the paintbrush. If that happens, chances are you've left an area selected but have forgotten to unhide it. As a result, the area you're trying to work in is protected, and nothing happens. If that kind of nothing happens to you, press CMD/CTRL+D to deselect all and try again. More often than not, you'll cure the problem.

Inverting the Selection

It's often easier to select that part of the image that you don't want masked because it's just a small section of the area that you do want masked. No problem. All you have to do is invert the selection. Then everything that wasn't selected is selected.

To invert a selection, press CMD/CTRL+SHIFT+I, or choose Select > Inverse, or choose Select Inverse from the selection context menu.

Changing a Selection into a Mask (Saving a Selection)

As I said some time ago, a selection and a mask are essentially the same. The difference, in Photoshop terms, is that a mask is a selection that has been saved to an Alpha channel, where it can then be used to reactivate the selection.

There are two ways to save an active selection as a mask:

- Choose Save Selection from either the Select menu or selection context menu.
- Click the Save Selection as Channel button at the bottom of the Channels palette.

You can activate any channel (whether it was originally intended to be a mask channel or not) by selecting the channel in the Channels palette and clicking the Load Channel as Selection button (see the following illustration). You can also do it by choosing Load Selection from either the Select menu or the selection context menu.

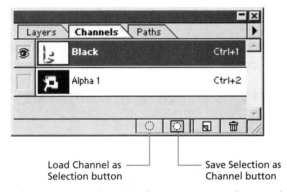

Load Channel as   Save Selection as
Selection button   Channel button

You can be much more versatile in loading a given mask as a selection if you choose Select > Load Selection, because the following dialog appears:

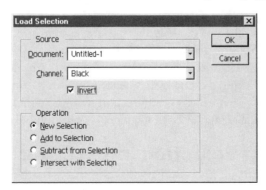

The Load Selection dialog allows you to load a selection from any open document window by choosing that document from the Document pop-up menu. The Channel pop-up menu lets you load any of the channels in that document as a mask. Finally, a set of radio buttons determines whether the mask will be loaded in one of four ways:

- As a new selection (dropping all prior existing selections)
- As an addition to any currently selected areas
- Subtracted from any currently selected areas
- Intersecting with any currently selected areas

Okay, okay, I know you can do all these things from the Channels palette. It's just that you have to remember the procedure. To move an Alpha channel (a mask is an Alpha channel) from one open image to another, drag its name bar from the originating document's Channels palette to the target document's window. The channel will appear in the target document's Layers palette and will also be the visible channel (the only one in the Channels palette with an eye icon in the left column). Click "on" the eye icon in the left column of the composite channel's name bar (the composite channel's name will be Black, RGB, CMYK, or whatever the name of the color mode is that you're operating in). Now the new mask layer is still selected, but you have a normal view of the image. The Channels palette should look something like this:

Click "on" the eye icon here.⎯⎯⎯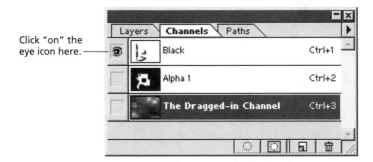

To load the new channel as an addition to the current selection, press SHIFT before clicking the Load Channel as Selection button.

To load the new channel as a subtraction from the current selection, press OPT/ALT before clicking the Load Channel as Selection button.

To load the new channel as an intersection with the current selection, press CMD/CTRL before clicking the Load Channel as Selection button.

Changing a Selection into a Layer Mask

Layer masks are different from ordinary masks in that they affect only the layer to which they are attached. What they do is make the layer to which they are attached transparent (to whatever degree the mask is transparent, of course). As you probably know, you can also make portions of a layer more or less transparent in other ways (such as erasing them), but those methods permanently change the transparency of the layer. Layer masks, on the other hand, can be turned on and off at will. They can even be discarded altogether.

Layer masks are versatile, and you can learn about them in more depth in the tutorial, "Using Layers," available on the Osborne Web site (www.osborne.com). Right now we'll just learn how to turn selections into layer masks and vice versa.

Start by having an active selection on the layer to which you want to add a layer mask. Make sure the Layers palette is visible (if not, choose Window > Show Layers). Click the Add Layer Mask button. The layer mask will appear in the name bar to the right of the image for that bar. Whatever is masked is transparent (see Figure 7-3).

The layer mask will also appear in the Channels palette and can be edited with any of the techniques that can be applied to editing any other mask.

1. Make your selection.
2. Click the Add Layer Mask button.

3. The layer mask appears here.

FIGURE 7-3   Making a layer mask from an existing selection

Moving the Selection Marquee

There are several good reasons why you might want to move a selection marquee without removing its contents:

- You can use the Edit > Paste Into command to paste the contents of the clipboard into multiple areas.
- You can fill the shape multiple times to create copies of background items such as Web buttons.
- You can stroke (paint along the marquee) the selection in different widths and colors in order to create a design, texture, or mask.

To move the selection border, you must make sure that one of the selection tools is active. Do *not* use the move tool; it will move the contents of the selection. Place the cursor inside the selection marquee and drag. If you want to move the selection in a straight line (perhaps you want to line up the outlines for the buttons you are going to fill), press SHIFT after you start dragging (pressing it before you start dragging will put the tool into "add to selection" mode). You can also nudge the selection's position in precise pixel increments with the arrow keys. Press SHIFT+ARROW to move ten pixels at a time.

If you want to copy the selection marquee without its contents, you have to save the selection. You can then load the selection into any other document by using the Load Selection command after dragging the contents from one area to another or by opening the other document and using the Load Selection command to load a selection from another document.

Here are the steps for copying the selection by dragging the Alpha channel mask from one open document to another:

1. Make your selection in the original document.

2. Without closing the original document, open the document you want to move the selection to.

3. Choose Select > Save Selection (or use the selection context menu and choose Save Selection). The Save Selection dialog appears, as shown here:

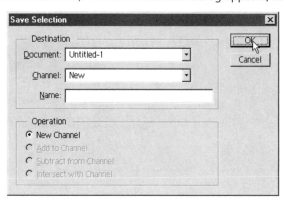

4. Since you want to save your selection to a new channel, just click OK. Alternatively, you could avoid the following drag-and-drop step by choosing your destination document from the Document pop-up menu in the Save Selection dialog. If you don't see the desired destination document listed, it's because it isn't a document that's currently opened in Photoshop.

5. From the Channels palette, drag the new Alpha channel's name bar (its icon will look like a mask in the shape of your selection) to your destination document's window. You will see the mask, and the Alpha channel will simultaneously appear in the Channels palette (which is now the Channels palette for the new document).

6. Make sure the new channel is still selected, and click the Load Channel as Selection button (the dotted circle icon) at the bottom of the Channels palette.

7. Select the composite channel's (e.g., RGB or CMYK) name bar to return to a normal view. You will see the selection marquee.

You can accomplish the same thing in another way by using the Save Selection and Load Selection commands:

1. Make your selection (or load an existing selection). To move it to a different document, open the document you want to save it to. In other words, both document windows must be open.

2. Choose Select > Save Selection, or choose Save Selection from the selection context menu.

3. The Save Selection dialog appears (see the previous illustration). From the Document pop-up menu, choose the filename of one of your other open documents. Since all you want to do is save the selection to a new channel, accept the default settings and click OK.

I've overlooked telling you how to move a selection from one layer to another because it's so easy that the solution seems obvious: while your selection is still active, use the Layers palette to select a different layer. This is just another way of reminding you that the active selection always works only on the active layer (unless that layer is an Adjustment Layer).

Moving and Copying the Selection's Contents

Moving the contents of a selection is just a matter of cutting and pasting, although several shortcuts speed up the process. It may also be important to be able to predetermine a precise placement for the copied pixels, so I'll show you how to do that as well. There are six predominant ways (Photoshop is so versatile that you can probably invent a few of your own) to move the contents of a selection in Photoshop:

• Use the Cut and Paste commands
• Use the move tool

- Use the selection context menu
- Use the Copy Merged command
- Use the Edit > Paste Into command
- Use the Layer Via Cut and Layer Via Copy commands

Using Cut (or Copy) and Paste to move a selection

If you've been using a computer for a while, the cut-and-paste method is so instinctive and so versatile that you'll probably use it more often than any other. After you've selected the area you want to move, you press either CMD/CTRL+X or CMD/CTRL+V, and a copy of the selection's contents is placed into a segment of your computer's RAM that the system has designated as the clipboard. This is a holding area for whatever was selected when you executed a Cut or Copy command regardless of what type of application you were using at the time. Whenever you paste (CMD/CTRL+V or Edit > Paste), the upper-left corner of the clipboard's contents are placed at the location of your cursor. As long as you don't execute another Cut or Copy command (some of which may be disguised under other names), you can continue to paste copies in a variety of places.

The clipboard will retain its contents even if you close your current document and open another—or even if you close Photoshop and open another application that's compatible with bitmapped graphics. So all you have to do to move your selected imagery to another document or application is to execute the Paste command once the target document is open and active.

If you cut and paste, you'll remove the contents of the selection from their original location with the Cut command. You can put the contents right back by immediately executing the Paste command, but if you move the cursor, it's too late. If you copy and then paste, the original contents will remain. Pasting will simply add new copies.

Each time you paste, the clipboard's contents are automatically placed on a new layer. This makes it very easy to use the move tool to drag the contents of the new layer to any position you want them to occupy. If you want to keep file size down and want to make your new layer part of another layer, link the two layers and use the Merge Linked command in the Layers palette menu to flatten just those two layers.

Using the move tool

Speaking of the move tool, you don't even need to use the Cut and Paste commands to move the contents of a selection to a new layer or to a new document. Just select the move tool (or press the CMD/CTRL key) and drag from inside the marquee (if you haven't selected anything, the entire layer will be moved). This will move the contents to a new position and cut them from the original position. While you are moving the selection, it becomes a "floater"; that is, it is temporarily suspended on an independent layer. As soon as you deselect it, it merges with its original layer. If you don't want that to happen, press CMD/CTRL+ SHIFT+J, and the floater will be converted to a new layer.

If you want to copy and move rather than cut the contents of the selection from their original location, don't use the move tool. You could, however, cheat. Use the Cut and Paste commands to put the contents of the selection on a new layer, and then use the move tool to change its location or document.

The move tool makes it really easy to move the contents of a layer or selection to another Photoshop or ImageReady document. Just open the other document and position the window of the originating document and the target document in such a way that you can see the contents of both. Then drag from inside the layer or selection to the target document and release the mouse button. When they are dragged to a new document, the moved pixels will find themselves on their own layer.

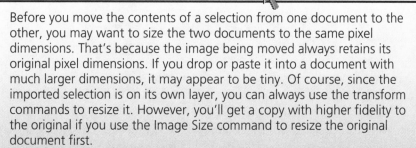

Professional Pointer

Before you move the contents of a selection from one document to the other, you may want to size the two documents to the same pixel dimensions. That's because the image being moved always retains its original pixel dimensions. If you drop or paste it into a document with much larger dimensions, it may appear to be tiny. Of course, since the imported selection is on its own layer, you can always use the transform commands to resize it. However, you'll get a copy with higher fidelity to the original if you use the Image Size command to resize the original document first.

Using the selection context menu

Five commands on the selection context menu can be used to move or copy either the contents of a selection or the selection marquee. Two of these are the Layer Via Cut and Layer Via Copy commands discussed a little later. The other three are transformation commands: Free Transform, Numeric Transform, and Transform Selection. These were all discussed in Chapter 5, except that little note was made of the fact that Free Transform and Numeric Transform can also be used to move the contents of a selection, and Transform Selection can be used to move the selection marquee.

The advantage in using any of the transform commands to move a selection or its contents is that you can also make other forms of transformations (such as rotating and scaling) in the same operation.

If you choose Free Transform (also available by choosing Edit > Free Transform), the eight-handled transformation marquee will appear. All you have to do to move the selection is place the cursor inside the marquee and drag the contents of the selection to their new location. There will be a hole, filled with either transparency (if you're selecting from a layer) or the background color (if you're selecting from the image on a Background layer, as in the following illustration).

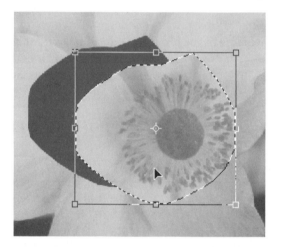

Numeric Transform (or choose Edit > Transform > Numeric) does exactly the same thing, but gives you the opportunity to set exact X/Y coordinates in pixels.

If you just want to move the selection marquee, Transform Selection (or Select > Transform Selection) lets you drag the selection with the same result as if you were using a selection tool to drag from inside the marquee.

Cross-Reference: Transformations are covered in detail in Chapter 5.

Using the Copy Merged command to copy from all visible layers

There I go again, giving it all away in the headline. Suppose you have an image of a flock of flying birds, and each of the birds is actually the same bird on a separate layer that's been scaled and transformed so that each bird looks a little different and is closer or farther away. Now you want to make the flock even bigger by selecting several of the birds and placing them on yet another layer. Surround the birds you want to copy with a lasso selection and choose Edit > Copy Merged. Everything that is visible within the selection will be copied to the clipboard. If you choose Edit > Paste or press CMD/CTRL+V, it will all be copied to a new layer.

Actually, if you're trying to increase the size of the flock, this operation creates a problem because you've also copied the chunk of sky that could be seen on the Background layer. All you have to do to solve that problem is to turn off the Background layer. To do that, click the eye icon in the left column of the Layers palette. The eye icon will disappear and the Background layer will be hidden. You could do the same for any other layers whose contents you didn't want to include in the merged copy. Figure 7-4 shows a "flock" of flowers with a leafy background that has been created by the same method as just described.

Using the Paste Into command

Whenever you need to frame your clipboard contents with specific parts of the surrounding image or to place them in a precise spot, you can choose Edit > Paste Into (CMD/CTRL+SHIFT+V). For instance, you might want to place someone's portrait inside a picture frame. When you use this command, the new layer that is automatically assigned to the pasted-in data is given a layer mask that is automatically made from the selection (see Figure 7-5).

Once you've used the Paste Into command, you can use the move tool to refine the position of the layer's contents. That's because Photoshop doesn't automatically link the layer mask and the layer, as would be the case if you had assigned the layer mask from a selection made after the new layer was pasted in. So now you know that a layer mask link (a chain icon between the thumbnail and

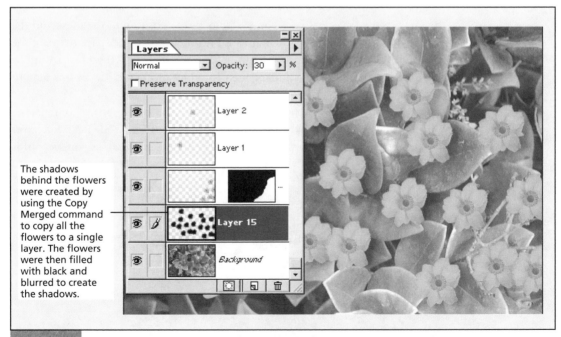

The shadows behind the flowers were created by using the Copy Merged command to copy all the flowers to a single layer. The flowers were then filled with black and blurred to create the shadows.

FIGURE 7-4 The same flower can be copied and placed on layers to create a field of flowers.

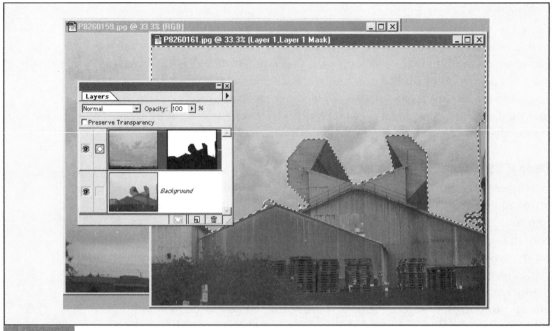

FIGURE 7-5 The bottom photo has been pasted into a magic wand selection that reflected the sky. You can see the layer mask that was automatically created by the Paste Into command.

the mask in the Layer palette's name bar) locks the position of the mask and the layer's contents together. If the link icon isn't there, click the space between the layer thumbnail and the mask thumbnail and it will appear. If you ever want to move the mask and the layer independently of one another, click the link icon to turn it off.

It's no longer on any menu, but you can also paste the clipboard contents behind the active selection by pressing OPT/ALT+CMD/CTRL+SHIFT+V. The layer mask will now mask the portion of the image that was selected, as you see in this illustration:

Using the new Layer Via Cut and Layer Via Copy commands

If you want to move the contents of your selection to a new layer in a single step, you can do it from the selection context menu by choosing either the Layer Via Cut (CMD/CTRL+SHIFT+J) or Layer Via Copy (CMD/CTRL+J) command.

If you want to send the new layer to another document, you can simply use the move tool to drag the new layer's name bar to another document window, and the new layer will automatically appear in the target document's Layers palette.

Commands That Modify Selections

Quite a few commands change the nature of the selection mask itself. You can make the borders of the selection mask graduate from complete opacity to transparency (called feathering); you can change the selected area into a selection that borders the selected area; you can round (bezel) sharp corners in a selection marquee; and you can change the size of the selection or change the orientation of the selection.

Making the Mask Edges Gradually Transparent

If you want the masked image to fade into its surroundings, you gradually change the opacity of the mask's surroundings. This is called *feathering a selection*. When you feather a selection and save it as a mask, you can see that the edges slowly graduate from black to white. Photoshop lets you easily control the distance over which this change occurs. This illustration shows a mask that has been feathered next to a mask that has not been feathered:

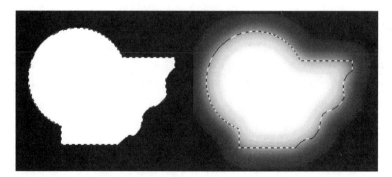

Note that the selection marquee is identical for both of the masks; the difference is that the one on the right shows what happens to the mask after the selection is feathered.

Feathering softens the edge of a selection by graduating it from opaque to transparent. The technique helps to blend composited images in a collage or montage. In a mask, white represents transparency, black opacity, and shades of gray are as semitransparent as the percentage of white they contain. You can see the effect of feathering in the illustration here, where the image of the boat was masked by a feathered selection on the layer above the leafy background.

To feather a selection, choose Feather from the selection context menu, or choose Select > Feather. The Feather Selection dialog, shown here, will appear. Enter the width (in pixels) for the feather in the Feather Radius field.

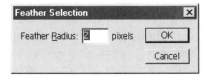

Modify > Border

The Border command lets you select an area that borders the current selection by a specified number of pixels. The original selection is no longer selected; the border is selected. In this next illustration, you see the original selection (I stroked it so you can see the shape of the original and its location in respect to the border) and then the selection as it looks after the border command is issued.

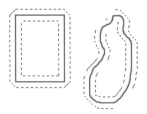

You can border any type or shape of a selection. If the selection happens to be a geometric shape, this command becomes a very convenient way to paint a border or a frame for a button or a Web portfolio picture. It's also an excellent way to create a glow along a shape made with the lasso. Keep in mind, however, that as the border moves away from a sharp corner, it becomes beveled.

To create a border selection, choose Select > Modify > Border. The Border dialog appears. Enter a number of pixels for the width of the border you desire.

Creating a glow with the Border command

Here's how you can use the Border command to create a glow around a selection:

1. Select the area around which you want to create the glow. Save the selection by choosing Select > Save Selection.

2. While the original selection is still active, press CMD/CTRL+J to lift the contents of the selection to a new layer.

3. In the Layers palette, select the original layer (click its name bar). Choose Select > Load Selection and (if necessary) choose Alpha 1 as the channel to be selected. Click OK.

4. Choose Select > Modify > Border. When the dialog appears, enter a number of pixels for the width of the border (make sure it's twice as wide as you want the glow to be), and click OK.

Now you want to feather the border selection so that when you fill it, the fill will graduate outward, simulating a glowing neon tube. In the Layers palette, click the Background layer's name bar to select that layer (otherwise, the next command won't work).

5. Choose the color you want to use (see Chapter 2). Now choose Edit > Fill. The Fill dialog appears. Choose Foreground Color from the Use pop-up menu and click OK. The selection and feathered border will look something like this:

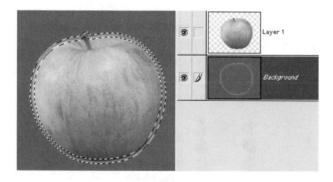

Modify > Smooth

The Select > Modify > Smooth command brings up a dialog that lets you specify a minimum radius curve between contiguous edges of a selection. It is useful for a couple of things, at least. First, it can let you create rectangular selections with rounded corners. Second, it can smooth the rugged edges that can result from making nervous selections with the lasso tool or correct but not very clean-looking edges that can result from a magnetic lasso, magic wand, or Color Range selection. I've smoothed both a lasso and a polygon lasso selection in this illustration so that you can see the effect. In both cases, the original selection has been stroked so that I could superimpose the smoothed selection over it.

There's one caveat about smoothing. If you're not careful, the rounding of the corners can cause some marquee edges to move away from the subject you're selecting, so you inadvertently get little pieces of the background. To eliminate the problem, zoom in to about 200 percent after you've done the smoothing and examine all the areas that come to a sharp point. Use the lasso tool and the SHIFT and ALT keys to add to and subtract from the selection.

Modify > Expand

Photoshop provides several ways to change the size of a selection. The Select > Modify > Expand command is the best thing to use if you want to push the edges out only slightly to improve the perceived accuracy of your selection. It's also useful if you want to stroke a wide line around your selected subject without cutting off your subject.

The thing you have to watch out for is that the more you expand the selection, the more likely it is that you will change its shape to an unacceptable degree. This is because the program expands outward a discrete number of pixels from the original pixels. So the corners of shapes end up being beveled because straight lines are drawn between the radii of the expansion. Having written that, I'm not at all sure it's clear, so here's an exaggerated picture:

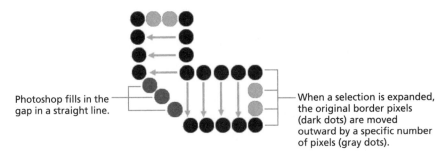

Photoshop fills in the gap in a straight line.

When a selection is expanded, the original border pixels (dark dots) are moved outward by a specific number of pixels (gray dots).

If you want to make big or asymmetrical changes to the selection, it's best to use the Select > Transform Selection command. It places a transform marquee around the selection, and you can change the selection (without changing its contents) in any of the ways that you can use Edit > Free Transform for changing the contents of a selection. Not only that, but it uses a vector formula to redraw the selection, so curves remain curves and corners remain corners.

Modify > Contract

Choosing Select > Modify > Contract shrinks the current selection uniformly in all directions by the specified number of pixels. You'll probably use this command quite often to trim away some of the unsightly halos that occur when a few too many edge colors are mixed with the colors of the edge of the object you have selected.

There are other ways to clean up the edges that result from making a selection and then moving the selection's contents. You can manually retouch edges of layers using the tools (especially the eraser). You can also get rid of stray black-and-white pixels on the edges of layers with the matting commands in the Layers menu.

Cross-Reference: The Layer Matting commands were introduced in Chapter 6 and are covered in more depth in the "Using Layers" tutorial on the Osborne Web site.

Professional Pointer

It's pretty common for objects in the real world to reflect the colors of their surroundings, especially at their outermost edges. If you make a precise selection of that object, you're bound to pick up some of those reflected colors. If you then place the object against a different-colored background, the reflected colors will make it impossible to blend the edges in a natural way. Here's the cure: Double-click the paintbrush to select it and bring up its Options palette. In the Options palette, choose Color from the blend mode menu. Place the paintbrush over a color in the (formerly) selected object and press OPT/ALT. The paintbrush temporarily becomes the eyedropper. Click to pick up the color, and then paint over the areas of reflected color. The lightness values will remain photographically correct, but the out-of-place reflected color will completely disappear.

Saving and Loading Selections

Making precise selections can take a lot of time. All it takes to lose those selections (often before they're even finished) is an accidental click of the mouse. So you're well advised to save your selections often. Also, there will be many times when the shape of the selection can be used over and over again, and once you've saved a selection, it becomes an Alpha channel that you can edit any way you like by hand.

Save Selection

The Save Selection command saves a selection as a mask in the Channels palette. It can be found in both the Select menu and selection context menu. Options include saving to any document; saving to any current channel; and operations for New Channel, Add to Channel, Subtract from Channel, and Intersect with Channel.

As soon as you execute the command, the Save Selection dialog opens. Options include loading from any document; loading from any current channel; and operations for New Selection, Add to Selection, Subtract from Selection, and Intersect with Selection. For instructions on how to use this dialog, see Figure 7-6.

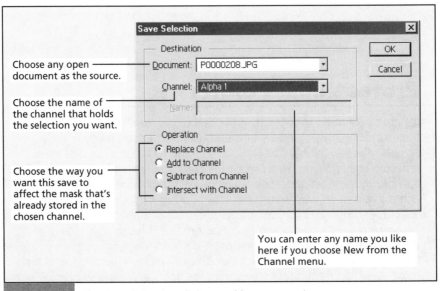

Choose any open document as the source.

Choose the name of the channel that holds the selection you want.

Choose the way you want this save to affect the mask that's already stored in the chosen channel.

You can enter any name you like here if you choose New from the Channel menu.

FIGURE 7-6 The Save Selection dialog and how to use it

Load Selection

Choosing Select > Load Selection revives a selection that has been stored as an Alpha channel. (Alpha channels are those not used by primary colors or the composite channel.) You can use the radio buttons at the bottom of the Load Selection dialog to add, subtract, or intersect the selection being loaded with any selections that are already active. Figure 7-7 shows the Load Selection dialog and how to use it.

Softening Selection Borders

More often than not, edges of selections that haven't been softened in some way will make composite images look as though they've been cut and pasted rather than naturally blended with their surroundings. The cut-and-pasted look is okay for some collage work; but for realistic montages, it just won't do. You want the viewer to believe that the Wells Fargo stagecoach is actually rolling down Wall Street. There are four basic ways to do this, each appropriate to particular situations:

- Feathering
- Anti-aliasing
- Mixed feathering
- Hand painting

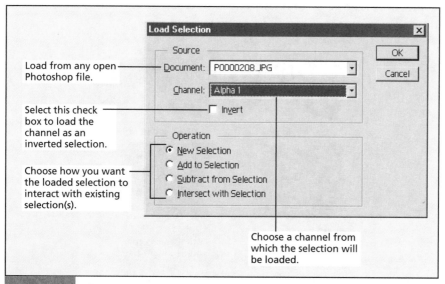

FIGURE 7-7 The Load Selection dialog and how to use it

Feathering

- **Advantages:** ☑ Can be applied to any selection or mask. ☑ Process is quick and easy. ☑ Makes a uniform graduated blend along all edges.
- **Disadvantage:** ☒ Blending is not tailored to specific sections of the edge, so it may look natural in some places and not in others.

The techniques for feathering were discussed earlier in the chapter in the section "Making the Mask Edges Gradually Transparent," which dealt with changes that you can make to the entire selection. There is one more thing worth adding here: you can feather the edges of a selection that was saved without feathering. Simply load the selection; choose Select > Feather; and, in the Feather dialog, enter the degree of feathering desired. If the selection was previously feathered (when it was first saved), you can feather it more but not less. For that reason, it's usually best to save at least one version of the selection that hasn't been feathered.

Anti-Aliasing

- **Advantages:** ☑ Much more subtle than feathering. ☑ Makes obviously pixelated (jaggy) edges look smooth.
- **Disadvantage:** ☒ Can cause halos when used in a selection that will lift the subject from a starkly contrasting background.

Anti-aliasing creates the illusion that edges are smoother than they really are by shading edge pixels so that they gradually shift into the color of the pixels that border the outside edge of the selection. Since it's a little hard to imagine what this means in practical terms, I've drawn you a picture:

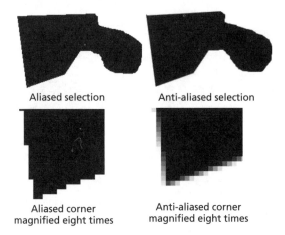

Aliased selection   Anti-aliased selection

Aliased corner   Anti-aliased corner
magnified eight times   magnified eight times

You might think you'd want to use anti-aliasing all the time, since the edges look so much smoother. Fact is, you can't. Since it's the nature of anti-aliasing to pick up some edge colors from the surrounding pixels, you may see some truly ugly halos when you place the resulting knockout against a background of a different color. This illustration shows an extreme close-up of edge pixels from an anti-aliased selection made from one color background and then placed against a background of a much different color:

Mixed Feathered and Sharp Edges

- **Advantage:** ☑ Can give you edges that blend or fade into transparency to a specific degree along a specific part of an edge.
- **Disadvantages:** ☒ It takes more time and practice to learn to do this well. ☒ Some manual mask retouching may be needed to make smooth transitions.

Imagine having to select a hand holding a glass of iced tea. The edges of the hand are fairly smooth, so the edge blend should be fairly abrupt. The glass of tea, on the other hand, becomes more transparent along its edges (it also becomes more transparent in other places, but we'll save how to do that for later). So what we want is a selection that is feathered around the edges of the glass and solid along the edges of the hand and arm.

There are several processes you could use to make a selection that had different feathering along different parts of edges. If it's a fairly simple hand-drawn selection, you can just draw part of the selection with the feathering set in the selection's Options palette, close that part of the selection, change the degree of feathering in the Options palette, press SHIFT, and then continue to draw. Figure 7-8 shows an example of an image drawn that way.

You'll notice in the figure that when the selection is filled with black, there is a feathered space between the two stages of the selection. This is fairly common, and there are two ways to cure it:

- In the selection tool's Options dialog, enter **0** for the amount of feathering. Then press SHIFT and make another selection inside the area where the preceding selections overlapped.

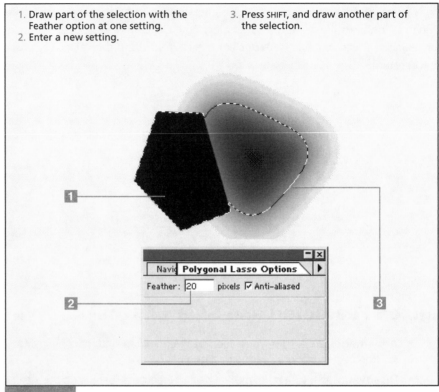

FIGURE 7-8 Feathering different parts of a selection to different degrees

- Edit the mask channel by painting in it. Paint a solid white over any areas that you don't want feathered. Step-by-step instructions on how to manually edit a selection mask will be found farther along in this chapter.

The other method for dealing with edges with different feathering is to make several separate selections and feather and save each individually. You can then use either the Load Selection command or the Channel palette's Load Channel as Selection button (in conjunction with a modifier key) to add, subtract, or intersect these separate selections with one another. You could then save the combined selections as yet another selection and manually edit it in a number of ways to further refine the selection. One advantage of making complex selection edges by combining saved selections is that it gives you a way to create an edge that's feathered only inside the selection. (Shrink the original selection and then feather.)

The following steps take you through the making of a complex feathered selection using the Channels palette. It uses the example I spoke of earlier—a hand holding a glass of liquid. You can supply your own file or download BOBHAND.JPG from the Osborne site. Figure 7-9 shows the picture after

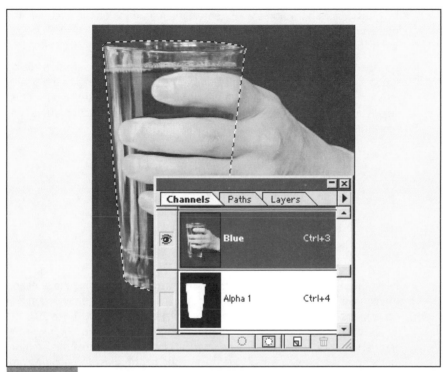

FIGURE 7-9 A selection after saving appears as a new channel.

selecting the glass and saving the selection. You can see the selection mask in the Channels palette, too.

1. Choose Window > Show Channels (or if there is already an open window containing tabs for Layers, Channels, and Paths, click the Channels tab). You'll probably find it faster to use some of the buttons at the bottom of the Channels palette rather than the menu commands for saving and loading selections. Besides, you'll be able to see how your selections look when they're saved and become mask channels.

2. Select the glass. Since this is a fairly hard-edged object, I used the pen tools, but the method isn't critical. When you've finished making the selection, click the Save Selection as Channel button at the bottom of the Channels palette.

3. Select the hand. I used the magnetic lasso with anti-aliasing. When you've finished, save the selection as a channel by clicking the button, as in step 2.

4. Now you want to feather the selection for the glass. In the Channels palette, select the channel that is the saved glass selection; then click the Load Channel as Selection button.

5. You're going to feather this selection and save it as a channel, but you want most of the feathering to take place inside the original selection marquee for

the glass. Since Photoshop always centers the feathering on the marquee, the feathering takes place on both sides of the selection. So we'll shrink the selection by half the feathering width before we actually feather the selection.

6. Choose Select > Modify > Contract. When the Contract Selection dialog appears, enter **10** (in real life, this number will vary according to the size of your image and the amount of feathering you want to impose), and click OK. Here, you can see the Contract Selection dialog and the selection after it has been contracted:

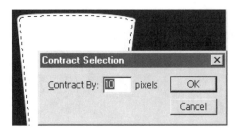

7. Select the lasso tool (press L), and then CONTROL/right-click inside the selection and choose Feather from the context menu. When the Feather Selection dialog appears, enter **20** in the Feather Radius field, and click OK. Since 20 is the radius, only about two-thirds of the feathering is going to occur inside the original selection. As you'll see when we get closer to the end of this exercise, that's good because we don't want the edge of the glass to become completely transparent—it would disappear.

8. Click the Save Selection as Channel button in the Channels palette. If necessary, scroll down so that you can see the newly saved channel. You'll see the silhouette of the glass, but this time the edges will be quite fuzzy.

9. Now you want to load the original, hard-edged selection of the glass. Click its name bar in the Channels palette. The image of the channel will take the place of the RGB image in your image-editing window. Click the Load Channel as Selection button. The original selection marquee will appear in the image and will stay there even if you switch channel or layer displays. Take a look at Figure 7-10.

10. Click the feathered selection's name bar to select that channel. Your image window will display the image of the feathered channel. The selection marquee for the original, unfeathered glass will still be active. Notice that some of the feathering takes place outside the marquee. We want to eliminate that; otherwise, we won't have a clean-edged selection. So we simply invert the hard-edged selection and then fill it with solid black. Press CMD/CTRL+SHIFT+I to invert the selection. Choose Edit > Fill, choose Black from the Use menu in the Fill dialog, and click OK. You'll notice that the mask now has a sharper edge before it starts graduating toward transparency.

11. Click the Load Channel as Selection button. A marquee appears that represents the feathered selection.

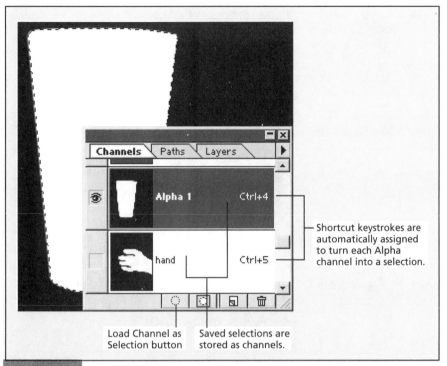

Shortcut keystrokes are automatically assigned to turn each Alpha channel into a selection.

Load Channel as Selection button

Saved selections are stored as channels.

FIGURE 7-10 The active channel has been loaded as a selection.

12. Click the name bar for the hand selection. The image-editing window now shows the mask for the hand. You want to add the selection for the hand to the selection for the feathered glass. Press SHIFT and click the Load Channel as Selection button. Notice that the marquee now includes the hand. Don't drop the selection.

13. Now you want to switch to the Layers palette. Either click its tab (if it's visible) or choose Window > Show Layers. You should see the original photograph with the marquee for the combined channels still active. It should look like this:

14. Now you're going to lift the contents of the selection to a new layer. Use the shortcut for the New Layer Via Copy command—CMD/CTRL+J. If you turn off all the other layers and select the new layer, it will look like this:

You'll notice that the edges of the glass go from being pretty transparent to opaque. If you put a background of a different color behind the glass, or one with a texture, the glass will look quite natural. Here it is with a new background:

In the next section, you'll see how to make some of the liquid more transparent, too.

Painting Feathered Edges

- **Advantages:** ☑ The easiest way to feather small portions of a selection border or to have many different degrees of feathering in small areas. 7 ☑ You can set the tool's Options for any level of transparency and give any degree of feathering to the edge of your brush.

- **Disadvantage:** ☒ Takes practice to perfect (some painting ability helps).

Adding some small areas of transparency or semitransparency to the edges of a selection mask can also add some realism to items that tend to reflect the colors of their surroundings. This is especially true of shiny metal objects with rounded edges. However, it is more common in not-so-obviously reflective material than you might think.

If you paint feathered edges with a brush, you'll often want to paint with a shade of gray because you want a particular level of transparency in the edge. Be sure to protect the edges of the mask by making a selection before you start painting. That way, you won't be giving transparency to areas of the mask that should be opaque.

One of the problems with using a brush to paint feathered edges is keeping the stroke steady enough. Figure 7-11 shows some techniques for feathering mask edges.

Cross-Reference: You'll find instructions for stroking a path in Chapter 6. Chapter 11 shows you how to make custom brushes.

The fastest way to select the edges of a hard-edged mask is to use the magic wand. You'll find lots more on manually editing selections by painting into their masks in the next section of this chapter.

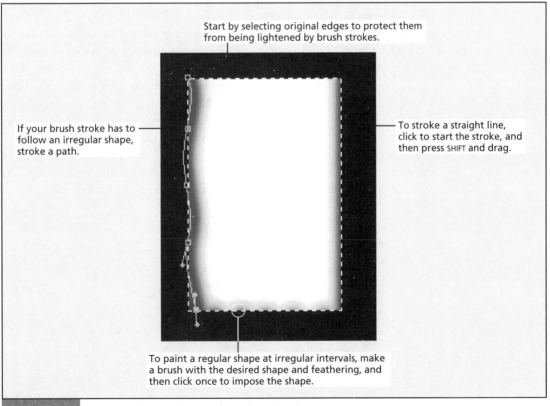

Start by selecting original edges to protect them from being lightened by brush strokes.

If your brush stroke has to follow an irregular shape, stroke a path.

To stroke a straight line, click to start the stroke, and then press SHIFT and drag.

To paint a regular shape at irregular intervals, make a brush with the desired shape and feathering, and then click once to impose the shape.

FIGURE 7-11   Methods for steady painting of mask edges

Editing Selections by Painting Masks

To hand paint a mask, make sure the Channels palette is visible. Select the mask channel you want to paint by clicking its name bar. Your image-editing window will now be filled with the selection mask rather than the image. You can use any of Photoshop's tools to alter the mask.

Any colors currently chosen in the current Swatches palettes will be interpreted as a shade of gray when you paint on or into a mask because all channels except the composite channel are grayscale images. Nevertheless, it's a good idea to press D to choose the default black foreground and white background colors. You can then control transparency with the Opacity slider on the tool's Options palette.

There will be times when you want to add some level of transparency to sections inside a selection. In those instances, you may find it handy to overlay the mask onto the image itself so that you can see which areas you want to paint over. In that case, be sure the mask channel you want to paint is selected by seeing that its name bar is highlighted (if not, click it). At the same time, click to turn on the eye icon in the composite channel. The mask will now be shown in red. When you paint into the mask, your strokes will appear in red (or whatever color you've chosen for Quick Mask previews—see the next section), but you will actually be painting grays into the mask.

You can judge the results of your painting at any time by clicking the Load Channel as Selection button, selecting the composite channel, pressing CMD/CTRL+J to copy the contents of the selection to a layer, and then switching to the Layers palette. Turn off all but the new layer to see the effect of your masking. If you aren't satisfied with what you see, click the Delete Current Layer button at the bottom of the Layers palette (the trash can icon). This illustration shows the result of painting inside the mask I made for the hand and glass of tea:

Changing a Selection
Using Quick Mask Mode

An even faster way to change the shape of a selection by using the painting tools is to use a Photoshop feature called Quick Mask mode. Quick Masks are temporary channels shown in a color that contrasts with the underlying image (the default is red).

To enter Quick Mask mode, click the Edit in Quick Mask button in the toolbox.

Professional Skills Summary

This chapter has told you virtually everything you need to know about how to modify a selection or its mask once you've made it. The primary lesson to be learned is that you should remember to save your selections. You can always make your file sizes smaller by deleting the extra channels when you're sure you'll no longer need them. The other extremely valuable lesson you should have learned is to keep the Channels palette visible when you're working with selections because it offers the fastest path to saving, loading, and modifying selections.

chapter 8

Bending and Twisting the Image

In this chapter, you:

- Wrap photos around 3D shapes
- Correct perspective distortion
- Use the distortion filters
- Stretch an image to fit needed space
- Learn to use morphing and shaping plug-ins

Wrapping Your Photos onto a Cube, Sphere, or Cylinder

Often, in the course of putting together a composite image, you will find that you need to wrap a logo around a bottle, you need to see a reflection in a curved surface (such as a hubcap), or you need to glue a product shot to a box or book cover.

Photoshop has only recently acquired the ability to do this. The secret lies in the 3D Transform filter that was introduced in Photoshop 5. It lets you project your currently selected layer onto a cube, cylinder, or sphere. You can then manipulate the image so that you can see it from different angles. You can also choose to light the image so that shadows are cast on the sides facing away from the light. Here's an image that has been projected onto a cube and then viewed from several different angles:

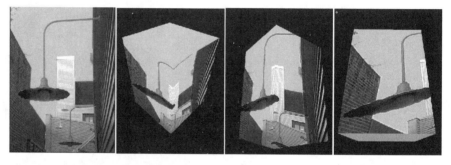

This is still a fairly basic (but very easy-to-use) means of molding your images to 3D shapes, but it's also good enough to do the jobs mentioned in the first paragraph of this section.

First, I'm going to show you how to map an image to each of the geometric shapes. Then I'll show you how to composite that image to the surface of an apple.

Using the 3D Transform Command

You can map any layer of any Photoshop file to the surface of a cube, sphere, or cylinder by using the 3D Transform command. These may seem like simple shapes, but you can make more complex shapes by combining shapes, and you can also use Photoshop's other bending and warping tools to further modify the shape before you combine it with another shape.

Start by loading an image that has some straight horizontal and vertical lines (or download PERSPECT.JPG from the Osborne site). The only layer this image needs to have for the moment is the background layer. Remember, though, that you can import an image to another layer via drag and drop, select that layer, project it onto one of these 3D shapes, and then blend that layer with one of the underlying layers to create the illusion that the image has the texture of a 3D surface.

1. Open the file that you want to map to 3D.

2. Duplicate the background layer by dragging it to the New Layer button at the bottom of the Layers palette.

3. Turn off the background layer by clicking the eye icon in the leftmost column of the Background layer name bar in the Layers palette.

4. Choose Filter > Render > 3D Transform. The 3D Transform dialog appears, as shown in Figure 8-1.

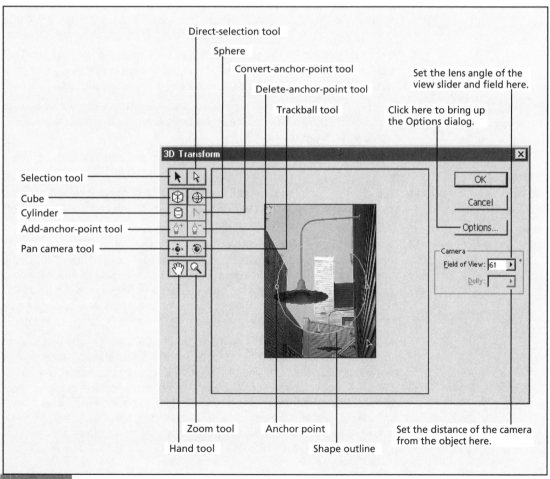

FIGURE 8-1 The 3D Transform dialog

5. Select the cylinder tool and drag diagonally in the preview area to make the shape cover the desired area of the image.

6. Click the Options button. The Options dialog will appear, as shown here:

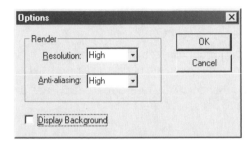

7. Choose the desired quality of resolution and anti-aliasing from the respective menus in the Options dialog. The higher the level of each, the longer it will take to render the result. On the other hand, the quality is usually worth the wait.

8. For our purposes here, be sure that Display Background is not selected. That is because we want our rendered 3D object to float on its own layer on a transparent background. Click OK to accept the Options settings.

9. Select the pan camera tool. The preview area will instantly show the object at the currently chosen Field of View and Dolly settings. This is likely not to be the view you want to see.

10. Drag the Dolly slider until the shape is framed as you'd like in the preview area.

11. Drag the Field of View slider until you see the level of perspective distortion you'd like. You may have to switch back and forth between these two sliders to get exactly the desired positioning.

12. To change both the horizontal and vertical rotation of the 3D object, select the trackball tool and drag in the preview area. To rotate the object about the horizontal axis, drag up and down. Drag from side to side to rotate it about the vertical axis. Be sure you don't rotate so much that you show an area too big for the image to wrap. To get more complete image wrapping, you'll need to use a third-party program (see the upcoming Professional Pointer).

13. Now we'll make the cylinder a bit more complicated. You can use pen tools to reshape a cylinder (but not the cube or sphere). Select the add-anchor-point tool and click on the right side of the cylinder to add a point. You can add as many new points as you like. If you add too many, select the delete-anchor-point tool to delete them. If you want a point to be a corner rather than a smooth curve, select the convert-anchor-point tool and click the point to be converted to a corner. To reshape the cylinder, select the direct-selection tool and drag the anchor points to new locations.

14. Any time you want to preview the results of what you've done, select the trackball tool again. You'll see the item previewed according to the last-used settings for the trackball, Field of View, and Dolly. When you're happy with the preview, click OK. Since the background layer has been hidden, you should see something that looks like this:

You will notice that the bottom of the cylinder is just a blank, light gray. The 3D Transform filter doesn't wrap images around the top and bottom of shapes. It also doesn't wrap them around more than 180 degrees of a cylinder or sphere. Also, there is no shading on the cylinder.

Shortcuts for 3D Transform Tools

You can use single keystrokes to select tools from the 3D Transform dialog's toolbox, just as you can from the main Photoshop toolbox. There are only six of these (see Table 8-1), so you'll probably be able to memorize them fairly quickly.

Tool	Keystroke
Selection tool	V
Cube tool	M
Sphere tool	N
Cylinder tool	C
Trackball	R
Pan camera tool	E

TABLE 8-1 3D Transform Tool Shortcuts

Professional Pointer

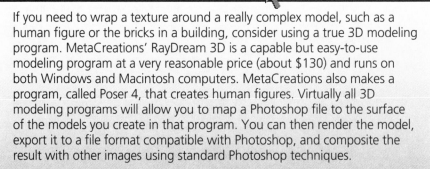

If you need to wrap a texture around a really complex model, such as a human figure or the bricks in a building, consider using a true 3D modeling program. MetaCreations' RayDream 3D is a capable but easy-to-use modeling program at a very reasonable price (about $130) and runs on both Windows and Macintosh computers. MetaCreations also makes a program, called Poser 4, that creates human figures. Virtually all 3D modeling programs will allow you to map a Photoshop file to the surface of the models you create in that program. You can then render the model, export it to a file format compatible with Photoshop, and composite the result with other images using standard Photoshop techniques.

Correcting Perspective Distortion

The portability and readiness of hand-held cameras has made them very popular. At the same time, they create a common problem when shooting buildings and other geometrically familiar subjects. That problem is called keystoning. (You may recall from Chapter 5, keystoning refers to the fact that parallel lines are farther apart when closest to the lens.) Here's an intentionally dramatic example of keystoning:

In the example, keystoning is used intentionally to dramatize the strength of the structure and to lead the eye across the composition. More often, however, it looks like a mistake or takes away from the strength of the geometry. This is most often a problem in product shots of cubical objects like boxes and radios and in architectural photography.

So that you can see what we're aiming for, here are "before" and "after" pictures of the same building in Berkeley, California:

Keystoned building

Keystoning fixed

1. Open your own image of a slightly keystoned building or box, or download BERKELEY.JPG from the Osborne Web site.

2. Double-click the hand tool (CMD/CTRL+0) to make your image-editing window fill as much of the screen as possible.

3. Now you want to zoom out so that you'll have room to work outside the image but inside the image-editing window. Select the zoom tool, press OPT/ALT, and click in the image until you have a border all around it.

4. We want to impose guidelines on the image so that we can tell when lines are straight and perpendicular to one another. Choose View > Show Rulers (CMD/CTRL+R). Press V to select the move tool, and drag vertical guidelines from the vertical ruler to the vertical edge(s) of the subject.

5. From the horizontal ruler, drag a guideline to a point that's parallel to a line you would like to be perfectly level. Ideally, this line should be at a height corresponding to the photographer's eye level.

6. Now you will rotate the image so that the horizontal guideline actually matches the horizontal line (real or imaginary) in the image. Select the entire image by pressing CMD/CTRL+A. Then press CMD/CTRL+T or choose Edit > Free Transform. Place the cursor outside one corner of the transform marquee and drag to rotate the image until the horizontal lines match. At this point, what

you see should look very much like the illustration here. Don't complete the transformation yet. Remember, the more you can do before completing a transformation, the higher the fidelity of the final transformation to the original image.

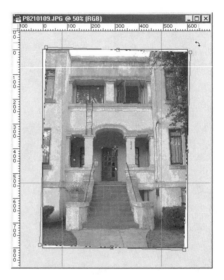

7. Press CMD/CTRL and alternate between dragging the right and left upper corner handles of the transform marquee until the vertical lines are as straight as you can make them. If you have some barrel distortion in the image, you won't be able to make a perfect match. Just come as close as you can. When your vertical lines look as straight as you want them to, double-click inside the marquee to render the transformation. Compare this illustration with the preceding illustration.

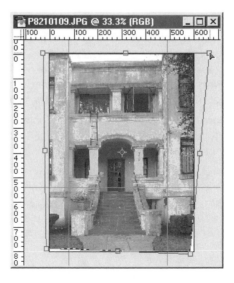

8. Once the transformation renders, you may still have curvature in some lines. You may be able to fix this, once again, with the Free Transform command. Select the rectangular marquee (press M—or SHIFT+M if the elliptical marquee is currently in view), and make a selection that encompasses only that portion of the image where the line curves.

9. Now press CMD/CTRL+T to bring up the free transform marquee in place of the selection marquee. Be sure you don't drag from inside the marquee, or you'll pull your image apart. Press CMD/CTRL and drag the handles at the corners of the image to straighten out the line. Be sure you don't drag the corners inside the image, or it will come apart. If that happens, use the History palette to back up. When your curved lines are as straight as you can make them, double-click inside the transform marquee to render the transformation, and then immediately press CMD/CTRL+D to drop the selection marquee.

> **Tip:** Step 8 won't work if you have obvious barrel distortion on both vertical and horizontal edges. In that case, you're better off leaving well enough alone.

Unfortunately, Photoshop doesn't yet give us any way to truly correct barrel distortion. A plug-in that is usually used for making large-scale distortions has a feature that can help immensely. The product is Human Software's Squizz. Squizz has a grid that you can move to indicate the direction of localized transformations.

Filters That Ripple and Bend

There are times when you want to distort the image in ways that affect only a particular area of the image or that create a surface detail. You will also want to create ripples, bubbles, and other distortions to create surface texture effects, such as a pebble being dropped into an otherwise quiet pond or the wind rippling the surface of the water. Photoshop's Distort filters are particularly adept at this sort of thing, although you can also use some of them to distort particular parts of the image in order to create such effects as beveled edges for frames. Heck, you can even create psychedelic distortions.

The Distort filters are Diffuse Glow, Displace, Glass, Ocean Ripple, Pinch, Polar Coordinates, Ripple, Shear, Spherize, Twirl, Wave, and Zigzag. Most of these are adjustable over a wide range of effects; but to give you a quick idea of what each does, take a look at Figure 8-2, which shows you the default settings for each of these filters when applied to the same subject.

The following sections describe how each of the Distort filters might be used to solve particular special effects problems or enhance a particular type of assignment.

Diffuse Glow

I think of Diffuse Glow as a mood filter. It softens the image by spreading the highlights and increasing the illusion of grain. Both the glow and the graininess

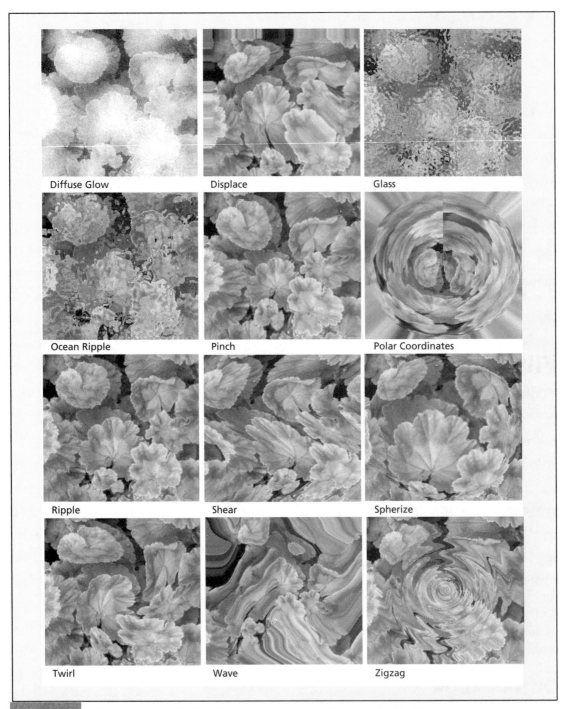

Diffuse Glow

Displace

Glass

Ocean Ripple

Pinch

Polar Coordinates

Ripple

Shear

Spherize

Twirl

Wave

Zigzag

FIGURE 8-2   Effects of the default settings for each of the filters under the Distort submenu

are adjustable. There is a catch, though. The "glow" color is the currently chosen background color. So be sure you choose the default background color to get a white glow. Of course, you may want to experiment with some other colors. Even black can be good if you want to set a dark or murky tone. Diffuse Glow can be an excellent filter for soft glamour portraits, sultry nightclub scenes, or heated desert battles.

You adjust the effect of this filter by dragging any or all of the three sliders and previewing a thumbnail of the image at the upper left of the Diffuse Glow dialog. All Distort filters (indeed most of the Photoshop filters) have this preview area in the same location.

To execute this filter, choose Filter > Distort > Diffuse Glow. Here's the dialog:

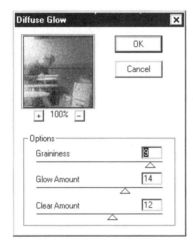

Here's an example of this filter being used to impart a mood to an image:

Displace

The Displace filter is used to shift parts of an image right or left, or up or down. The amount of displacement depends on the brightness values in another image. This second image is called a *displacement map*, but it can be any Photoshop file—including the image itself.

Essentially, this filter lets you create custom distortion effects. It's also very effective at letting you create a major distortion mess. However, you can create two useful effects with a fair amount of predictability: brush stroke effects and bending effects. I'll show you how to do both in a moment. The two exercises will also give you an idea of the versatility of this filter; but beware—you might be tempted to spend outrageous amounts of time experimenting.

The Displace filter works by using a monochromatic image to determine the vertical and horizontal offset that will be applied to a matching part of the image. Brightness values below 128 produce a negative displacement; values above 128 produce a positive displacement. A single-channel image shifts along the diagonal described by the settings in the horizontal and vertical sliders. Two-channel images use one channel for horizontal displacement and the other for vertical displacement. To bring up the Displace dialog, choose Filters > Distort > Displace. Here's what you'll see:

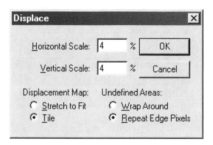

The following exercise creates some examples of distortion effects. Keep in mind, though, that the results you get will vary enormously, depending on your settings and on your displacement maps.

To make a map that will give a brush stroke effect to the image (or layer or selection), follow these steps:

1. Open your target image. The first thing to do is to create a displacement map that's the same size as your image. This will make it easier to see where the displacements will occur. If *you* don't care, Photoshop doesn't care what size the displacement map is. It can be tiled or stretched to match, as long as you click the appropriate radio buttons in the Displace dialog. Anyway, press CMD/CTRL+A to select all, press CMD/CTRL+C to copy the image to the clipboard, and then press CMD/CTRL+N to create a new image. The New dialog will appear.

2. In the New dialog, choose Grayscale from the Mode menu and click the White radio button. Photoshop will have automatically chosen all the correct

settings for the rest of the dialog; so click the OK button, and a new, empty window will appear.

3. Press D to select the default colors. Then select one of the brush tools, and make random brush strokes all over the new, blank window. Choose several shades of gray and continue doing this until you get bored.

4. This is a good place to try combining some artistic filters. Meantime, just make a fun mess. Mine looked like this:

Cross-Reference: Learn how to effectively combine filters in Chapter 10.

5. Save the mess as a displacement map—meaning you choose File > Save As, and then make sure Photoshop is chosen as the file type and name the file anything you like. Later, you can retrieve this displacement map for use with any other image that's the same size.

6. Switch to the window for the target image and choose Filter > Distort > Displace. The Displace dialog will appear. You should experiment with all these settings, but start with the default 10% Horizontal and Vertical displacements. Since the image is the same size as the target image, the settings for the displacement map radio buttons will have no effect. Choose Repeat Edge Pixels under Undefined Areas and click OK. Your results should be similar to this:

Try choosing Image > Image Size to reduce the size of your displacement map to about 10 percent of its original size, and repeat the process in the previous exercise. But this time, click the Tile radio button in the Displace dialog in step 6. You'll get a much different texture.

Okay, so now let's try the technique that leads to bending the image in a more gentle way. You can use variations on this technique to create a variety of reflections and dream-state effects.

1. You can use the same image, and use the same technique as in step 1 in the previous exercise to create a new image the same size as the current image.

2. In the new window for the image, make a marquee selection that leaves about a 10 percent margin all around the image. Choose Select > Feather (OPT/ALT+CMD/CTRL+D) and enter a feather radius of about 30 pixels. The marquee will now have rounded corners.

3. Select the paint bucket tool and fill the selection with black. It will graduate to white at the edges.

4. Click the double-headed arrow to swap the foreground and background colors. Make another marquee selection inside the darkest area of the image. Now select the radial gradient tool and drag from the center of the selection to the closest point on the right edge of the selection. Your result should look something like this:

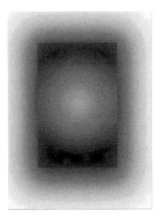

5. We're using basic shapes here so that you can readily see the effect. You will be able to control your bending by the size, location, and gradation of the shapes you create.

6. Follow steps 5 and 6 in the previous exercise, and you will see the following result:

If you're in the mood to experiment further, you'll find a slew of premade displacement maps in the Photoshop plug-ins folder. Open these files to see what they look like, and then try running them on a couple of images with a variety of settings. If you create an effect you see a practical use for, let me know, and I'll post it on my Web site or on the Osborne site.

Glass

The Glass filter makes a distortion that looks like the pebbled or wavy glass you'd see in a shower door and in some office windows. I've used it to romanticize a too-blatant nude and to "frost" the windows in some interior shots in which the view out the window wasn't all that attractive. It can also be a cool way to give an alien a bad complexion or to make the surface of water look wafted by a gentle breeze.

By the way, this filter is a more versatile version of the Ocean Ripple filter, so I won't dwell on that too much when we come to it. Here's the basic look:

The lovely thing about using this filter instead of Ocean Ripple is that you can use another image as a texture map. The only qualification is that it be a PSD file, so any of the images that you created for use as displacement maps can double for use here.

To load an image as a texture, choose Load Texture from the Texture pop-up menu in the Glass dialog (shown in the following illustration). A file-loading dialog will appear, and you choose the desired file by using the browsing method standard to your operating system. The other adjustments are self-explanatory and lend themselves to easy experimentation.

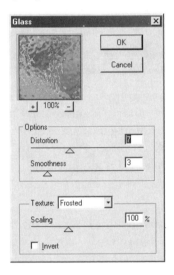

Ocean Ripple

The Ocean Ripple filter creates the same effect as Glass, but with only two settings. Neither setting is for smoothness, and you can't load a texture from a file you created. On the other hand, it's quick and simple. Here is the dialog:

Ripple

Ripple is even simpler than Ocean Ripple, but it looks much more like ripples in water than like pebbled glass. It's more like a beginner's Wave filter (coming up next) and gives you a nearly instant means of making objects look like they're being reflected in water or wet pavement. Here we see the rose's reflection, made by copying the top half of the image to a new layer, flipping it, and running the wave filter on the new layer:

The settings consist of only one slider and a Size pop-up menu with a choice of Small, Medium, and Large.

Wave

Now if you really want to control the ripples, or waves, or whatever we're calling them this week, use the Wave filter. This thing has enough controls to please a fighter pilot. You can choose up to 999 wave source generators (think of riverboat paddlewheels), set a range of random wavelengths and heights (Amplitude), and choose whether the shape of the waves will be curvy (Sine), sharply peaked (Triangle), or square edged. Finally, you can scale the wave effect to a percentage of the picture between 1 and 100.

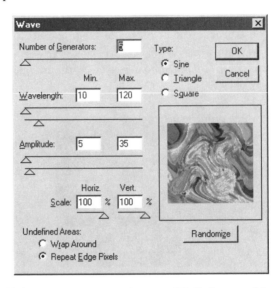

What does all this mean in practical terms? Well, for one thing, you could acquire a new hobby. More seriously, you can create surface effects that are reminiscent of the variable ripples in water, and you can sand or warp a posterized image so that it looks like stained glass, as shown here:

Professional Pointer

Sometimes, it can be hard to make a subtle enough adjustment to get the effect you want. Photoshop provides a solution. You can reduce the effect of any filter, adjustment, brush stroke, or fill by a specific percentage. Just choose Filter > Fade (whatever you did last). A dialog appears that lets you enter a percentage.

ZigZag

When it comes to waves and ripples, Photoshop puts you into overload. Believe it or not, the ZigZag filter actually adds quite a bit to the mix. It makes several variations on "pebble in a pond" circular waves.

If you want to make the circular waves' perspective appear to match that of a body of water (or the person's navel?), make an oblong rectangular selection. Then choose Select > Transform Selection. Press CMD/CTRL and drag the top corners in to squeeze the selection into a keystone shape. Photoshop will force the waves to fit inside the selection. Here's how it looks for all three of the ZigZag filter's wave types:

| Pond Ripples | Around Center | Out from Center |

Here's the ZigZag dialog. Drag the sliders and you instantly see the result in the preview area.

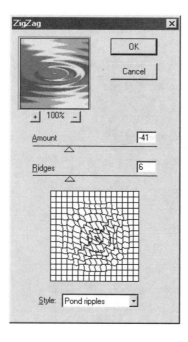

Pinch

Pinch and Spherize are another couple of closely related distortion filters. These filters let you distort the image according to a grid. Pinch sucks everything in toward the center, as though it were flowing down a drain, while Spherize makes the image look as though it were printed on rubber and stretched around a ball.

There are two main differences that distinguish the Pinch from the Spherize distortion. First, the Pinch filter pulls or pushes the image into a shape that is more reminiscent of a rounded-top cone than of a ball. Second, the "cone" gradually rises out of the image. If you make a selection, the center of the cone will be in the center of the selection.

Professional Pointer

Although most of the demonstrations in this chapter show the effect of a distortion on the entire image, don't forget the power of being able to make these distortions within a selection. It takes practice, but if you mix distortions inside of selections you can create whole new life forms.

To suck up or blow out the image, choose Filters > Distort > Pinch. When the Pinch dialog appears (shown next), drag the slider to the right or enter a negative number in the Amount field to suck the image in. To blow the image out, drag the slider to the left or enter a positive number.

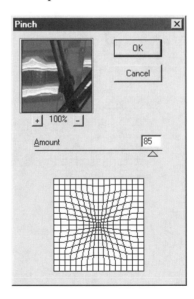

The following image of windows and trolley cables has been made to rise and sink in different places by making a rectangular selection and then running the Pinch filter at both positive and negative settings:

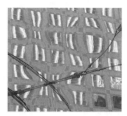

Spherize

In addition to wrapping the image around 180 degrees of a ball, you can wrap the image around a cylinder using the Spherize filter. You can also use negative numbers so that you can wrap the image to either a concave or convex surface.

Practical uses for this filter are many. For one thing, you can use it to correct barrel distortion that results from wide-angle lens shots. In fact, I'll show you how to do that in a minute. You can also create all manner of reflections that might be seen on chromed surfaces, or you can do things such as curving a tattoo so that it looks as though it wraps around an arm.

In the Spherize dialog, shown next, the Amount slider travels from –100 to 100. Positive numbers make the sphere bulge outward; negative numbers make it concave. The choices on the Mode pop-up menu are Normal (spherical, that is), Horizontal Only (horizontal cylinder), and Vertical Only (vertical cylinder).

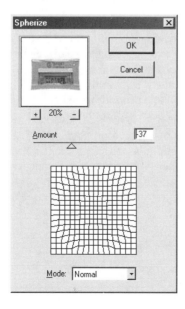

Now we want to correct for barrel distortion. It's a very common problem when shooting with lenses whose focal length (on a 35mm camera or digital equivalent) is 35mm or less (less is wider angle). The storefront that appears in the preview area of the Spherize dialog was photographed with a 35mm lens. Notice that the sides of the building (the top and bottom edges are particularly noticeable) bulge outward slightly.

Here's how to fix barrel distortion:

1. Load a picture of a building or a box that shows evidence of barrel distortion. If you don't have an image you've been wishing you could fix, download STORFRNT.JPG from the Osborne Web site.

2. Use the Free Transform command to correct the perspective distortion. If you haven't learned to do that, there's a tutorial earlier in this chapter in the section "Correcting Perspective Distortion."

Once we've leveled the structure, it's plain that the top and bottom edges of the building curve outward. It's a fairly subtle phenomenon in this instance, so we have to make sure we don't overcorrect. The correction is made by mapping the image to a concave portion of a sphere. We can know exactly what the borders and shape of that sphere are, as long as we first make an elliptical selection. Otherwise, Photoshop will position the sphere so that it is centered in the image and just touches the longest sides. Other advantages of making an elliptical selection are that you can make the sphere an ellipsoid, and you can soften the edges of the sphere so that they curve gradually in or out of the image. Okay, so now that we've taken that little intermission to give you some background, onward with correcting barrel distortion.

3. Since we're going to make a very subtle distortion, we're only going to use a very small part of the sphere. It's easier to do this if our image doesn't cover the whole sphere. For that reason, we'll give ourselves more room by enlarging the canvas. Make sure your background color is white by pressing D. Choose Image > Canvas Size. In the Canvas Size dialog's New Size section, enter figures that double the width and height of the selection, and click OK. You will see a white border surrounding your image.

4. Select the elliptical marquee tool. (Press M—or SHIFT+M if you have to cycle through the other marquee tools to get to the elliptical marquee.) Drag diagonally from the upper-left corner of your canvas until the selection touches two sides of the image. If the image isn't centered in the marquee, drag from inside the marquee to reposition it. Now your image should look like this:

5. Choose Filter > Distort > Spherize. Set the dialog approximately as shown here. Zoom out the preview so you can see how the building is "bending." Enter a small negative number in the Amount field. Then press OK.

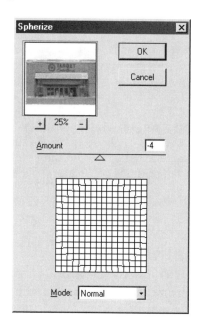

6. Your corrected image still has the oversized canvas. Also, in order to straighten some of the interior lines, you may have overcorrected the borders. Select the crop tool, and drag to place the crop marquee so that it will trim your image evenly. Then double-click to complete the crop and save the image. It should look like this:

Professional Pointer

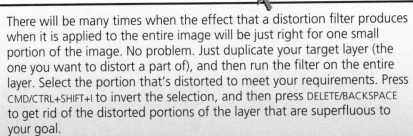

There will be many times when the effect that a distortion filter produces when it is applied to the entire image will be just right for one small portion of the image. No problem. Just duplicate your target layer (the one you want to distort a part of), and then run the filter on the entire layer. Select the portion that's distorted to meet your requirements. Press CMD/CTRL+SHIFT+I to invert the selection, and then press DELETE/BACKSPACE to get rid of the distorted portions of the layer that are superfluous to your goal.

Polar Coordinates

The Polar Coordinates filter distorts things in such an extreme way that you might at first have a tough time imagining what on earth you could use it for. I've found three worthwhile purposes for it:

- Rolling text into a circle
- Making radial gradients from rainbows
- Turning images into abstract backgrounds for portraits and product shots

Each example illustrated here shows the "before" on the left and the "after" on the right. Here's an example of the "text into a circle" trick:

You'll notice that the center of the circle is what was formerly the top center of the image. Had the text been at the bottom of the image, it would have been spun into a larger circle. Now here's what happens when you use the Polar Coordinates filter on a gradient. Try experimenting with gradients on slants, too.

Notice that the beginning and end of the gradient come together at a very sharp point. You can cure that by putting a selection around the sharp edge, feathering it, and then applying the Gaussian Blur filter (blurring techniques are discussed Chapter 10). Okay, now for the abstract. We do this by choosing the Polar to Rectangular radio button in the Polar Coordinates dialog, shown here:

Now here's the resulting abstract. You could make it even more abstract by running some of the other filters discussed in this chapter over it. In fact, the combination of filters you might effectively employ is endless.

Shear

Shear is another of Photoshop's oddly named distortion filters. I say it's oddly named because it's more appropriate for introducing precise vertical bends into an object than for shearing. If you just want to shear, which is to make the image lean to one side, you can do it more quickly with the Free Transform command.

The Shear dialog, shown here, lets you indicate the number and extent of the bends in the image by clicking the dark vertical line to place a control point and then dragging that control point. You can also drag the top and bottom of the line if you want to make the object lean to one side or the other.

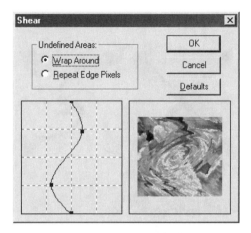

If you want to bend the subject in a horizontal direction, you first have to choose Image > Rotate Canvas > 90° CW/CCW, or if you want to rotate a layer, choose Edit > Transform > Rotate 90° CW/CCW. Then run the Shear filter, and repeat the rotate command to turn the canvas or layer back to its original orientation.

Twirl

The Twirl filter effect is straightforward enough. It just puts a spin on things. All you have to do is choose Filter > Distort > Twirl. Drag the slider, and the preview area will show you how tight the spin has become, as shown here:

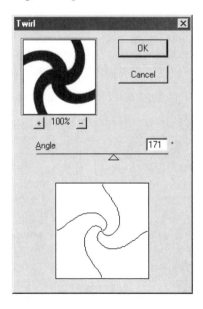

Click OK to see the effect, as in this example:

Making Images Fit into Prescribed Areas

Usually when you distort an image, you are doing it on a specific part of the image, or you are molding one image to make it appear to be the surface of something in another image. The one remaining trick, then, is to make the distorted or transformed image appear in the right place. Here's how to do that:

1. Place the image (or the part of the current image) that you are going to stretch on its own layer. If you are adding one image to another, open both images. Activate the image to be distorted, and select the layer to be distorted. Then select the move tool and drag the image to the window of the target image. This will automatically create a new layer. If you want to stretch part of the current image, duplicate the layer and name the duplicate "distort."

2. Perform your preferred distortion.

3. Select the target area that you want to map the distortion into. You are going to use this selection to knock out the distortion, so make sure your selection techniques are such that the edges blend smoothly.

Cross-Reference: See Chapters 6 and 7 to find out how to blend the edges of selections.

4. Move the distorted layer into the proper position within the selection. Temporarily lower the transparency of your distortion layer so that you can clearly see the image you are going to blend it with. To do that, select the distortion layer in the Layers palette. Next, select the move tool and use it to move the layer. When you have the layer in position, press CMD/CTRL+I to invert the selection and DELETE/BACKSPACE to remove the unwanted portions of the distortion.

5. Use the distorted layer's blend modes menu to blend the distortion with the underlying image. The mode you use will depend on the effect you're after, but I find Multiply is the one that works best most often. Finally, adjust the distorted layer's brightness and transparency to fine-tune the blend.

That's all there is to it.

Morphing and Shaping Plug-ins

Several plug-ins let you brush distortions into exactly the areas where you want them. The three most prominent are MetaCreation's Goo (no longer a standalone toy, but a full-fledged KPT-X Photoshop plug-in or part of KPT 6), Valis Group's Flo' series of products, and Human Software's Squizz. Each plug-in has unique strengths, but all have many overlapping features. Collectively, they can be used for anything from pulling the features in a face into a caricature, to creating images that make a metamorphosis from one form to another. Goo is especially good at the caricature sort of thing and presents an easy interface. The other two are also good at that sort of "pixel pushing," but also have more sophisticated talents. Flo' is an excellent morphing tool. Squizz lets you move the points and lines in a grid so that you can correct for all sorts of optical distortions in an image.

To find out more about what you can do with this type of product, check the manufacturers' Web sites. Flo' is at www.valisgroup.com. Goo is at www. metacreations.com. Squizz can be found at www.humansoftware.com. Goo and Squizz are available for both Windows and Macintosh computers; Flo' is Mac only.

Professional Skills Summary

This chapter discussed ways and reasons to reshape all or part of your images. The bulk of the chapter covered the 3D Transform filter's ability to bend the image around geometric primitives and the dozen filters in the Distort filters group. There was also a discussion of how to make these distortions fit within specified areas of another image. Finally, some guidance was included on where to find third-party plug-ins capable of doing much more sophisticated warping and morphing. The next chapter is all about adding text to images.

Incorporating Text

Photoshop is the very cornerstone of image editing and manipulation for anyone in publishing, photography, multimedia, or any other discipline in computer graphics. When you see the interesting, beautiful, and often quirky images on the Web, on CD-ROMs, and in books and magazines, you will know those images most likely were once mere pixels on a Photoshop canvas. But the wonder and power of Photoshop does not end with pictures. Sometimes, a word is worth a thousand pictures. In this chapter, we will explore Photoshop's versatility in creating text effects.

Photoshop lets you impose the same effects on text as on images. All the same rules apply, whether you're doing Web work, experimenting with filters, or preparing for print output. Even if you create text in a vector-based application (Adobe's Illustrator, for example), Photoshop will rasterize it as soon as you import it. Although bitmapped text is more difficult to edit, Photoshop lets you do things with text that you can't do in vector drawing programs, such as FreeHand and Illustrator.

Entering Text

Photoshop gives you two options when typing new text: filled or outline. Text is filled with the foreground color chosen in the foreground color selection box at the bottom of the toolbox. (To get the default black/white combination, click the Default Foreground and Background Colors icon in the lower-left corner, or press D on the keyboard.) Photoshop automatically places this text on a new layer as editable text, and this text can be given typesetting controls such as kerning, leading, and tracking. All of the typesetting controls will be explained in the following sections.

Alternatively, selecting the type mask tool from the type tool flyout creates the outline of the text without filling it in and places it on the currently active layer rather than on its own layer. This is handy for lifting the interior of the type selection (usually an image) to a new layer, where it can be treated independently, using any of Photoshop's commands. To lift the contents of the text marquee to a new layer, place the cursor inside the marquee and press CONTROL+click/right+click; then choose Layer Via Copy or press CMD/CTRL+J. The type mask tool can also be activated when the regular type tool has been chosen by selecting the Edit in Quick Mask Mode button in the toolbox (the right-hand button directly below the foreground and background color selection boxes). In the following illustration, the normal type tool is chosen, as well as Quick Mask mode, and the entered text is in the shape of a selection marquee filled with red—the default Quick Mask color.

Type tool

Edit in Quick Mask
Mode button

Working in Quick Mask text mode makes it possible to paint around the shapes
of letters. The marquee masks off the shapes of the letters. If you then use any of
Photoshop's brushes or fills, only the area outside the letters will be painted.
Here's what the effect looks like at its most primitive:

When you're ready to enter text, select the type tool (the uppercase *T*) in the
toolbox and place the cursor where you want the text to appear within the image.
Clicking in the image opens the Type Tool dialog, shown in Figure 9-1. Type the
text in the white area at the bottom of the dialog. Notice that you can observe
changes in type size by clicking the zoom in (+) and zoom out (−) buttons below the
large text-entry field. This helps you see exactly what you're doing, as you do it.

Professional Pointer

If you are creating text for the Web, you will have the most versatility with
aliased text, which you can drop onto any background without worrying
about halos. However, if you really want to have that smooth-edged anti-
aliased feel when you create, say, floating text—*très* popular on the Web—
simply create the text on a background of the same color as the target Web
page background, with the Anti-Alias option selected. The text will not
only look blended and smooth, but will also have that cool floating effect.

Using Typesetting
and Type Tool Dialog Controls

Here's a quick reference for what all the controls in the Type Tool dialog can do for
you. Photoshop 5 was the first version to approach real typesetting capabilities,

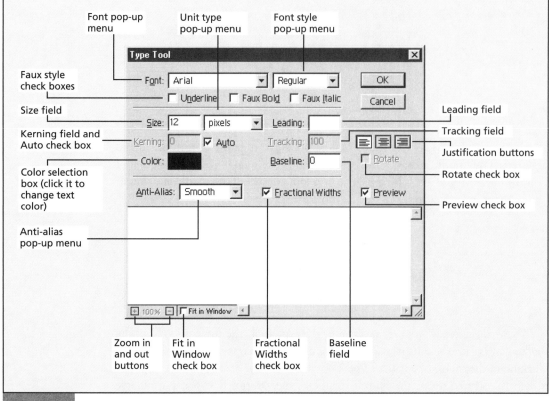

FIGURE 9-1 The Type Tool dialog

though ultimately all text is shown at the same bitmap resolution as the image on which you are currently working. It is also the first version that lets you edit and re-edit text, as long as you haven't rendered it or flattened it. Actually, I think I already said that, but it's worth repeating.

Font pop-up menu

The Font pop-up menu lets you choose from any font (bitmapped, PostScript, or TrueType) installed on your system. Photoshop uses the real font outline to shape your type, but actually records it as a bitmap.

Font style pop-up menu

The style menu, immediately to the right of the Font menu, lets you choose from whatever extra styles (such as Italics, Bold, Bold Italic) the typeface designer decided to include with the typeface chosen in the Font menu. A few typefaces have no styles or very limited styles.

Faux style check boxes

In version 5.5, Photoshop has made it possible to add styles to typefaces that aren't specifically designed to have them. All you have to do is select one or more of the three check boxes under the Font pop-up menus. Yes, that means you can have underlines, bold bold, and extra slanted italic for typefaces that already have built-in bold and italic styles.

Size field and unit type pop-up menu

The Size field lets you enter the type size in either points or pixels, depending on which of these two unit types you choose from the pop-up menu.

Kerning field and Auto check box

Kerning is a typesetter's term for setting the spacing between individual letters. If the Auto check box is selected, kerning is done according to the type designer's specifications for the font you are currently using. However, you may want to tuck the *o* a little more under the *T*. If so, place the cursor between the two letters you want to kern manually and deselect the Auto check box. Then enter a number in the Kerning field (it will turn white to indicate that it's ready for manual entry). A positive number will spread the letters farther apart; a negative number will pull them closer. If you like, you can individually kern the space between each letter in this manner.

Color selection box

The color shown in the color selection box is the color of your type on its layer. By default, the color shown in the swatch is the same as the current foreground color. I watch lots of folks cancel the Type Tool dialog and then change the foreground color and then go back to entering text. There's no need to go to all that trouble. Click the Color field, and your system's Color Picker dialog will open. Use the standard routine to pick a color (refer to Chapter 2 if you don't know how to use the color picker), and both the swatch and your text will immediately change to that color. You can use the same technique to change the color of a text layer at any time.

Leading field

Leading is the space between lines. More precisely, it's the distance between the baseline of two lines of type when measured with the current font size unit (points or pixels in Photoshop's case). The automatic default is 125 percent of the current type size. If you want to change that, you must first select the line(s) of type you want to respace and then enter a specific unit size in the Leading field.

In the illustration here, the leading for the top paragraph is 18 pixels; that for the bottom is 8 pixels.

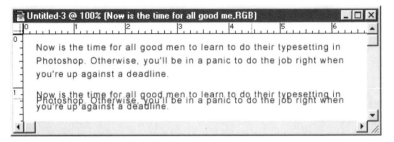

Tracking field

Tracking, like kerning, has to do with the spacing between letters. But kerning can only be applied to the space between two pairs of letters at a time. Tracking will place an equal distance between all the letters in as much of the text as you select.

To set tracking to anything other than the default, enter positive numbers to space letters farther apart or negative numbers to tighten them up. If you're familiar with typesetting terms, *ems* are used by Photoshop to measure the distance between letters. If precision isn't paramount, you can just eyeball the preview until you like what you see. Here are the same two lines of text. Tracking is set to −40 ems in the top paragraph and is normal in the bottom paragraph.

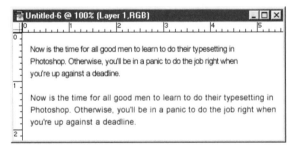

Baseline field

The Baseline setting changes the height of letters in respect to the normal location of the bottoms (the *baseline*) of letters that don't have hanging stems (such as *j*, *y*, and *g*). Raising and lowering type in respect to the baseline results in super-scripts and subscripts, like this:

$$B^2 \quad H_2O$$

To change the baseline, highlight the text you want to change and enter a number in the Baseline field of the Type Tool dialog. Positive numbers shift the baseline up, negative numbers shift it down. The units you are entering correspond to those currently chosen for the font being used—either points or pixels.

Justification buttons

The three buttons under the Cancel button are for left, centered, and right justification of multiple-line text. If you click the left alignment button, text will start at the position of the cursor and push out to the right. Click the center alignment button, and text will spread equidistantly from either side of the cursor position. Click the right alignment button, and text will push from the cursor to the left. This illustration uses the vertical line to show the position where the cursor was clicked for each of the three buttons:

<pre>
    |Left
 Cen|ter
Right|
</pre>

Rotate check box

The Rotate check box is grayed (out of commission) unless you have chosen either the vertical type tool or the vertical type mask tool. If this box isn't selected, letters are upright and placed directly under one another. If you want the whole line of type rotated 90 degrees, select the Rotate check box. Here's a line of type done each way:

Anti-Alias pop-up menu

Anti-aliasing, as you may have read by now, is the mixing of pixels with the background color in order to create the illusion of smoothed edges. Photoshop 5.5 allows you to choose from four levels of anti-aliasing: None, Crisp (very slight),

Strong, and Smooth. Here is a 300 percent blowup of 12-pixel black text at each of the four levels:

None
Crisp
Strong
Smooth

Fractional Widths check box

This new feature in Photoshop 5.5 is placed here especially to help those who must set small type for the Web. It's also a little confusing, because the check box means the opposite of what it says. If the check box is selected, fractional spacing is turned *off*. Font designers generally tweak the spacing of their letters to such an extent that they specify some fractions of a unit. This makes larger type look more polished, but there is the danger that very small type will run together and become more difficult to read. If you are setting itty-bitty type, select the check box before you apply the text. All the text on the layer will be spaced fractionally or not. It makes no difference whether you've preselected text.

Preview check box

This feature is so handy that I rarely turn it off. As long as the Preview check box is selected, you will see the placement of each letter on a layer the instant it is typed. If it is not selected, you'll be able to type extensive text much more quickly. Note that there is no check box for the type mask tool. If you discover you need to relocate the marquee text, choose the lasso and drag from inside the marquee.

Zoom in and out (+/−) buttons

If you'd like to make room to see more text inside the text entry box at one time (or want to see your text closer up to examine its edges), click the zoom buttons at the extreme lower left of the Type Tool dialog. The + button zooms in, and the − button zooms out.

Fit in Window check box

If you're having trouble seeing all your text in the text entry window, you can cure the problem in one click. Just select the Fit in Window check box. The text will automatically become smaller as the lines of text become longer. They will also continue to get smaller as you enter too many lines to fit vertically.

Editing Text

Any time you think about rendering text or merging text layers, be sure to stop and carefully proofread your copy. It will be your last chance to edit it (unless you can clone over it with the rubber stamp and reenter it). As long as you leave text on its own layer, you can go back and make any changes you like.

To reedit text, double-click the name bar for the text you want to change. The Type Tool dialog will reopen. You can change any of the settings to change the way the type looks. If you want to edit the words, highlight any words you want to replace and type over them. If you want to insert words, place the cursor where the new words will be tucked in, and start typing. When you've finished making changes, click OK.

Importing 3D Text

You may want to use a true 3D model of text in your composition. If that is the case, you will have to compose and model the text in a third-party 3D program or use a third-party filter.

If you already use a 3D modeling program, you will have the greatest flexibility in determining how your 3D text will look. Use the program to create the model of the text, and then export the file to a Photoshop-compatible, bitmapped, still-image format.

You don't need a professional 3D modeling program to get 3D text, however. There are a couple of fairly inexpensive Photoshop-compatible plug-in programs that will do the job. My favorite is Xaos Tool's TypeCaster, which is a bargain if you buy it as part of their Total Xaos package. If you have trouble finding Xaos Tools after this book comes out, search the Web for Onflow Corporation. At the time of this writing, they had just taken over Xaos Tools. Anyway, TypeCaster will let you render any Type 1 PostScript or TrueType font with textures, bump maps, and multiple lights. You can scale, rotate, and manipulate 3D text, and add depth by creating bevels and extrusions. You can see text from TypeCaster here:

Another choice is Vertigo Software's 3D HotTEXT 1.5.

There are also several much lower cost 3D programs that will create 3D text, sometimes even place it on a curve, and let you rotate it before you export it.

Open the file in Photoshop while the file you want to place the type in is also open. Drag the image from the window of the 3D image into your target composition's window. It will automatically become a layer. Select the text from its background, invert the selection, and then delete the contents of the inverted selection. Your 3D text is now on a transparent layer. Use the transform commands to scale, proportion, rotate, and move the text into the desired place, and then double-click inside the transform marquee to apply the transformation. Your end result might look something like this:

Tweaking the Text

After you have the text the way you want it, how can you fine-tune it to have exactly the appearance you seek? This is where you can draw on your other Photoshop skills. Probably the most important tool you will use is the move tool for positioning the text at the exact spot where you want it to be in the image composition. To call it up, click it in the toolbox, press V, or press CMD/CTRL while working with any other tool.

You can also "nudge" text into more precise positioning by using the arrow keys. To adjust the location of text in single-pixel increments, select the text layer to be moved, select the move tool, and use the arrow keys. Each time you press one of the arrow keys, the layer will be moved in that direction by one pixel.

If you want to move a single letter, don't make a rectangular selection unless you're sure there are no overlapping parts of letters. You can also use the arrow-key method to move part of a word.

Another way you can position a text layer is by using the transform functions to scale, stretch, rotate, or skew the text. If you want to perform distort and perspective transformations, you first have to render the text. You can choose either Edit > Free Transform or Edit > Transform, and then choose a specific transformation type. You can also go straight to Free Transform by activating the layer you want to transform and pressing CMD/CTRL+T.

In addition, using Edit > Transform > Numeric lets you perform several transformations at once, but with much more precision than with Free Transform. Transform Numeric presents you with a dialog that lets you enter exact measurements for each type of transformation, and then executes them all at once when you click OK. Any transformation properties that have been left at zero will remain unaffected for that type of transformation, so it's very easy to perform only one or two types of transformations at once, if that's all that's required.

A variety of text transformations are shown in Figure 9-2.

Cross-Reference: For more on transformations, see Chapter 5.

Text Effects You Can Create After Rasterizing

It's only been since version 5 of Photoshop that text was entered onto an editable layer with typesetting controls. It's a wonderful feature, but there are still times

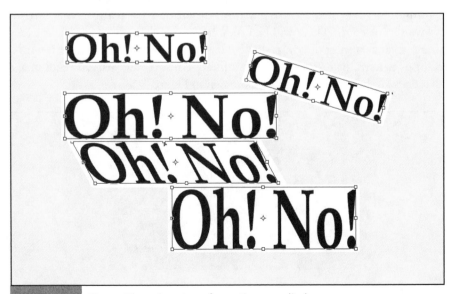

FIGURE 9-2 Text with various transformations applied

when it's worthwhile to rasterize your text (turn it into a bitmap) so that you can treat it with the full panoply of Photoshop commands.

The next sections list some simple procedures you can use to spice up any text you rasterize. You'll find you can use portions of these procedures or combine different formulas to create your own statement.

Professional Pointer

Once you've merged a text layer with an image layer, flattened the image, or rendered a text layer, Photoshop thinks of your text as an image, and so should you. The correct text treatment is very important in completing your whole graphic message. Choose effects and fonts that give emotional impact to the words. Don't be afraid to mix and match filters. Try to find substitutes and other ways to do things—one of my favorites is to feather a selection of text instead of anti-aliasing. And above all, observe what's out there, and then find the things *you* like to do. Just make sure that in the course of all this experimentation, your text is as readable as you need it to be.

Customized Drop Shadow Effects

Drop shadows are so effective at making text seem to leap from the page and at helping to separate text from its background that the effect has almost become a cliché. Photoshop now lets you create drop shadows by using the Layer > Effects commands (for more information, download "Using Layers" from www.osborne.com). There will be times, however, when you want to do tricky things such as setting the drop shadow text in another font, or filling it with a color or pattern, or texturing it with a filter. This exercise will create an image that does all three of these things, as shown in Figure 9-3.

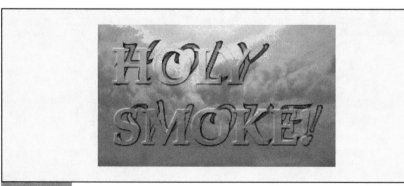

FIGURE 9-3   A drop shadow set in a different font from the main text

1. Create your text on a background image with the type mask tool, and lift the text to its own layer (CMD/CTRL+J). Such layers will automatically have a transparent background (represented as a checkerboard pattern in Photoshop).

2. In the Layers palette, click the eye icon for the background layer. The background layer will be hidden, so that you can easily see your new text layer, as shown here. (We'll turn the background layer back on later.)

3. Create another new layer (click the New Layer icon in the Layers palette), and with the new layer selected, click with the type tool to set a new line of type. When the Type Tool dialog opens, choose a different font at approximately the same font size.

4. Enter the text you entered in step 1 and click OK. Its marquee will appear on the new layer. This is going to be your shadow. If you want its edges to be a little blurred, choose Select > Feather and enter a radius of softness.

5. While the text marquee is still active and the new layer is still chosen, choose Edit > Fill. In the Fill dialog, choose Black from the Use menu. The new marquee text will turn black.

6. It's unlikely that the new text will line up precisely with the original. Select the move tool and drag the contents of the layer until you get the two lines of type to line up at their base as close as possible.

7. Choose Edit > Transform > Skew to stretch and slant your shadow text until it takes the approximate shape you want.

8. You may still have to move some letters individually. To do so, select them with the lasso tool and move them with the move tool.

9. Try out a special effect filter for your text by choosing one from any of the submenus on the Filter menu. If you have third-party filters installed, you can use them as well.

Cross-Reference: For much more on using filters, see Chapters 10 and 11. Also, see the Filter Gallery (part of the second color insert of this book) for a visual catalog showing each of Photoshop's filters applied to the same image.

10. Click the eye icon to turn on the background layer. Your original text will probably disappear because it blends into the background.

11. One thing you could do to make the original text stand out is to press CMD/CTRL+click its thumbnail in the Layers palette. This will automatically place a marquee selection around the text. Create a new layer by clicking the Create New Layer button at the bottom of the Layers palette. Choose a contrasting foreground color, and then choose Edit > Stroke. In the Stroke dialog, enter a stroke width that is wide enough to be visible given the size of your text and the resolution of your image, and then click OK. Your text will be outlined in a contrasting color.

12. A more subtle technique might involve the use of layer effects, which can be applied to either rendered or outline (unrendered) text. In Figure 9-3, I used the Bevel and Emboss effect to make the text seem as if it were punched out of the sky. To experiment with this, choose Layer > Effects > Bevel and Emboss. When the Effects dialog opens, as shown in Figure 9-4, you can experiment with any of the many settings in the dialog. You can add even more effects on top of that effect by choosing them from the effects pop-up menu at the top of the dialog.

Casting Shadows with Text

One type of shadow you can't create with layer effects is a perspective shadow that looks as though it were cast from a light positioned high overhead or behind

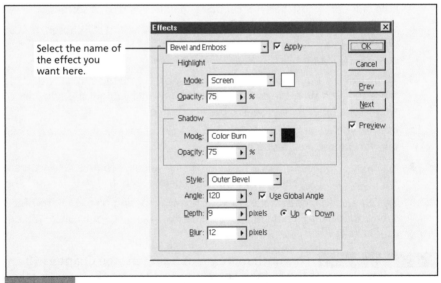

FIGURE 9-4   The Effects dialog for Bevel and Emboss

the text. However, thanks to Photoshop's transformation tools, it's easy to create these effects. Here's what we're aiming for:

As you can see, this type of shadow can add considerable drama and focus to your text. As you're about to see, it isn't all that difficult to do, either.

1. Enter the text you want to cast the shadow from. If you like, add a layer effect to it. (I used the Bevel and Emboss effect to round and highlight the edges of the original text in the example.)

2. Drag the new text layer to the New Layer button at the bottom of the Layers palette, or choose Duplicate Layer from the Layers palette menu. Another copy of your text layer will appear in the Layers palette. Select the new layer.

3. Select the move tool and drag the new layer's image slightly away from the original layer so that you can see it.

4. Color the text in the new layer black. Double-click the new layer's name bar to open the Type Tool dialog. Now click in the color selection box, and pick black as the new color.

5. Now you want to turn the new text upside down. Choose Edit > Transform > Flip Vertical. Use the move tool to position the upside-down black layer so that the baselines of the two layers meet.

6. Now stretch and skew the shadow layer. Press CMD/CTRL+T to execute the Free Transform command. Press CMD/CTRL again while you drag the lower center handle to simultaneously stretch and skew. (At this point, you may once again need to use the move tool to reposition the shadow layer so the baselines of the two layers meet.)

7. With the shadow layer still selected, drag the Layers palette's Opacity slider to around 75%.

8. Now you want to blur the shadow more and more as it moves away from the letters that cast it. CMD/CTRL+click the shadow layer's thumbnail to put a selection marquee around the text on that layer. In the toolbox, click the Edit in Quick Mask Mode button. Press D so that your foreground color is black and

your background color is white. Select the linear gradient tool and drag from immediately under the shadow letters to just above them, as shown here:

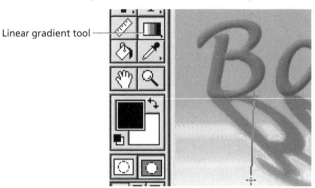

Linear gradient tool

A rubylith (reddish) gradient will fade to white across the width of the shadow text.

9. Press Q to edit in standard mode. You will see a selection marquee around what, in Quick Mask mode, had been the darkest part of the gradient. You have created a temporary gradient mask that will cause the blur filter to have less effect as the mask becomes darker (more opaque).

10. Choose Filter > Blur > Gaussian Blur. A message box will appear asking if you want to render the layer. Click OK. When the Gaussian Blur dialog appears, make sure the Preview check box is selected, and drag the Radius slider until you see the degree of blurring you desire in the shadow. Click OK.

And there you have it.

Filling Text with a Pattern, Texture, or Image

A great way to get a truly original effect is to have your text filled with a pattern or texture. Here is a simple procedure for filling your text.

1. Click the New Layer button to create an empty layer. (The reason for creating an empty layer is to throw it away later without disturbing anything else in the composition.)

2. Fill the layer with any texture pattern you like. To do this, open a file that contains an area you want to define as a pattern (you can define a pattern from just about anything—a line drawing, a texture file, or even a photograph). Select the rectangular marquee tool and drag its cursor to select a

rectangular area that will define the pattern. Choose Edit > Define Pattern. (This will be your default pattern until you close the program or define another pattern.) Now go back to your empty layer, choose Edit > Fill, and then choose Pattern from the Use pop-up menu.

3. You could lift type from the pattern by entering it with the type mask tool, but you wouldn't be able to render the type mask, which you'll need to do before you use it to lift the pattern or photo. So select the type tool and click in the image. Enter your text and make any desired overall transformations. (If you've been doing the preceding exercises, you should know how to do that.) Of course, the type will be created on its own layer. What you should see on your screen is the text over a pattern and two layers; one for text and the other for the pattern, like this:

Tip: If you own Kai's Power Tools, you'll find a wealth of easily accessed textures in the Texture Explorer. Alternatively, this layer could be a photograph. If you use a photo, rather than filling with a pattern, you will not need to use the Edit > Fill command; just start with a photo and create a new layer from it.

4. From now on, you are going to work with rendered text so that you can use other filters and some Photoshop commands that don't work on editable type. Choose Layer > Type > Render Layer. The T icon in the layer's name bar will disappear, and text will no longer be editable.

5. Now we're going to impose a special effect. Select each letter separately and apply the Pinch filter. (Decide on the effect you're going for, depending on the message. In this example, I alternated pinching in and pinching out for every other letter.) To do that, choose Filter > Distort > Pinch. When the Pinch dialog opens, enter **50** in the Amount field and click OK. Then select the next letter and repeat the Pinch command, only this time enter **–50** in the Amount field. As with all other Photoshop filters, there's lots of room for experimentation. Anyway, keep it up until you've distorted every other letter.

6. When you get the shape you want for the text, CMD/CTRL+click the text layer's thumbnail in the Layers palette. This will cause the text to be selected. You now have two options:

   • Select the pattern layer in the Layers palette and then press CMD/CTRL+J to lift the pattern to a new layer. Now delete the original text layer, so the lifted pattern shows up.

   • Use your favorite Photoshop or third-party texturing or artistic filter to fill the selection with a different texture pattern that contrasts with that used for the background.

7. Because the background is so busy, the text won't be easy to read unless it's raised from it. Let's just impose a quick drop shadow with the layer effects. Choose Layer > Effects > Drop Shadow. The Effects dialog appears with Drop Shadow chosen as the type. Adjust your settings to those shown in the following illustration. As long as the Preview check box is selected, you can see the effect you're getting. Take the time to experiment with the settings—you'll learn a lot in a short space of time.

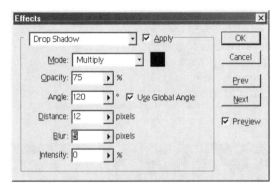

8. You can use the Effects dialog to impose more than one effect on the layer. From the pop-up menu that now reads Drop Shadow, choose Bevel and Emboss. For the moment, accept the default settings and select the Apply check box; then click OK. Your patterned and distorted type will now have a raised effect.

9. That's probably enough effects to be pushing the boundaries of good taste. For the purposes of learning, however, we'll push them just a bit further. Next, set the Layers palette to Difference mode, and with the selection still active (or repeated), choose Select > Modify > Expand, and expand the selection by two pixels. Choose Edit > Stroke. When the Stroke dialog opens, click the Center radio button and enter a stroke radius of **2** pixels. Thanks to the Difference mode, this gives an eerie outline effect around the text, which adds quite a bit of drama without detracting from the text. Here's how the text in this example looks now:

Professional Pointer

There are millions of simple filter tricks to enhance your text effects. Try applying a filter a couple of times; or, for an interesting, original effect, try putting some filters together that ordinarily aren't used together.

Transparent Text

Sometimes a more subtle effect is desired—perhaps the goal is simply the appearance of a word or phrase over an important image, as shown in the following illustration. To do this, use the type mask tool to enter your text over the layer that contains your image. Use the lasso to position the type marquee exactly where you want the type to appear, and then press CMD/CTRL+J to copy the contents of the marquee to a new layer. To make the text show up, apply a layer effect to the new layer. Experiment with the effects and choose one (or more) that makes your text readable and achieves your design goals.

Floating Text

To create the appearance of text hovering above a geometrical plane, only the transform function and a little manipulation of the move tool are needed.

1. After creating the ideal text for your message, duplicate its layer by dragging its thumbnail to the New Layer button in the Layers palette.

2. Do this for each of the two text layers: choose Layer > Type > Render Layer. This is necessary because you want to apply a perspective transformation, which can't be applied to text.

3. Now you want to transform the two layers so that the text seems to disappear toward the horizon. You want the layers to have exactly the same transformation applied, so click the link icon in the Layers palette to link them.

4. Now choose Edit > Transform > Perspective and stretch the text (this will affect the text in both layers, since the layers are now linked) to look like this:

5. Now you want to make one layer the cast shadow of the other. Unlink the two layers (click the link icon in the Layers palette).

6. Select the move tool and drag the text to move one of the layers to a spot where it appears to be the cast shadow of the other.

7. CMD/CTRL+click the thumbnail of the shadow layer to select the text. Press D to select the default colors and X to switch foreground and background. Select the linear gradient tool and drag a vertical line from just above the letter selection marquee to just below it. Your letters should now be filled with a dark gray to light gray gradient, so that the shadow looks as though it fades into the distance.

8. Now you should blur the shadow slightly. Choose Filter > Blur > Gaussian Blur. The Gaussian Blur dialog opens. Move the Radius slider until you see a slight blur in the shadow letters, and click OK.

9. To make the perspective more convincing, make the tops of the original text lighter in color. Select the top layer of text. Select the Preserve Transparency check box in the Layers palette. Select a lighter color from the picker and dust the letters with a large airbrush at about 60% pressure.

10. The result is text that appears to float as it stretches back into the horizon, as shown here:

Professional Pointer

To make the perspective look more authentic, the top text that floats above the shadow should be transformed to a tighter perspective so that it leads to the same horizon line as the shadow. To do this, make a new layer, select the line tool, and draw along vertical lines of the shadow type to where they cross. This establishes a horizon vanishing point. Draw these same lines from the bottom of the top type to the same vanishing point. Transform the top type to conform to this perspective.

Neon Text

You can even make text look as though it glows in the dark, kind of like a neon sign.

1. Type the text, using a bright foreground color.

2. Select the text (CMD/CTRL+click the text layer thumbnail in the Layers palette) and invert the selection CMD/CTRL+SHIFT+I (or choose Select > Inverse).

3. Choose Select > Feather and set the radius to about 4 pixels. (This may vary depending on the font size and image resolution you have chosen.)

4. Choose Layer > Type > Render Layer to render the text layer.

5. Fill with the foreground color (OPT/ALT+BACKSPACE), which should be black. (If the foreground color isn't black, first make it so by changing the foreground and background colors in the toolbox to the default [press the D key].) You should end up with text that looks something like this:

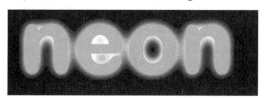

Movers and Shakers

To create the impression of speedily moving text, take these steps:

1. Type the text in italics. The direction of "movement" will be left to right, so use the move tool to move the text toward the right side of the canvas.

2. Choose Layer > Type > Render Layer to render the text layer.

3. The first filter to apply is Wind. Choose Filter > Stylize > Wind. When the Wind dialog appears, click the Wind radio button and the From the Right radio button.

4. Next, choose Filter > Blur > Motion Blur. When the Motion Blur dialog appears, set the angle of motion to **0** and the distance for the blur to travel to **10**; then click OK.

5. Finally, to give that extra bit of motion appearance, choose Filter > Distort > Shear and create what appears to be a sideways *u* by dragging the handles in the grid. When the Shear dialog appears, change the settings to look like this:

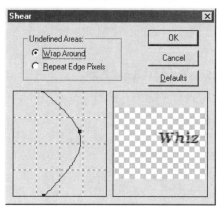

When you've finished, you'll have text that looks like it's going to fly right off the page. See?

Action!

To give just a little movement to your text, try the following steps:

1. On a white background, type your text in any color, and then choose Layer > Type > Render Layer.

2. Make sure the text layer is selected, and then select the Preserve Transparency check box.

3. Double-click the linear gradient tool. In the Linear Gradient Options palette, click the Edit button. The Gradient Editor dialog will appear. From the scrolling list, choose the Orange, Yellow, Orange gradient. Make sure you've chosen the linear gradient tool, and drag a line vertically through your active text layer.

4. Use the Shear filter (Filter > Distort > Shear) or the Edit > Transform > Skew command to slant the text to give it the feel of motion.

5. Use layer effects to create a drop shadow. It might look something like this:

Repeating Text Patterns

Here's a quick and dirty way to make repeating text:

1. Type the text you want to repeat, render the layer, and make a rectangular selection around it.

2. Choose Edit > Define Pattern.

3. Delete the original text layer.

4. Create a new, empty layer.

5. Choose Edit > Fill and specify Pattern in the pop-up menu.

6. For the example shown here, I also applied a perspective transformation (Edit > Transform > Perspective) to make it a little more interesting. Please note that transforming anti-aliased text sometimes gives a strange, undesirable smudge effect.

Professional Skills Summary

This chapter has given you all the references you need for entering and controlling the appearance of editable text. In addition, you've learned how layer effects can benefit the appearance of text and all about how you can further customize the look of text by first turning it into a bitmap—that is, by rendering it.

From here, we move on to Part III of this book, "Special Effects." The next chapter is all about effects that look as though they happened at the time the picture was shot or processed.

Part III

Special Effects

Photographic Effects

Even the best photographers have been rudely surprised at what came out of the lab when the film was processed. Often, these "surprises" are not because of anything that occurred in the darkroom, but are due to the technological process of making the photograph itself. We get lens flares when we don't want them and can't get the sun to produce them when we do want them. The color temperature of the prevalent light turns out to be different from what we expected. (Color temperature meters help, but we don't all own them.) Speaking of color temperature, have you ever absentmindedly shot a roll of "daylight" film indoors, under tungsten light?

Fixing unexpected problems that occur in the camera is usually pretty easy for Photoshop. Yet it isn't the only reason to use Photoshop's lens and film effects. On the other hand, sometimes you want to intentionally introduce problems to give the image the feeling that it was shot in difficult, unusual, or especially attractive circumstances. For instance, excessive "film grain" and a loss of color saturation could give a photo of a disco scene a documentary feel.

Using Photoshop to Create a Lens Flare

Lens flare is something photographers generally try to avoid. They buy lens hoods or have assistants shade the lens so that the glare doesn't obliterate the detail in the picture. Sometimes, however, an apparent defect in the photo indicates a condition that existed at the time of the shooting that sets a mood or enhances a message. One such defect is lens flare—the phenomenon that occurs when a bright light source (such as the sun or a police officer's flashlight) shines directly into the lens.

Imagine that you're creating an ad for Orange Blossom Diamond Rings and have a beautiful moody back-lit close-up of a couple just after he placed his ring on her finger. Flares from the sun (shot through crinkled cellophane) complement the subject. But you want to add a star flare to draw attention to the diamond. Also, having been shot at sunrise on Chicago's lakefront, the bit of dawn blue that crept into the faces and clothes of the models needs to be warmed to the occasion.

Photoshop's tools make introducing a realistic-looking lens flare quite simple. You can get the effect you want with one of Photoshop's built-in filters and one custom brush. Here's how to bring this effect into play:

1. Download the file DIAMRING.JPG from the Osborne site (or load one of your own images).

2. Choose Filter > Render > Lens Flare. The Lens Flare dialog appears. Move the crosshair to the spot where you want the bright light (the sun, in this case) to appear. The wonderful thing about introducing an effect rather than shooting with real lens flare is that you can place it wherever it best strengthens the composition, as you can see here:

Artistic Filters

COLORED PENCIL

CUTOUT

DRY BRUSH

FILM GRAIN

FRESCO

NEON GLOW

PAINT DAUB

PALETTE KNIFE

PLASTIC WRAP

This gallery contains samples showing each of Photoshop's filters applied to an image of a pink flower. All filters were run with the default colors, so filters that make use of the foreground and background colors used black as the foreground color and white as the background color. Note that some filters do not return to their original settings, but to the last-used settings. Therefore, the settings used here may not be the defaults.

POSTER EDGES

ROUGH PASTELS

SMUDGE STICK

SPONGE

UNDERPAINTING

WATERCOLOR

Blur Filters

BLUR

BLUR MORE

GAUSSIAN BLUR

MOTION BLUR

RADIAL BLUR

SMART BLUR

Brush Strokes Filters

ACCENTED EDGES

ANGLED STROKES

CROSSHATCH

DARK STROKES

INK OUTLINES

SPATTER

SPRAYED STROKES

SUMI-E

Distort Filters

DIFFUSE GLOW

DISPLACE

GLASS 1

GLASS 2

GLASS 3

OCEAN RIPPLE

PINCH 1

PINCH 2

POLAR 1

POLAR 2

RIPPLE

SHEAR

SPHERIZE 1

SPHERIZE 2

TWIRL

WAVE 1

WAVE 2

WAVE 3

ZIG ZAG 1

ZIG ZAG 2

ZIG ZAG 3

Noise Filters

ADD NOISE

DESPECKLE

DUST & SCRATCHES

MEDIAN

Pixelate Filters

COLOR HALFTONE

CRYSTALLIZE

FACET

FRAGMENT

MEZZOTINT 1

MEZZOTINT 2

MEZZOTINT 3

MOSAIC

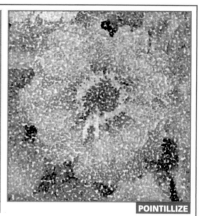

POINTILLIZE

Render Filters

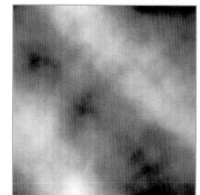

3D TRANSFORM 1

3D TRANSFORM 2

3D TRANSFORM 3

CLOUDS

DIFFERENCE CLOUDS

LENS FLARE 1

LENS FLARE 2

LENS FLARE 3

LIGHTING EFFECTS

Sharpen Filters

SHARPEN

SHARPEN EDGES

SHARPEN MORE

UNSHARP MASK

Sketch Filters

BAS RELIEF

CHALK & CHARCOAL

CHARCOAL

CHROME

CONTÉ CRAYON

GRAPHIC PEN

HALFTONE PATTERN 1

HALFTONE PATTERN 2

HALFTONE PATTERN 3

NOTE PAPER

PHOTOCOPY

PLASTER

RETICULATION

STAMP

TORN EDGES

WATER PAPER

Stylize Filters

DIFFUSE

EMBOSS

EXTRUDE 1

EXTRUDE 2

FIND EDGES

GLOWING EDGES

SOLARIZE

TILES

TRACE CONTOUR

WIND

Texture Filters

CRAQUELURE

GRAIN 1

GRAIN 2

GRAIN 3

GRAIN 4

GRAIN 5

GRAIN 6

GRAIN 7

GRAIN 8

GRAIN 9

GRAIN 10

MOSAIC TILES

PATCHWORK

STAINED GLASS

TEXTURIZER

Blend Modes

This gallery contains samples showing each of Photoshop's blend modes applied to the pink flower image. The original color image was copied to a new layer and made into a textured, black-and-white image with the Chalk & Charcoal filter. Then, the Color blend mode was used to paint a section of the layer with each of the RGB primary colors. The lower-left portion of the image was left as monochrome (that means one color, not necessarily grayscale).

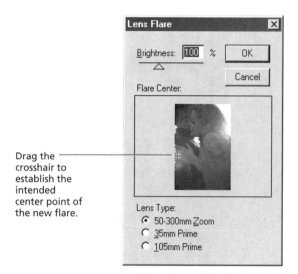

Drag the crosshair to establish the intended center point of the new flare.

3. Experiment with the Lens Type radio buttons to see how many lens flare effects you can achieve with this one filter. I chose the 50-300 Zoom button.

4. Adjust the brightness slider until you like the brightness of the preview. When you've made your decision, click OK.

5. Work on a selection of duplicate background layers containing a variety of flare opacities, choose the layer that best allows the shape of the ring to "read through" the flare, and then flatten the image.

6. If you're using the downloaded sample image, you can make the day seem a bit warmer by choosing Image > Adjust > Color Balance and experimenting with the sliders shown here:

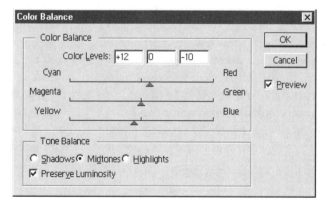

You can see the final results of the image manipulation in Figure 10-1.

FIGURE 10-1 Final image of engaged couple shows flare added to diamond ring

Creating a Fish-Eye Effect with Photoshop's Tools

When the fish-eye lens was first introduced, every 35mm pro with the bucks just had to have one. Soon every imaginable subject, from a dizzying view atop a Golden Gate Bridge tower down to portraits, was being shoehorned into this 180-degree view of the world, and as a fad it soon wore itself out. But when the message is right, the fish-eye lens effect still tells a story like no other—whether you want to texture-wrap the Taj Mahal onto a soccer ball, or make a city filled with skyscrapers look like a porcupine's spine.

You can create the fish-eye lens effect you want with one of Photoshop 5.5's built-in filters and a marquee tool. Here's how to carry out this effect:

1. Download the SHIP_SEA.JPG file from the Osborne site, or use one of your own files. Open the file you'll use in Photoshop.

2. Drag a circle selection around the area of the picture you want to appear on your world, using the elliptical marquee tool while holding down the SHIFT key.

3. Choose Filter > Distort > Spherize. Set Amount to 100% and Mode to Normal, and click OK, as shown here:

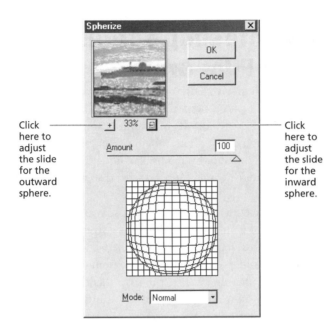

Click here to adjust the slide for the outward sphere.

Click here to adjust the slide for the inward sphere.

4. With your circle selection still active, press CMD/SHIFT+I or choose Select > Inverse. Set the background color to white (or your choice of color) and press DELETE. Save your work.

5. To achieve an inward sphere, retrace all of the above steps, but change Amount to –100%. Now you've got both an outward and an inward sphere, as you can see here:

Inward sphere   Outward sphere

Another method to achieve a similar result would be to use 3D Transform. Choose Filter > Render > 3D Transform.

Cross-Reference: 3D Transform is treated in more detail in Chapter 8.

Using Photoshop's Tools to Match Film Grain

Sometimes the problem with a digital image, like a digital audio recording, is that it's too perfect. It's been despeckled, smoothed, sharpened, and retouched until it loses its original grittiness. If you want to capture the feeling that the picture is dated, or that it is an art photo (obvious film grain was once a hot trend in photo illustration), or one shot by a journalist under fire, you will probably want to intentionally introduce grain. This is one of the easiest and most variable effects in Photoshop.

Imagine that you have a stock photo. Because you want to use the photo in a book on the history of your family to illustrate a story about relatives in the old country, you want this very well photographed and immaculately processed picture to look even older—and definitely homemade.

Real film grain is uneven, because the silver halide particles in the negative clump together at the points of greatest exposure and scatter in the darker areas, so you don't want to introduce noise evenly. Almost any kind of random noise will produce a more authentic look. If you use Photoshop's built-in Add Noise filter, set Gaussian distribution in the dialog to achieve greater unevenness. Choose the level of noise that your own taste dictates. Here are the individual steps required to create film grain:

1. Load the photo file you want to work on. If you need a guinea pig, download CORNWALL.JPG from the Osborne site.

2. If the photo is to be reproduced on a spot-color or four-color page, it also makes sense to add a little color toning, which would further contribute to the aged look. Sepia toning was often used in photographs around the turn of the 20th century; however, in the 1940s and 1950s machine-processed snapshots tended to have an almost bluish tint. Let's go with sepia. Choose Image > Mode > Grayscale. You will see a message box asking if you want to discard color information. Click OK.

3. Choose Image > Mode > Duotone. When the Duotone Options dialog appears, choose Monotone from the Type menu and click the right-hand Ink 1 box, as shown here:

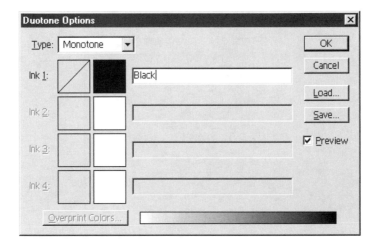

4. This will bring up the Color Picker dialog. Move the slider all the way to the red at the top, and click the selection circle in the colored square about two-thirds down and all the way to the right, as shown here. Then click OK. Click OK in the Duotone Options dialog.

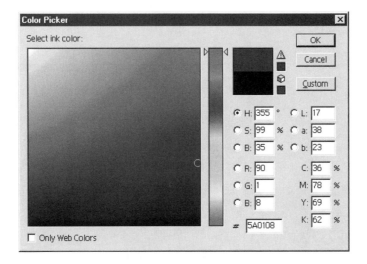

You now have a sepia monotone photo.

5. Next, choose Filter > Noise > Add Noise, and the Add Noise dialog opens. Set the slider to 50, select Gaussian and Monochromatic, and click OK, as shown here:

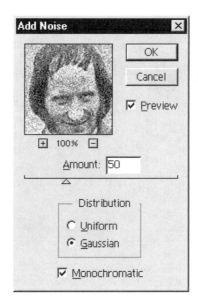

The photo is now a noisy sepia tone, as you can see in Figure 10-2.

FIGURE 10-2 Finished sepia-toned photograph with "film grain" added

Using Photoshop Tools to Control Focus by Blurring the Background

One of the oldest tricks in the traditional photographer's kit is controlling *depth of field*. This refers to the range in a photograph between the nearest point and the farthest point at which objects remain in focus. In most cases, depth of field is controlled by the lens aperture *f*-stop. You can direct the viewer's attention by keeping the lens focused on the subject and letting everything closer to or farther away from the subject go out of focus. This is best done by employing a "long" (100+ mm) lens in combination with a large *f*-stop aperture (which is a small *f*-stop number, such as f:3.5). (This is a problem when shooting with digital cameras that cost under $5,000 because their 35mm-equivalent focal lengths are actually much shorter. Therefore, they have "too much" depth of field.) You can use Photoshop to simulate this effect in images where there's just too much "stuff" surrounding the subject you want the viewer to concentrate on. The best part is, with Photoshop, even items on the same distance plane as the subject can be made to appear out of focus.

Here's the situation I faced when I created the illustration for this exercise: I was shooting a travel brochure story on the Middle East and had been assigned a photograph of a chef serving an Israeli breakfast by the swimming pool of a four-star hotel in Tel Aviv. It was shot outdoors in the bright sun with a wide-angle lens—stopped way down. Nearly everything—foreground and background—is in focus. In other words, there's no way to throw the background out of focus, but the background is way too busy.

First, you'll use Photoshop's selection tools to isolate the subject(s) from the background. Then you use a blur filter. The exact effect you will get depends on the particular blur filter you use. The two most popular are Gaussian Blur and Motion Blur.

Because you're going to use Photoshop to fuzz out the background, you don't need to blur the foreground in the process. This foreground helps to set a relaxed and conversational tone for the photo that's in keeping with its context in an interview. Besides, in this case that's where all the yummy food is.

In this exercise, you'll select the chef and the other objects in the foreground of the sample image and copy them to a new layer. This will let you erase the edges of the selection with a brush and see the old background through the transparent area of the new layer. Then you'll run a blur filter on the original layer. Finally, you'll use an adjustment layer to color correct the photo.

1. Load your image or download TELACHEF.JPG from the Osborne site.
2. With the polygon lasso tool, select as much of the background as you can without coming too close to the edges.

3. When you've finished making the selection, place the cursor inside the selection. CONTROL+click/right-click to bring up the context menu, and choose Invert.

4. Once more, place the cursor inside the selection, and CONTROL+click/right-click, and then choose Layer Via Copy from the context menu.

Your main subjects are now seen on a new layer in the Layers palette (if it isn't showing, choose Window > Show Layers).

5. In the Layers palette, with the background layer selected, choose New Layer from the flyout. Select the new layer, press OPT/ALT, and then press DELETE/BACKSPACE to fill the new layer with the foreground color. (An outrageous color such as bright pink makes it easier to see what you're going to do next.) In our example, the image now looks like this:

6. Select the eraser tool from the toolbox. Carefully brush away the unwanted edges of the newly created layer. Select the zoom tool and zoom in tight to retouch the edges so you can see exactly what you're doing, keeping two fingers on the shortcut keys for the Undo command (CMD/CTRL+Z) in case you suddenly make an erratic stroke.

Tip: Instead of the freehand action of the eraser tool, you may prefer another selection tool, such as the polygon lasso or the elliptical marquee, when following around a fairly geometric shape.

7. Make your selection and press DELETE/BACKSPACE to make the selection transparent. If you're satisfied with the way the edge looks, delete the middle layer (the one with the plain background).

What you see now looks as though the original photo hasn't been touched.

8. Select the bottom (background) layer and choose Filter > Blur > Gaussian Blur. In the Gaussian Blur dialog, set Radius to 5 pixels, as shown here, or you can experiment with more or less blur until you get the look you like. Click OK.

The picture is now much improved, but there's a halo at the edges of the selection where the underlying image was blurred.

9. Select the burn tool. (Or if you prefer, use the rubber stamp tool to pull cloned areas over from just outside the halo.) Choose a brush that's fairly large from the Brushes palette, and with the background layer selected, darken the halo to make it go away (not that a great chef doesn't deserve a halo).

10. Now flatten the layers. To avoid a cutout look and help the foreground settle into its new blurred background, select the zoom tool and come in close. Select the rubber stamp tool, and soften any harsh edges where the two images meet.

    Now, warm up the image by correcting the color balance to remove some of the blue.

11. From the menu bar, choose Image > Adjust > Color Balance. In the Color Balance dialog, move the Yellow-to-Blue slider slightly toward Yellow. You will see an immediate preview in your image window (assuming Preview and Previous Luminosity are selected). When you are pleased with the results, click OK and save.

You can see the final result in Figure 10-3.

Using Photoshop to Sharpen the Focus of Your Images

Even the best photographers have varying ability to hold the camera steady or to see the image in the viewfinder clearly. As a result, you are often presented with images of less-than-ideal sharpness. True sharpness means better definition of detail in the image. There's nothing Photoshop or any other image-editing program can do to create information from an image where there was none. You can, however, create the impression of having more definition by heightening the contrast between adjacent pixels, thus sharpening the edges of those pixels.

FIGURE 10-3   Photograph of the Tel Aviv chef with the background blurred

Another process that happens frequently in Photoshop also causes loss of sharpness: resampling. Any time you make the image larger or smaller—and any time you make a transformation (such as rotation), the program has to arbitrarily decide which pixels stay and which go. In the process, some detail inevitably gets smudged.

The other common cause of image softness is low-cost digital cameras. A number of factors contribute—snapshot-camera–quality optics, low capture resolution, and heavy image compression. Sharpening filters can help all of these problems. Photoshop has several of them—as well as a sharpening brush. There are also sharpness enhancements in several third-party filter sets.

Sharpening Filters

Sharpening filters come in two main categories: pixel sharpening and unsharp masking. There is a way you can usually tell them apart: "Unsharp masking" is often incorporated or implied in the name of the filter. "Pixel-sharpening" filters simply increase the contrast between adjacent pixels of different colors. The chief difference between the effect of the sharpening filters of various manufacturers is the degree of contrast imposed by the specific filter and the amount the color has to change before the program notices the difference and increases the contrast. Photoshop's own Sharpen Edges filter is one such filter, increasing contrast only when there is a plainly visible difference between the colors of pixels in one area and those in another.

Photoshop 5.5's resident pixel-sharpening filters—Sharpen, Sharpen More, and Sharpen Edges—are found under the Filters/Sharpen submenu.

Unsharp Mask filter

The Unsharp Mask filter sharpens the contrast between edges, but it masks areas of little change so they don't become too pixelated. The Unsharp Mask filter is the only sharpening filter that is adjustable. The following list describes what kind of adjustments can be made with the various controls.

- **Amount slider** Controls how much sharpening will be applied. This can be varied between 1 and 500. Don't apply so much sharpening that you start to see pixelated edges or banded colors.

- **Radius slider** Determines how many pixels out from the target pixel the effect will be applied. A greater radius results in less sharpening and less pixelization. You want to balance this control with the Amount control.

- **Threshold slider** Determines to what extent colors must differ from one another to be included in the sharpening process. The range is 1–255, because there can be up to 256 levels of gray in a single channel.

Techniques for Sharpening Focus

In this example, you're working on the cover of a Hawaii travel flyer. You want to feature a close-up of an islander, one with just the right *joie de vivre*. You've sorted through a couple dozen sheets of slides, and, *crickey!*, there she is on your light table, except she's just a tad soft focus. Could a sharpening filter help? Maybe, but sometimes none of these filters is the complete answer. For instance, you might want more definition in the hair without making the skin look like sandpaper.

> **Tip:** If the image is quite blurry due to too much movement during exposure—or because it is severely out of focus—nothing can save it. In fact, trying to run a sharpening process could produce sickening results.

You are going to use a few nifty tricks to fix this photo. First, you are going to get rid of some of the artifacts in the image by filtering the Blue channel—the channel most affected by artifacts. You'll just blur that "schmutz" out of existence. Next, you switch from RGB to Lab color, which has far different characteristics from RGB, even though it is still three channels. You'll take advantage of the fact that Lab color uses two of its three channels for information that has nothing to do with sharpness. By blurring those channels and sharpening the Lightness channel, you get rid of artifacts while sharpening in the same operation.

Here's why this works: In Lab color, one channel carries the lightness information. Generally looking like a fairly high-contrast black-and-white photo, the

Lightness channel will be sharpened dramatically. The other two channels, A and B, carry color information. Because sharpness isn't critical to this information, you'll blur those channels to eliminate some of the noise and color shifting in the digital image, adding visual smoothness to the blends in the photograph.

1. Load your file or download the file OAHUGIRL.JPG from the Osborne site.

2. Choose Image > Mode > Lab Color > Channels.

3. If the Channels palette isn't showing, select Channels from the menu bar. In turn, select A channel and B channel. To get rid of any JPEG artifacts and smooth out the photograph's blend areas, it's a good idea to slightly blur one or both of these channels. The best way to accomplish this is by choosing Filter > Noise > Dust & Scratches. The Dust & Scratches dialog appears. You might have to experiment a little with the blur. I found that setting Radius to 3 and Threshold to 1, as shown here, worked pretty well for this image at this resolution:

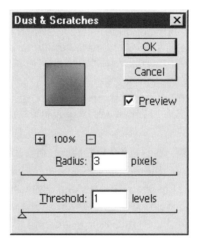

Click OK when you've blurred this layer just enough to minimize edges (and, therefore, noise patterns). Surprisingly enough, the blurring causes the image to look noticeably cleaner.

4. Now, in the Channels palette select the Lightness channel. Choose Filter > Sharpen > Unsharp Mask. In the Unsharp Mask dialog, set Amount to 150, Radius to 1, and Threshold to 0, as shown here:

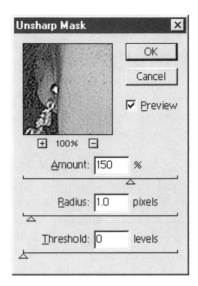

Click OK, and select the RGB combination channel. If the sharpness looks good, click OK or press CMD/CTRL+Z to undo your work. If necessary, go back into Unsharp Mask and experiment with settings until you have what you like. Then click OK.

5. The job is almost finished. Choose Image > Mode > RGB Color.

The final image can be seen in Figure 10-4.

FIGURE 10-4 A much sharper photograph of the girl in Oahu, Hawaii

Adding Motion Blur to Your Photographs

A photographer's trick that is closely related to sharpening focus is motion blur. The photographer swings the camera at the same speed as a moving subject while shooting with a slow shutter speed. The result is that (most of) the subject stays relatively sharp, while the surrounding scenery becomes a streaked blur. Not only does this technique keep attention focused on the subject; it greatly increases the feeling of speed in motion. Except for which filter you use, the procedure for executing motion blur is quite similar to background blur.

What good is a shot of Superman flying if there are no streaks shooshing out of his cape? The man might as well be hanging from the set by guide wires. Some of today's cameras have shutter speeds of up to eight thousandths of a second. That's fast enough to make even the speediest motorcycle racers look like they're posing on their bikes with the kickstands down. Speaking of which, what if you shot a famous racer in the studio, sitting on his bike, with the kickstand down, and now you want to montage him onto a racetrack? You'd best find a way to get this guy movin'. This is a job for motion blur.

Let's imagine that for last year's winter issue you illustrated a story about a florist's holiday catalog. They had you shoot flowers in the snow in Minneapolis at five below. An accidental touch in that cold shatters a flower like Baccarat crystal. You really needed a floral warehouse in your van to complete the job successfully.

So, what now? This year it's to be high fashion along Chicago's lakeshore drive, and you guessed it. Five below again, and they don't call it the Windy City for nothing! Your outside world is covered with frost. What fashion model in her right mind would risk a frostbitten nose for love or money?

You just shot a beautiful scene of frosty trees along the shore drive, and it's back from the lab. Should you shoot the model in the studio and use the scenic shot in rear-screen projection, or have the lab perform some of their compositing magic? Both involve heavy outside costs. Besides, you're liable to end up with that stilted frozen-action look. Let's check the file. Aha! You find a few nice model tests taken last summer on the roof of the photo studio. One looks like the pose might work. You need to pull the two shots together without looking stiff. Hmm? Photoshop and its plug-in friends to the rescue.

There are plenty of other lessons in this book on the techniques of selection and masking, so I'm assuming you've been preparing the knockouts and sharpening to prepare yourself for the motion-blur techniques. If you want a sample image to work on, you can download FROSTLAK.JPG and BLUMODEL.JPG from the Osborne site.

Here are the specific steps:

1. Load the two files you are going to composite.

2. To size the image to fit on the frosty lake background, choose Image > Image Size. Make sure the DPI of the model image matches the DPI of the frosty lake background.

3. Select the magic wand tool, set Tolerance to 10, and select the white background area. Choose Select > Inverse (or press CMD/CTRL+SHIFT+I). Select the move tool and drag the foreground image over to a position on the background image, as shown here:

    A new layer will automatically form. It is always prudent to make backup duplicate layers of both images, placing one set on the bottom of the Layers palette. Press CMD/CTRL and click the eye icon to turn off each backup image.

4. Select the zoom tool and zoom in on a section of the model's figure, as shown next. Select the eraser tool so you can go around the edge of the

image using a smaller soft brush to clean up the extra edge pixels, thus making the figure fit in against the background.

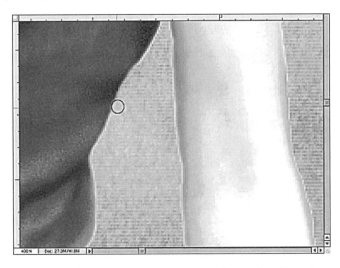

5. In the Layers palette, press CMD/CTRL+J or choose Duplicate Layer from the flyout to create a copy of the subject's layer, and select the top layer.

6. With the top model figure layer still selected, draw a selection around the figure of the model, leaving a lot of extra room away from the image. Choose Filter > Blur > Motion Blur, and in the Motion Blur dialog set Angle to 0 degrees and Distance to 200 pixels. Click OK, and the image will turn very blurred with horizontal streaks, as you can see here. In the Layers palette, set the Opacity for the blurred image to 70%.

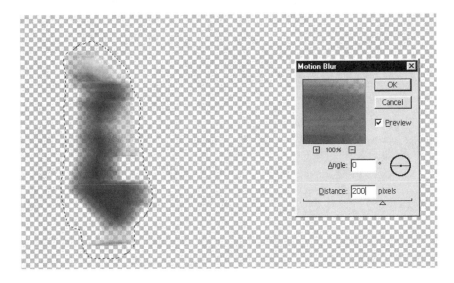

7. Select the move tool from the toolbox, and move the blurred image to the right by choosing its layer and repeatedly clicking the RIGHT ARROW key until the relationship between the blurred and sharp images of the model looks best.

8. With the blurred layer still selected, select the eraser tool from the toolbox, choose a large soft brush from the Brushes palette (Window > Brushes), and clear away any excess blurred image from the leading (left) edge of the model's image to allow full sharpness of the second layer model's image to come through. Be careful not to intrude too far into the desired parts of the blurred image. Keep your other hand on the shortcut keys for the Undo command (CMD/CTRL+Z) to correct any misguided erasures.

9. Be sure the three active layers are the correct ones and that they are in the correct order from top to bottom. Then you can delete the two inactive bottom backup layers. Choose File > Save a Copy (which automatically flattens in JPEG format), and then be sure to save your Photoshop PSD file to preserve a copy containing your final layers.

Your photograph of a fashion model strolling barefoot alongside Lake Michigan at five below zero is done. You can see the result in Figure 10-5.

FIGURE 10-5 Finished blurred-action photograph

Creating a Motion Zoom

Think of motion zoom as a vignette that gives the viewer the feeling of having been startled into noticing the subject of the photo: "Ohmigosh! There's that thing I've been looking for all my life!" Another use for motion zoom is time and space travel—the feeling that you've been catapulted toward or away from something at warp speed.

You've been asked to illustrate a book for children about a witch who lives under a waterfall in a sylvan forest. You already have a studio shot of a model with fuzzy hair wearing somewhat gypsylike clothing. She's holding a string shawl over her head in a pose that makes the shawl look like the wings of a butterfly. From your travel files you find a waterfall photo shot with a slow shutter speed, giving the water a texture of soft cotton candy. You put the two together. The montage looks lifeless—no feeling of movement, nothing to tie in with your story's action—so you start playing around in Photoshop and discover radial blur.

In the process of finding a solution to your illustration problem, you will learn a few selection and layer tricks while you learn to make practical use of motion zoom.

1. Start by loading an image of your own (or download FLYWITCH.JPG from the Osborne site). Then load a background image of your own (or download WATERFAL.JPG from the Osborne site).

2. Select the move tool from the toolbox. Position the windows for the two open files so you can see both. Select the FLYWITCH.JPG window to activate it, and drag the witch into the WATERFAL.JPG window.

3. In the Layers palette, select the witch's layer. Select the magic wand tool and set Tolerance to 30. Click outside the witch, selecting everything but the witch.

4. Choose Select > Modify > Expand. The Expand Selection dialog appears. Enter **1** in the pixels field and click OK. Press BACKSPACE; the halo disappears.

5. Select the move tool, and position the witch where you think she looks best compositionally, as shown in Figure 10-6.

So far, the image is pretty, but not very dynamic—in fact, not even very believable. Let's go to the Radial Blur filter (also known as the zoom filter) and see if we can improve the feeling of movement.

6. In the Layers palette, select the background layer and press CMD/CTRL+J, or choose Duplicate Layer from the Layers palette flyout. (If you work on the duplicate layer and mess up the image, you can just throw out the layer.)

7. From the toolbox, select the elliptical marquee tool and drag a circle around the figure of the witch. CONTROL+click/right-click inside the circle and choose Select Inverse from the context menu. CONTROL+click/right-click inside the selection and choose Feather from the context menu. Set feathering to around 20 pixels.

FIGURE 10-6 After eliminating the background, drag the figure of the witch
(right) over to the waterfall (left).

8. Choose Filter > Blur > Radial Blur. The Radial Blur dialog appears. Set Blur Method
to Zoom, Quality to Best, and Amount to 39. Click OK. Press CMD/CTRL+D to drop
the selection. Now draw a circle around the figure of the witch, as shown here:

This is a much more dramatic result, but the forest and waterfall scene is so blurred it's hard to identify. Some of the dreamy quality of the light has been lost.

9. In the Layers palette, make sure the background copy layer is selected and move the Opacity slider to about 70%.

Ah, this is getting good. But you can make it even better. How about giving a little upward motion blur to the witch, making her blend better with the surroundings and really appear to fly.

10. Press CMD/CTRL+J or choose Duplicate Layer from the Layers palette menu to create a copy layer of the witch's layer; then select the top layer.

11. Select the lasso tool and draw a selection around the figure of the witch leaving a lot of extra room away from the image. Choose Filter > Blur > Motion Blur, and in the dialog set Angle to 0 degrees and Distance to 200 pixels. Then rotate the circle so the diagonal line parallels the upward motion you want the witch to make. Click OK, and the figure of the witch will become very blurred with diagonal streaks, as shown here:

12. Select the move tool from the toolbox and move the blurred image down and to the right by alternately pressing the DOWN and RIGHT ARROW keys until the relationship between the blurred and sharp images of the witch looks best.

13. Then, with the blurred layer selected, grab the eraser tool from the toolbox; select a large soft brush from the Brushes palette (Window > Brushes); and erase any excess blurred image from the leading parts of the witch's image, allowing full sharpness of the second layer witch's image to come through. Be careful not to intrude too far into the desired parts of the blurred image.

FIGURE 10-7 The finished image of the witch flying from her waterfall

Keep your other hand on the shortcut keys for the Undo command (CMD/CTRL+Z) to correct any misguided erasures.

14. Press CMD/CTRL+F to repeat the Radial Blur filter. Press CMD/CTRL+D to drop the selection. Voilà! You've nailed it.

Figure 10-7 shows the final result.

Controlling Lighting and Shadows in Composites

Let's face it, we don't live in a perfect day-to-day world. It's one thing shooting with the time and equipment of carefully staged studio lighting, yet quite another to move along, clicking off roll after roll while following the machinations of a pair of models up and down a hill. All the while that great arc light in the sky keeps moving, changing color as it ducks behind a cloud. A little help with the lighting is bound to be needed.

Suppose a pharmaceutical firm has asked you to lay out an ad for their antihistamine medicine—the kind of ad in which a subject (or actor?) walking through a field of mustard sets forth sneezing in rapid-fire bursts. A search of your images brings up a test shoot of a couple of models running in a field of yellow; and, as luck would have it, portraits were taken at the end of the day as well. Your idea is to montage two actions of the couple in the field, and then feature a large portrait of the girl. Fortunately, the sun's direction matches; however, the portraits have a lot of sunset coloring.

In this exercise, we will explore ways to modify and correct lighting discrepancies, to make images appear to belong with each other.

1. Start by loading your own three original photographs, or download COUPLHIL.JPG, COUPLRUN.JPG, and GIRL_SUN.JPG from the Osborne site. Choose Image > Image Size. Resize each photograph to match. Make sure they also are the same DPI. I assume that you have already analyzed the photograph's compatibility as to direction and quality of lighting and relative size of figures when placed together. If not, now's the time, before you get too far into the work.

2. Place the file containing the girl's portrait alongside the file that is to be the principal background. Select the polygon lasso tool and quickly select as much of the background around the girl as you can without coming too close to the edges of her shape. When you've finished making the selection, place the cursor inside the selection. Press CONTROL+click/right-click, and then choose Select Inverse from the context menu.

3. Select the move tool, and then drag the selection of the girl into the background. The girl is now seen on a new layer in the Layers palette (if it isn't showing, choose Window > Show Layers from the menu bar). Position the girl where you want her in the layout.

4. In the Layers palette, with the background layer selected, choose New Layer from the flyout menu. Select the new layer and press OPT/ALT; then press BACK-SPACE to fill the new layer with the background color. (An outrageous color such as bright pink makes it easier to see what you're going to do next.)

5. Select the zoom tool. Zoom in tight so you can see exactly what you're doing. Select the eraser tool and choose an appropriately sized soft brush from the Brushes palette. Carefully brush away the unwanted edges of the girl's image, as shown next, keeping two fingers on the shortcut keys for the Undo command (CMD/CTRL+Z) in case you suddenly make an erratic stroke. Watch the head especially closely and take care to keep the stray hairs, while letting the background show through. When you're satisfied with the way the edge looks, go to the Layers palette and delete middle layer (the plain background).

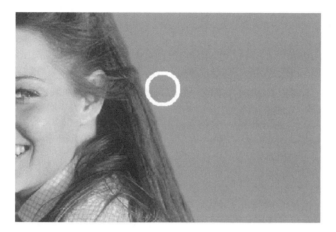

6. Select background number two and select the lasso tool to draw a selection of the area you wish to bring onto background number one. Drag the selection of background number two onto the composite, as you can see here. The arrangement of layers in the Layers palette of the composite should be the girl layer (top); the selection from background number two (middle); and background number one (bottom).

Drag the selection from background two to its position on the composite file.

7. Before you do any more detail work, you need to balance the color of each image with the other images. Choose Image > Adjust > Color Balance to bring up the Color Balance dialog. Color balance each layer so the layers appear in color relation to one another.

Now it's time to give form, shadows, and highlights wherever your keen eye tells you it's appropriate. We'll do this next. Before you start, remember to sandbag your efforts by duplicating the layer of the girl (choose Duplicate Layer from the Layers palette menu). Be selective. Don't get carried away. But if you do, you can always choose Window > Show History and delete the last action.

8. From your bag of tricks, you can use the paintbrush, burn, dodge, rubber stamp, or eraser tool to improve the image. Brighten the eyes and teeth by gently burning in a shadow here, or dodging a highlight there. Maybe lighten the flowers in the man's hands to draw attention.

9. To select the girl's teeth, use the lasso tool. To lighten or add contrast, choose Image > Adjust and then choose the Curves, Levels, or Brightness/Contrast commands, as necessary. To take a little of the sun's yellow out of her teeth, choose Image > Adjust > Color Balance. A before-and-after comparison is shown here:

Check out the results of all your work in Figure 10-8 to see how the layout turns out.

FIGURE 10-8 The composite of the two couples and the portrait in one scene

Focusing Attention with the Lighting Effects Filter

As a photographer I have usually looked askance at lighting effects filters, much as graphic designers tend to look at clip art—they tend to see it as gimmickry. However, when understood and used appropriately, these filters can bring effective results, adding an exciting touch to your visual, without which the final image might have fallen short. They deserve to be included in your bag of tricks as long as they don't become your bag.

When I first entered the inner sanctum of the Lighting Effects filter, I was amazed! I do mean, it is *a maze*. It would take an Einstein to calculate the number of combinations available. Be not daunted. Just start playing with the 16 styles; 3 light types with sliders; 4 properties, each with sliders like matte to shiny, plastic to metallic; plus R and G and B texture channels. With these you also get a thumbnail screen to modulate to your heart's content. Start by loading an image from your file to have a ball with the Lighting Effects filter. (You can also download DUNEBUGY.JPG from the Osborne site if you wish.)

The Lighting Effects filter is no Tinker Toy, but you will need to tinker and toy with it if you want to learn what you can do with what it can do. Dive in, have fun, and use your creative imagination. See the Filter Gallery for a sample of what you can achieve with this filter.

Professional Skills Summary

In this chapter, you learned how to produce a flare when it wasn't there, distort a normal photo through a fish's eye, add grain that wasn't on the film to your shot, make soft focus become sharper, get a still subject to move—even zoom—and to bring different lights and shadows together in a composite image.

The next chapter shows you how to add artistic effects and textures that look like those produced by artists and their paraphernalia from the past and present—and maybe you'll even concoct a few looks not yet in use.

Creating Photopaintings

"Painterly" techniques let you leave evidence of the artist's hand (such as real brush strokes), they let you make and enhance original art if you can draw and paint, or they give you a few good tricks for producing dramatic effects on a photo. Your image may not technically be a painting, but it is something just as interesting—or better yet, something you couldn't get by any other means.

Let's face it: sometimes a photograph is too realistic to evoke the emotion that the assignment calls for. There are also times when the job calls for creating artwork from scratch, by drawing and painting, rather than scanning or digitizing a photograph. Photoshop provides several techniques for turning photos into new works of art:

- Painting brush strokes over a photo
- Applying Photoshop's native filters to make all or part of a photo or scanned drawing look as though it had been hand painted in some sort of natural media, such as charcoal, pastels, watercolors, or oils
- Using the history brush and the brand-new art history brush to create painterly effects that were never before possible.

Even more exciting, there is nothing to stop you from using these techniques in combination with third-party products by

- Applying filters such as Xaos Tool's Paint Alchemy and Segmation
- Exporting what you've done in Photoshop up to a point into a natural media paint program such as MetaCreations' Painter or Right Hemisphere's Deep Paint plug-in.

Photoshop isn't a natural media paint program like MetaCreations' Painter (and doesn't feature natural media brushes like those found in such programs as Corel PhotoPaint 9). Nevertheless, you can create artwork that isn't based on a photo. Just grab the brush tools and start painting, or start by sketching with traditional tools, and then scan the sketch into Photoshop.

Tip: It's much easier to emulate brush strokes if you acquire a pressure-sensitive digitizing tablet, such as one of those made by Wacom.

Why Use Photoshop 5.5 as a Paint Program?

Though Photoshop was never intended to be a natural media emulator like MetaCreations' Painter, many people who create art from scratch use Photoshop as their tool of choice. You can collect an infinite number of custom brushes, and use the dodge, burn, sponge, rubber stamp, and eraser in a somewhat paintbrush-like manner.

One good reason to paint in Photoshop, as opposed to a natural media program, is to make use of Photoshop's versatility and power. In Photoshop, you can spend time on a few details and then repeat them, making seamless tiles; you can clone areas of texture in random ways; and you can combine layers in complex ways using blend modes, transparency, and textured or gradient layer masks.

Layers give you endless possibilities for combining artistic effects and for interactively limiting a variety of effects and filters to specific areas of the image. As you add each element to your design, whether scanned or painted from scratch, place it on its own layer. Move it, tweak the color, hide it until you're satisfied, save it all as a Photoshop document, and then choose Image > Duplicate and select the Merged Layers Only box to make a copy with just one layer. Choose Layers > Flatten Image and save in the appropriate format.

Professional Pointer

I've made illustrations with 50 or more layers, but if you're working in limited memory, you'll want to compromise by creating a set of related layers, merging them, and then moving on.

Natural media like charcoal, watercolor, or oils have a certain random quality that can create "happy accidents." Art painted in Photoshop using nothing more than the default brushes is prone to an overly smooth, plastic quality. However, you can easily add interest to brushwork by

- Adjusting the default brush settings
- Creating custom brushes
- Using the art history brush
- Painting with the history brush from a snapshot of a filtered layer

Adjusting the Default Brush Settings

You can adjust the default brush settings to create new sizes, make elliptical shapes, change the angles of brushes whose shapes are disproportionate in height and width, or change the "softness" (edge feathering) of the brush. To do so, choose Window > Show Brushes to bring up the Brushes palette. Double-click the brush you want to change, and the Brush Options dialog appears. You can then change the brush's diameter, hardness, oval angle, and roundness. The Brushes palette and the Brush Options dialog are shown in Figure 11-1.

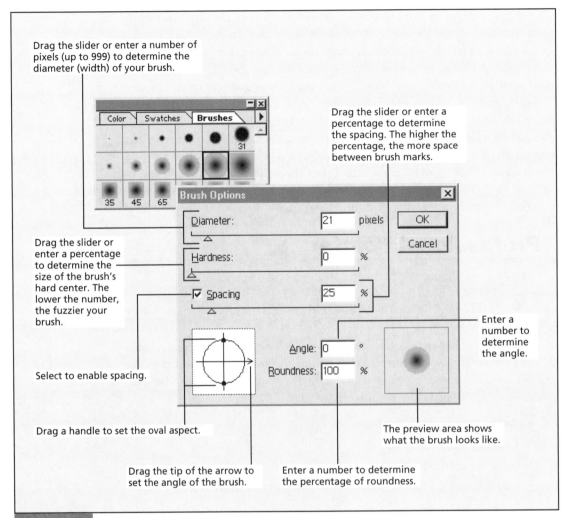

Drag the slider or enter a number of pixels (up to 999) to determine the diameter (width) of your brush.

Drag the slider or enter a percentage to determine the spacing. The higher the percentage, the more space between brush marks.

Drag the slider or enter a percentage to determine the size of the brush's hard center. The lower the number, the fuzzier your brush.

Enter a number to determine the angle.

Select to enable spacing.

Drag a handle to set the oval aspect.

The preview area shows what the brush looks like.

Drag the tip of the arrow to set the angle of the brush.

Enter a number to determine the percentage of roundness.

FIGURE 11-1   The Brush Options dialog for default brushes

Like most palettes, the Brushes palette has its own menu. The functions of the Brushes palette menu are described in the next section and later in this chapter in the section "Making and Loading a Custom Brush Palette."

Making Custom Brushes

You can create several types of special effects, especially atmospheric, particle, and artistic effects, by making your own brushes. Unlike default brushes, custom brushes are defined from a selection and can only be the size, shape, and angle at which you define them. Custom brushes can be any shape; in fact, they can be made from anything you can create in Photoshop. You can save them in the Brushes palette or organize them into palettes that you create. (See "Making and Loading a Custom Brush Palette," later in this chapter.) You can even make several special-purpose brush palettes for certain jobs.

To make your own brushes from scratch and create your own brush palettes, you make a custom brush from a selection. Even though the image you select as a brush may be in color, the brush will be grayscale after it has been saved as a brush. You can create brushes out of silhouettes or shapes made with brush strokes from existing brushes.

The easiest way to make your own brush shapes is to create a new file with a white background and then open clip art from vector files in Illustrator (AI) or Encapsulated PostScript (EPS) format. Strong shapes filled with black work best, but just about anything will do. Virtually all illustration programs (for example, CorelDRAW!, Adobe Illustrator, Macromedia FreeHand, Deneba Canvas, and MetaCreations' Expression) are capable of exporting their files as either AI or EPS format; so you can experiment with any of the clip art that comes with these programs.

The strokes in custom brushes can be only one width if you paint with a mouse. If you use a pressure-sensitive pen, you can use the pen pressure to vary the size of the brush. If you don't have a pressure-sensitive pen, you'll need to make several sizes of the same brush, as follows:

1. Select the image, copy the selection to a new layer, and then duplicate the new layer several times.

2. Use the move tool to drag the layers apart (you want to have plenty of space between the images on each layer), and then transform each layer to a progressively smaller size.

3. Flatten the image by choosing Layers > Flatten Image.

Now you're ready to define each size of the brush as a new brush.

4. Drag a rectangular marquee around the portion of the image you want to define as a brush (see Figure 11-2).

5. From the main menu, choose Window > Show Brushes (unless the Brushes palette is already visible), and select an empty spot on the Brushes palette.

6. Choose Define Brush from the Brushes palette menu. The new brush shape will magically appear in the chosen brush slot, as shown in Figure 11-2.

7. Place the brushes in the palette in order of size. Then, when you're painting, you can vary the size of the brush by pressing the [and] keys while you're using the mouse.

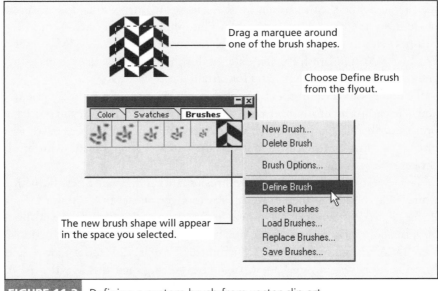

Drag a marquee around one of the brush shapes.

Choose Define Brush from the flyout.

The new brush shape will appear in the space you selected.

FIGURE 11-2 Defining a custom brush from vector clip art

8. Double-click the new brush to bring up the Brush Options dialog for a custom brush. The Brush Options dialog for custom brushes is different from the one for default brushes. It contains only two check boxes:

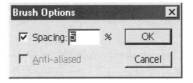

If you want to enable spacing between brush marks, select the Spacing check box and enter a value in the Spacing field. The value in this field is a percentage of the brush's width that the brush must travel before it paints again. Select the Anti-aliased check box if you want angled or rounded edges of the brush to be smooth (rather than pixelated).

9. When you've finished making the settings, click OK.

Ideas for Custom Brushes

Practiced artists have learned that there are some commonly useful categories of custom brushes. Adobe provides quite a few of these on the CD-ROM that accompanies Photoshop. In the following sections you'll find more that are favorites of mine. Some of the custom brushes below are texture brushes, and some are variations of the default or "standard" brushes.

FIGURE 11-3 A custom brush was used to make the star in this image.

Almost every command and tool in Photoshop can be made to create some kind of special effect. Custom brushes are no exception. For example, you can create what I call an "atmospheric brush": raindrops, snowflakes, flames, sparkles, dust, and so on. The list is potentially endless. Brushes can have color and transparency, they can be used to paint on a transparent layer, and they can be used with 17 different blend modes. Figure 11-3 illustrates the use of one atmospheric brush—a sparkle—to make the star you see in the sky.

Sparkle brush

You should make this brush in numerous sizes and with a different number of sparks in the spokes. Add it to your permanent library if you like.

1. Click in a blank area of the Brushes palette. The New Brush dialog will appear. This is actually the same dialog as the Brush Options dialog for default brushes.

2. In the dialog, set Diameter to 45 pixels, Hardness to 0%, Spacing to 25%, Angle to 0° (zero degrees), and Roundness to 9%. Click OK.

You have now made a new brush. You can change any of the characteristics of this brush (as described in step 2) at any time—just double-click the brush in the Brushes palette.

3. In Photoshop, from the main menu, choose File > New (or make a new white layer that you will delete when you've made the brush or brushes).

4. In the New dialog that appears, set Resolution to 72 dpi and make the image just big enough to hold several brushes at actual size—400 × 500 pixels usually seems about right to me. In the Contents box, choose the White radio button. Click OK.

5. From the toolbox, select the paintbrush.

6. From the main menu, choose Window > Show Brushes (unless the Brushes palette is already visible). From the Brushes palette, choose the new brush (a long, flattened, soft-edged oval at 0 degrees). If you didn't make the brush, make it now.

7. Click in one corner of the new file. (Be sure not to drag, or it will smear the brush stroke.) The result should look like this:

8. In the Brushes palette, double-click the same brush. The Brush Options dialog appears. Enter **90** in the Angle field. Click OK. In the palette, the brush will now be shown in a vertical position.

9. With the paintbrush selected, click once to make a vertical stroke that crosses the diagonal stroke. Repeat step 8 (changing the angle each time) and this one until you have several "spokes" in your sparkle, like this:

10. From the toolbox, select the rectangular marquee. Drag a rectangle around your sparkle. Press CMD/CTRL+C to copy the sparkle to the clipboard and CMD/CTRL+V to paste it to a new layer. The new layer automatically becomes the one that is selected. From the main menu, choose Edit > Transform > Numeric.

11. The Numeric Transform dialog appears. Deselect the check boxes for Position, Skew, and Rotate. The Scale check box should be selected, and the Constrain Proportions check box should be selected. Type **75** in the Width box. The Height box will automatically change to 75. Click OK. You've made a smaller sparkle on a new layer, but you may not be able to see it. From the toolbox, select the move tool and drag until you see the new sparkle.

12. Repeat steps 8 and 9 (you don't need to change anything in the Numeric Transform dialog because you'll automatically reduce the sparkle 75 percent each time you repeat the steps) until you have four to eight brushes ranging in size down to tiny.

13. Flatten the file by choosing Flatten Image from the Layers palette flyout. If you've created new layers above the other art you've been working on in order to paint this brush shape, click the eye icon next to each of the pre-brush-making layers, and choose Merge Visible from the Layers palette flyout. The results of what you've done so far should look like this:

14. From the toolbox, select the rectangular marquee. Drag a selection around each sparkle. From the Brushes palette flyout, choose Define Brush. Repeat this step to make a new brush of each size of sparkle.

15. Delete all the other brushes in the palette and save the sparkle brushes as SPARKLES.ABS. Now you will be able to add these special effects brushes to any other brush palette, simply by choosing Load Brushes from the Brushes palette flyout.

You can use these sparkles to enhance your images in countless ways—from "brightening" the chrome on a car's bumper, to placing a constellation in a night sky, to putting a gleam in the eyes of two lovers. You can vary these sparkles (and any other atmospheric brushes) in endless ways, for example, change their color or transparency, filter the layer they're painted on, or use image controls on their layer. Now, think about making smoke, raindrops, snowflakes, or laser beams. Also, this brush works really well in conjunction with a lens flare filter.

You can also get quite a bit of variety into a basic brush such as the one we've just designed by texturing it with a filter. Once you've captured your basic brushes, choose a filter. Try several filters; you will get a variety of worthwhile effects. Motion Blur filters can be very effective. Here, I ran the Palette Knife filter on the sparkle brushes:

Calligraphy brush

Even if you don't have a tablet and stylus, you can get more from a default brush shape by making the equivalent of a calligraphy pen held at a 45-degree angle to the paper. To make this "calligraphy" brush, take these steps:

1. Click in an empty space in the Brushes palette or choose New Brush from the flyout. Set Diameter to 25 pixels, Hardness to 100%, and Spacing to 1%. Set Angle to 45 and Roundness to 25%, and click OK. The preview of the brush should look like this:

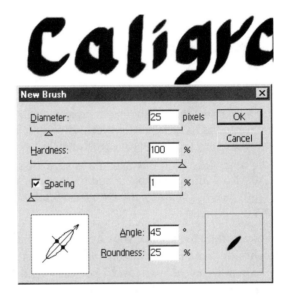

2. Select the paintbrush tool and try making a variety of lines with it by moving the mouse or stylus at different angles or in loops. Notice that you get automatic thicks and thins. (If you're using a stylus, double-click the paintbrush tool in the toolbox to open the Options palette, and turn off all of the Stylus pressure settings for now.)

If you can hand letter, you can get some very acceptable results with this. Try making some "calligraphy" brushes at different sizes to compare effects. If you're painting with this, you may be annoyed at not being able to rotate your brush. But you can! Just repeat the two steps above, but change the angle setting by 15 degrees each time. Then you can rotate the brush by using the [and] keys to change the angle of the brush.

Set of rake brushes

A set of brushes made from any custom brush that you define that has this oblong shape will achieve similar effects. I created a series of brushes that would give me cross-hatching effects similar to what you can achieve with a nibbed pen, especially when combined with a pressure-sensitive tablet, so that the strokes can be easily varied in size. What I like about this brush is being able to draw five "lines" at once, which really speeds up getting cross-hatched strokes. The brushes shown here are rotated in 45-degree increments, but I suggest you do them in 10- or 15-degree increments:

Here's how you make a set of six "rotating" custom rake brushes:

1. This brush has to be made on a blank white document. Press D to choose the default foreground and background colors. Open a new grayscale document at 500 pixels wide and 200 pixels in height, and set the background to white. We'll use this space to make an oversized copy of the basic rake brush.

2. Choose Window > Show Info. From the Info palette flyout, choose Palette Options, and choose Pixels from the Ruler Units pop-up menu in the Mouse Coordinates section. Choose New Layer from the Layers palette flyout. Use the elliptical marquee tool while holding down the SHIFT key to constrain a circular selection 60 pixels wide. Fill it with black, as shown here:

3. Press CMD/CTRL+D to drop the selection.

4. Select the rectangular marquee tool and place a selection around your big dot. Then press CMD/CTRL+J twice in succession. This will create two new layers, each with a dot. Select each layer in turn, but before you select the next layer, use the move tool to drag the dot in that layer so that all the dots line up in a row, like this:

5. Select the first layer. Choose Edit > Transform > Numeric to open the Numeric Transform dialog. Select the Scale and Constrain Proportions check boxes, and set the Width and Height fields to 70 percent. This shrinks the dot on the new layer to 70 percent of the original size.

6. Select the next dot's layer and open Numeric Transform again. The scale factor is still set to 70 percent, so just click OK. Now repeat the command again. Each dot is now 70 percent smaller than the dot to its left.

7. Hide the background layer by clicking off the eye icon in its bar in the Layers palette.

8. Now merge the three dots onto one layer by choosing Merge Visible from the Layers palette flyout, and then choose Duplicate Layer from the flyout.

9. The new layer is still selected. Choose Edit > Transform > Rotate 180 degrees. Choose the original layer of dots, and select the move tool. Move the dots to the left until the big dots merge in the middle and look like this:

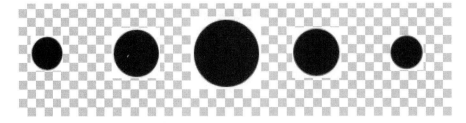

10. Merge the visible layers and choose Filter > Blur > Gaussian Blur. In the Gaussian Blur dialog, set Radius to 4.

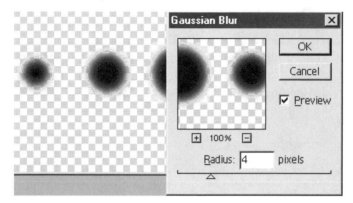

11. Click the eye icon in the Layers palette to show the background layer. From the Layers palette menu, choose Flatten Image.

12. Choose Edit > Transfrom > Numeric. In the Scale area, select the Constrain Proportions check box and set either of the fields to 10 percent. Make sure neither of the check boxes for the other transformation types are selected, and click OK.

13. Duplicate the layer and use Numeric Transform to move it 15 pixels along the X axis. Turn on Rotate and set it to 30 degrees.

14. Duplicate the layer, move 15 pixels, and rotate 30 degrees for each of the other four copies, until you have the six positions required for the set:

15. For each of the six shapes, make a selection with the rectangular marquee tool, and choose Define Brush from the Brushes palette flyout.

Making and Loading a Custom Brush Palette

Since you can make such a variety of brush shapes and textures, you'll eventually get tired of scrolling all over your huge brush palette (it can hold an unlimited number of brushes). It would make a lot more sense to have brush shapes and patterns divided by category (for example, water, sparkles, and textures). In order to do that, you will have to learn to make, save, and load whole custom brush palettes.

To make a new brush palette file:

1. Delete all the default brushes one at a time. The fastest way to do this is to select a brush, CONTROL+click/right-click while the cursor is over the brush, and choose Delete Brush from the context menu.

2. Use the procedure for defining a brush (see "Making Custom Brushes," earlier in this chapter) to make as many new brushes as you want for this palette.

3. From the Brushes palette flyout, choose Save Brushes. A file save dialog appears. Photoshop will automatically open the Brushes folder, but you can change the directory path if you like. Name the palette. Photoshop will automatically assign the correct file type (ABR for Windows). Click Save.

To append brushes from an existing file, just choose Load Brushes from the Brushes palette flyout. Browse to select the file containing the brushes you want to append, and either double-click the filename or click OK.

To restore the default brushes, choose Reset Brushes from the Brushes palette flyout. You will be presented with a message box asking you to confirm whether you want to replace the current brushes with the default brushes. Choose OK to replace the entire palette with the default palette, or choose Append to append the default brushes to the current palette.

Using the Art History Brush

The art history brush is a brand-new tool in Photoshop 5.5 that can pick up colors from a History palette snapshot and spread those colors over a certain radius and style. The result looks like an impressionist painting. In fact, if you push its limits, you can turn a photograph into a pure abstraction. There are ten stylized strokes that you can pick from a menu in the Art History Options palette. All ten strokes are shown in the chart in Figure 11-4.

To choose the state or snapshot that the art history brush will use, click the history brush source box in the leftmost column of the History palette in that state or snapshot's name bar. The history brush icon will appear there, as shown here:

History brush source box

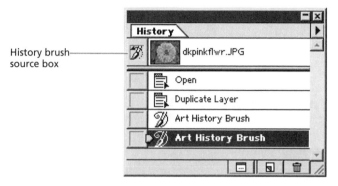

FIGURE 11-4 Stroke styles for the art history brush. The original image is shown at lower right.

As is the case with the history brush, you can use the art history brush to paint from any snapshot or any state in the History palette. The art history brush takes its color from the location of the center of the cursor as it corresponds to the same location in the chosen history state or snapshot. The fidelity of the color to that of the original will deviate within a range set by the Fidelity slider in the History Brush Options palette.

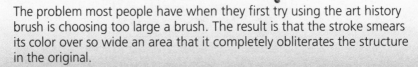

Professional Pointer

The problem most people have when they first try using the art history brush is choosing too large a brush. The result is that the stroke smears its color over so wide an area that it completely obliterates the structure in the original.

You can get some really interesting effects from the art history brush by using it in conjunction with user-defined and custom brushes. You can also "paint" on a blank canvas. If you have a pressure-sensitive pen, be sure to use it—you'll have a lot more flexibility. All of these techniques are demonstrated in the following exercise.

1. Load an image that you'd like to use as the basis for a painting. If you have to rotate the image to set it upright because a camera or scanner stored it on its side, choose Image > Rotate Canvas > 90° CW/CCW.

2. If you have rotated, cropped, resized, or otherwise changed the image, make a new snapshot. Choose Make New Snapshot from the History palette menu.

3. You want to create a new background layer to paint on. Double-click the current background layer name bar in the Layers palette and press RETURN/ENTER to accept the default layer options. Choose Layer > New > Background. Fill the new background with a slightly off-white color, like that of watercolor paper or canvas. You will be painting on this new layer, so be sure it stays selected. Click the eye icon in the layer's name bar to turn off the original (or discard the layer if you don't think you will want to use it for another purpose).

4. Double-click the art history brush (it's grouped with the history brush in the toolbox) to select it and open its Options palette.

5. Set the source for the art history brush. If the History palette isn't visible, choose Window > Show History. If necessary, scroll to the top of the palette so that you can see the snapshot(s). Then click the source box in the leftmost column of the snapshot's name bar. A history brush icon will appear.

6. From the Art History Brush Options palette, choose a moderately tight style (Dab, Tight Short, or Tight Curl).

7. From the Brushes palette, choose a fairly small brush. (If you're using a mouse, start with a very small brush.) Start painting in the area where you expect your main subject to be. You will gradually start to see your image appear in a painterly style, like this:

8. You may want to choose a looser style for areas where you want to hide detail or where detail isn't nearly as important. You can make it even looser by choosing both a looser style and a larger brush.

9. You should also experiment with the Tolerance and Area controls in the Art History Brush Options palette. Tolerance controls the degree to which you can paint into areas that differ considerably from the history source. Be sure it's set fairly low, or you won't be able to paint on your "canvas." Area determines the size and coverage of the individual strokes.

10. If you want the strokes to fade toward the edge of the canvas, use the Opacity slider when you paint near the edges.

11. When you're pretty close to what you want, choose an even smaller brush and an even tighter style and start painting in sharper details in the areas where you want to focus the viewer's attention. Once you've done that, your painting should look more like this:

12. If you want to give your strokes an impasto effect (make them look as though you used very thick paint), choose Filter > Render > Lighting Effects. In the Lighting Effects dialog, choose Directional as your lighting type and Blue as your texture channel.

Cross-Reference: For more information on the Lighting Effects filter, see Chapter 10.

13. If you want to give the painting a canvas texture, choose Filter > Texture > Texturizer. The Texturizer dialog will appear. From the Texture menu, choose Canvas. From the Light Direction menu, choose the lighting angle that matches the texture you've already imposed with the Lighting Effects filter. When you're happy with your settings, click OK. The result should look something like this:

Using the History Brush to Create the Look of Natural Media

The history brush is most often used to restore part of the image that you've altered (probably by mistake). However, you can also create numerous natural media textures with Photoshop's built-in filters and then paint those textures in with the history brush. Of course, if you want to get really sophisticated, you can combine the techniques for the art history brush described in the previous section with the following history brush techniques:

1. Open the document and do any needed transformations, retouching, or image adjustments.

2. From the Filters menu, choose a filter whose effect you want to be able to "paint in." Run the filter on the new layer. Double-click the new layer's name

bar to bring up the Layer Options dialog, and enter a new name for the layer that corresponds to the filter effect.

Cross-Reference: See the Filter Gallery in the color insert for examples of various filter effects.

3. In the History palette, choose Create New Snapshot from the History palette menu. When the New Snapshot dialog appears, enter a name that corresponds to the filter you ran, so that you can quickly identify the effect.

4. Repeat steps 2 and 3, above, several times. Each time, choose a different filter. (By the way, if you are lucky enough to have a copy of Xaos Tool's Paint Alchemy, you can get much more variety in natural brush stroke looks.) As soon as you've run a filter and created a snapshot of it, delete that step from the History palette so that you can run a different filter on the original image.

5. Now, for the effect you want to paint from, click the history brush source box in the leftmost column of the snapshot name bar.

6. You're going to paint in strokes from other states. Select the history brush from the toolbox, and then double-click it to make sure the History Brush Options palette, shown here, is visible. If you select the Impressionist check box, you'll get a "smeary" variation of the effect whose snapshot you've chosen. This can be a good way to vary the texture of your strokes.

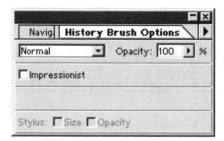

7. Make sure your background layer is selected, and paint with the history brush. It will reproduce the effect in that snapshot on your original image. If you overdo an area, just select the snapshot of the original image and paint it back in.

8. Paint other areas of the image by clicking the history brush source box for several other effects that you ran. Figure 11-5 shows the original and the painting I made after running the Crayon, Dry Brush, Ink Outlines, and Palette Knife filters, creating a snapshot of each, and then painting the results in.

Original   Painting

FIGURE 11-5 The history brush was used to paint in several filter effects from several different History palette snapshots.

Photopainting with Photoshop's Filters and Layers

Before the history brush came along in Photoshop 5, a favorite technique of photopainters (especially yours truly) was to copy the background layer several times, and then run a different artistic filter on each layer. By turning off all but two of the layers (clicking the eye icon in the layer's name bar), I could erase away part of a layer with the eraser tool so that the layer below showed through. Then I experimented with blend modes and transparency of the two layers involved, made the next layer above those two visible, erased all but the parts of that layer that I wanted to add to the competition, and then went to the next layer—and so forth.

Professional Pointer

You can use a user-defined brush as an eraser by choosing Paintbrush in the Eraser Options palette and selecting the brush from the Brushes palette.

The use of the history brush doesn't totally eliminate the usefulness of that technique. Because you are progressively blending layers instead of simply painting in different areas, the overall effect can be quite different. Figure 11-6 uses this layer-blending technique.

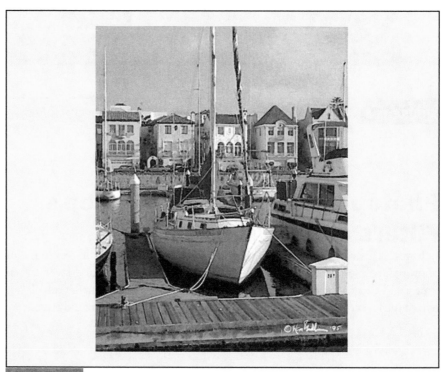

FIGURE 11-6 Numerous layers were created and then blended together to create this painterly effect.

Professional Skills Summary

In this chapter, you learned the main techniques for using Photoshop 5.5 as a painting (as opposed to a photo-editing) tool. You learned ways to adjust the default brushes and to create your own custom brushes so that you can paint from scratch using strokes that look more textured and "painterly." You also saw the three major techniques for quickly turning photographs into professional-looking paintings: using the art history brush, using the history brush in conjunction with Photoshop's artistic filter effects, and combining filtered layers so that different areas of the image are treated suitably.

Part IV

Printing and Publishing Your Work

Managing Your Images

What's to Manage?

It doesn't do you much good to have the world's most widely accepted professional image-processing software if you can't find the image you need to process. If you're just starting—with Photoshop and with digital imaging—managing images may not be much of a problem because you don't yet have that many images to manage. Of course, if you're learning Photoshop to manage your stock agency's catalog or your corporation's employee mug shots, you already understand the problem. In any case, it won't be long before you have way more images than you can find at a moment's notice. One of the main reasons that images can be so hard to find is that you only have a filename to go on. A filename such as AUT_0651.JPG doesn't tell you much, as you can see here:

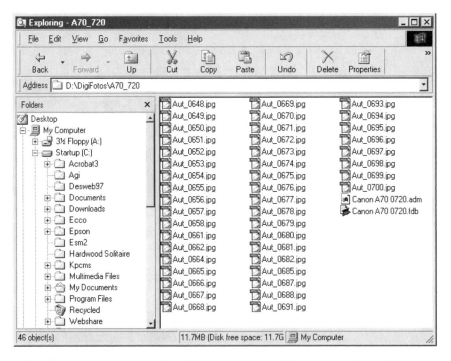

Finding images is especially difficult if you use Windows and don't have image thumbnails in your Explorer views (the Windows equivalent to the Mac's file manager). But even if you're a Mac person and you do have thumbnails in your directories, there will be times when the thumbnails are just too small to distinguish one shot of a given subject from another. After all, often the telling difference is something as small as the sincerity of a smile or the presence of a bumblebee on the petal of a flower. So the first thing you want to do is to create a readable catalog of images. For those of you who are photographers, this is the equivalent of a traditional contact sheet.

Professional Pointer

In traditional photography, a contact sheet is a print made by placing negatives facedown in tight contact with a sheet of photographic paper. The sandwich is then exposed to light and developed. The result is a series of images the same size as the negative, all appearing in the same order as they were photographed. You can also see the frame numbers that were on the edge of the film, so you can readily select the image you want to print.

As your image collection grows, you'll discover that you can find images much more quickly if you store them in categories. Generally, this means copying files into several directories (folders) and then storing them offline via removable disk (floppy, CD-ROM, Zip disk, etc.). I'll show you at least one logical process for doing that in this chapter.

The next step in making your collection efficient is to link it to a database so that you can search for images by keyword. Imagine a catalog of flowers. Imagine how fast you could find the right image if each were assigned a title, a species name, a Latin name, the type of lighting, geographical location where the species was popular, and possibly several other categories. Then you could search for a particular type of image by keyword. The database would then bring up a visual (thumbnail or contact sheet) catalog of all the likely candidates. Although Photoshop allows you to enter descriptive text that gets embedded with an image, which provides some rudimentary search capabilities, it doesn't come with a built-in image database. However, you can purchase third-party programs for image management that will give you all those capabilities. Extensis Portfolio and Canto Cumulus are excellent examples of such programs.

Photoshop 5.5 is capable of using batch automation (the same technology that makes the contact sheets) to help you manage images in a couple of other important ways. First, you can publish something known in the industry as a *job print*, in which one image is printed several times on the same sheet of paper—often in two or more different sizes. Job prints are also called *package prints* and are typically sold by wedding, portrait, and industrial photographers as a convenient and economical way of ordering multiple copies of different-sized prints.

Photoshop 5.5 can also automatically make thumbnails and Web-sized illustrations from a whole folder of images (even if they're not all in the same format) and then create the links and the necessary HTML to instantly publish the images to a Web site. The process is very similar to that of making a contact sheet.

The Contact Sheet II Command

Contact Sheet II is a big improvement over the Contact Sheet command in Photoshop 5, thanks mostly to one little check box in its settings dialog that lets you automatically add the correct filename as a label for each thumbnail.

Adobe originally introduced batch actions (described in Chapter 2) in version 5 along with the Contact Sheet command batch action. Even in version 5, I found the Contact Sheet command useful for quickly showing an art director the results of a day's shoot or for making job prints of a limited number of subjects. Still, there was a major shortcoming: there was no way to automatically label a thumbnail. That meant you had to open each file, look for the corresponding printout in the thumbnail sheet, and then use the type tool to enter a label. Talk about maddening tedium.

Even with Contact Sheet II, there are still a few shortcomings. When you label with the filename, the size of the image automatically shrinks to about half the size that the same settings would have produced without the label. That's because long filenames can take up lots of space, and the program has to allocate all the space you might possibly use.

Professional Pointer

You can enter long descriptive filenames for images, and they can serve as captions. Just remember to shorten the filenames and reprint the contact sheet if you plan to distribute these images on a cross-platform CD-ROM. Most cross-platform CD-ROMs are in ISO 9660 format, which requires that filenames have eight alphanumeric characters, followed by a three-character extension. A period (usually called a "dot") divides the filename and the extension. This is almost the same rule as for MS-DOS filenames except that MS-DOS filenames can contain certain symbols. You will also have problems with posting long filenames to your Web site. You can download a shareware program called HTML Rename! from Shareware.com that automatically legalizes long filenames.

Making a Contact Sheet

Making a contact sheet is easy, and for most purposes, many of the steps that you set up initially can be left at their default settings. However, before you make a contact sheet, you need to do a little preparation.

1. Put all the images that you want to catalog into the same folder. It's a good idea to open all the files and make sure they're stored in upright, or portrait, orientation, since many of us shoot scenes with the camera turned vertically. (Kodak's digital cameras automatically rotate the image when the camera stores it—a very nice feature.) Although the Contact Sheet II command opens each file individually and then places it on a layer where it's resized, the layers are all flattened by the time the command finishes executing. Therefore, there's no way to rotate a side-lying image after the fact.

2. While you have all the images open, you might also want to run a basic correction on them before storing them. Photoshop's Image > Adjust > Auto Levels command is particularly handy for this. Once you've rotated and corrected each file, use Save As to save the corrected image to the contact sheet folder while leaving the original intact. That way, you have a corrected image that's easy to read on the contact sheet, and the unchanged original still resides in the original folder.

Cross-Reference: Refer to Chapter 2 for step-by-step instructions on creating action scripts that you can use not only to automate this entire process, but also to insert pauses so that you can decide whether to rotate and whether to correct. You can even insert a pause before saving the file so that you can rename the file with a long filename to use as a more descriptive label.

3. Now for the easy part. Choose the File > Automate > Contact Sheet II command, enter the settings you prefer in the resulting dialog, and click OK. Here's what the dialog looks like:

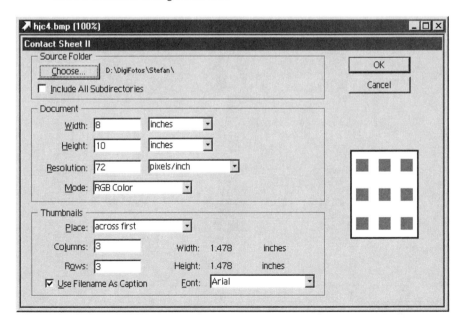

Now you wait a while. Photoshop opens each image individually, resizes it, and places and aligns it on the contact sheet. As each image is placed, it is labeled. The command will use as many pages of the size you designate as it takes to make contact proofs of all the images in the chosen folder. When the process is done, each page is a separate, open, but unsaved file, as shown in Figure 12-1. If you like what you see, store the images in whatever folder suits your purposes.

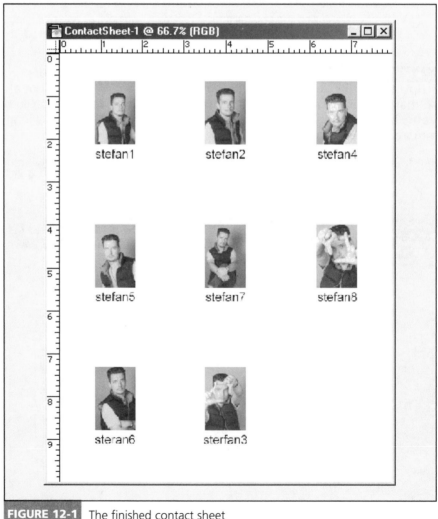

FIGURE 12-1 The finished contact sheet

Professional Pointer

If you want to store the contact on a floppy, save it as a JPEG image to cut down the file size. If you're putting a collection of images on the floppy, you'll probably also want to make JPEG versions of the files, with each one scaled to fit the screen. If you happen to own Kai's Power Tools, you'll find a small program on its CD called QuickShow. Quick-Show is so small that you can put it, a JPEG-compressed contact sheet or two, and a couple dozen images on a floppy. Double-click the Quick-Show icon, and it will automatically run a slide show of all the images on the floppy.

Copying images into multiple thumbnail catalogs

It may help you to place images into more than one thumbnail catalog. Then you can find them more quickly. It will also be easier to show a potential client a category of photos, and you will be able to put collections of categories of photos into their own directories or CD-ROMs. If you want to place the same images into multiple catalogs, you will need to place copies of the files into new directories, and then follow the instructions above to make a new thumbnail sheet for each new directory.

Making a Storyboard

You can use the Contact Sheet II command to automatically make a storyboard. A storyboard is a sheet or mounting board that uses a series of images to show step by step, or frame by frame, the visual state of a story or process at each important point in the progress of the whole. Storyboards are used to plan the shooting of films and TV commercials and are also excellent devices for helping map out the design of almost anything visual, such as a comic strip, magazine, or Web site. If you want to make the storyboard pictures bigger than is typical of contact sheet images, that's no problem. Just choose fewer rows and columns in the Contact Sheet II dialog, and don't elect to use the filenames as captions. Having said that, the real trick here is getting the batch action in the preliminary step to put the illustrations into the proper sequence. The following illustration shows you what a storyboard made in this way might look like.

It's a long way home through the desert Joe stops at a diner Will Joe diet home?

Before you run the Contact Sheet II command to create your storyboard, make the following preparations:

- Make (or collect) the storyboard illustrations.
- If some of the images aren't digital, they will have to be scanned or photographed.
- Scale and correct the images, if necessary, using the Image > Adjust > Auto Levels command.
- Open all of your images at once, and open each so that you can see the order you want to place them in, left to right and top to bottom.
- Create a new folder and rename each of your files as the number of the sequence in which it should appear: 01, 02, 03, and so on. If there will be more than 99 files, make sure to have two leading zeros ahead of the single-digit numbers and one leading zero ahead of the double-digit numbers, for example, 001, 009, and then 088, 099. (To this folder, load all the images that will be in your storyboard into Photoshop, and follow the steps shown in Figure 12-2.)
- Save or move all the files to the new folder.

Now you're ready to build your storyboard using the following steps. Figure 12-3 is a visual map of how to do this.

1. Choose File > Automate > Contact Sheet II.
2. In the dialog, click the Choose button and navigate to the folder in which you've stored the files that make up the pictures for your storyboard.
3. Under Thumbnails, enter a number of rows and columns that will make the files as large as you want them to be. (If you have a large-format printer, you may also want to use a large paper size, such as 11 × 17 or 16 × 20. If that is the case, enter different dimensions in the Width and Height fields under Document.)

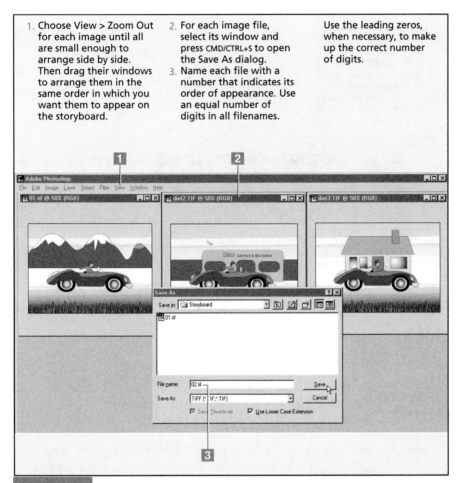

1. Choose View > Zoom Out for each image until all are small enough to arrange side by side. Then drag their windows to arrange them in the same order in which you want them to appear on the storyboard.

2. For each image file, select its window and press CMD/CTRL+S to open the Save As dialog.
3. Name each file with a number that indicates its order of appearance. Use an equal number of digits in all filenames.

Use the leading zeros, when necessary, to make up the correct number of digits.

FIGURE 12-2 Numbering images so they appear in the correct sequence

4. After you click OK, when the command is run, you will see a picture in which each frame of the storyboard appears in the proper sequence. Now just take the type tool and label each frame with descriptive text or dialogue, as called for in the storyboard.

5. Print out the storyboard so that it can be presented to your colleagues or clients.

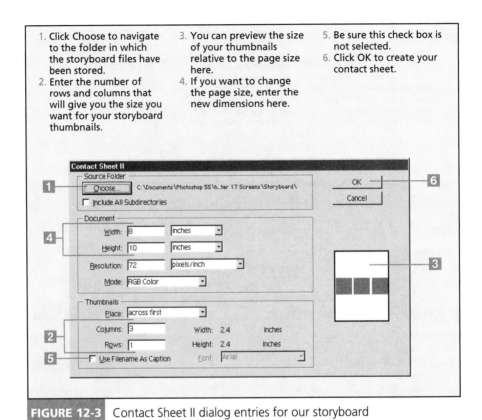

1. Click Choose to navigate to the folder in which the storyboard files have been stored.
2. Enter the number of rows and columns that will give you the size you want for your storyboard thumbnails.
3. You can preview the size of your thumbnails relative to the page size here.
4. If you want to change the page size, enter the new dimensions here.
5. Be sure this check box is not selected.
6. Click OK to create your contact sheet.

FIGURE 12-3   Contact Sheet II dialog entries for our storyboard

When you enter the text for captions under the storyboard pieces, it may not line up as neatly as you'd like. Since Photoshop enters each caption on its own layer, you can select the move tool and then drag the text into place while its layer is still active (or by reactivating its layer). One way to ensure that the text is aligned to your design is to use guidelines and have the text snap to them. Another way is to make use of the Layers > Align Linked command. Figure 12-4 shows you how to do that.

Adding Data Fields to Images

It is often faster to search text for keywords or a photographer's name than to hunt through dozens of contact sheets. Some third-party tools for making contact sheets and managing images let you attach the contact sheet to a database. If you're not yet ready to invest in one of those products, some of which are described in the next section, Photoshop does give you a way to attach a valuable amount of text to almost any image. This text follows guidelines established by the Newspaper Association of America (NAA) and the International Press

1. Select the move tool and use it to drag the contents of each layer into position immediately after entering text. If you move the text later, you must reselect its layer first.

2. Select one of the layers you want to link.
3. Click the link icons for layers you want to align. (Make sure layers you don't want to align don't show a link icon here.)

4. Choose Align Linked, and then choose one of the alignment commands from the submenu.

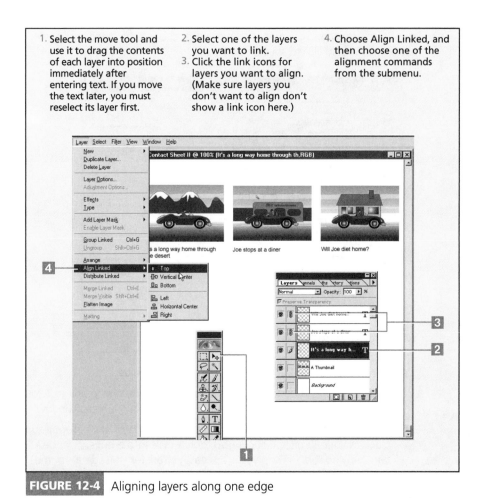

FIGURE 12-4 Aligning layers along one edge

Telecommunications Council (IPTC) for identifying transmitted text and images. The text you enter can also be automatically read by some of the third-party image management packages.

Windows users can add text information to files saved in the Photoshop TIFF, JPEG, EPS, and PDF formats. Mac users can add file information to files in any format. How? Follow the bouncing ball, or at least these steps:

1. Open the file you want to add text to and make sure it is the active window. If necessary, use the Save As command to convert the file to a type that will accept text.

2. Choose File > File Info, and the File Info dialog will appear.

3. From the Section pop-up menu, shown here, choose the category of information you would like to start entering.

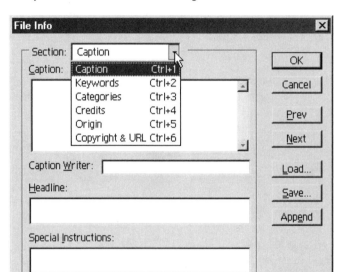

4. Enter the information called for in the labeled fields.

5. Click the Append button to append, or change, the text to any text you have previously entered for the file you have open in the active window.

6. You will almost certainly want to reuse portions of this information (such as your name and copyright) for later File Info entries. (See the accompanying tip.) Also, you can easily transfer this data to most third-party information managers.

Tip: You can also load information from a previously saved Info file. Just click the Load button and follow the on-screen instructions.

Third-Party Image Management Tools

If you need more sophisticated image management tools than what Photoshop 5.5 offers, you have quite a few to choose from. Your choice will depend on the exact features you need, all of which include some means of making contact sheets from folders of images. At the higher end, you will also get built-in data management features. Most of the programs with such features will be able to read the File Info that you have previously created for your image. It will then put it into a form that will be much easier to search and read.

I have listed a few third-party image management products here. They're roughly arranged in order of price. Features vary quite a bit and change faster than new book editions, so you would do well to visit the Web site for each product in order to get the most up-to-date information.

- **Thumbs Plus, Cerious Software (http://www.cerious.com)** Windows-only shareware that offers a nearly indispensable organizational benefit. You can drag files from one directory (folder) to another by opening the thumbnails you've made for both folders. You can also use the program to do basic editing.

- **Image Book, published by Gamut Imaging (http://www.gamutimaging. com)** ImageBook is a Photoshop plug-in. In addition to making contact sheets, the program specializes in printing thumbnail-illustrated covers for CD-ROMs and Zip disks. Gamut also produces a separate image database management program. Approximate retail price is $89.95.

- **Extensis Portfolio, Extensis (http://www.extensis.com)** Portfolio is based on what was formerly Adobe Fetch. It has grown quite a bit these days and is also the most widely used application of its type. It's now a full-fledged, cross-platform image and data cataloging system. The catalog reader is freely distributable. Portfolio will also create automatic Web portfolios. Approximate retail price is $199.95.

- **Kudo Image Publisher, Imspace (http://www.imspace.com)** Originally a Mac-only program, Kudo Image Publisher is now available for Windows as well. This one also publishes to the Internet. Its specialty is cataloging CD-ROM content. It also creates self-running slide shows. Approximate retail price is $999.00.

- **Canto Cumulus, Canto Software (http://www.canto-software.com/ home/index.html)** This is a heavy-duty image and image data management tool used by many stock photo agencies and major corporations. You can even add voice annotations to media assets (multimedia files, including image files and voice annotations), automatically e-mail chosen assets, and create multimedia slide shows. Single-user versions start at $99.95. Prices for network versions are negotiable, depending on the number of users.

Scaling Images to Fit a Publication

Whether you're preparing a print catalog, or storing images for an employee database, or collecting images for use on a Web site, you probably have a requirement for files that fit within a given size and resolution range. Of course, you need to meet these requirements without changing the aspect ratio (the ratio of height to width) of the original. With a single batch command—the Fit Image command—Photoshop will automatically scale an entire folder of images to fit within that range. The upcoming tutorials will show you how. First you see how

Tip: As you create or find images you want to perform the batch command on, put copies of them into one file folder. The Fit Image command, like all batch commands, works only on images in one specific folder (and, optionally, its subdirectories).
Important: Make sure you put them in a different folder than the one containing the original images. If you leave the originals in the target folder with the copies, they will be permanently rescaled, which will prevent you from ever being able to recover all the detail in the original.

to record an action that defines what your parameters should be and rescales the current image. (You also find out how to customize that action by editing it should it become necessary later on.) Then you perform a batch command that will execute that action on the entire folder of images.

Creating an Action to Define the Image Parameters

To define the parameters for each of your images, follow these steps:

1. Choose File > Open. Open one of the images in your folder. If there are other open image windows, make sure the window for the file you just opened stays active (the title bar is highlighted)—don't click in any of the other open windows until after you've finished recording the action.

2. Record an action that rescales the current image. Choose Window > Show Actions to show the Actions palette. From the Actions palette flyout, choose New Action.

3. A dialog will appear and you will be asked to name the action. Enter a name for the action (**Fit Into** will do) and click the Record button. Do *not* choose a color or a function key.

4. Choose File > Automate > Fit Image, and the Fit Image dialog will appear, as shown in the following illustration. Enter the width and height (in pixels) within which the resampled image must fit. Note that you're not specifying the dimensions of the image. You are saying that the largest dimension must match its equivalent and the other must be smaller than its equivalent. Click OK. The image in the active window will now be rescaled.

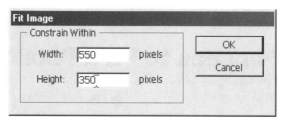

5. Click the Stop Recording button at the bottom of the Actions palette.

Editing the action for different parameters

You can edit the Fit Into action you recorded in the preceding section whenever you change the dimensions of the file size you want to fit within the desired parameters. If you find you need to do this, the process is quite straightforward and is accomplished by following these steps:

1. Open the Actions palette and select the Fit Into action.
2. Open a file for the action to operate on.
3. Click the Plays Current Action button in the Actions palette. This will cause the command to execute, and the Fit Image dialog will appear.
4. Enter a new set of dimensions in the Fit Image dialog and click OK. The file will be rescaled. The new dimensions have also automatically been entered into the action so that the next time you use this action, it will use the new dimensions.

Creating a Batch Command to Execute the Action on Several Images

Now that you have created the Fit Into action to perform the File > Automate > Fit Image command on a single image, you will see how to perform a batch command to execute the action on the entire folder of images:

1. Choose File > Automate > Batch. The Batch dialog will open.
2. Choose the set and action that you have just made from the top two pop-up menus.
3. Click the Choose button and navigate to the folder in which the images you want to fit were previously stored.
4. In the Destination section, choose Folder, and then click the Choose button to navigate to the folder in which you want to store the results of the action.
5. From the Errors pop-up menu, choose Stop for Errors.
6. Click OK. The entire folder of images will be automatically processed to fit inside the dimensions you specified.

Picture Packages: Printing Multiple Images on a Sheet

Given the cost of supplies for color printers, you'll soon find that it makes economic sense to squeeze more than one copy of an image onto a sheet of paper. If you want to reproduce several of the same image on a single page, Photoshop 5.5 has automated the task for you with the Picture Package command. If you want to create a single page with several different images on it, you'll find that's quite easy to do as well. I'll show you how to do both actions here.

Creating Multiples of One Image on the Same Page

If you want to create a job print (that's what wedding and portrait studios call a print that contains several copies of the same image), you use Photoshop 5.5's new Picture Package command, aptly named since a picture package is another trade term for a job print. Anyway, here's what you do:

1. Open the file you want to create a package of. Actually, this is an optional step since you can have the Picture Package command open the file for you. However, opening the file yourself allows you to make any adjustments to the image before you package it.

2. Choose File > Automate > Picture Package. The Picture Package dialog appears, as shown here:

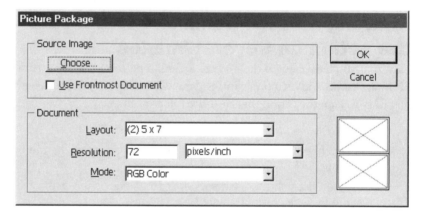

3. Select the Use Frontmost Document check box, and Photoshop will package the image in the currently active window.

4. Choose the package layout you want from the Layout menu.

5. Enter a printing resolution (about 240 dpi if you are using an Epson inkjet at 1,440 dpi on photo-glossy paper).

6. Pick a color mode that's suited to the printer you'll be using (see your printer manual) and click OK.

The finished printout will look something like what's shown here:

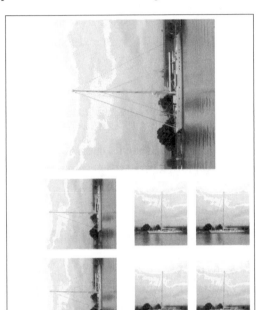

Creating a Single Page with Several Different Images

If you watched Photoshop put your job sheet together and you understand how both the drag-and-drop and layers features work, you've probably already figured out how to make up a page with several different images on it. Here's the drill:

1. Put copies of the images you want to package into a new folder. You'll probably want to name the folder, but that's not a requirement.

2. If you did the exercises in "Scaling Images to Fit a Publication," use the action you recorded there. Edit it to work for the size that you'd like the individual images to fit within.

3. Use the Batch command to run the Fit Image command, as described in the earlier section, "Creating a Batch Command to Execute the Action on Several Images."

Tip: You could use the technique described in this section to create a scrapbook. Use the type tool to label the photographs. Use a three-hole punch on the printout and place the result in a three-ring binder.

4. Open all the rescaled images at the same time. The quickest way to do that is to open the file folder on the desktop (Mac) or in the Explorer (Windows), select all the files, and drag them into an open Photoshop window.

5. Create a new file that is the size and resolution you'd like to print your combined image to. In the New File dialog, make sure you choose to have a white background.

6. Select the move tool and use it to drag each of the rescaled and opened images onto the new file. As you move each file into place, be sure to position the images where you want them.

Unless you think you might need the images you copied into the new folder for some other purpose, you should trash the new folder to avoid needlessly over-crowding your hard drive.

Creating Linked Thumbnails for a Web page

For the longest time I thought it would be so cool to put up a private Web portfolio of the results of a shoot so that the client(s) and other participants could view and judge the results from their own offices. Friends who have done this tell me that they often make more money because clients (or a client's client) see photos that they decide they can use for other purposes. The problem is to find the time to get everything organized to do that effectively. Now that Photoshop 5.5's new Web Photo Gallery command is ready to do it all for me, you can bet that I'll be making use of this feature.

In fact, if you have a WYSIWYG HTML editor, such as Adobe GoLive or Macromedia FireWorks, it's easy to edit what Photoshop does automatically. So it's even a good idea to start with this feature when you're designing a portfolio for your primary Web site or for a client.

Quite a few of you have done this sort of thing manually many times. You'll be the ones most impressed with how easy Photoshop 5.5 makes the job for you with the new Web Photo Gallery command. Prepare for the job by doing the following:

- Place copies of the files you want in the portfolio in a new folder. Open them all and make sure they are rotated upright.

- Create a new folder as the destination for the Web-processed files and the accompanying HTML.

- If necessary, rename the copied files so that their names follow ISO 9660 rules. You rename your files so that they will behave properly in the Web environment.

When you finish running the Web Photo Gallery command, you will end up
with two sets of files: a set of small GIF thumbnails and a set of larger gallery images. The thumbnails will be arrayed on a single screen so that your viewers can
quickly see the subjects pictured in your portfolio and choose which they'd like
to see at a larger size. You can really maximize the performance of the gallery files
if you first optimize them in ImageReady (see Chapter 13 for details on image
optimization). To produce your Web gallery, as just described, choose File > Automate > Web Photo Gallery, which will open the Web Photo Gallery dialog.
Then follow the steps shown in Figure 12-5.

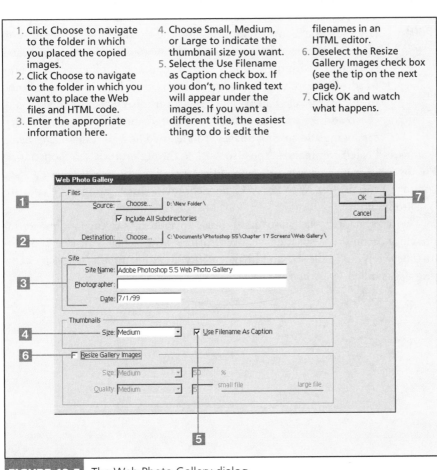

1. Click Choose to navigate to the folder in which you placed the copied images.
2. Click Choose to navigate to the folder in which you want to place the Web files and HTML code.
3. Enter the appropriate information here.
4. Choose Small, Medium, or Large to indicate the thumbnail size you want.
5. Select the Use Filename as Caption check box. If you don't, no linked text will appear under the images. If you want a different title, the easiest thing to do is edit the
filenames in an HTML editor.
6. Deselect the Resize Gallery Images check box (see the tip on the next page).
7. Click OK and watch what happens.

FIGURE 12-5 The Web Photo Gallery dialog

Tip: If you want good performance and appearance for your gallery images, you should first optimize them using ImageReady. If you wait until you're running the Web Photo Gallery command to select the Resize Gallery Images check box, Photoshop will reprocess them. There's a better-than-even chance that you will end up with an unnecessarily large number of compression artifacts. That will give your picture a bad case of the uglies.

You may want to change the look of this page or the contents of links later. If you know how to edit HTML code, you can simply edit the code that Photoshop has automatically produced for you. If you want to make it easy on yourself, I suggest you get your hands on Macromedia Dreamweaver or some other well-designed WYSIWYG HTML editor that doesn't produce or demand nonstandard code. You can then use the commands in the program to quickly change any of the design characteristics of the page.

Professional Skills Summary

This chapter was all about the importance of managing images properly and about some of the strengths and shortcomings of Photoshop 5.5 in that respect. First, you learned how to make contact sheets and storyboards with the Contact Sheet II command. Next, you saw how to add file searching capability using the File Info command. Some third-party image management tools were also recommended.

To address size and resolution requirements often necessary when cataloging and storing images, you learned how to scale images using actions and batch commands. You also worked through tutorials demonstrating Photoshop's image organization capabilities, including the new Picture Package command and the new Web Photo Gallery command for creating a Web portfolio automatically.

The next chapter talks about how to use ImageReady to prepare images for presentation on the Web. It emphasizes learning how to make the best compromise between image file size and image quality. Maximizing this necessary compromise is called *image optimization.*

chapter 13

Optimizing Web Graphics

In this chapter, you:

- Optimize Web images in Photoshop 5.5 and ImageReady 2

- Find out which product to use when

- Consider performance vs. appearance, using the 2-Up and 4-Up views

- Learn about the Web image formats (JPEG, PNG-24, PNG-8, and GIF) and their byte costs

- Learn tools and commands unique to ImageReady

- Make navigational and logo graphics

ImageReady 2 is a complete application for preparing images for use on Web pages. Once sold only as a standalone program, ImageReady is now available only as part of Photoshop 5.5. The program looks and feels so much like Photoshop that you'll often forget whether you're working in one or the other. Nearly everything you've learned to do in Photoshop can be done the same way in ImageReady. Furthermore, Photoshop has new Web optimization capabilities that make it nearly as capable at optimizing Web graphics as ImageReady.

Optimization, when used in association with Web graphics or sound, refers to the process of achieving the most workable compromise between quality and byte size for an image or sound file. This compromise is important because it takes time for data to be transferred over standard voice phone lines and modems. Moreover, the majority of viewers are still using 56K and 28.8K modems. Any time it takes more than ten seconds for an image to appear, you're in grave danger of losing your viewer to a faster-moving site.

This chapter covers the decisions involved in optimizing Web graphics, and the process of preparing files for use on the Web. Because ImageReady lets you preview several optimization choices in comparison with one another or to the original image, the emphasis here will be on using ImageReady.

Photoshop vs. ImageReady

It makes little difference whether you optimize your image in Photoshop or ImageReady, because the tasks involved in both programs are nearly the same. The big difference between the two is that the optimization process is, overall, more interactive in ImageReady. What do I mean by interactive? All you have to do to see an optimization preview is click the tab for the view you want. So you can see the results of all the optimization settings as you make them. You don't have to save the file and then reload it to see the results of your choices.

Regardless which program you use, you never have to resort to the old-fashioned method of creating several versions of the file, saving each individually, and then reopening them to see which settings strike the best balance between image quality and download speed. Instead, you instantly compare versions side by side. Only when you've settled on a "keeper" do you actually save the file.

Your optimization tasks are done a bit more directly in ImageReady than in Photoshop:

- In ImageReady, you are able to click a tab conveniently located right there in the image-editing window. This takes you from the original to an optimized (2-Up or 4-Up) view.

- In Photoshop, you have to first choose File > Save as Web. Once you've done that, you can't continue to edit the image being optimized. You can, however, resize the image right on the spot—no need to choose the Image Size command before saving for the Web.

Professional Pointer

Although you can jump directly from Photoshop to ImageReady by clicking the Jump To button, the size of the image in Photoshop is generally several times that of the typical Web image you'd be editing in ImageReady. That's because even those illustrations featured on a site are seldom larger than 400 × 300. An image of that size destined for print (which is what Photoshop is typically used for) would be several megabytes. Unless you have a lot of memory and a fast computer, the first thing you'll want to do in ImageReady is reduce the size of the file to its Web destination size. But before you do, be sure to save a different version from the original. Otherwise, you'll never be able to regain the data you threw out in reducing the size of the file.

This file-size issue will make a great deal more sense if you compare the optimization screens for both Photoshop and ImageReady. In Photoshop (Figure 13-1), you can see the optimization settings at the right. In ImageReady's image-editing window (Figure 13-2), however, that's not the case—you get to the optimization

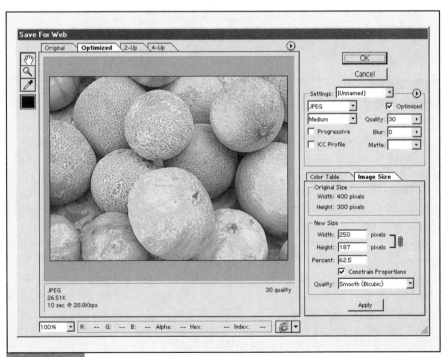

FIGURE 13-1 Photoshop's Save for Web dialog is very similar to ImageReady's interface for optimization.

In ImageReady, you can edit a file you're optimizing and the edits are instantly reflected in the optimized views of the file.

settings in a separate Optimize palette. You resize an image in the same way as if you were doing it from the regular Photoshop image-editing window—by choosing Image > Image Size.

Whether you're optimizing in ImageReady or Photoshop, by clicking the appropriate tab at the top of the window, you can see the original file, or the version resulting from the current optimization settings, or a side-by-side view of the original and the currently chosen optimization setting, or four views of the image—each showing any optimization setting you choose. (You'll learn all about how to make these optimizations in this chapter.) The side-by-side views make it possible to immediately judge the trade-offs in image quality resulting from various choices in the optimization and file-type settings for any file.

ImageReady also uses the status line to report the download speed for the chosen optimization(s). Figure 13-3 shows the 2-Up and 4-Up views.

FIGURE 13-3 The status line at the bottom of each view shows the download speed for each level of optimization.

Optimizing a Photograph for the Web

Photographs and other continuous-tone, full-color art are generally optimized to the JPEG format. That is because JPEG is the only one of two universally accepted Web file formats that can display a full 16.8 million colors, and because JPEG can compress color files to data sizes that are but a fraction of the original's. The problem with JPEG is that it's "lossy," which is to say that it manages its high level of compression by throwing out a lot of color information and then substituting pixels that are "close enough." Of course, the more you compress the file, the more likely that "close enough" will resemble garbage.

Thumbnails are the exception to the "photo = JPEG" rule. If an image is around 100×150 pixels, it can contain a maximum of 1,500 colors—far from the 16 million in the average photo. The 256 colors in a GIF file, plus a little *dithering* (intermingling colors to create the illusion of another color), will generally do a good job of simulating all the colors well enough to let the viewer know whether it's worth the wait to see the larger image. Furthermore, the browser doesn't have to spend time running the JPEG algrorithm to decompress the file, a process that takes just about as long for a small image as for a larger one.

Of course, quality will suffer somewhat—you just need to settle on an acceptable level of compromise, just as you do for all Web graphics. There is no law that says you can't use JPEG for thumbnails; just remember that viewers tend to click quickly out of a slow-moving site.

The Optimization Settings

The optimization settings for JPEG can be seen in Figures 13-4 (Photoshop) and 13-5 (ImageReady).

- **Optimize flyout menu**   Options available on this menu let you save and delete settings (saved settings will appear in the Settings menu). You can also choose to optimize your file to a specified size, and Photoshop or ImageReady will automatically choose the best settings for that size. Of course, you can always use the other optimization controls to modify these settings. Finally, there's an option to have the program automatically calculate higher levels of compression for all but the currently selected optimization (but originals are never altered).

- **Settings menu**   This pop-up menu lists the most common settings for each of the supported Web file formats: JPEG, GIF, PING 8, AND PING 24. You can also enter your own settings. The number of settings and their nature changes depending on the file format you choose.

- **File format menu**   This menu lets you choose one of the optimized Web formats supported by Photoshop and ImageReady.

- **Quality menu**   For file compression, the choices are Low, Medium, High, and Maximum. Your choice determines the initial automatic setting for the adjacent Quality field, but you can change that setting to intermediate values.

- **Quality field and slider**   Initial setting depends on quality-level selection. You can use this setting to modify the compression level. Enter a number between 1 and 100, or click the arrow button and drag a slider until the number you want appears.

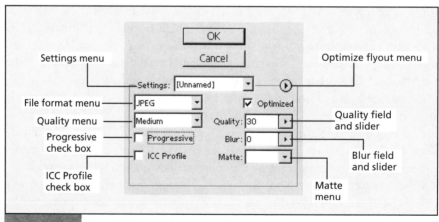

FIGURE 13-4   The JPEG optimization settings in Photoshop

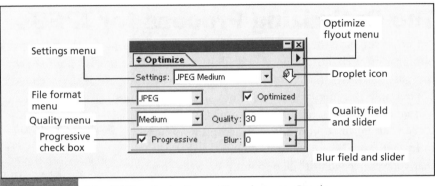

FIGURE 13-5 The JPEG optimization settings in ImageReady

- **Progressive check box** Select this box if you want a low-resolution version of your file to be seen while the high-resolution version is downloading. This works best for medium- to large-size Web images.

- **ICC Profile check box (Photoshop only)** Preserves the ICC profile generated by Photoshop so that browsers recognizing the profile can adjust the color accordingly. Not all browsers can do this, but if the color of your image is important, you might find it worthwhile to make sure that a profile has been created and that you save it with your Web image.

- **Matte menu** Lets you choose a color to match your HTML page's background color so that transparent portions of the original image can be simulated. Note that this is not true transparency. If you display the image on a background that's a different color from the matte color, the matte color will simply appear as solid-color "blotches" within the image. Of the two universal Web file formats, only GIF supports true transparency by assigning a single solid color to be transparent, rather than to match a background.

- **Blur field and slider** Hard edges can't be compressed too much without showing really bad artifacts (blotchiness due to overcompression). If you soften edges, you will get a more highly compressed file. You can use this setting for images where detail is unimportant or when you need a look that is more flattering or romantic. Enter a number between 0 and 2, or click the arrow button and drag the slider to set the blur.

- **Droplet icon (ImageReady only)** This icon appears in several of ImageReady's palettes. You can click it to create an icon on your desktop that will apply the current settings to any file (or folder full of files) that is dropped onto it.

The Optimizing Process for JPEGs

Now that you have the basics, it should be easy for you to go ahead with actually optimizing a Web illustration. A Web illustration, by my rules, is a photo or continuous-tone image that's large enough to be a visual feature of the Web page. For example, this might be a news photo, or an example in an artist's portfolio, or a product illustration for a Web auction.

You can do the optimization either in Photoshop or in ImageReady. We're going to do it in ImageReady so that you can see what it's like to jump between the two applications and so that you get used to resizing your image before you start optimizing. Otherwise, the steps are nearly identical. (If you choose to do this in Photoshop, start by choosing File > Save for Web, and then continue with the steps in this section.)

Note that much of the process for optimizing in other file formats and for other purposes is the same as in this exercise. Since we don't have room to repeat them all in every exercise, this is one exercise that you should read all the way through.

> **Tip:** If you are doing the Web optimizing in Photoshop, you can reduce the size of the file right in the Save for Web dialog (click the Image Size tab and adjust the settings as desired). This dialog saves the optimized version of the file, *not* the original. Just be sure to give the file a new name in the Save Optimized As dialog.

1. Load the image you want to save for the Web. If you want to use the same image I used, download BUSSHAK1.JPG from the Osborne site. (This is an image from a Kodak DC265 digital camera. As is, it's way too big for Web use and we need to reduce it. But you don't want to risk not being able to use it for print later. To keep that from happening, immediately duplicate the file and reduce its size before jumping to ImageReady, where we will do our Web optimizing.)

2. Choose Image > Duplicate. The Duplicate Image dialog will appear:

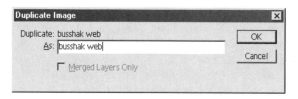

3. Enter a new name for the file so that your adjustments won't overwrite your original—or just accept Photoshop's renaming with the word "copy" added to the original name. (I usually just substitute the word "Web" for the word "copy" in the new filename. That way I'll instantly understand the purpose of the copy the next time I see it in the directory.)

4. Click OK. Another window containing the original image will appear. Just to ensure that you don't get them mixed up, close the original file.

5. Choose Image > Image Size to open the Image Size dialog, which is shown in Figure 13-6.

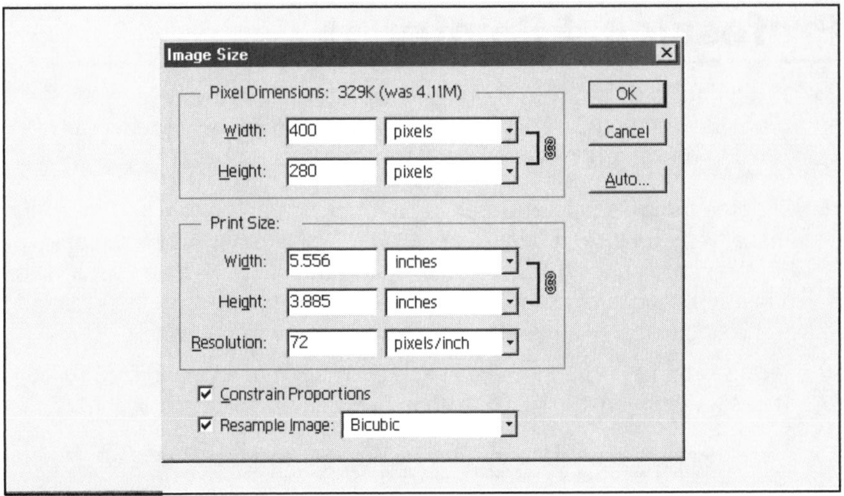

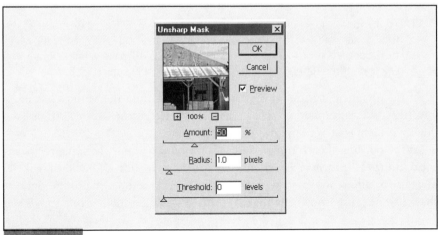

FIGURE 13-6 The Image Size dialog

6. Under Pixel Dimensions, enter the number you'd like for the image's largest pixel dimension. The other dimension will automatically size itself in proportion (unless you've deselected the Constrain Proportions check box). That's all there is to resizing for the Web. Click OK.

7. After changing the size of the image, usually you have lost some edge sharpness, and the picture will seem very slightly out of focus. The default settings in the Unsharp Mask filter usually fix the problem without further ado. Just choose Filter > Sharpen > Unsharp Mask. The dialog retains the last settings you used, so you may have to return them to the defaults shown in Figure 13-7. If not, just click OK.

FIGURE 13-7 The Unsharp Mask dialog

Professional Pointer

If you're going to do many Web images, put these first seven steps into an action (see Chapter 2). Then all you'll have to do is press a function key to resize and sharpen your images for the Web.

8. Click the Jump To Default Graphics Editor button at the very bottom of the ImageReady toolbox. If ImageReady 2 is the only other Adobe Graphics or HTML editor you've installed, it will open automatically. If you've installed other applications or assigned other graphics editors to work here (see the Photoshop manual), a menu will appear. Choose ImageReady 2.

9. Because you have changed the image originally loaded and didn't immediately save them afterward, Photoshop presents the following dialog:

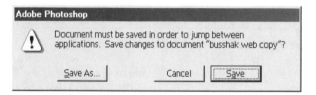

You have already renamed the file, so just click the Save button. Otherwise, you could click the Save As button and give the file a new name, location, or both. Click OK and ImageReady will open. Photoshop will stay open as well. (Notice how similar the two interfaces are.)

10. Since we know we want to use JPEG optimization, choose Window > Show Optimize to bring up the Optimize palette, shown earlier in Figure 13-5. (Actually, it's probably already up. You'll rarely want to turn it off because you'll need to test any changes you make.) From the Settings menu, choose JPEG High.

11. To do your optimization, switch to the 4-Up view. Click the 4-Up tab at the top of the image-editing window. By default, the original image is shown in the upper-left window. As soon as you switch to 4-Up view, ImageReady will calculate three different optimizations, as shown in Figure 13-8.

At the upper right is the optimization you chose from the Settings menu. At lower left is an optimization at half the quality percentage. At lower right, the quality percentage has been lowered another 50%.

At the bottom of each image view is information about that image. First is the optimized file format chosen for that view (yes, you can choose different file formats for different views), with the quality percentage setting to the right of that. The next line shows the file's optimized size, and the last line shows the

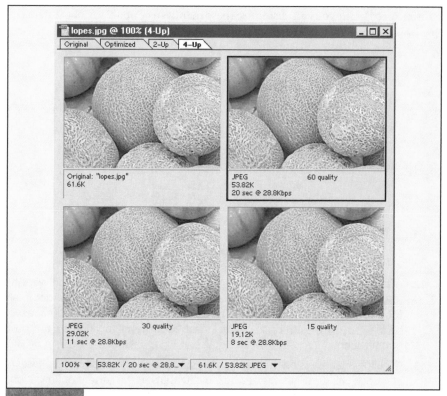

FIGURE 13-8 The 4-Up view always shows the original and three different optimization settings.

amount of time it will take to load over a typical modem. (The default modem speed is 28.8 Kbps because that is still the speed at which the majority of viewers browse the Web.)

In the status bar at the bottom of the screen, the size currently selected in the zoom menu is shown at the left end. To the right of that are two information menus: a document information menu in Photoshop, and an image information menu in ImageReady. In Figure 13-8, both information menus contain the same information (file size and estimated

Tip: Now, here's the thing you must remember: Each individual photograph will differ as to how much compression it can take before its appearance becomes unacceptable. It's strictly a subjective opinion and one that depends on the sharpness of your eyesight. If you don't trust your own judgment, call in a colleague or have someone else do the job.

transfer speed). But you can customize these menus to contain any of the items in the drop-down list shown here:

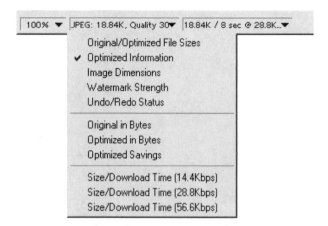

12. After setting your information menus to show the information you want to see, choose 100% from the zoom menu in the status bar. This will zoom all four views to 100%. After all, this is the zoom level at which your image will be viewed on the Web, so it's the best zoom level for judging the best optimization.

13. Click the image version that seems closest to making the best compromise. A black box will surround this view to indicate that it is the current optimization, and its stats will appear in the status bar. This is the view that will change when you alter the settings in the Optimize palette.

14. In the Optimize palette, drag the Quality slider to a setting low enough to change the transmission speed. If the image becomes unacceptably messy, move the slider back up slightly.

15. Drag the Blur slider slowly to the right to soften the image. Stop when and if the image seems unacceptably out of focus. Many images can't stand any blur at all. If yours can, you'll notice that the file size becomes smaller and the transfer speed becomes faster.

16. Since this is a larger image, you'll want to select the Progressive check box. Transfer speed probably won't be affected at all. If it goes up slightly, it's probably a worthwhile trade-off because the rough version of the image will load much faster.

    (If you're optimizing in Photoshop, at this point you should select the ICC Profile check box. It doesn't seem to cost much if anything in download speed, and it increases the chances that the destination browser will display your picture as you've intended.)

17. Now you need to examine the full-screen version of the file to make sure you haven't overdone the optimization. Do that by making sure your preferred optimization view is selected and then clicking the Optimized tab.

18. If you're satisfied, save the chosen optimization. From the File menu, choose either Save Optimized or Save Optimized As. The latter is safer because you get a chance to rename the file. You will probably also want to save versions in other sizes for other pages or as thumbnails, so it's a good idea to add a code to each filename that gives you a clue about that version's use.

Other Options for Optimization

In addition to the settings and options in the typical optimization scenario described in the preceding section, the Optimize palette flyout gives you a few others worth mentioning. To reach this menu, click the right-facing arrowhead in the upper-right corner of the palette.

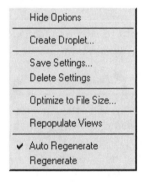

Create Droplet

The Create Droplet option lets you make optimization tasks automatic by reusing the settings you've just chosen. It will open a file-saving dialog that gives you a chance to rename the droplet, which ImageReady automatically names to correspond to the currently selected file format and Quality setting. You can do the same thing by simply clicking the droplet icon in the Optimize palette.

Once you've saved the droplet, drag the droplet icon from the Optimize palette to your desktop. You can then automatically optimize any folder/file by choosing the move tool and dragging the file onto the droplet icon, or by choosing the file from the directory window and dragging it onto the droplet icon. If you drag a folder onto the droplet icon, you optimize all the files in the folder to correspond with the settings for that droplet. You can have multiple droplets, each with different optimization settings. You can also create droplets for actions in ImageReady, and you can drop an Optimize droplet into an action droplet to include those optimization settings in the action. Pretty powerful for such a teeny little thing, eh?

Optimize to File Size

Optimize to File Size is the most powerful command on this menu. It lets you choose a specific file size and then automatically makes the settings needed to compress the file to that size.

You start by selecting any of the choices on the Settings menu or the Optimize file format menu. Then in the Optimize palette menu, choose Optimize to File Size to open this dialog:

Here you choose whether to start with the current optimization settings, or to force the program to choose between GIF and JPEG formats. Then enter the file size (in kilobytes) that you want to aim for and click OK. Next thing you know, you'll see your file reduced (by whatever means necessary) to meet the target size.

Professional Pointer

Choosing Optimize to File Size is particularly handy when speed takes precedence over image quality. Reduce an image to a size beyond any hope of maintaining quality and you might even end up with something that looks like an etching or a mezzotint. You'll have to decide whether the mistake is interesting or counterproductive.

Repopulate Views

This is a little like figuring out who's on first, so listen up: Choosing Repopulate Views causes all views but the selected one to be recalculated. Since the original and the currently selected view are not recalculated, if you want to recalculate all the views at a lower Quality setting, select a view with a lower Quality setting than the view with the highest Quality setting. The selected view will then be moved into the view for the first level of optimization, and the other view(s) will be recalculated at one-half and one-quarter of that value. Because the selected view isn't recalculated, Repopulate Views works in 2-Up only when the original isn't one of the two views.

Auto Regenerate

When you turn on the Auto Regenerate option, a selected view is recalculated the instant you change any Optimize setting. You may want to disable this feature if you are making several changes in settings for the same view. That way, you won't have to pause for recalculation for each of the changes. On the other hand, because Web images are small and today's computers are fast, I tend to leave this option selected at all times. It just makes the optimization process more interactive.

If you want to leave Auto Regenerate turned off, you can choose Regenerate when you are ready to recalculate the selected views. This command regenerates only the selected view.

Save Settings and Delete Settings

The Save Settings and Delete Settings choices allow you to save optimization settings so that they will appear on the Settings menu, or to delete the current settings from that menu.

Optimizing Photographs with PNG-24

The PNG formats, PNG-8 and PNG-24, were invented partly to overcome shortcomings in the GIF and JPEG formats. You'll want to consider using PNG-24 when

- You need transparency in a true-color photo
- You need multilevel (that is, feathered or graduated) transparency
- You want to prepare an image for use in Flash
- Image quality takes precedence over all other considerations
- Your target site is on a high-speed network with uniform, up-to-date browsers (or at least browsers that have a PNG plug-in installed)

Aside from these advantages offered by PNG-24 over JPEG, there are some disadvantages to consider as well. PNG-24 files are almost always significantly larger than JPEGs (and can never be as highly optimized); and only the latest generations of browsers have built-in PNG-24 compatibility. The first limitation means that the files will take longer to upload. The second means that you risk excluding a significant percentage of potential viewers.

Having said all that, if you decide to use the PNG-24 format, here's how to go about it.

1. Start by reading or reviewing the foregoing tutorial on optimizing JPEGs. It will give you a good grounding in the general optimizing process.

2. Load your Web-sized file into either Photoshop or ImageReady. If you want to stay in Photoshop, choose File > Save for Web. If you plan to make animations, slices, rollovers, or image maps from the Web image (these are covered in Chapter 14), jump to ImageReady. Either way, the Optimize settings will be the same.

3. From the Settings menu in the Optimize dialog or palette, choose PNG-24.

4. If you want to create transparency in the image, erase the background of the selected layer to transparency. You can use any of the methods described in Chapters 6 and 7, but the transparency should be in the layer, not in an Alpha channel or layer mask. If you have a mask you want to use for transparency, turn it into a selection, invert the selection, and then press DEL/BACKSPACE to erase the contents of the inverted selection. That layer should be selected in the original view so that what you see in the optimized views is the image against a transparent background, like this:

PNG-24
1.663M
606 sec @ 28.8Kbps

5. It's best to select the Interlaced box in the Optimize palette. As you can see just above, the PNG-24 file is going to take lots longer to load.

6. You will also want to disable Auto Regenerate in the Optimize flyout, because you'll quickly discover that it takes considerably longer to generate an optimized PNG-24 file. Nor is there any way to choose a higher level of optimization, since PNG is intended to be a comparatively lossless image compression format.

Professional Pointer

A few photographers and artists of my acquaintance are giving viewers an option to click a large PNG-24 version of a file so that they can better judge the quality of the original. That way, folks who aren't interested, or who don't have the necessary DSL or cable modem connection or a compatible browser, won't be trapped into wasting their time. On the other hand, the PNG-24 option lets an ad agency or rep on the other side of the world, and who has a T-1 connection, see what they need to see without your having to travel there. If you choose to offer this option, be aware that there's a greater risk of image theft when you provide a high-resolution image. Another possibility is to place those images on a URL that can be accessed only by authorized users with the proper password.

Optimizing Graphics with GIF and PNG-8

Graphics and images composed of hard lines with solid color (the sort of thing typically produced in programs such as CorelDRAW! and Adobe Illustrator) are best optimized to the 256-color (or less) GIF format. PNG-8 format works nearly as well, but many older but still widely used browsers won't be able to recognize the format. Exceptions to this advice for using GIF or PNG-8 format would be the more complex illustrations that make extensive use of gradients and blends.

GIF and PNG-8 are virtually lossless compression formats that achieve most of their efficiency because they limit the number of colors to 256. This technique maintains clean and sharp edges (something JPEG is notorious for messing up) and doesn't produce artifacts in large areas of solid or near-solid color. It makes GIF and PNG-8 nearly ideal for decorative text, buttons, navigational graphics—that sort of thing.

Another reason you might want to use GIF or PNG-8 is that you can make specific areas of the image transparent. GIF permits only one level of transparency, so you want to avoid anti-aliased selections when assigning that color. Otherwise, you end up with an unsightly halo where the anti-aliasing retains pixels that blend with the old background's color—as you see along the edges of these letters:

Both PNG formats (-8 and -24) allow multiple levels of transparency, so the image can blend into the underlying HTML page.

The drawback to optimizing files in GIF format is that it is inferior to JPEG in terms of compression ability. However, if you're working with a very limited range of colors or with smaller images (such as buttons and thumbnails), the files are likely to be so small that any size advantage afforded by JPEG is offset by clumpy solid areas, soft edges, and the browser's having to take a bit more time to decompress the JPEG file.

The secret to optimal GIF (and PNG-8) optimization is to use as few colors as possible. If a graphic contains mainly two colors with some slight shading, you may be able to get away with as few as four or five colors in the optimization—especially if you specify dithering to "invent" nonexistent colors by scattering pixels in a pattern. When this pattern is viewed from a normal reading distance on screen, it can resemble a color that's not even in the color (swatches) table for this image.

Now that you know what you're shooting for, let's optimize a GIF file. Figure 13-9 shows the file we're going to optimize, along with the Optimize palette as it appears when GIF has been chosen as the optimized file format. This image is a button with some text on it. Even with 32-color, which is way more than we really need, upload time is only about two seconds. We want to get that down even further, though. Remember, even on a simple Web page there are usually lots of buttons and other small graphical elements.

1. Make a button and apply a style that gives the object some depth. Don't use a style that uses a drop shadow. If you're too lazy to make your own, download BUTTON.JPG from the Osborne site.

2. Click the 2-Up tab and select the right-hand view.

3. From the Settings menu in the Optimize palette/dialog, choose GIF 32 Dithered. Choosing a dithered format lets you accommodate fading in the highlights and shadows without having to use too many colors.

4. The first thing you want to do is reduce the number of colors as much as possible without sacrificing the look of the button. Using the Colors menu, choose progressively smaller numbers of colors until you get to an unacceptable level. Then go back up one level. You have just determined how few colors you can use, without ever having to experimentally save and open files.

5. If the shading and shadows have become a bit blotchy, drag the Dither slider to the right to increase the amount of dithering. Stop when the problem is reasonably cured. You can also try the choices in the Diffusion menu. If your image had no shading, you would choose No Dither. Other choices are

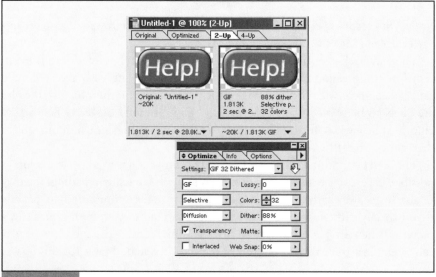

FIGURE 13-9   The Optimize palette's settings for GIF format

Pattern (a set pattern of pixels is used to simulate colors not in the palette) and Noise (the dithering is totally random).

6. For the Color Reduction Algorithm (middle menu on the left), choose Web. This will ensure that your chosen colors will be seen the same way by virtually all browsers.

7. The Transparency check box is probably already selected. ImageReady and Photoshop automatically recognize when part of the layer is transparent. If your button did have a drop shadow, you'd want to use Matte instead of Transparency. Matte fills the transparent area with the HTML page's background color; you should know what that color is so you can choose it from the swatches that appear when you click the Matte menu button.

8. Because this graphic is so small, you can leave Interlaced unselected without slowing things down much.

9. Drag the Web Snap slider to 100%. This will shift all the colors to the closest Web-safe color.

10. Once again, we save the best for last. Although GIF is a lossless format, Photoshop and ImageReady can make it somewhat lossy and thereby reduce the files even more than would be possible in most other programs. This button is too small to save us much that way, but try dragging the Lossy slider to about 50%. You'll notice slightly more dithering, but the file size drops by about eight percent. (If you are optimizing as PNG-8, the Lossy slider won't be available to you.)

11. Okay, enough nitpicking. Make sure the optimized view is selected and choose File > Save Optimized As. Or, if you're doing this in Photoshop's Save for Web dialog, just click OK.

What ImageReady Can Do That Photoshop Can't

Many of ImageReady's tools and commands duplicate those in Photoshop, so we'll focus here on the following features that are uniquely ImageReady's:

- Drawing geometric shapes such as rounded rectangles
- Animated GIFs
- Image slicing
- JavaScript rollovers

Three palettes in ImageReady are miniature Web applications in themselves: the Animation, Slice, and Rollover palettes. None of these exist at all in Photoshop.

Animated GIFs

The Animation palette, shown here, is a program for creating Web animations in animated GIF format. You can automatically create animations using image layers as individual frames in the animation. You can automatically create animations for rollover states. You can optimize animations so that the animation file stores only those parts of the image that change from frame to frame. You can also tween motion and fades between frames.

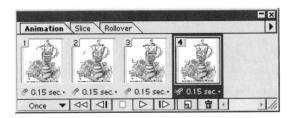

Cross-Reference: You learn all about how to make animated GIFs in Chapter 14.

Image Slicing

Image slicing is the process of dividing an image into smaller images. When the slices are subsequently loaded onto a Web page, they join one another seamlessly. Then each of these subimages can be optimized independently, allowing you to further optimize them where possible. In addition, designated slices can be turned off or made to contain text, so that the overall image loads much faster. Finally, each slice can be linked to another part of the Web page or even to an entirely different Web site.

ImageReady's image slicing operations reside in the Slices menu (which has no equivalent in Photoshop) and in the Slice palette, shown here:

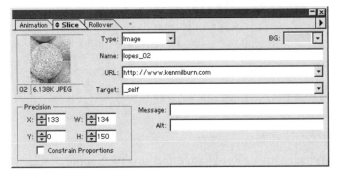

Cross-Reference: Image slicing is covered in Chapter 14.

Rollovers

A *rollover event* is what happens to change an image as a result of a change in the state of the mouse cursor. States are

- Normal (the cursor isn't in any particular position)
- Over (the cursor is over the designated target area)
- Down (the mouse button has been clicked and held)
- Click
- Out (the cursor has moved out of the target area)
- Up (the mouse button has been released after being held down)

Each of these states can display a different look for the target area or button. You just use Photoshop or ImageReady to change the color of, transform, give a layer effect to, or animate that object. In the Rollover palette shown here, none of the state images has yet been edited to change its appearance, but you can do so in any way you like.

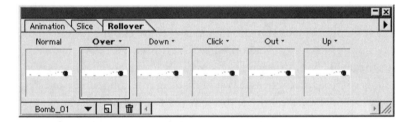

Image Maps

Image maps are images that contain selected areas designated as hotspots—areas in which something happens when the mouse cursor is in a particular state. These areas serve a purpose similar to image slices, but there are some important differences. First, hotspots can be any shape; you're not limited to rectangles. So in an image of a house, the garbage can could be one hotspot, the mailbox another, the front door yet another. Each of these hotspots can be linked so that clicking a hotspot takes the viewer to another part of the page, another HTML page within the same site, or to an altogether different site.

ImageReady's Tools and Commands

Now that you know what ImageReady and Photoshop have in common, and the unique abilities offered by ImageReady, let's go through each of ImageReady's menus. When we've finished, you'll have a good idea of when it makes sense to jump back and forth and when it makes sense to stay put.

File Menu

Two commands have been added to the File menu in order to make it easy to save the file's currently selected optimized view. Save Optimized simply saves the file under its current name and adds the extension for the file type. Save Optimized As lets you change the name and location of the file before saving it.

The dialogs for these two commands offer additional options over their more standard counterparts: You can elect to save an HTML file for the image, save only those slices that have been selected, or simply save the image (if an image has been sliced, it is actually several sequentially numbered images).

By the way, you don't need to write the HTML file that is saved with the image. ImageReady writes the code for you, according to what you've done with that image in ImageReady. For example, you may have sliced the image—in which case, you need an HTML table to hold the slices together on a Web page. However, don't expect ImageReady to create a Web site for you. You (or your site designer) will incorporate the HTML written by ImageReady into the HTML for the site. You can also do that in a WYSIWYG site-authoring program such as Adobe's GoLive or Macromedia's Dreamweaver.

The Update HTML command updates the HTML code you have saved for an image file according to any changes you've made in size, color, links, and so forth.

Export Original Image Info is the same as Photoshop's Save a Copy command: it duplicates the original, flattens the duplicate, and then lets you save it in any of the supported formats.

HTML Background lets you save the current optimized image as a background image in an HTML page. You could then import that page into your HTML editor and place other graphics and text in front of it.

The Preview In menu lets you see, in the browser(s) of your choice, the image displayed on the HTML code generated by ImageReady. Your operating system's default browser automatically appears on this menu. You can also install as many others as you have online (see next section).

Professional Pointer

Images intended as backgrounds for Web pages should be as simple as you can make them. They should have no more than three or four colors and these should be as flat as possible. Also, the greater the expanses of flat color, the more highly compressed the image can be. Otherwise, your background could take tens of seconds or even minutes to load—an unforgivable Web-design sin.

Installing browsers in the Preview In menu

All it takes to install a browser in the Preview In submenu is to create a shortcut or alias for that browser and drag it to the Preview In folder. The Preview In folder is inside the Helpers folder, which is inside the Photoshop program folder. In Windows, the Photoshop program folder is found inside the Adobe folder, which is inside the Program Files folder. Of course, all of this assumes that you accepted the default installation for these folders.

Edit Menu

On the Edit menu, in addition to the Undo and Redo commands, there's an Undo/Redo command. It undoes a redo command. (Seems silly when you can always use the History palette anyway—and you gain a lot more control in the process.)

Copy HTML Code copies the HTML code for the current document to the clipboard. Executing this command brings up a dialog presenting quite a few options. You can copy all or only selected slices. You can include or exclude the JavaScript code for slices in the document. Once you've used this command, you can insert the HTML code into any HTML editor by switching to that application, placing the cursor where you want to insert the code, and pressing CMD/CTRL+V to Paste.

Copy Foreground Color as HTML places the hexadecimal value for the Foreground Color onto the clipboard. Then all you have to do to enter that hex value into an HTML document is switch to that document in its editor, place the cursor where you wish the color to appear, and press CMD/CTRL+V. This same command exists in Photoshop—it's just in a different location, on the Color palette menu.

Image Menu

In addition to the Duplicate Image command, the Image menu contains a Duplicate Optimized command. Duplicate Optimized, as you've probably guessed, makes a copy of the currently selected optimization of the image. You can accomplish the same thing by pressing the OPT/ALT key and dragging the desired optimized view out of its window. It will immediately appear in a new window of its own.

In addition to the Crop command, there's Trim. Trim is handy for cropping out color or transparency that's outside the subject or graphic. This makes for smaller files and less hassle aligning graphic elements properly on a Web page. That's because the transparency or background color around the edges of the subject will no longer "push" the subject away from the alignment by the number of rows of pixels of that color.

The Flip Canvas command has the same Flip Horizontal and Flip Vertical commands as are available on the Rotate Canvas menu in Photoshop.

The Master Palette command in the Image menu lets you create, save, and load a master color palette to be applied to all the frames in an animated GIF, regardless of the source of the original image for a given frame and what its original palette's colors might have been. To create a master palette:

1. Choose Image > Master Palette > Clear Master Palette. This option won't be available if a master palette doesn't currently exist—in which case, don't worry about it.

2. Select one of the images whose colors you want to add to the master palette. This could be any image in any open window. Choose Image > Master Palette > Add to Master Palette. Any colors in the current image that aren't already in the master palette will be added.

3. Repeat the Add to Master Palette command for all images you want to add to the master palette.

4. In the Optimize palette, choose GIF as the optimization format. Then choose the number of colors and the palette type.

5. Choose Image > Master Palette > Build Master Palette, then Image > Master Palette > Save Master Palette. Be sure to save the new palette in the Color Tables folder so that you can access it when choosing colors in the Optimize palette.

6. To load a previously saved master palette, choose Window > Show Color Table and select Load Color Table from the Color Table palette menu.

Layer Menu

There's a reason why Remove Layer Mask is unique to ImageReady. In order to access the command, your active layer must have a layer mask. When you choose Remove Layer Mask, this dialog appears:

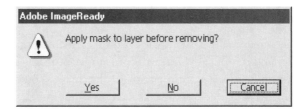

If you click Yes, the layer becomes transparent in the formerly masked area. Now when you save this layer as optimized, the transparent area can automatically be designated as transparent or matte.

Tip: There is no such thing as a background layer in ImageReady. If you jump over from Photoshop, the background layer automatically becomes Layer 1 and you can make or give it transparency without further ado.

If you want to move the position of one layer in respect to the others, choose the Set Layer Position command on the Layer menu. Why would you want to do that? Why, so that you can create a "slide show" animated GIF—you just put a long pause between frames. If you want each slide to appear in a different position relative to the last, this is the command that lets you do so. You just position the layers, then put the layers into an animation. Detailed instructions for making animated GIFs are in Chapter 14.

Slices Menu

There is no Slices menu in Photoshop, so every command on this menu is unique to ImageReady. They'll all be covered in the discussion on making image slices in Chapter 14.

Select Menu

There's no way to load or transform a selection from the Select menu, but you can choose the command Create Slice from Selection. ImageReady will automatically create a user-slice from the outside boundary of the selection, even if it's feathered. Then the rest of the image is subdivided into auto-slices. Once again, complete instructions for making and using slices are in the upcoming Chapter 14.

Filter Menu

ImageReady's Filter menu is identical to Photoshop's.

View Menu

Given the fact that ImageReady operates in views, it's no surprise that there are unique commands on the View menu. The most superfluous one is Show Optimized, which does exactly the same thing as if you clicked the Optimized tab in the image-editing window.

One View command I really wish was also in Photoshop is Resize Window to Fit. It makes the size of the window match the size of the image at its current zoom level. You get the smallest possible window that doesn't hide part of your image in one click. Right handy.

The Actual Size command is just another name for the Photoshop command called Actual Pixels.

In case you were wondering how (for presentation purposes) to hide all that text that appears under the optimized views, just select Show/Hide Optimization Info to toggle the information on and off. Also, when the info display is off, you'll have more space to preview more of the image, so you can better judge the quality of the image when comparing multiple views.

Window Menu

Another command I wish were in the same place in Photoshop is the Reset Palettes option. Having this option on the Window menu is much handier than having to choose File > Preferences > General and click the Reset Palette Locations to Default button—which also works in ImageReady. In either case, all of the available palettes will appear in their preassigned places.

This menu also contains Show/Hide commands for all of the palettes that are unique to ImageReady: Optimize, Type, Color Table, Layer Options, Effects, Styles, Animation, Slice, and Rollover.

Help Menu

Uh, oh. Keyboard Shortcuts *is* a unique command, but it doesn't do anything except bring up Help Topics. Watch for an update soon ☺.

Making Navigational and Logo Graphics

You can make great-looking navigation buttons and logo graphics in either Photoshop or ImageReady, thanks to Photoshop 5's introduction of layer effects. No longer do you have to depend on third-party filters such as Blade Pro and Alien Skin's Eye Candy to get "instant" drop shadows and beveled edges. Here are the effects you can create on a simple button shape with layer effects:

All of these effects, save the gradient, are available in both Photoshop and ImageReady (Layer > Effects). Each effect is highly variable via a palette of settings.

In ImageReady, however, adding effects gets even slicker. There's a Styles palette (Window > Show Styles), shown here:

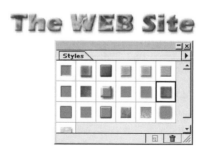

You can drag any style from the Styles palette onto any shape on a transparent layer, and that style will automatically be applied. Conversely, you can use any combination of layer and filter effects on a layer, and then click the New Styles icon at the bottom of the Styles palette, and the new style will appear in the palette. It can then be applied automatically to any other layer at any time. Too cool for school.

Professional Skills Summary

In this chapter, you learned how to optimize images for the Web in all four of the formats supported by Photoshop 5.5 and ImageReady 2. You also learned about features unique to ImageReady and how to use them. We didn't cover the mechanics of making animated GIFs, image slices, rollover events, and image maps—you'll see how to do all that in the very next chapter.

chapter 14

Using ImageReady for Special-Purpose Web Graphics

In this chapter, you

- Learn to create GIF animations for use on the Web

- Create image slices for fast loading

- Go interactive using rollover states

- Find out how to make image maps

You had something to sell, so you built a Web site. Then you did a little Web research to check out the competition, and found that the sites you kept returning to were more interesting, more fun, because they involved you more and downloaded much faster. On the best sites, stuff happened depending on the location *and* the state of your mouse. And everything downloaded so-o-o very much faster. It dawns on you that your site just doesn't have this same ability to grab the viewer's attention.

But ImageReady 2's other talents can give you the kind of interactivity and attention-grabbing techniques you've been looking for. In Chapter 13 you discovered ImageReady's image-optimization capabilities and its seamless partnership with Photoshop. In this chapter we'll look further into using ImageReady to implement the following special-purpose techniques: animation, image slicing, rollover events, and image maps.

Animating GIFs

In your stock photograph file you locate a Hubble astronomical photo of a "galaxy far, far away," and a NASA shot of Earth taken from far out in space. Using your flatbed scanner, you direct-scan a souvenir Native American dreamcatcher you've had hanging in your office. Then you take a 28-200 zoom lens, place it lens down on the glass of your flatbed scanner, scan it, and are delighted with the results. Next you prepare the lens, globe, and dreamcatcher digital images as knockouts in Photoshop, and you have the four elements with which to prepare your animation:

- The galaxy photograph (NEBULABG.JPG)
- The lens (NIKOLENS.JPG)
- The photo of Earth (BLUEARTH.JPG)
- The scanned dreamcatcher (DREAMCAT.JPG)

In the following sections, we'll use these elements to construct a GIF animation in ImageReady.

Making an Animation

The first task is to create the basic animation file. First, we'll place our files on individual layers in Photoshop, and then resize the overall image for the Web. Then we'll jump to ImageReady, where we'll begin creating the animation.

1. Start by downloading NEBULABG.JPG, DREAMCAT.JPG, BLUEARTH.JPG, and NIKOLENS.JPG from the Osborne site. Or, if you have similar elements in your own files, you may find using them to be more productive and educational.

2. Open the NEBULABG.JPG (galaxy) image to use for the background layer.

3. Open DREAMCAT.JPG (the dreamcatcher). Use the move tool (there's only one layer) to drag it over to the open NEBULABG.JPG file. The dreamcatcher becomes Layer 1.

4. Close DREAMCAT.JPG and open BLUEARTH.JPG. Use the move tool to drag the entire BLUEARTH.JPG layer over to the open NEBULABG.JPG file. The Earth image automatically becomes Layer 2.

5. Close BLUEARTH.JPG and open NIKOLENS.JPG (the scanned lens). The lens image automatically becomes Layer 3.

6. Close NIKOLENS.JPG. You now have four layers, arranged as shown in Figure 14-1.

Professional Pointer

The larger the animation image, the more download time is required and, as you add frames to the animation, this problem only multiplies. A site with slower-than-average downloading can be a major cause of viewer drift. So decide carefully on an image size you judge to be memory-reasonable. Take a look at some other Web sites, and you'll notice that animations are rarely larger than 150 × 200 pixels; many very effective ones are much smaller than that.

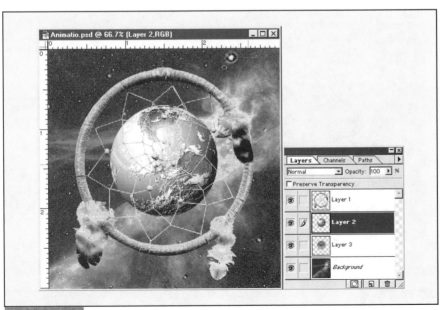

FIGURE 14-1 Start the GIF animation by creating four layers in Photoshop

7. Now we need to size our main image file. Choose Image > Image Size. Select the Resample Image option. In the Print Size settings, set Resolution to 72 pixels/inch (ppi). For Width, type **3** to make a 3 × 3-inch print size.

8. To create the animation, we need to use ImageReady. Click the Jump To button at the bottom of the Photoshop toolbox. Photoshop asks you to save your file (unless that was the last thing you did before clicking Jump To). Save the file, naming it EARTHANI.PSD. If you don't save your file before you leave Photoshop, ImageReady will ask you to return to the Photoshop file to save it.

9. ImageReady opens, with your file displayed in the image-editing window. You want the Original view; if you're not already there, select the Original tab at the top to display this view.

10. Choose Window > Layers. In the Layers palette, click the eye icons to turn all the layers off except for Layer 0 (background), as shown in Figure 14-2.

11. Choose Window > Show Animation. The Animation palette will appear, as shown in Figure 14-3. Select the zoom tool and click inside the image in the Original tab, to enlarge the image for better viewing.

12. Select frame 1, and then click the Duplicates Current Frame button to create a copy of the galaxy frame. In the Layers palette, select Layer 2 (the globe). Click the eye icon for Layer 4 (background) to turn it off.

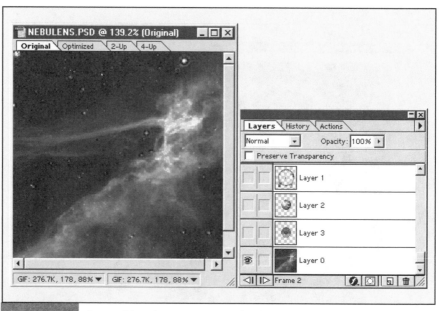

FIGURE 14-2 Start with only Layer 0 turned on.

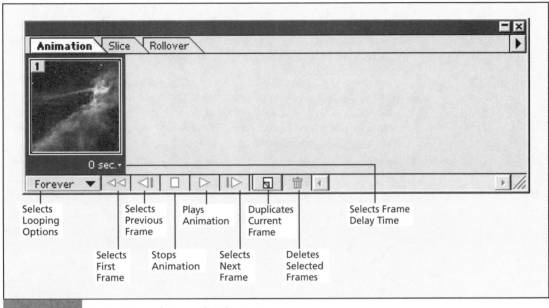

FIGURE 14-3   Animation palette and its buttons

13. In the Animation palette, select frame 2. Open the Actions palette, choose Spinning Zoom In, and then click the Plays Current Action button (the right arrow button at the bottom of the Actions palette). ImageReady now automatically generates a series of 12 globe frames sized sequentially from tiny to full size. In the Animation palette, click the Plays Animation button to view the animation effect so far.

14. If you haven't done so already, save your ImageReady file (File > Save As) and assign a name to this work file.

The animation at this point appears to spin straight toward the viewer from out of nowhere, and this is not what you want. The desired effect is for the globe to come in from off-screen, spinning closer and closer as it travels to the center of the screen. So you need to change the location of the globe in the frame with the smallest globe.

Tip: You can use the Plays Animation button whenever you wish to check on an animation's progress as you work.

15. Select frame 2 (the smallest globe image), and then select Layer 2 Copy from the Layers palette. Select the move tool and drag the smallest globe into the top-left corner of the frame. With frame 2 still highlighted, click the eye icon on for every globe in the sequence.

16. Now select Layer 2 Copy 2, and with the move tool drag the next-larger globe to the smaller globe in the frame's corner. Overlap the smaller globe at a point close to the direction in which you want the globe to spin (see Figure 14-4). Select Layer 2 Copy 3 and drag the next globe in the sequence to overlap the

other globes in the corner, so that the series of globes are proceeding toward the center of the screen (the planned direction of their movement). Repeat this procedure for all copies of the layer until you reach the last globe in Layer 2, which will remain in place without being moved. Frame 2 should now look as it does in Figure 14-4.

17. Now all the frames show all the globes. What we want, though, is for each globe to appear one at a time so that it will seem to grow as it moves to the center of the screen. Select frame 3 and then SHIFT+click frame 13, to high-light this series of frames. Drag them to the trash.

18. Select frame 2, and click 11 times on the Duplicates Current Frame button.

19. Again select frame 2, and in the Layers palette click off all the eye icons for the globe layers, except for Layer 2. Next, select frame 3, and click off all globe eye icons except for Layer 2 Copy 2. Then select frame 4, and click off all globe eye icons except for Layer 2 Copy 3. Repeat this procedure along the frames, each time leaving only the eye icon of the next globe in the se-quence—the last being frame 13, Layer 2.

20. This is a good time to test your movement effect. From the Selects Looping Options pop-up menu, choose Once.

Now you're going to add and animate the dreamcatcher, superimposing it over the globe and causing it to fade in.

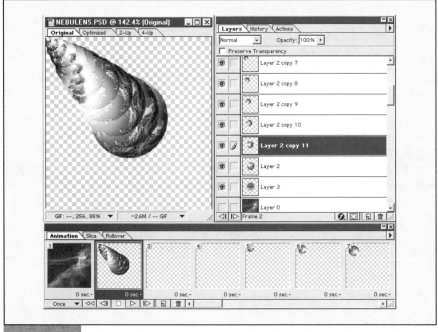

FIGURE 14-4 All the globe layers have been sized and dragged into position

21. Select each frame one at a time and click the eye on for Layer 0 (background).

22. Select frame 13 and click the Duplicates Current Frame button once.

23. Select frame 14, and in the Layers palette select Layer 1 (dreamcatcher image). Choose Tween from the Animation palette menu.

24. In the Tween dialog, choose the Selected Layer radio button. Under the Parameters list, select the Position, Opacity, and Effects boxes.

25. In the Tween With pop-up menu, choose Previous Frame and type **5** in the Frames to Add field. Then click OK. ImageReady will automatically add five in-between fade-in frames of the highlighted layer (dreamcatcher), as you can see in Figure 14-5.

26. Now you need to make the globe zoom out. Turn on Layer 2 (globe) and Layer 0 (background) in each of the in-between frames.

27. Select frame 19 in the Animation palette and click the Duplicates Current Frame button once. Select frame 20. Select Layer 2 (globe) from the Layers palette and click the eye icon off for Layer 3 (lens). Click the Duplicates Current Frame button once.

28. Select frame 21. Select Layer 2 from the Layers palette.

29. In the Actions palette, choose Zoom Out and then click the Plays Current Action button.

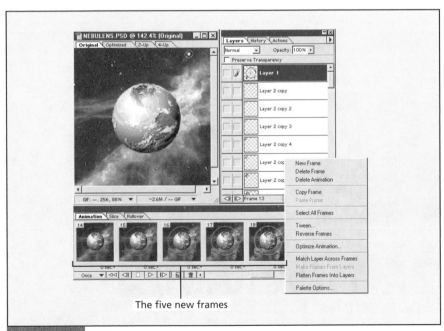

The five new frames

FIGURE 14-5   Superimposing and fading-in the dreamcatcher

Because the Zoom Out action (which is installed when you install Photoshop and ImageReady) is preprogrammed, ImageReady automatically adds the frames needed to complete the zoom out of the globe, all the way through frame 32, as shown in Figure 14-6.

30. Click the Duplicates Current Frame button to make a copy of the current frame (32). Select this copy; it will be frame 33. In the Layers palette, select Layer 1 (the dreamcatcher) and click off its eye icon. Choose Tween from the Animation palette flyout. In the Tween dialog, choose the Selected Layer radio button from the Layers list. Under the Parameters list, select the Position, Opacity, and Effects boxes (actually, they're probably already selected, but make sure). In the Tween pop-up menu, choose Previous Frame and type **5** in the Frames to Add field. Then click OK. ImageReady automatically adds five in-between frames to complete the fade-out action of the highlighted layer (dreamcatcher).

31. Turn on Layer 3 (lens) and Layer 0 (background) in each of the in-between frames.

32. Let's run the animation to see how it looks. In the Animation palette, click the Plays Animation button.

In the original scheme, this was to have been the final position for the lens. But, after playing the animation, you can see that a nice finishing touch would be to have the lens shoot forward, fill the screen, and then superimpose our logo on top of the larger lens. Let's do it.

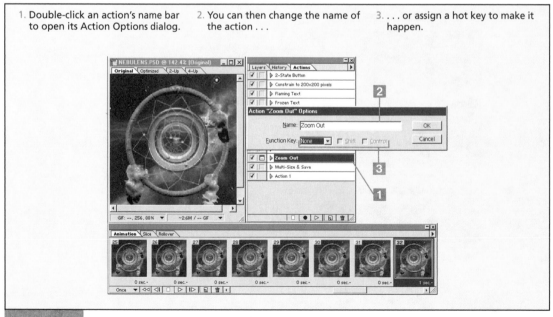

FIGURE 14-6   Creating the Zoom Out action for the globe

33. In the Animation palette, select frame 38. Click the Duplicates Current Frame button and select the new frame (39). Then select Layer 4 in the Layers palette. In the Actions palette, choose Zoom In. Then click the Plays Current Action button.

34. In the Animation palette, click the Plays Animation button again and watch the lens zoom in to fill the frame.

35. Select frame 59, and then SHIFT+click and select frame 39 to highlight this sequence of frames. Choose Reverse Frames from the Animation palette flyout. Select frames 51 through 45, one at a time, clicking off the Layer 3 eye icon in each frame.

36. Select frame 39, and then SHIFT+click frame 44 to highlight this sequence of frames. Drag them to the Trash.

The final effect will be to have the logo appear in front of the lens.

37. Select frame 45 from the Animation palette, click the Duplicates Current Frame button, and select frame 46. Select the type tool and right-click/double-click to bring up the Type palette. Set the typeface and other type parameters as you wish. In the toolbox, right-click/double-click the foreground color selection box to bring up the Color palette. Choose a color for the logo type and click OK. Using the type tool, type the text of the logo onto the frame.

38. Look directly below each frame in the Animation palette, and you will see "0 sec" followed by a tiny down-pointing triangle. Click that triangle to display the Selects Frame Delay Time pop-up menu:

| No delay |
| 0.1 seconds |
| 0.2 |
| 0.5 |
| 1.0 |
| 2.0 |
| 5.0 |
| 10.0 |
| Other... |
| ✔ 0 seconds |

The frame delay selector is metered in tenths of a second; choose 1.0 from the list to set the delay at one second. Do this for each of frames 19, 32, 38, and 45. Do the same for frame 46, except set this frame to a two-second delay.

Professional Pointer

It's a good practice to add a brief pause between the animation's runs, so the animation won't keep repeating over and over so quickly. To do this, select the first and last animation frames, and set longer times in their Select Frame Delay Time flyouts.

39. Click the Plays Animation button to see how your animation runs.

Now you need to get the animation ready for the Web page.

40. When you are satisfied with the animation, choose Window > Show Optimize to open the Optimize palette. In the Settings menu, choose GIF 32 Dithered. Accept all the default settings. Select the 4-Up view, and wait for ImageReady to generate each optimization view (Figure 14-7).

41. In the status bar at the bottom of the window, set the information fields (left to right) to show 100% magnification, Optimized Information, and Optimized Information. (You'll need to click the down arrows in these fields to open the flyout lists of available settings.)

42. Examine each optimization view, choose the best combination of dither and download time, and click to select that optimization. At the top of the view screen, click the Optimized tab to see the full-screen version of your optimization.

43. Choose File > Save Optimized As. Choose a file location, type a filename, and click Save.

Cross-Reference: To get an idea how this animation will look in color, refer to images 14-5 to 14-9 in the Image Gallery, which show five of the frames for this Animation sequence.

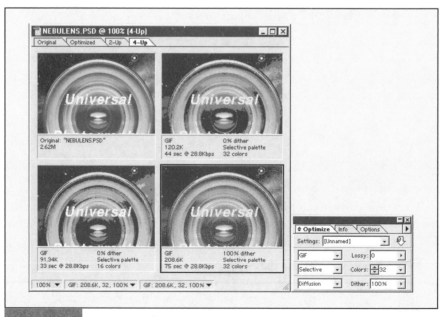

FIGURE 14-7   Optimizing the animation in the 4-Up view

Professional Pointer

To make sure your effects will function properly on the Web, always preview the finished product in a browser. That way you can return to ImageReady if you need to make changes. Start in ImageReady, choosing File > Preview and selecting the name of your installed browser. Then test-view your new animation at the speed it will play when placed in your Web site page. Be aware that type and graphics will display differently when viewed on various platforms, so if you have access to viewing on "the other one," by all means do so (or have an "other-platform" friend check it out for you). You will get a more complete sense of how others will be seeing your site. Avoids a lot of surprises after you've published.

Saving your animation as a movie

You also have the option to save your animation as a QuickTime movie. To do that,

1. Click the Original tab on the view screen.

2. Choose File > Export Original to open the Save: ImageReady dialog (Figure 14-8).

3. In the Format pop-up, choose QuickTime Movie. Then type a filename and choose a destination folder.

4. Choose Save, which will bring up the Compression Settings dialog.

5. In the Compressor box, choose Photo-JPEG and Best Depth; in the Quality box, choose High. Click OK.

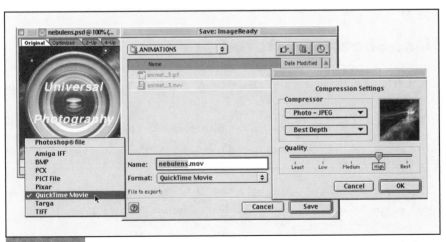

FIGURE 14-8 The settings for saving your animation as a QuickTime movie (or as sequentially numbered files in a number of still image formats)

Slicing Images for Fast Loading

One way to add interactive characteristics to your Web site starts with *image slicing*—a method of cutting up an image into seamless rectangles for much faster loading, with local control of optimization and other effects. Once an image is sliced, each slice may have an associated link and/or an assigned rollover event.

You may be wondering why a sliced image would load faster (since it's now several images) than one that wasn't sliced. Some of this acceleration is just the vewer's perception—because a small section of an image will load almost immediately, the image seems to be loading faster because we *see something* sooner. More important to this discussion is that often the slices can actually be *made* to load the whole image faster because some slices can be deleted or substituted for a text block (there's that much less data to load). Also, sections of the image that contain inconsequential information or large areas of solid color can be highly compressed, while the sections containing important details are given very little compression.

A slice is a section of an image that is automatically placed into a borderless cell in an HTML table. For this reason, all slices have to be rectangles. However, they don't need to be the same size, since the program will automatically create slices to fill any gaps.

Image maps can also have interactive mouse events assigned to their segments, so you may wonder why you'd use a slice rather than an image map. As mentioned, the chief advantages is that if an image is sliced, each slice can be optimized individually. Also, the individual slices can be animated, so you can make your button actions much livelier. On the other hand, the divisions of an image map can use irregular or oval shapes.

User-Slices and Auto-Slices

There are two types of slices: *user-slices* and *auto-slices*. Auto-slices are created by the program to fill in the blanks after you've create user-slices. You can also promote an auto-slice to a user-slice. User-slices can be either Image slices or No Image slices.

- *Image slices* display data and can contain rollover states.
- *No Image slices* can contain solid color and/or HTML text. Background color and text are invisible in ImageReady and can only be viewed in a browser.

Each user-slice can be optimized separately and can be edited, moved, duplicated, combined, divided, resized, deleted, arranged in stacking order, aligned, and snapped to other slices.

An automatically generated slice is an *auto-slice* and can also be an Image slice or a No Image slice. All auto-slices are linked together and share the same optimization.

An auto-slice can be promoted to a user-slice by choosing the slice select tool ( ) in the ImageReady toolbox, just to the right of the slice tool ( ); selecting the auto-slice; and choosing Slices > Promote to User-slice. (You can also CONTROL+click/right-click the slice and choose Promote to User-slice from the context menu.) The Slices menu also contains the Duplicate Slice and Divide Slice commands. Duplicated or divided slices will automatically become user-slices.

To change the borders of a slice, choose the slice select tool, click the slice to select it, and then drag the handles that appear in the marquee around the slice. A handy way to duplicate a user-slice is choose the slice select tool and drag from inside the slice. To combine slices, choose Slices > Combine Slices. The optimization settings of the first slice selected will determine the settings of the combined slices.

Professional Pointer

When you choose File > Save Optimized, ImageReady will produce an HTML file plus a folder named IMAGES that contains a set of files—one for each slice in the image document. These slice files must be saved, stored, and used together or the effect will not work in a Web page.

Creating Slices

To begin the image-slicing process, you'll first need to select, launch, size, and optimize an image of your choice in ImageReady (see Chapter 13). For your practice here, you can download the sample file DIAMRING.JPG from the Osborne Web site. When you have your image displayed, choose Window > Show Slice to bring up the Slice palette (Figure 14-9), and then choose Show Options from the flyout.

There are three ways to create slices: from guides, from a selection, or by drawing them directly in an image.

Creating slices from guides

Guides are the nonprinting guidelines that you can utilize to aid your placement of text and layers. You can automatically create slices that fit the intervals between guides. Such slices are always user-slices. To create slices from guides, choose View > Create Guides to bring up the Create Guides dialog. Figure 14-10 shows this dialog and the DIAMRING.JPG image with several slices made. By

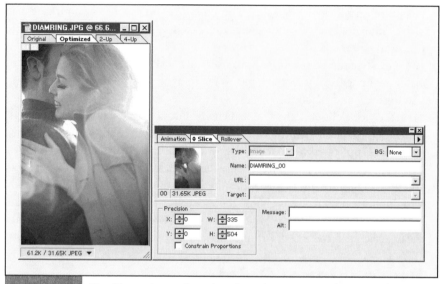

FIGURE 14-9 The Slice palette after choosing Show Options from the flyout

experimenting with various combinations of the buttons and values in the Horizontal Guides and Vertical Guides sections, you will very quickly learn how to create guides to make slices.

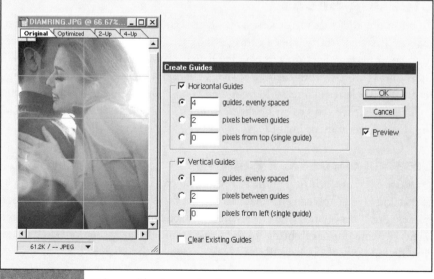

FIGURE 14-10 Using guides to create slices

Creating slices from a selection

To create a slice from a selection within an image, first use the rectangular marquee tool to make a rectangular selection. Then choose Slices > Create Slice from Selection. You can use a nonrectangular selection tool, but your slice will automatically become a rectangle based on the width and length of the selection, as you can see in Figure 14-11.

Drawing slices directly in an image

To draw a slice inside the image, select the slice tool from the toolbox. ImageReady will then automatically display a default auto-slice.

Drag the slice tool from the corner of the area where you want a slice. (To constrain to a square, press SHIFT while dragging. To drag from the middle, press ALT/OPT.) If you happen to drag outside the document, the slice will be clipped at the edge. However, if you move an existing slice beyond the document's edge, the full slice remains preserved.

In Figure 14-12, note that only the slice selected is shown in the thumbnail display in the Slice palette.

A user-slice can overlap another user-slice. ImageReady will regenerate the underlying slice to make room for the overlapping slice. Both slices may still be selected.

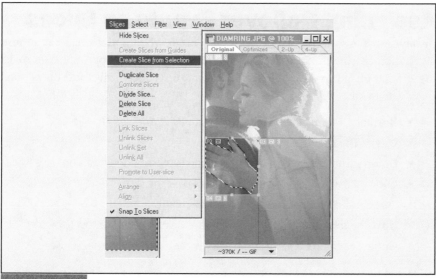

FIGURE 14-11   The Slices menu and the created slice

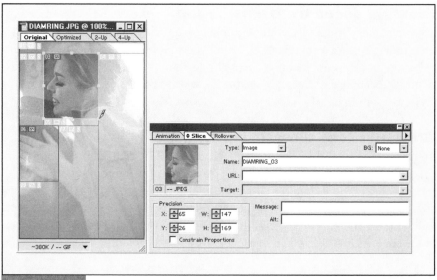

FIGURE 14-12   Only the currently selected slice is shown in the Slice palette

So now you know how to make slices. Now I suppose you want to know how to assign rollover events to them? Coming right up.

Assigning Rollover Events to Slices

Rollover states (also called *mouseover events*) occur when a user drags the mouse over a slice, causing the slice to animate or otherwise change appearance, or making another image appear elsewhere. Here are the rollover states and the actions that cause them:

- **Normal**   The movement of the cursor hasn't affected the slice.
- **Over**   The cursor is over the slice.
- **Down**   The mouse is over the slice and is pressed down but not released.
- **Click**   A fast single mouse click occurs over the slice.
- **Out**   The cursor has moved out of the slice.
- **Up**   The mouse button is released after being held down over the slice.
- **None**   Nothing happens, no matter what is done with the mouse.

Any of these events can be made to reflect a change in the target image or can bring up another image on the screen. The Rollover palette and its buttons are

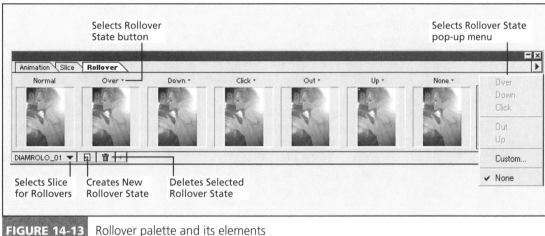

FIGURE 14-13 Rollover palette and its elements

shown in Figure 14-13. Notice that it shows several states assigned to the rollover events in the previous list.

Thus you can display an animation as a rollover event, and even use a rollover event to cause an image in a different slice to change.

Creating Rollovers

Imagine that you're a graphics designer whose travel agency client wants to promote honeymoon travel packages to engaged couples. You've been asked to produce this page for the agency's Web site. Looking for a way to highlight destinations, you've decided to feature a rollover element right in the middle of the page. For resources, you've got a moody sunset shot from a local photographer's sample file, showing a couple in a romantic embrace; plus you've gleaned five or six scenics from a collection of stock agency submissions.

Follow these steps to create your rollover element:

1. Select and launch images of your choice in ImageReady. For this exercise, you can download DIAMROLO.JPG, FORTRESS.JPG, HAWAIIAN.JPG, MOONWALK.JPG, SHIPCRUS.JPG, and CHORLINE.JPG from the Osborne site.

2. Select the DIAMRING.JPG file as your background image. Choose Image > Image Size. In the Image Size dialog, designate the width and/or height. Type in a specific number of pixels, depending on the size of your Web page, or type a percentage in the Percent field.

3. Choose File > Save Optimized As and save the image to a dedicated folder; re-name the folder DIAMROLO (or a name of your choice). *Don't forget:* All image files and HTML files for a rollover need to be kept together in one folder.

4. Choose Window > Show Rollover, and then Window > Show Layers, to bring up the Rollover and Layers palettes.

5. Since the DIAMRING.JPG is to be your background, select its image file. This image will now appear in the Rollover palette's thumbnail. ImageReady will provide a full-frame auto-slice as a default slice. Choose Slice > Promote to User-slice.

6. To add some dimension to the layout, let's add enough transparent area outside the background image so that the travel images will be visible partially beyond the edges of the background image when the mouse action occurs. Choose Image > Canvas Size. In the Canvas Size dialog, indicate the width and height dimensions in the exact, preplanned amounts needed for your final slice layout.

Professional Pointer

Always plan out your rollover layout *before* adding the transparent areas. You will not be able to add to the transparent layout area, nor use the crop tool to subtract from it, once you begin building your rollover. If you try this, you will scramble the generation data in the document, and the rollover will no longer work properly.

7. Click OK. You now have transparent space around the background image, enabling you to create your slice image layout, as shown here:

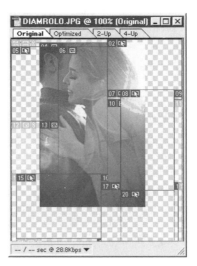

Now let's add titles, then effects, to each travel image one at a time.

8. Select the type tool in the toolbox, select an image, click in the image to place the start of the type, and type a title directly onto the image. (You don't

need to use a Type dialog, as you would in Photoshop.) Click OK and the text will appear on its own layer. Next, choose Layers > Effects and pick one or more layer effects for the text. When finished, flatten the image and optimize. Repeat these steps for each image (see Figure 14-14).

9. One at a time, select the travel destination images; and for each image, follow the steps shown in Figure 14-15 to enhance the images with the Bevel and Emboss effect.

10. Choose the Original tab at the top of the background image and at the top of each travel image. (Most of the toolbox tools don't work in the Optimize view, or the 2-Up and 4-Up views.)

11. Now you want to arrange for these images to appear in the original sliced image when a rollover event occurs. Start by choosing the slice select tool and selecting the background image. Then select the slice tool and draw a

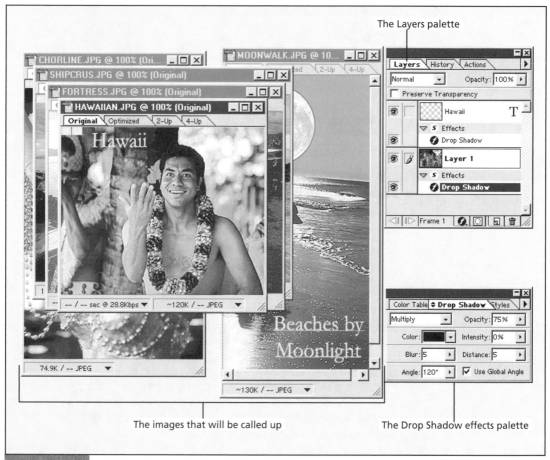

The Layers palette

The images that will be called up

The Drop Shadow effects palette

FIGURE 14-14 The pictures we're adding text to, and the palettes that are used

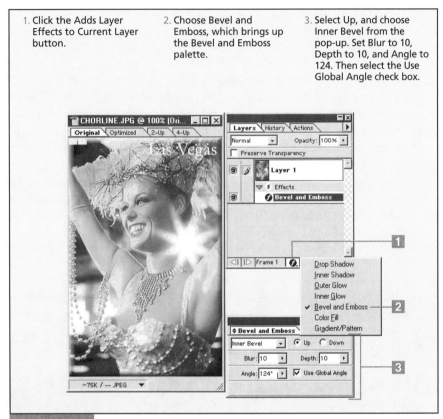

1. Click the Adds Layer Effects to Current Layer button.

2. Choose Bevel and Emboss, which brings up the Bevel and Emboss palette.

3. Select Up, and choose Inner Bevel from the pop-up. Set Blur to 10, Depth to 10, and Angle to 124. Then select the Use Global Angle check box.

FIGURE 14-15 Adding a bevel and emboss effect to the images

user-slice approximately the shape of the image to be inserted in the slice. In the Slice palette, take note of the width and height of the selected slice. Return to the Rollover palette and select the image you want for the slice. Choose Image > Image Size and resize the selected image to match the slice shape. Click OK.

12. With the slice select tool, select the slice. In the Rollover palette, click the Creates New Rollover State button. The first state will always remain a fixed Normal setting. Select the second state and leave it set to the default (Over), as shown in Figure 14-16. The states for Normal and Over in the palette will now display the slice. Next, choose the move tool and select the image from the Original tab in it's file window; then drag and drop it into the slice (see Figure 4-16). In the Rollover palette, if the correct sequence has been followed, the Normal state's thumbnail will now display the slice, and the second state will now display the image.

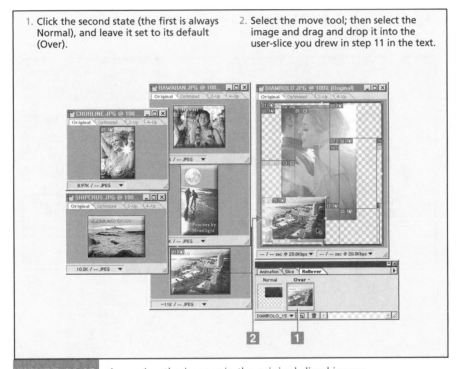

1. Click the second state (the first is always Normal), and leave it set to its default (Over).

2. Select the move tool; then select the image and drag and drop it into the user-slice you drew in step 11 in the text.

FIGURE 14-16   Arranging the images in the original sliced image

With the move tool still selected, you can now move the image around inside the slice, as shown here:

Move tool

13. With the slice select tool, select the slice and drag its handles to adjust its shape to fit to the image, as shown in this before-and-after example:

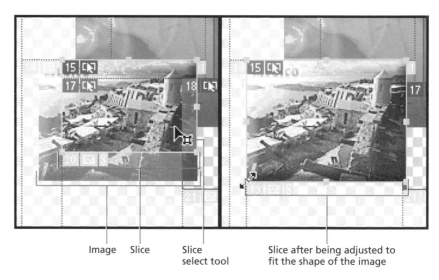

Image   Slice   Slice   Slice after being adjusted to
                          select tool   fit the shape of the image

Tip: Both the slice and the image can be moved about in the layout, but a slice and its contained image move independently.

14. Repeat this procedure (steps 11 through 13) for each travel image until the slice layout is complete.

15. This is a good time to preview the performance of this first action (rolling the mouse over the slice) in your browser. But before you do, choose Save Optimized. Then choose File > Preview In and select your browser from the resulting flyout. Your browser will open and display the sliced image. Move the mouse into the slice with the roll-over event assigned, and it will happen—as shown in Figure 14-17.

Now when your travel client wants to see if you've been busy, sit her down in front of the two newly engaged lovers hugging in a sunset. Hand her the mouse. When she rolls the mouse around the edge of the scene, exotic destinations pop up right and left, top and bottom.

Now you understand how to create rollover events. So let's not stop while we're on a roll (sorry, I just couldn't resist). There's still one more trick to put up your sleeve.

Professional Pointer

When you preview a rollover event in a browser from within ImageReady, as you just did, you will see the rollover's HTML text displayed right below the active image. This can be very handy.

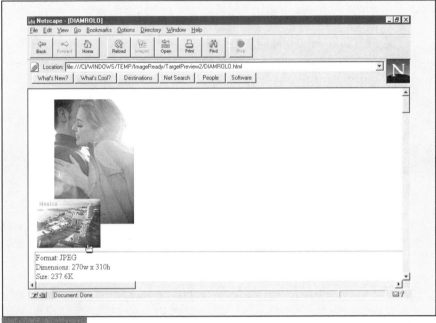

FIGURE 14-17 Here's how one of the rollover events looks when previewed in Netscape Navigator

Making Image Maps

Let's say you're an illustrator on the staff at a medical library. You work on their Web site and have produced an illustration showing a cut-away view of inflamed tissue. Various areas of the illustration are explained in more detail on other linked pages of the library's Web site, and there's a lot of product information available on other Web sites. To take advantage of all this material, you need to create an *image map* with *hotspots* to link portions of the illustration with these other locations.

As we've already pointed out, image maps have one property in common with slices: the capability to specify a URL link. This enables the viewer, by clicking one or more hotspots in the image, to go to another page in the Web site; another Web site; or an image, text file, audio, video, or other multimedia element. Slices can only be rectangular, whereas image maps let you utilize rectangles, polygon shapes, or circles and ovals to designate the hotspots.

In ImageReady, you set up the designated hotspots by assigning them to layers. Since layers can have transparency, Photoshop designates only the nontransparent area of the layer as a hotspot. These are regular Photoshop layers, so you need to make sure that the nontransparent areas of your layers don't overlap. Otherwise,

▶ Tip: When working with image maps, do not use slices containing URL links or rollover states. These slice links or rollover states will likely fail because they will conflict with the links assigned to the image map slices.

when the mouse cursor rolls into the overlapping area, it won't know which assigned link is the right one. A specific layer must be created for each hotspot. The image map data is saved in the document's HTML file. (And remember, everything must be kept in a folder with the optimized image, or the image map will not function.)

In ImageReady, client-side and server-side image maps can be created in HTML preferences. Client-side image map links are interpreted by the browser and usually load faster. However, they may not be recognized by some very early browsers. Server-side image map links are interpreted by the server and so can be recognized by any graphical browser.

Here are the steps for creating an image map:

1. Open an image in ImageReady, or download MEDICILL.JPG from the Osborne Web site. Choose File > Save Optimized As and save the image to the folder that will contain all the file elements of your image map. If any slices are present, remove them by choosing Slice > Delete All Slices.

2. With the selection tool of your choice, draw a selection containing the area you want to be an image map/hotspot. Keep in mind that image maps cannot extend beyond the edge of the image. Press CMD/CTRL+J to lift the contents of your selection to a new layer.

3. A new layer, Layer 2, is added in the Layers palette. It contains the opaque selection in place, surrounded by the transparent area. Select the Preserve Transparency check box. Then open the Optimized tab.

4. Choose Layer > Layer Options. In the Layer Options dialog, shown here, use the default settings for Opacity and Mode, and select the Use Layer as Image Map box. For the Shape, choose Polygon (or whichever shape you used) and set the Tolerance slider to 2.0. Type a complete URL address in the space provided; the address is automatically saved. It can then be accessed by clicking the down-arrow button. Click OK.

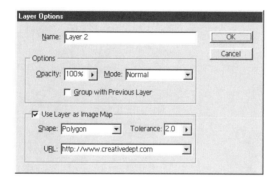

5. Back in the Layers palette, when you see your linked URL displayed in Layer 2, choose File > Save Optimized As. Select the boxes for Save HTML File and Save Images. Leave the Save Selected Slices Only option disabled. Click Save.

6. Before you add more image map layers, it's a good idea to preview your work in a browser to see what you've accomplished so far. To do this, drag the document's HTML file to your browser and drop it on the browser icon.

What's that? You say it worked? I knew all along you'd do it! So, what are you waiting for? Now you can make all the image maps your heart desires. Just repeat what you did for Layer 2.

Professional Skills Summary

In this chapter you learned how to use ImageReady 2 to create a GIF animation for your Web page, how to slice images into smaller parts for faster loading and linking, how to create mouse rollover events, and how to create an image map.

And now that we've reached the end of the book, I hope you've found it to be a ready reference for accomplishing the most-often needed Photoshop tasks in a professional manner. Please stay in touch. If you have suggestions for the next edition, please send the author an e-mail at kmilburn@pacbell.net.

Index